Communicating at Work

CREATING MESSAGES THAT GET RESULTS

THIRD EDITION

Ron Blicq

RGI INTERNATIONAL

Toronto

Canadian Cataloguing in Publication Data

Blicq, Ron S. (Ron Stanley), 1925–
Communicating at work: creating messages that get results
3rd ed.

Includes index.
ISBN 0-13-085830-7

1. Business writing. 2. Business communication I. Title.

HF5718.3.B58 2001 808'.06665 C00-930760-5

Authors' Note: The names of people and organizations in this book are imaginary and no reference to real persons is implied or intended.

Weblinks are included as end-of-chapter references and may occasionally present alternative points of view. Because the World Wide Web is a dynamic medium, Web site addresses may sometimes change over time.

ISBN 0-13-014599-8

Vice President, Editorial Director: Michael Young
Executive Editor: David Stover
Marketing Manager: Sophia Fortier
Executive Developmental Editor: Marta Tomins
Production Editor: Julia Hubble
Copy Editor: Valerie Adams
Production Coordinator: Peggy Brown
Page Layout: Janet Zanette
Art Director: Mary Opper
Interior Design: Lisa Lapointe
Cover Design: Lisa Lapointe

1 2 3 4 5 05 04 03 02 01

Printed and bound in Canada

Contents

Part 2
Writing Business Correspondence

Part 3
Writing Business Reports and Proposals

Part 5
Getting Your Words Onto Paper

Preface

Communication is an extraordinarily important aspect of every enterprise. A business has to deal with customers, suppliers, other businesses, government departments, and the general public on a day-to-day basis. If the business maintains good communication with all of these people, the enterprise tends to prosper. But if the business ignores the importance of good communication, causing mistakes to occur, a deterioration of product quality, and missed deadlines, customers may feel they are dealing with a poorly organized enterprise and may choose to take their business elsewhere.

This book, divided into five parts, takes a look at how you can improve your effectiveness as a communicator, and so enhance your image in the eyes of those with whom you will do business. It takes a practical approach that experienced business administrators would immediately endorse.

- Part 1 examines the effects of poor business communication, and then shows you some easy-to-apply techniques that will help you get off to a fast start every time you write.
- Part 2 shows you how to use these techniques when writing business letters and interoffice memorandums, with particular emphasis on the preparation of letters in which you have to *persuade* the reader to accept your suggestions and react in the way you want.
- Part 3 focuses on short and long business reports, and semiformal proposals. Again, you are shown how to use the techniques demonstrated in Part 1, but this time to prepare incident reports, conference reports, progress reports, and investigation reports.
- Part 4 demonstrates the importance of effective presentation if you are to convey a confident, knowledgeable image of both yourself and the company you work for. It shows you how to select the proper format for letters and reports, how to design your information so it will enhance a report's appearance and effectively support your words, and how to present information before a small or a

large audience. It also has a whole chapter on how to write a strong resume and present yourself well at a job interview (Chapter 11).

- The final part—Part 5—is a resource section that offers numerous hints on how to refine the words you use when you write, from selecting the correct word or expression to presenting it in a well-structured sentence and a fully developed paragraph. It includes a chapter that recommends designing your letters, reports, and proposals so they present a visually appealing image that encourages their recipients to read them. It also describes how to write efficient email, suggests how to use non-gender-specific language, and talks briefly about factors you need when communicating with an international audience.

The book offers ready-to-use formulas, called writing plans, for many types of letters and reports. For each, it also provides a model letter or report that has been written using the appropriate writing plan, and comments on how the original writer used the plan to create an effective communication. These writing plans and models will help you write the letters and reports in the exercises at the end of most chapters in this book, and eventually write effective letters and reports in a business setting.

I want to thank the students of the technology division at Red River College in Winnipeg, who pilot-tested many of the exercises in Chapters 3 through 7, and the instructors of the technology communication department for their advice, help, and continued understanding.

New to this Edition

The third edition of *Communicating at Work* has been updated with the following features:

- A completely new chapter (Chapter 6) that focuses on how to write business proposals, and provides two model proposals as examples.
- The chapter describing the formal report (now Chapter 7) contains a new contemporary report.
- The seven guidelines previously in the same chapter as the Glossary of Business Usage have been integrated into Chapter 12: "Writing Businesslike Language."
- A new section in Chapter 13 ("The Personal Aspects of Business Writing") describes the importance of designing information well.
- The Glossary of Business Usage is now a separate entity at the end of the book.
- Over forty percent of the writing assignments are new.

RB

Supplements

Instructor's Resource Manual with Transparency Masters

Accompanying this text is an Instructor's Resource Manual based on the author's extensive teaching and workshop experience. It includes teaching tips for each chapter, suggested answers for many of the text exercises, and Transparency Masters for use in the classroom.

Test Item File and Computerized Test Item File

A Test Item File supplies over 30 questions for each chapter, including multiple choice, true/false or matching, and short answer. The Computerized Test Item File has a variety of features which allow instructors to sort questions and add new questions of their own.

The Write Stuff: An Interactive Grammar Program

This text is accompanied by an interactive grammar program on disk, which is a concise overview of grammar and usage: parts of speech, types of sentences, errors in sentence structure, subject-verb agreement, pronouns, punctuation, and mechanics (capitals, numbers, spelling, usage problems). Stimulating interactive exercises for each chapter focus on the main writing errors that college and university students tend to make.

PART 1 Taking a Businesslike Approach to Communication

The Importance of Clear, Concise Communication

chapter 1

At 11:45 a.m. Dan Tesluk wanders into the cafeteria at North Western College. It is the day after Labor Day and he has just enrolled in the first semester of a two-year Business Administration program. He searches for an empty seat along the rows of crowded, noisy tables until he sees Kim Hessletine's red-sleeved arm beckoning to him.

"Hi!" he greets her, plopping into a chair on the opposite side of the table and piling his books in front of him. "I didn't know you were coming here."

"I'm taking Computer Analyst-Programming," Kim replies. "Two years of drudgery at a self-service gas bar was enough for me! How about you?"

Dan says he has been working in his father's printing shop. "My Dad expects me to take over the business when he retires," he explains. "But I'm not sure I want to." He confides to Kim that he doesn't like to hurt his father's feelings, but he would prefer to strike out on his own—carve his own niche in the business world. "That's why I chose Business Administration. I want to see what else is out there. Look around a bit. Then if I don't find anything I'll go back into Dad's business. My time won't have been wasted."

They compare timetables.

"What's this?" Dan explodes, pointing to a 1:50 p.m. slot on his timetable. "Another English course!"

Kim leans forward and peers at the paper. "You mean 'Communication Skills?'" she asks.

"Yeah! But that doesn't fool me. They've just given it another name."

"It's on mine, too," Kim agrees, less upset than he is. "Four hours a week."

"But why do I have to take English *again*?" Dan argues. "I've had 12 years of it!"

Dan's reaction is not uncommon. Many students question why they need a course such as "Communication," "Report Writing," or "Business

Strong communication skills are the first step toward promotion

Correspondence"; they feel that the English composition courses they took in high school prepared them to write and speak well enough. Unfortunately, some students—like Dan—may not discover until after they have graduated and are working that without a strong business communication course behind them they are missing an essential component that will help propel them up the promotion ladder.

IN THIS CHAPTER

You will learn how to
- recognize the effects of poor communication,
- identify the components of a complete communication system, and
- identify and meet your readers' and listeners' needs.

The Effects of Poor Communication

Janice Willard and Marnie Topoloski have both worked for Multiple Industries in Owen Sound, Ontario, for four years. They are roughly the same age and have similar education and work experience. As well, both hope to be promoted to the department supervisor's position next month, when their present supervisor is transferred to another division. But one has a much better chance than the other.

Janice is known to be a quiet, knowledgeable, highly productive worker who frequently comes up with new ideas and is popular with other members of the staff. Her only problems are an inability to explain a process clearly and a tendency to write rather long-winded, rambling reports when one of the office systems breaks down.

Fair? Possibly not. But managers judge employees by what they see and hear

Marnie is much less reserved than Janice and is equally popular with the staff. Although she seems to be a productive worker, she has much less imagination and only occasionally conceives a new idea. But where Janice tends to be inarticulate, Marnie can always direct her thoughts into coherent sentences, both when she writes and speaks. Consequently, management has noticed her far more than Janice and feels she already possesses the credentials that will make her an efficient supervisor. Marnie's memos to her supervisor and other department heads have created an image of a straightforward, confident person, a "paper" image that has been reinforced by the coherent, confident way she speaks when she has to request materials or equipment, or to explain a procedure.

This image was corroborated when she and Janice applied for the supervisor's position. Both prepared neat application letters. Janice clearly described her education and the positions she had held, but there she stopped. Marnie not only listed her education and work experience, but also described how she felt her background would help her in the new position, and outlined a course in industrial supervision she planned to take at night to ensure she would become an effective supervisor.

When they were interviewed, Marnie again appeared as the better candidate. Although Janice answered questions directly, she hesitated to go into too much detail because she feared she would have difficulty finding the right words and would seem disorganized. Instead, she appeared reticent and uncommunicative, creating the impression that she was unassertive and would not be able to direct other people's work. Marnie, on the other hand, spoke clearly and definitely, not only responding with the required answer to each question but also providing additional information to show she had a sound grasp of the subject. The communication skills she had learned at college, and had honed further on the job, served her well.

Janice needs to read Chapter 11

You may think that selecting a person based primarily on her ability to communicate clearly and persuasively is unrealistic, an unfair way to assess a person's overall capabilities. But what other tool can management use, particularly an employer seeking a new employee?

We tend to take speaking and writing for granted. After all, we learned to speak at an early age and to write some four or five years later. Over the next 10 to 12 years we were encouraged by teachers to write good prose, mostly as essays, and occasionally to speak in front of the class. Often we found writing to be drudgery and speaking to be terrifying. As a result, many of us entered adulthood with a built-in dislike of writing and a gigantic fear of public speaking. And we carried this resistance into college.

Do you hate to write? Or fear public speaking?

Unless we correct these inhibitions early, there is a strong possibility we will carry them with us into the business world—where they can become expensive!

The Costs of Poor Communication

Inadequate communication is far more costly than most people realize, and often the costs are hidden. Janice, for example, was unaware that her inability to write and speak effectively was preventing her from being promoted. She shrugged her shoulders and warmly congratulated Marnie, feeling that next time it would be her turn. But unless she takes steps to improve her communication skills, probably by enrolling in courses on effective writing and speaking, that promotion will be a long time coming.

A lost promotion is not only a missed opportunity but also a financial loss, for most promotions carry with them an increase in pay.

Within business itself the costs of poor communication can be even more significant. Willard Jamieson sells medical equipment and prosthetic appliances to hospitals and medical centres. He has an office on 8th Avenue in Edmonton, and a small warehouse on the south side of the city where he stores the equipment he orders from various manufacturers.

On October 14 Willard received a telephone call from Gary Schultz, the purchasing agent for Westside Health Centre in Regina. Gary said he wanted to place an order for 30 Micro-Rove control units for motorized wheelchairs.

"What price are you asking?" Gary asked. "I want to quote it on the purchase order."

Willard put him on hold while he looked up the catalogue price ($395) and then calculated the total price for 30 Micro-Roves ($11 850). Then he deducted a 12% discount because it was a bulk order.

"That's $347.60 each," he told Gary.

"Or $10 428 for the lot?" Gary replied. "For 30 units?"

"Right!" Willard agreed.

"Don't we get a discount," Gary asked, "if we're buying that many?"

"Sure, you get 12%."

Making assumptions can be costly

"Great!" Gary murmured, as he jotted down the figures. "I'll fax you a purchase order."

"Thank you," Willard replied.

"One more thing," Gary added. "Would you mind dropping me a note confirming the price?"

"Sure will," Willard agreed. And he did, that very afternoon. He wrote:

Willard's letter only *seemed* clear . . .

Dear Gary:

Our price for 30 Micro-Rove wheelchair control units will be $347.60 each or $10 428 for the 30. A discount of 12% applies. Shipping costs from Edmonton to Regina will be extra. Delivery date will be October 24.

Thank you for the order.

Sincerely,
Willard Jamieson

The purchase order from Gary Schultz rolled out of Willard's fax machine two days later, and without examining it closely he dropped it into a file folder.

Three days after that the 30 Micro-Rove units arrived from the supplier and Willard immediately reshipped them to Regina. Two days later his secretary typed and mailed an invoice to the hospital.

The next week Willard received a telephone call from Wanda Hendrix, the supervisor of accounts payable at Westside Health Centre. "There's a discrepancy between your invoice and our purchase order," she announced. "The invoice is higher. Can you explain the difference?"

"Shipping costs, I expect," Willard ventured.

Wanda was doubtful. "Shipping would hardly cost $1251.36."

"Oh, no," he replied, and dug out his copy of the invoice. "Shipping was $34."

And then he looked at the purchase order. "I can see the problem," he said. "There's an error on the purchase order. The unit price is $347.60, which *includes* the discount. But your purchasing agent has deducted a further 12%. That makes the difference of $1251.36."

"I can't buy that!" Wanda retorted. "There's a letter from you here quoting $347.60 as the unit price. There's no indication that the discount has already been deducted. In fact you say, 'A discount of 12% applies.' It's perfectly clear."

"Yes, but that's not what I meant!" Willard gasped.

. . . yet its lack of clarity proved expensive

Saying one thing and meaning another is not conducive to good communication, as Willard discovered. Not making himself clear cost him over $1200.

Incidents like this cost time and money, create aggravation for both parties, and cause one party to lose confidence in the other as a conveyor of information. But, surprisingly, such incidents are not rare: every day businesses encounter problems created by poor communication. Some are humorous and easily resolved. Others are complicated, time-consuming, and costly. Still others—more than there should be—create misunderstandings that sometimes result in incidents that harm people and damage equipment.

Recipe for a near disaster!

When Air Canada flight 143—a Boeing 767 flying nonstop from Ottawa to Edmonton—ran out of fuel at 41 000 feet (12 500 metres) over Lake Winnipeg, a surprised Captain Bob Pearson had to *glide* his controlless aircraft and its alarmed flight crew and passengers to an emergency landing 24 minutes later on a disused runway at Gimli's small airport. The fuel shortage was found to have been caused by a combination of unclear operating instructions and a misunderstanding between the flight crew and the refuellers (the new 767 was the first aircraft in Air Canada's fleet to have its fuel measured in litres rather than gallons). Incredibly, the incident ended safely with only a few bruises to the passengers as they slid down the escape chutes. But if it had not been for the captain's skill, it could just as easily have resulted in a disaster. Indeed, six months later the investigation board chairman, Mr Justice George Lockwood, declared in his 199-page report, "The evidence of a failure of communication at all levels . . . is alarming."

The Communication Circuit

When company owner Gisèle Villeneuve notices there is only one blank ink cartridge remaining in stock for the seven computer printers, she tells Danny Chang to order a new supply. Her request represents one-way communication.

If Danny has not previously ordered ink cartridges, he may ask Gisèle:

How many do you want?
From whom do we normally buy them?
How soon do we need them?

His reply provides two-way communication.

And when Gisèle answers, she completes the communication circuit illustrated in Figure 1-1.

Good communication depends on effective feedback

In a complete communication system, after the message has been transmitted the sender and receiver reverse their roles so that the receiver can provide *feedback*. Feedback informs the original sender that the message has been received and that it either has been understood or needs clarification. (If Danny fully understands what he has to do, he most probably acknowledges Gisèle's request by saying, "I'll get right on it." Such a response provides *positive* feedback.)

Feedback is an essential component of a complete communication system. It helps prevent errors from occurring if a transmission is vaguely worded, as Gisèle's is, and it helps counteract circuit noise.

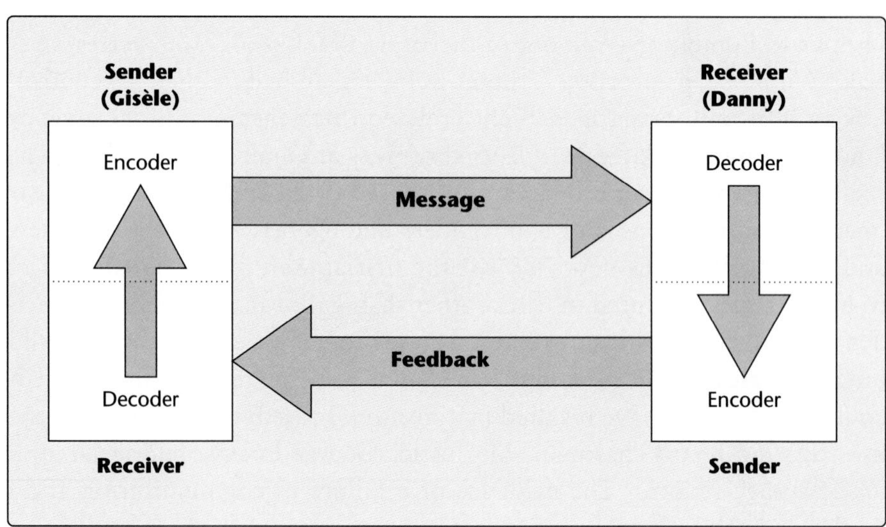

Figure 1-1 The ideal communication system

The Effect of Noise

Circuit noise inhibits a message from transmitting properly, just as the noise from a band in the college pub prevents you from hearing what the person next to you is saying. The effect that circuit noise has on the quality of a transmitted message is shown in Figure 1-2.

Noise can take many forms. It can be physical noise, created by people or equipment. It can be perceptual or "ethnic" noise, created when the receiver's upbringing or personal experience is dissimilar to that of the transmitter. Or it can be personally induced psychological noise, created by the receiver's state of mind at the time he or she receives the message.

Physical noise may be the hum of a poorly insulated air-conditioning system, the voice of the person at the next desk arguing with someone over the telephone, or the hiss of a jet passing overhead. Perceptual noise may simply be the use of an expression familiar to the speaker or writer but not to the particular listener or reader. For example, if I describe a grouchy person as "having got out of the wrong side of his bed this morning," most people would understand exactly what I mean. But if I say the same thing in front of people for whom English is a newly learned language, one of them may whisper to the others, "What does it matter which side of the bed he got out of?" Personal or psychological noise can be caused by worry about a terminally ill parent, anguish over an early-morning argument with a spouse, or concern about an imminent interview for an important promotion. All of these are likely to affect a listener's or reader's concentration.

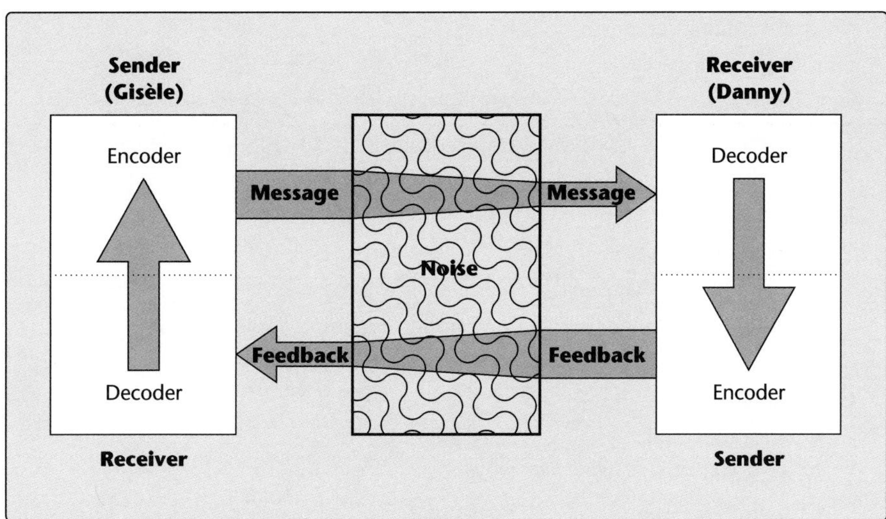

Figure 1-2 The actual communication system

Circuit noise inhibits both transmission and feedback

When you communicate information, you need to be aware of the factors that affect how readily your readers and listeners will understand what you have to say. If you recognize that "noise" may influence reception, you can seek ways to counteract it. Often, this means finding a method of communication that both suits the information you have to convey and fits your readers' and listeners' needs.

Types of Communication

You can communicate in three ways: by writing, by speaking, or by using a visual aid such as a picture. Sometimes these methods are used alone, and at other times two or all three are used together. The three methods are listed in Table 1-1 with a comment on the method's potential for providing immediate feedback.

Only face-to-face communication offers immediate feedback

You can immediately infer from Table 1-1 that listeners and readers can offer immediate feedback only when someone is *speaking* to them. In other communication modes—written and pictorial—there is either no feedback or, at the very best, there is a delay (as there would be if a reader wants clarification of a letter containing unclear statements). Under these conditions even the often-quoted adage that "a picture is worth a thousand words" is

Table 1-1 The relationship between communication methods and their potential for providing immediate feedback

Type of Communication	Potential for Immediate Feedback
Written Communication	None
Oral Communication—	
Conversation	Very good
Lecture Formal talk	Delayed; depends on willingness of speaker to accept questions
Visual Communication—	
Pictorial (chart, diagram)	None
Personal (body language)	Very good (assuming "actor" is present, i.e. not on film or videotape)
Combination of Methods—	
Written and Oral	Very good
Written and Pictorial	None
Oral and Pictorial	Very good
Written, Oral, and Pictorial	Excellent

invalid (unless the originator of the message can be present to respond to viewers' questions).

Interactive computer-based training (CBT) and hypertext, however, permit a user to *interact* with written and pictorial data presented on a computer video monitor, by either clicking a mouse or touching a specific part of the screen. The user's ability to "talk" to the system—to interact with it and thus either obtain or provide instant feedback—both promotes better learning and challenges its viewers.

Meeting the Receiver's Needs

Carl Hinkstrom has been having recurring problems with a Neostat packaging machine. In the past two years he has had to call in a service representative 13 times to repair or adjust the Neostat, and he is beginning to doubt the service person's ability. He decides to write to the manufacturer to complain about the service he is getting. (Neostat does not have a local office and contracts with a small company, Equipment Maintenance Services Limited, to service its equipment.) But when Carl tries to compose an email letter, he has difficulty getting started. First he writes:

Writing the opening words: often a problem!

> I am writing about our Neostat packaging machine, model 2044, which we have owned for two years and bought as a reconditioned unit under the terms of . . .

And there he stops, feeling he is missing the point. He deletes the words from his screen and tries again:

> Two years ago we purchased a reconditioned model 2044 packaging machine that seemed at first to give good service but lately has become somewhat of a problem. The unit was bought on our purchase order No. 21634 and sold to us on your Sales Invoice No. 2236. The Neostat came with a three-month warranty and I must admit for the first four months gave no trouble at all. The problems seem to have started after the 500-hour servicing recommended in the operating manual, which was performed on . . .

Again Carl stops. "That's not what I meant to say," he murmurs, deleting the words.

Twenty minutes later Carl still has not written the letter, so he gets up from his desk and walks down the hall to the coffee shop. His frustration is understandable and certainly not unique. But why has he found writing a straightforward letter such a problem?

Carl's false starts happen because he has omitted an essential step in the communication process. Angered by the servicing problem, he has tried to write solely from his own frustrated viewpoint rather than from the reader's inquiring viewpoint.

To avoid false starts, which are common to all writers of email, letters, memos, and reports, you must *first identify exactly whom you are writing to*. Then you can focus your writing because you will have an image of that person in front of you. Without it you will be writing in a vacuum and, like Carl, you will become frustrated by your inability to fashion satisfactory opening sentences and paragraphs.

To identify your reader, ask yourself four questions:

Step 1: Know whom you are writing to

Step 2: Ask questions about your reader

Step 3: Step into your reader's shoes

Step 4: Focus your message

1. *Who is most likely to act on or react to my message?* Sometimes you will know exactly whom you are writing to. But if you are writing to an organization in general, perhaps requesting information about a new product, you must decide who in that organization would be the logical person to respond to your communication.

   In Carl's case, he has not written to the manufacturer of the Neostat before, so he has to assume that the customer service manager, or a person with a different title but holding an equivalent position, would most likely handle his complaint.

2. *What does my reader know now (about the situation I will be describing)?* Knowing how much your reader knows about you and the problem or situation will give you a starting point. If the reader is familiar with the situation, you can briefly refer to previous events or email messages and then launch into the details you need to present. But if the reader is unfamiliar with the circumstances, you have to start much further back and bring the reader up-to-date.

   In Carl's case the answer will be, "The reader knows very little." Carl can assume his reader will be familiar with the Neostat 2044, but probably does not know the company Carl works for, may not know the name of the company providing service in Carl's area, and has heard nothing previously about the service problem.

3. *What does the reader want to know?* If you are writing in response to a reader's query, you will already know what the reader wants to hear from you. But if you are initiating an exchange of messages, you have to consider what the reader most wants to know.

   In Carl's case, the customer service manager will want to know of any problems that have developed in the equipment the company manufactures and services.

4. *What does the reader need to be told?* Answering this question will help you provide relevant information, as opposed to a lot of details that are of considerable interest to you but only of marginal interest to your reader. Often, your familiarity with a project or problem may prevent you from seeing just how much information a reader needs. You want to avoid offering too few details, so that the reader becomes

annoyed because he or she has to call you for clarification, or providing so much information that the reader becomes bored and is deflected from seeing the point you are trying to draw to his or her attention.

Carl needs to describe the history of events so that the reader will understand the severity of the problem. But at the same time he must be objective and not allow his irritation to become overly evident.

From the ideas presented so far, you may think that these questions and the answers they generate apply only when you are about to write an email, letter, memo, or report. But in practice you will find the four questions are just as applicable when you have information to convey orally—to a customer, to management, or to other employees. How the questions are used to identify a listener or an audience is described in Chapter 10.

TO SUM UP

Poorly executed communications can prove frustrating, time-consuming, and costly. Written communications are particularly important because the writer normally is not present to answer the reader's questions.

Instant feedback is an essential component of a complete communication circuit, but interference may affect how clearly the message is received.

Clear identification of the reader or listener, and his or her information needs, can help you focus your communication before you write or speak.

EXERCISES

Exercise 1.1

For each of the following situations, identify whether the transmitter (writer, speaker, or illustrator) can obtain immediate feedback from the receiver (reader, listener, or viewer).

1. Ann Wenderby shows a parking plan to staff members and is pointing to each person's new parking location.
2. In Truro, Nova Scotia, Phil Karlowsky writes an email to Kerry Mittern in Montreal, inviting him to attend a high school reunion.
3. Rita Tremmerling telephones Sudbury Industries to ask the personnel manager if there are any job openings.

4. Mavis Wolenchuk, in Calgary, sends a list containing names and dates by Priority Post to a hotel in Vancouver, requesting room reservations.
5. Bill Williams and Sandra Pickering sit at personal computers in Ottawa and Windsor, Ontario. The computers are part of a local area network (LAN). Bill types, "I will be in Windsor one week from today. Will you have lunch with me?"
6. Julie Shearer, in Edmonton, sends a drawing of a site plan by fax to her head office in Toronto. On the bottom of the drawing she has written, "Please let me know as soon as possible if this plan has your approval."

Exercise 1.2

Is it easier to write an email or letter that will be read by only one person (such as your supervisor) or an email or letter that will be read by several people (such as the members of a parent-teacher committee)? Explain why.

Exercise 1.3

What four questions should you ask about your reader before you start writing a letter or report?

Exercise 1.4

Think of a situation you have observed, or are aware of, in which poor communication caused a delay or a costly error. Describe the situation and the result in one paragraph.

WEBLINKS

The Communication Process
spider.hcob.wmich.edu/bis/faculty/bowman/comproc.html
This article discusses the communication process and the importance of effective communication. Topics covered include language and meaning, communication and behavior, and relationships and rapport.

Revision in Business Writing
owl.english.purdue.edu/Files/90.html
Part of Purdue University's Online Writing Lab, this page covers the importance of revising your writing. The principles discussed are language, conciseness, clarity, tone, attitude, audience, organization, grammar, punctuation, and spelling.

International Association of Business Communicators (IABC)
www.iabc.com
The IABC provides products, services, activities, and networking opportunities to help people and organizations achieve excellence in business communication. This site includes access to some stories from their award-winning *Communications World* magazine, covering trends and issues in the business communication area.

Getting Off to a Fast Start

chapter 2

Marie Dassault is a marketing analyst for Independent Research Labs Limited. She finds her assignments varied and interesting and, unlike Carl Hinkstrom (in the previous chapter), has no difficulty getting started when she writes her research reports. She identifies her readers and sets to work.

Louise Fournier—Marie's manager—pushes her chair back from her desk and shakes her head. She has been poring over a 73-page draft of a report titled *Analysis of Traffic Patterns in City Malls and Customer Response with Respect to the Feasibility of Installing Self-Serve Video Machines*.

"Terrible title!" she murmurs, reaching for her telephone. "Can you come down for a moment, Marie?" Louise asks. "I'd like to go over your report with you."

Louise knows what is wrong: Marie tries to say too much, to cover all the bases rather than be selective. The title of her report is typical of the pages inside: all the information is there, but it is buried in too much detail. Marie knows who she is writing to, but not how to focus her information.

"You've got all the information here," Louise explains, "but I still need to ask questions. And so will your client."

"All right," Marie agrees. "What have I left out?"

"It's not so much what's missing—I think you've covered everything that has to be said—but I had difficulty in recognizing the most important information when I came across it."

Louise explains that it is not enough simply to present information to a reader. "You have to focus your reader's attention on the critical issues: what the reader most needs to be told. If you don't, your reader may miss important points and draw the wrong conclusions."

IN THIS CHAPTER

You will learn how to

- identify the most important information you have to convey and draw your reader's attention to it,
- organize the details,
- write the first draft, and
- edit your own writing.

Focusing the Message

Focusing a reader's attention on the most important information means

1. clearly identifying the main message before you write (first identify your reader and his or her concerns, as outlined in Chapter 1), and
2. placing the main message *right at the start,* where the reader will see it immediately.

The Climactic Method

"Do you remember being taught the 'climactic' method of writing in high school?" Louise asks.

"Only vaguely," Marie admits. "We used it to write essays, I think."

"Exactly!" Louise says. "And you're still being influenced by it."

Louise draws a sheet of paper toward her and draws the horizontal and vertical axes of a graph. Below the horizontal axis she writes "Time," and to the left of the vertical axis she writes "Information."

"In the climactic method of writing," she explains, drawing the curve shown in Figure 2-1, "you develop your case carefully and logically until you have presented all the details the reader needs to fully understand your point. This information becomes your main message, which you place at the end of the document."

"It's like writing a story," Marie exclaims.

Don't make the reader wait for the Main Message

"Exactly!" Louise says again. "But business readers don't want to wait until the end of a letter or report before they find the most important information. Neither do they want to dig around and search for it. They expect to find the main message right up front."

The Immediate Method

Louise takes another sheet of paper and sketches in and labels a second pair of axes. "For business writing you have to forget about the climactic method," she explains, drawing the curve shown in Figure 2-2, "and use what we call the 'immediate' method. This means you have to bring the main message forward, so the reader encounters it in the very first paragraph."

Put the Main Message right at the start

From her filing cabinet Louise takes several letters and pushes one across the table to Marie. "Here's an example of a letter written using the climactic method."

Marie reads the letter (see Figure 2-3). "I see what you mean," she says. "You have to read right to the end to find Martin Kenny's answer to your question."

"Right," Louise agrees, and she pushes a second letter toward Marie. "Now here is one written using the immediate method."

Marie reads the second letter (see Figure 2-4). "Now I see what you mean," she says. "The answer you want is right up front."

Louise explains that Thanh Nguyen obviously knows he should identify and focus attention on the main message, whereas Martin Kenny probably is still being influenced by the climactic method he was taught at school. "That's the difference between effective and ineffective conveyors of information," she adds. "One speeds up understanding while the other hinders it—or at least builds in a delay."

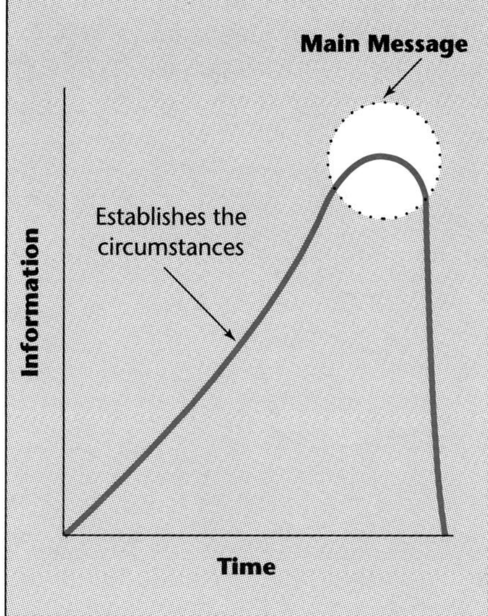

Figure 2-1 The climactic method of writing

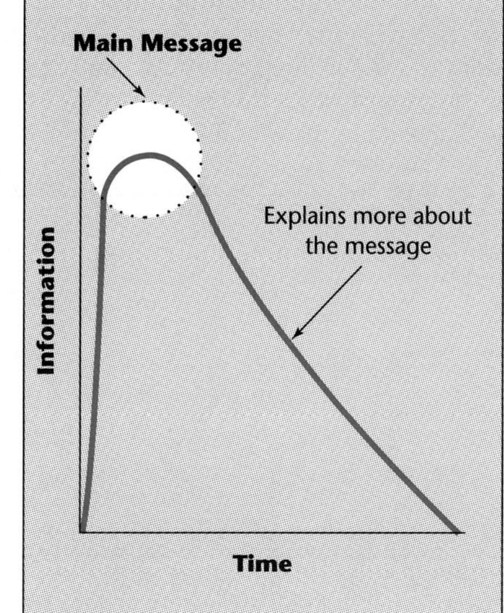

Figure 2-2 The immediate method of writing

Martin Kenny
1806–210 Pan-American Blvd
North Vancouver BC V7F 2R6

February 15, 2001

Ms Louise Fournier
Manager, Atlantic Division
Independent Research Labs Limited
Saint John NB E2R 3B5

Dear Ms Fournier

With reference to your inquiry of January 12, in which you asked if I had experienced any adverse effects from using Brand X Windshield Washer, here is the information you requested.

My experience with Brand X goes back some four years. Initially I started using it when I owned a Honda Civic. That was until about 15 months ago when I sold the Honda and bought a Toyota Tercel. Now, I don't know if other drivers have had the same problem, or if it's just a coincidence, but there was a difference that I noticed at about the same time that I changed from one car to the other.

Main Message delayed! (Wastes reader's time)

The difference should not have anything to do with the cars, because the effect is on me. All through the years I owned the Honda I could handle Brand X without any effect. But from about 15 months ago, when I first started driving the Tercel, I began to notice that, if I splashed Brand X on my hands as I was refilling the storage tank, the next day I would have a rash on my fingers and wrists that would last for 24 hours. As for the cars, I can see no difference in the windshield washing capability of Brand X on either car.

I hope this is the information you want.

Sincerely

Martin Kenny

Figure 2-3 A letter written using the climactic method (the main message is at the end of the letter)

Thanh M Nguyen
247 Lansing Road
Nanaimo BC V9T 4M8

January 29, 2001

Ms Louise Fournier
Manager, Atlantic Division
Independent Research Labs Limited
Saint John NB E2R 3B5

Dear Ms Fournier

I have noticed no change in the windshield washing quality of Brand X over the three years I have used it, but recently I have been aware that if Brand X is splashed on my hands it causes a rash.

Up-front Main Message captures reader's attention

My comments are in response to your letter of January 12, 2001. I have been using Brand X as a windshield washer for my Olds Achieva since I bought the car in May 1998, and it has always seemed to clean the windscreen as efficiently as any other windshield washer. When the liquid started to affect my hands is more difficult to pin down, because I did not at first recognize there was any connection between Brand X and the occasional rash I was experiencing. I am sorry I cannot be more exact.

Regards

Thanh M Nguyen

Thanh M Nguyen

Figure 2-4 A letter written using the immediate method (the main message is at the start of the letter)

Writing the First Words

"There's a technique journalists use to start their news stories," Louise suggests, "and I think you will find it useful." She tells Marie about her cousin Leanne, a reporter for the local newspaper. When Leanne sits down to write a news item, the first words she types are

The secret to getting started. Ssssh!

I want to tell you that . . .

Then she completes the sentence, inserting information she feels will catch readers' attention and provide them with a capsule-size summary of the event she has to report, like this:

> *I want to tell you that . . .* an early morning fire in a warehouse at 2108 Hanover Avenue caused an estimated $200 000 in damage and obstructed eastbound rush-hour traffic for two hours.

When she is satisfied with her opening statement—her *main message*—she removes the six opening words ("I want to tell you that . . . ") so that when her story is printed it looks like this:

> **Fire Creates Traffic Chaos**
>
> An early morning fire in a warehouse at 2108 Hanover Avenue caused an estimated $200 000 in damage and obstructed eastbound rush-hour traffic for two hours.
>
> The alarm was turned in at 5:28 a.m. by a male caller who did not identify himself. Fire Chief Svensen . . .

Louise says that Leanne calls *"I want to tell you that"* her six hidden words. They are always there, helping her start with an informative opening sentence, but her readers never see them.

"Since talking to Leanne I have used the six 'hidden words' whenever I write an email message, letter, or report," Louise tells Marie. "They get me started and prevent me from saying something uninformative as my opening sentence." She places the tip of a finger on the first sentence of Thanh Nguyen's letter (in Figure 2-4) and asks Marie to insert the six hidden words in front of it.

How Thanh Nguyen started his letter (in Figure 2-4)

"I want to tell you that," Marie reads, "*I have noticed no change in the windshield washing quality of Brand X over the three years I have used it, but recently I have been aware that if Brand X is splashed on my hands it causes a rash.*"

"See how it works?" Louise asks. Marie nods. Louise asks her to place *I want to tell you that . . .* in front of Martin Kenny's opening paragraph (see the letter in Figure 2-3).

Marie reads, "*I want to tell you that... with reference to your inquiry of January 12, in which you asked if I had experienced any adverse effects from using Brand X Windshield Washer, here is the information you requested.*" And then she adds, "It doesn't *say* anything!"

"Nothing useful," Louise agrees.

Identifying the Details

"Of course, it's not enough just to present a main message," Louise continues. "You also have to identify the details that follow, and arrange them in a coherent order that will make sense from the reader's point of view."

She suggests dividing the remaining information into three compartments:

- the **Background**, in which you describe the circumstances that have led up to your writing the email, letter, or report,
- the **Facts and Events**, in which you amplify what you have said in the main message, and
- the **Outcome**, in which you describe the result.

Then Louise takes out a third sheet of paper and draws a triangle, as shown in Figure 2-5. "We call this the *writer's pyramid*," she explains.

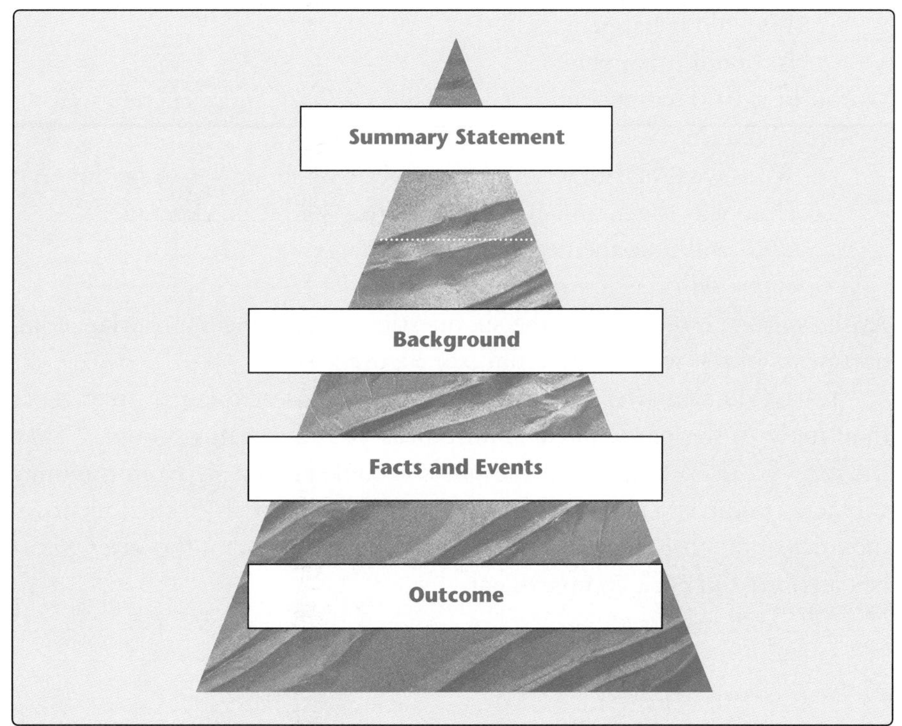

Figure 2-5 The writer's pyramid

The writer's pyramid: your key to planning effective email, letters, and reports

"The top contains the main message, or **Summary Statement**. The remainder contains all the information you need to support what you have said in the Summary Statement."

"That's fine," Marie agrees. "But how do you decide what goes into each compartment?"

"Just answer six questions," Louise replies, and she jots down

Who?
Where?
When?
What?
Why?
How?

She tells Marie that she assigns the six questions to the three compartments and repeats some of the questions:

- In the Background section she answers *Who? Where? When?*:
  Who was involved?
  Where did they go, or where did the event happen?
  When did it happen?
- In the Facts and Events section she answers *What? Why? How?*:
  What happened?
  Why did it happen?
  How did it happen?
- And in the Outcome section she answers *What?* and sometimes *How? Who? When?*:
  What was the result? or *What* will be done, or has to be done?
  How was the action effected? or *How* will it be effected?
  Who will take the necessary action?
  When will the action take place?

Align the questions (and their answers) with the appropriate writing compartments

As she speaks, Louise writes the six questions beside the appropriate compartments of the writer's pyramid (see Figure 2-6).

Ask and answer only *relevant* questions

"You seldom answer all the questions," Louise explains, "just those that apply to the particular circumstances you are writing about." Then she draws a third letter from the pile she took previously from the filing cabinet. On the left-hand side of the letter (see Figure 2-7), she jots down the titles of the three compartments and the questions that the letter writer has answered in each compartment.

Developing an Outline

Michael Chagal is the Southside branch manager of High Gear Truck and Auto Rentals Ltd. When he planned to write a memo announcing the

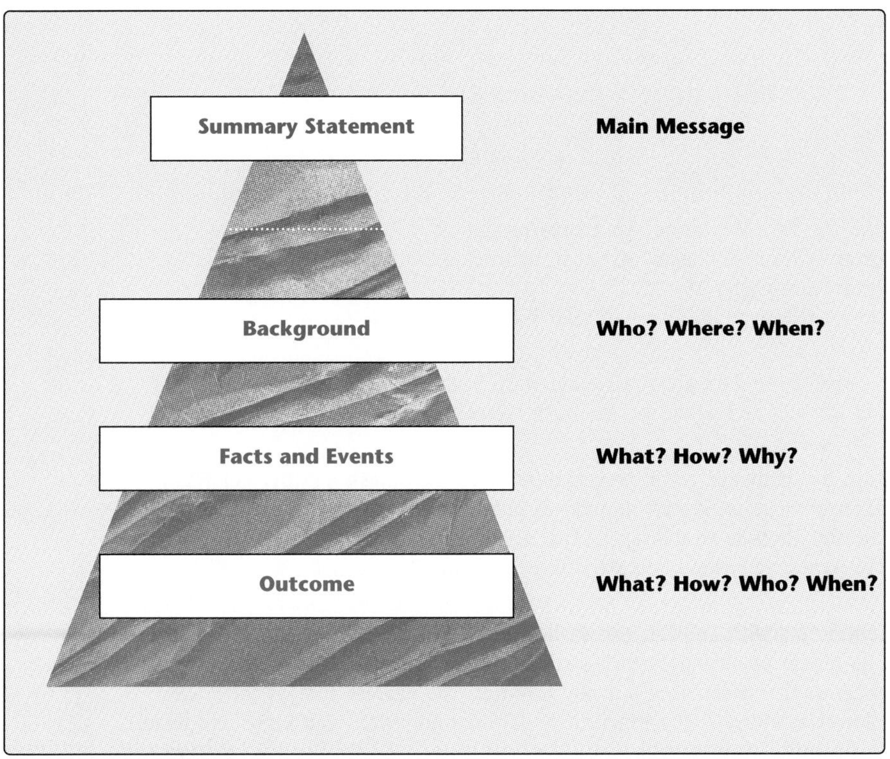

Figure 2-6 Typical questions to be answered in each writing compartment

branch's need to negotiate a new vehicle washing contract with a different car wash company (see Figure 2-7), he first jotted down the headings and subheadings shown in Figure 2-8. These headings helped him write his memo quickly and easily, and present his information logically and coherently.

The best way to create a writing outline for a longer letter or report is not to force it. Because events happen chronologically, we tend to report them in a chronological sequence, which is not the best way to approach the task.

Loosen up how you develop your writing outline

"The smart thing to do," Louise explains to Marie, "is to *disorganize* your planning. Sit in front of a blank screen, or take a sheet of lined paper, and settle down somewhere where you won't be disturbed for 10 minutes. Now type in or write any topics, in any order, you think you should write about in your report."

She tells Marie not to worry if the items are not in sequence, or if on closer inspection some seem irrelevant. "You'll look after that later. At this stage you must have a completely open mind, uncluttered by details, so that your brain freewheels. It's called brainstorming, and it's the best way to explore all the aspects you need to cover."

High Gear Truck and Auto Rentals Ltd.

Memorandum

To: Fern Whitmore, Area Superintendent
From: Michael Chagal, Manager, Southside
Date: February 15, 2001
Subject: Impending Change in Car Wash Availability

Summary Statement
(Main Message)

We need to find an alternative car wash because our contract with Splash and Dry will end when the car wash closes in six weeks.

Background
Who?
When?
What?

Sven Ingamundsen, who owns and operates the Splash and Dry Car Wash, plans to retire on March 30 and has put his property and the business up for sale. There is no guarantee that the buyer, when one comes forward, will want to continue operating the car wash.

Facts and Events
What?
Why?
How?

Contracting with another car wash means sacrificing convenience and incurring higher operating costs. Splash and Dry is only 100 metres away, directly across the street from our rental outlet; the nearest competitor is 2.8 kilometres away, at the junction of Gateway Boulevard and Kingsland Road. Splash and Dry charges us only $3 per vehicle; my initial enquiries show that the competition will charge at least $1 more per vehicle.

A possible alternative would be for High Gear Truck and Auto Rentals to purchase or lease the Splash and Dry property and to continue operating the car wash. This, incidentally, would also provide us with much needed parking space for our fleet.

Outcome
What?
Who?
When?

If you feel purchasing the business is a viable alternative, I will discuss selling price and a possible lease price with Ingamundsen. In the interim I will enquire about contract rates with the three car wash facilities that are within 5 kilometres of our Southside outlet, and will report my findings to you on February 28.

Michael

Figure 2-7 A memorandum divided into writing compartments

Summary Statement	
Car wash closing Need to find new one	
Background	
Who? When? What?	Ingamundsen retiring Closing shop March 30 Find replacement
Facts and Events	

What? Why? How?	Find suitable alternative
	Why is it a problem?
	  Others much farther away
	  Others have higher prices
	Possible alternative is to buy car wash

Outcome	

What? Who? When?	Enquire about prices
	  Property purchase
	  Contract with other car washes
	Report by February 28

Figure 2-8 A simple writing outline

Jot down main thoughts; insert them into the compartments

Louise types in an instruction and the six blocks shown in Figure 2-9 appear on her computer screen. She explains that they represent the six steps of her outlining method. She tells Marie that identifying the reader is an essential first step. "Knowing your reader will help you establish your purpose for writing in step 2, type or write some headings in step 3, and then decide which headings are truly relevant in step 4."

In step 4, Louise crosses out any heading she now considers irrelevant. Then, between the remaining headings, she inserts a few additional subheadings wherever she feels a need to enlarge upon a particular topic.

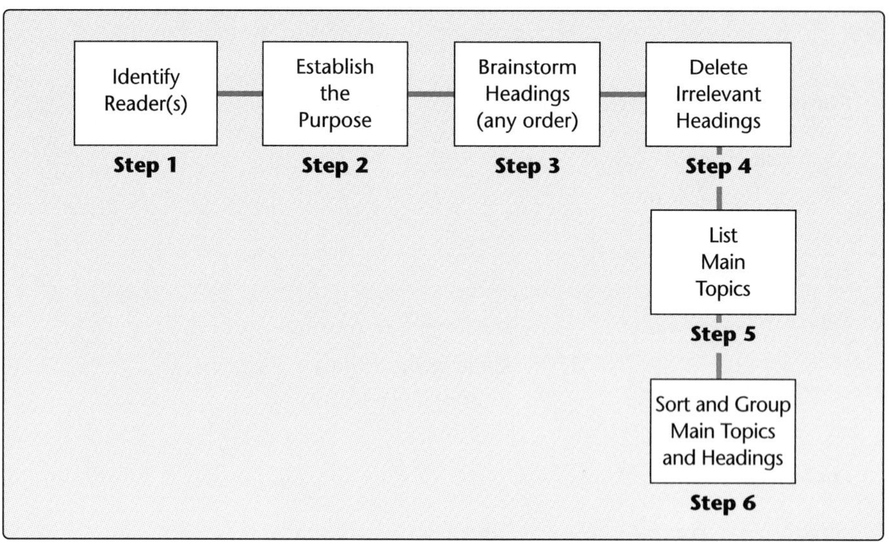

Figure 2-9 The six planning steps for outlining a long letter or report

Refrain from organizing until late in the planning stage

Not until steps 4 and 5 of the outlining process does Louise do any organizing. In step 4 she examines the remaining headings to identify what general topic areas are becoming apparent. These she lists on a separate sheet as five or six primary topic headings (step 5) and arranges them in a logical order. Finally, she returns to the first list and identifies which of its headings and subheadings fit under each of the primary topics she has just identified. She forms them into groups and arranges each group into a logical sequence under its primary topic heading (this is step 6). Figures 2-10 and 2-11 provide examples of Louise's outlining method.

"You can outline with pen and paper, or you can do it with a computer," Louise adds. "I like outlining on screen, because it gives me the freedom to move headings around, insert new ones, and erase irrelevant ones without creating a mess, as I would if I were to work on paper."

Writing the Whole Document

Getting started is difficult, whether you write with a pen or keystroke at a computer terminal. Either you stare at a blank sheet of paper with only horizontal lines to relieve its monotony, or you face a blank screen with only a cursor blinking at you from its top left-hand corner. Both situations inhibit writing.

For many business writers, the problem has been aggravated by a well-meaning person in their past drilling into them that *they need to be organized* when they write: to start at the beginning and "set the scene," to

Outline for "Use of Suntan Parlors" (STPs) Report

Who commissioned survey?	-identify -purpose -developed questionnaire
Survey details	-types of STPs -survey dates
Letter of authority	-quote or attach
Health hazard	-awareness -concerns
Number of surveyors	-(data)
Number of people surveyed	-age groups -locations
How many use STPs?	-do } by age group -don't } -why or why not? -satisfied? -health concern?
What does it cost to use STP?	-(data)
Which season is most popular?	-(data)

Figure 2-10 Louise Fournier's "brainstormed" outline

work through the body of the text and establish all the facts in a logical (which usually means chronological) order, and to finish by drawing a conclusion that evolves naturally from the facts they have already articulated. Some businesspeople write well this way, finding the road map prescribed by the outline a comfortable route to follow. But far more find that starting at the beginning seems to block their creativity.

Find a Quiet Place to Write

Follow a four-step writing plan

Finding the right place to write may seem unimportant, yet where you write can have a marked effect on how much and how well you write. The "right" place is a location where you will not be disturbed by outside sounds, where

Outline for "Use of Suntan Parlors" Report

Background

Survey Purpose
Who Commissioned Survey?
Description of Suntan Parlors (STPs)
- -How they operate
- -Is there a health hazard?

Survey Details

Development of Questionnaire
Survey Dates
Locations of Survey Sites
Number of People Surveyed
- -Age distribution

Responses
- -Number using STPs (by age group)
  - -Identify main user group
  - -Degree of satisfaction
  - -Concern about health
- -Number not using STPs (by age group)
  - -Reasons for not using

Analysis of Results

Figure 2-11 Louise Fournier's revised outline

other people cannot intrude, where you cannot be reached by telephone, and where you will not be distracted by other work that needs your attention. (If you write with pen and paper, this is reasonably easy to do. But if you write at a computer keyboard, usually you have to work at a set place—unless you are fortunate enough to work on a portable computer.)

Step 1: Strive for continuity

Your objective should be to write uninterrupted for 60 to 75 minutes. In the first 10 to 15 minutes you get started—you loosen up your writing hand—and the final 10 minutes you wrap up and "set the scene" for the next writing session. The middle 35 to 50 minutes are for really productive writing, when nothing must derail your train of thought. (It can take no more than a brief call from your travel agent, asking whether you want an early morning or mid-afternoon flight home from Quebec City, to divert your attention.)

Continuity is essential. If, as you write, you cannot remember the name of a person, a date you need to quote, or how to spell a word ("ingenious" or "ingenuous," for example), do not stop to research the name or date, or to consult your dictionary. Just write "name" or "date" or "ingenious" in the appropriate place in your narrative and insert "(?)" after the word, so you can find it easily later on when you look back over your draft.

Start in the Middle

Step 2: Write first what you know best

Just as you may think you have to prepare an outline chronologically, you may also think you have to write chronologically. But that is not true. The best place to start writing is *anywhere* but at the beginning. The first sections of a letter or report are the Summary Statement and the Introduction. In all but very short documents, you will probably have difficulty writing these introductory sections when you do not yet know what the following sections contain. Instead, look over your outline and select the topic that you know best, or that interests or challenges you most, and write about that topic first. Words will come more easily and you will seem to reach the middle—the most productive—part of your 75-minute writing session more quickly.

Don't Stop to Edit

Step 3: Avoid *all* interruptions

No matter where you start, you will probably find the first paragraphs you write do not please you. Recognize what professional writers already know: they revise the first two or three paragraphs more than any other. But they also know how dangerous it is to stop and try to improve those paragraphs before they write any more, for if they do they may never get past the first screen. They keep typing, saying to themselves, "I know my first paragraphs are not satisfactory, but I will not attempt to change them now. I'll leave that until later, when a lot more has been written." And when they do go back, often after the remainder of the letter or report has been written, they find they can much more easily refashion those early paragraphs.

Similarly, resist the temptation to stop every so often to reread what you have written. Almost always you will find sections that do not please you, and you will be tempted to rewrite them immediately. Again this will affect your writing continuity. Worse, you may become dissatisfied with the way your whole letter or report is shaping up, which in turn may reduce your enthusiasm for writing it.

End with the Next Start

Most of us like to "compartmentalize" our work when it is part of a project, to tie up the loose ends before we get on with something else. But if we carry this practice into our writing, we may be inhibiting our ability to start easily the next time we place our hands on the keyboard or put pen to paper.

Step 4: Plan the next writing session

You may find it satisfying to wrap up each writing session knowing you have completed a particular section of your document, but you would do better to go a little further and leave a few ends untied. When you write the concluding sentence that marks the end of a writing section, you probably press "Save" with a sigh of relief. But when you return the next day, ready to write another section, you have to wind yourself up all over again. To lessen the amount of "rewinding" you have to do, after ending one section immediately jot down a few words, either on screen or on paper, outlining what you plan to say when you start the next section. Write just enough so that you will be able to pick up the threads easily.

When you do return, read the last page or two of the section you completed the previous time (but try to resist the temptation to edit what you wrote!). Then use your notes to help you write the first paragraphs of the new section. You will find you restart much more readily.

Revising Your Own Words

There is more to reading and revising than simply taking a freshly written draft in one hand and a blue pencil in the other, especially when revising one's own words, which can be more difficult to edit than those written by someone else. (In Chapter 13 I recommend that you print a hard copy of your draft, and edit or proofread on paper rather than on screen.)

Step 1: Wait

Pause before you proofread, then read with a plan

The first step in the revision phase is to put your draft aside for long enough so you can read your words *objectively*. If you read them while you are still keyed up from the writing experience, you will be able to hear your own voice behind the words, causing you to overlook spelling errors, awkwardly constructed sentences, or vague or ambiguous statements. What you really need is to see what your readers will see: cold, clinical type. Pass the file through a spell-check program, print a hard copy, and use that to check your work.

Step 2: Read

There are two reading stages: a straight-through read with no stops to revise the document, and a slow, careful read to identify where changes are required and to incorporate them.

Your first reading should be done without a pen or pencil in your hand. The idea is to gain a feel for the whole document, which can be particularly important if it is long and you have written it over several sittings. This initial reading also lets you view your letter or report in the same way your readers will see it. If you stop to make changes, you will miss gaining that first overall impression.

Step 3: Revise

Your second—and subsequent—readings should be done carefully and methodically. Now you are searching for specific faults, for words that are misused or misspelled, sentences that are unclear or poorly structured, and paragraphs that lack continuity or are loosely knit. By the time you have finished, you should have made six "quality checks."

Check for Accuracy

As you read and revise your words, remember to verify that names, addresses, telephone numbers, quantities, dates, and similar specific details have been transcribed correctly. Never *assume* they are correct. For example, if when keystroking you inadvertently transpose the figures 421 and write them as 412, unless you go back to your original data and check that every detail you have quoted is correct, such an error will probably remain undetected through every level of editing and proofreading.

Don't let your knowledge of the subject blind you to errors in your words

Your readers will expect you to present accurate information. If they find just one inaccuracy, they will tend to view everything you write with suspicion. If they find another, they will seriously question your reliability as a conveyor of information. Neither you nor your employer can take that risk.

Check for Clarity

Your familiarity with a project can cause you to write sentences that, although perfectly clear to you, are misunderstood by or are incomprehensible to your readers. For example, in mid-July, accountant Derrick Bursa sent this one-sentence email to all of the company's employees:

> To all employees
>
> May I remind you that your July and August expense accounts must reach the Accounting Department by August 31; after that you will not be paid until next year.

Derrick meant that expense accounts received after August 31 would be paid with funds drawn from the next *financial* year, which was to start on September 1. He was not expecting a flood of email messages—and even some telephone calls—from indignant employees demanding to know why they should have to wait three months for their September expense accounts to be paid.

Although Derrick's unclear message did not incur any visible costs, it proved frustrating, aggravating, and time-consuming. He had to explain his message to over 20 callers, and then spend even more time writing a second, clearer email message to everyone.

What could Derrick have done to check that his message was clear? And what can he do in the future? He could try a technique practised by two supervisors in a major business enterprise in Edmonton. Whenever either of them writes an important letter or report to a client, she first sends a draft copy to the other supervisor to read. In this way she obtains an opinion from an objective (unbiased) reader.

Check for Brevity

Check: Does the reader need *everything* I have written?

You can identify whether you are trying to explain too much by asking two additional questions about the reader:

1. *Does my reader need all the details I have supplied?* To answer this question, you must first establish how much your reader knows about the project or circumstances you are describing. If you have already identified your reader (see pages 10–11), this question normally can be answered easily.

2. *Could some of the details go in an attachment, rather than in the body of the email, letter, or report?* Much will depend on whether the reader will need to refer to the specific details as he or she reads. A useful compromise is to place the full details in an attachment and just a summary of the key points in the body of the document.

Check for Simplicity

The best business communicators know they should avoid using jargon or long words when equally sound but simpler short words are available. Some business writers use long words because they think the words sound businesslike. (They write "an error of considerable magnitude" when they could just as easily say "a large error," or they refer to "staff remuneration" and the "corporate superannuation scheme" when they would be understood by everyone if they were to write "employees' pay" and the "company pension plan.") Others use big words because they have seen their bosses use them and so think it is the proper way to write. But all they succeed in doing is making themselves sound pompous or a little unsure, as though they are hiding their ineptness behind the big words.

The key to simplicity is to use short words rather than long words and to avoid overworked expressions such as "at this point in time" when you really mean "now." (For a list of common overworked expressions, see Chapter 12, page 343.)

Check for Continuity

There should be a logical flow from item to item within the document. The reader should sense the naturalness of the flow, yet be unaware of it. If you plan your letters and reports using the pyramid method suggested in Chapters 3 through 7—whether they are being sent electronically or on paper—you can feel reasonably sure you have achieved a logical flow of information. If you also identify your readers accurately, you will be more likely to write well-developed introductory information that helps them understand the details that follow.

Check for Correct Tone

Check: Am I "talking" to my reader(s)?

Adopting the correct tone means writing at the right level for a particular reader (or group of readers). You neither want to aggravate knowledgeable readers by providing them with details they already know, nor frighten off less knowledgeable readers by skimping on details that may seem obvious to you but are essential to them. You will find it easier to adopt the correct tone if, before you start writing, you thoroughly research your readers, their needs, and their primary interests. Then when you sit down to write, say what you have to say as naturally as you can. Use these four guidelines to help you:

1. *Be sincere.* Make your readers feel you are personally interested in them and their concerns and sincerely want them to have a thorough understanding of the topic you are describing. This information is not something you can *say*, but something you can convey through the enthusiasm within your words.

2. *Be direct.* Level with your readers. Tell them the main news immediately, whether good or bad. Save all the explanatory details until later in the communication.

3. *Be definite.* Decide clearly what you have to say, then say it without hedging or explaining more than the reader needs to understand your message.

4. *Be human.* Let your readers feel there is a real person writing the letter or report, not a computer or a business organization. Use the personal pronouns and emphasize the "you" and "your" more than the "we"

and "our." If you are writing an email or an informal or semiformal letter, and know the reader personally, use "I"; if you are writing a semiformal or formal report, or an email or letter in which you are representing your company's point of view, use "we."

Know When to Stop

Check: Have I proofread enough?

How many times should you revise a document before you decide it is good enough to send out? Much will depend on the importance of the document and who will read it. If you are writing a short email or memorandum to your supervisor in which you describe a computer error that caused several customers to be billed twice, you will probably read and revise the draft just once. If you are writing a letter of explanation and apology for the double billing to one of your company's customers, you might read and revise the letter twice. But if you are writing a proposal for your company to conduct a study for a client, or a detailed report describing a survey of the client's products, you will be more careful and so read and revise several drafts before mailing the document.

TO SUM UP

To write more easily, and at the same time create informative letters and reports, you should

- clearly identify your readers and what they most need to know,
- loosen up when you develop your writing outline (brainstorm),
- if possible, write where you will not be interrupted,
- summarize the most important information in the opening paragraph, and
- search for specific faults each time you read and revise your draft.

EXERCISES

Exercise 2.1

What is the *first* step you should take when planning a letter or report? Why is this step so important?

Exercise 2.2

Which of the two report planning methods do you feel would work best for you: the traditional "organized" method, or the proposed "brainstorming" method? Explain your choice.

Exercise 2.3

Label the compartments of the writer's pyramid.

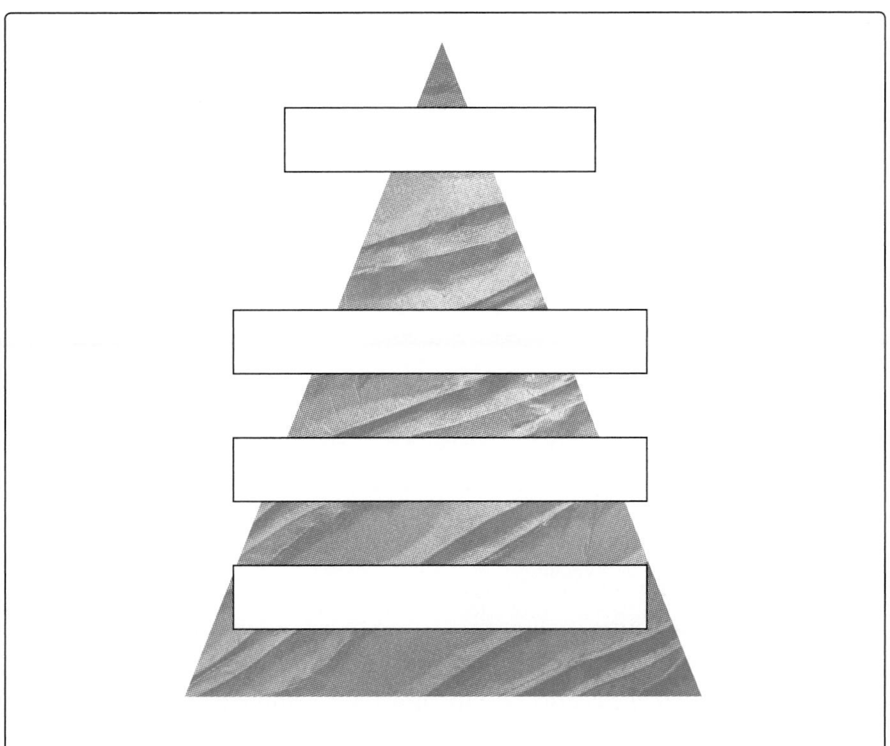

Fill in the blanks!

Exercise 2.4

What are the "six hidden words" used by newspaper reporters to start the first sentence of each article they write?

Exercise 2.5

Does a reader learn the most important information more quickly when an email or letter is written in the climactic method or the immediate method? Explain why.

Exercise 2.6

If you have a long project report to write, and have a portable computer you can use or are going to handwrite the report, where would you choose to do the writing? Explain why you would choose that location.

Exercise 2.7

As you write the long project report in Exercise 2.6, should you write just one or two pages at a time, and then read the page(s) over and make any necessary revisions before going on to write the next one or two pages? Or should you write the whole report without making revisions until the whole document has been written? Explain why you would use one or the other approach.

Exercise 2.8

Which of the four guidelines for setting the right tone do you feel is most important? (The guidelines are as follows: be sincere, be direct, be definite, and be human.) Why do you feel it is most important?

Exercise 2.9

Why is it more difficult to revise a report you have written yourself than to revise a report written by someone else?

Exercise 2.10

Is it better to edit your own work on a computer screen or on paper? Explain why.

WEBLINKS

The Craft of Writing

www.inkspot.com/craft/

This site provides a wealth of resources to help improve your writing and writing habits. Visit the section on inspiration to find tips on how to overcome writer's block.

Organizing Your Thoughts

www.cs.unc.edu/~jbs/sm/Part1_organizetd.html

Read about how to organize your ideas and the importance of preparing an outline to structure your writing.

Verify and Revise

www.cs.unc.edu/~jbs/sm/Part1_verifyrev.html

This site provides checklists and questions to consider when revising your writing.

Informative Letters and Memorandums

chapter 3

At 6:15 p.m., Marita's telephone rings. She is alone in the office and normally does not expect to receive calls in the evening after the office has closed.

"Business Learning Systems," she announces. "Marita Estavo speaking."

"It's Terry," a male voice replies. "Terry Wing. I tried calling you at home . . . "

"I had some paperwork to catch up on," Marita explains. She is marketing manager for BLS, and Terry is one of her sales representatives. "Where are you?"

"Montreal." Terry can hardly keep the excitement out of his voice. "I've got great news! Tormont Canada Incorporated has placed an order for 300 Modular Learning Programs."

"Three hundred! Well done, Terry."

"Not just the software," Terry explains. "They're buying the hardware too: video monitor, playback unit, CD-ROM . . . the whole lot!"

"Now that *is* an order!" Marita replies enthusiastically, aware just how good this quarter's sales charts will look.

"But there is a catch . . . " Terry continues. "They want the first 100 units to be in their plant in just two weeks. And then 100 more every two weeks after that. I had to guarantee we can meet those dates, just to get the order. We can, can't we?"

"It'll be tight, but we'll manage," Marita assures him. "We'll just have to."

"They want a letter from you—a guarantee—confirming both the price and the three delivery dates."

"I'll do it right away," Marita tells him. "I suggest you call Tormont in the morning, or go and see them. You can say you have spoken to me and my letter is already in the mail. Better still, I'll fax a copy to them."

Marita writes down the price and delivery dates that Terry quotes, then hangs up the telephone and turns to her computer. "Hmmm . . . " she muses as she boots up the system. "I really have *three* letters to write: the confirmation letter to Tormont, accepting its order; a memorandum to our

A major sale starts the paperwork

production department, instructing them to set the wheels in motion; and an announcement to the company president, informing him we've landed the sale. I had better get busy!"

IN THIS CHAPTER

You will learn how to plan and write informative letters that do not need a reply from the reader. Specifically, you will learn how to write letters that

- confirm an arrangement or the outcome of a discussion,
- give instructions,
- pass information along or make an announcement,
- provide a reference about someone you know,
- accompany a document or shipment, and
- thank someone for doing something.

Planning Informative Letters

Like Louise Fournier in Chapter 2, Marita Estavo uses the pyramid technique to plan her letters and memorandums. She keeps a writing plan stored on disk for each situation she is likely to encounter, and calls up the appropriate plan when she has a particular letter to write. After typing in a command, the pyramid shown in Figure 3-1 pops onto the screen.

She uses this writing plan to organize information-type letters into compartments. In each letter, Marita

- opens with a **Summary Statement** (preceded by the six hidden words "I want to tell you that . . . "),
- continues with **Background** information that helps the reader understand what has happened previously and why she is writing,
- continues with **Details** that amplify and provide evidence for what she has said in the Summary Statement, and
- finishes with a **Closing Statement** that offers a *useful* final remark (rather than a low-information "duty" remark such as, "I trust that the above information meets with your requirements").

Some letters, such as those that convey information, fit this writing plan exactly. For others, such as an instruction, she relabels some of the compartments.

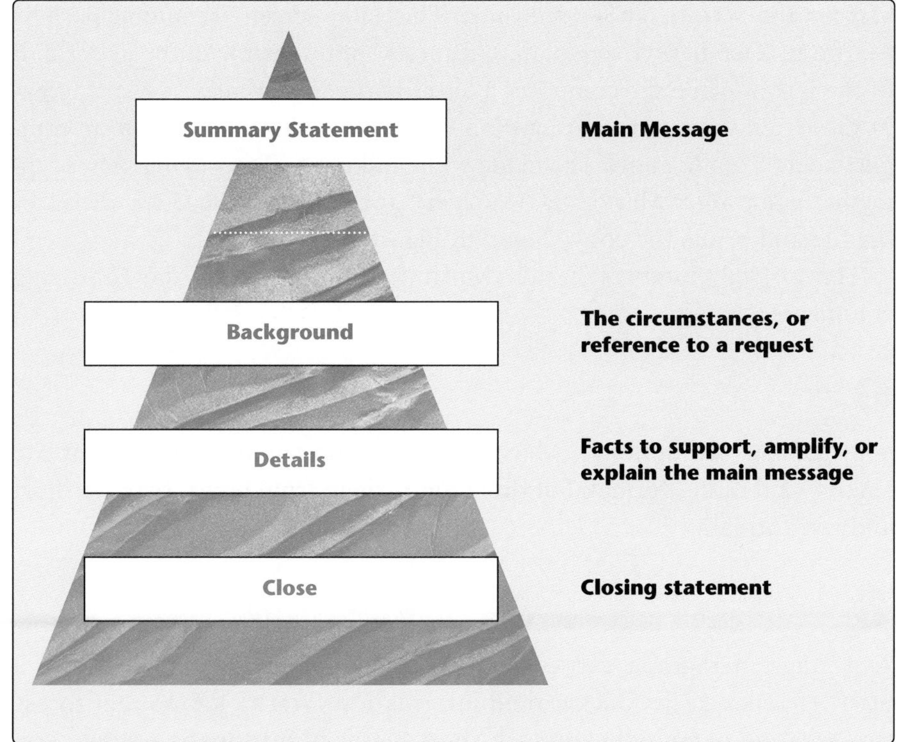

Figure 3-1 A basic writing plan for information-type letters

Informative letters do not ask the reader to respond

Confirming a Contract or Arrangement

Marita types in a three-stroke command. "For the letter to Tormont Canada Incorporated I'll use the writing plan for a confirmation letter," she murmurs. The writer's pyramid on the screen remains the same as in Figure 3-1, but it contains the following information:

- A **Summary Statement** very briefly states that the writer is confirming a previous tentative agreement.
- A **Background** section refers briefly to the circumstances and any previous events or correspondence. (In short confirmation letters, the Summary Statement and Background are often combined into a single paragraph.)
- A **Confirmation Details** section clearly defines the facts and figures that both parties have agreed to. A confirmation letter may be the first step in drawing up a legal agreement such as a purchase order or contract.
- A **Closing Statement** offers a brief remark such as, "Please call me if you have any questions."

Marita presses another key and a horizontal line appears across the centre of the screen. Simultaneously, the pyramid moves into the upper

Keep pyramid writing plans accessible

half of the screen, above the line. This split-screen technique permits Marita to keep her writing plan, outline, or notes visible in the upper half of the screen while she composes a letter in the lower half. As Marita keys in the letter, using the writing plan as a guide, she fills in its four compartments from the notes she made while talking to Terry Wing. After typing her name and "Marketing Manager" at the foot of the letter, she saves the file and prints the copy shown in Figure 3-2.

The circled numbers beside Marita's letter refer to the following comments:

Subject lines are optional. Marita uses a subject line in letters that are lengthy and rather formal, but often omits them from letters that are short and less formal.

2

This single paragraph carries both Marita's **Summary Statement** and a brief reference to the **Background** information. Marita knows that to use two separate paragraphs for such short pieces of information would create a fractured effect.

These are the **Confirmation Details.** Because a confirmation letter is a statement rather than a contract, it should spell out only the details of immediate concern to the reader. For a major order like this, when M Doucette receives the confirmation letter he will arrange for Tormont either to prepare a contract or raise a purchase order that provides specific details of what is being ordered, and how and when the products or services are to be delivered.

Marita correctly uses numerals rather than bullets for these items. Generally, numbers should be reserved for items that represent steps or are part of a sequence.

In her **Closing Statement** Marita thanks the customer for placing the order, but does not gush or become overly effusive. She retains a natural, friendly, businesslike tone throughout.

Business Learning Systems Limited

200 Riverside
London ON N6J 1A8
www.bls.com

Tel: (519) 489-7240
Fax: (519) 489-7249
email: m.estavo@bls.com

March 22, 2001

Eugene P Doucette
Manager, Information Services
Tormont Canada Inc
1870 rue de Moulpied
Montreal QB H2R 8K3

Dear M Doucette

1 **Acceptance of Order for 300 BLS 210 Learning Systems**

2 I am confirming our acceptance of your order for 300 Modular Interactive Learning Systems model BLS 210, placed with our representative Terry Wing on March 21, 2001.

3 Each BLS 210 Learning Program will consist of

- Playback unit 801 with infrared remote control,
- Color video monitor model 444 with 350 mm diameter screen,
- All associated cabling,
- Software for the 12-module Supervisory Management Program, and
- Online operating instructions (plus a 110-page manual).

Use bullets when the sequence is unimportant

Our price will be $910 for each complete BLS 210 Learning System, or a total of $273 000 for the 300 systems. This price includes shipping costs and a six-month warranty on all parts and labor. It does not include federal and provincial taxes.

The units will be shipped surface express, in three 100-system shipments f.o.b. your plant, with delivery on the following dates:

4
1. First shipment: April 9, 2001
2. Second shipment: April 23, 2001
3. Final shipment: May 7, 2001

Use numerals to denote sequence or to prioritize items

5 Terry Wing and I very much appreciate your order. Terry will be contacting you regularly to ensure that delivery is on schedule and operation of the units is satisfactory.

Regards

Marita Estavo

Marita T Estavo
Marketing Manager

Figure 3-2 A comprehensive confirmation letter

This confirmation letter is not the first Marita has written today. She belongs to the Southern Ontario Association of Marketing Managers (SOAMM), which meets once a month, and she takes an active part in the Association's activities by arranging for business equipment demonstrations and guest speakers at the Association's meetings. One week ago she visited Erin Caterers in London, Ontario, to discuss prices and catering arrangements for a forthcoming SOAMM social event. Last night she presented her findings at a SOAMM executive meeting, and the committee authorized her to go ahead. This morning she wrote a short email to the caterers to confirm that the Association wants them to cater the event (see Figure 3-3).

Marita's first paragraph combines **Summary Statement** and **Background** information, confirms the arrangements, and just briefly refers to the events that led up to the letter being written. The second paragraph is a **Closing Statement** that outlines what has to be done next. Marita omits the Confirmation Details compartment because there is no point in listing detailed arrangements that will be spelled out in the caterers' quotation.

Use short confirmation letters to establish arrangements *in writing*

Many confirmation emails and letters are as short as this one, and frequently follow spoken arrangements made with a business associate. You may want to confirm the date and time of an airline flight, lunch meeting, building inspection, or conference. Or you may simply want to remind a sometimes forgetful business associate that you have a joint appointment, and a confirmation letter or, better still, an email, is a more polite and less obvious way of offering the reminder.

If you have had an informal meeting or a teleconference with two or more people, it's an excellent idea to summarize the decisions you reached and the plans you made for taking some form of action, and sending a copy to each participant. Use an abbreviated form of the compartments in Figure 3-1:

Summary Statement:	Write a sentence starting with: "Summary of . . . (*meeting* or *teleconference*)," and state the purpose of the discussion.
Background:	List who took part.
Details:	List, in point form: • decisions reached, and • actions to be taken (including by whom and by when).

To: k.oherlihy@erincaterers.on.ca
C: laurie.malan@soamm.on.ca
From: m.estavo@soamm.on.ca
Date: March 22, 2001
Re: Catering SOAMM Social

Kevin

The executive committee of the Southern Ontario Association of Marketing Managers (SOAMM) has agreed to engage Erin Caterers to cater the Association's spring social evening in The Round House of Grosvenor Park on Friday, May 25. The arrangements you and I discussed on March 19 were considered ideal.

If you will send me a detailed price and facilities proposal, I will forward it to the Association's treasurer.

Marita Estavo

Program Chair

In a short confirmation letter you can combine writing compartments

Figure 3-3 A simple confirmation letter sent by email

Writing an Instruction Letter

The production manager at Business Learning Systems is Emilio Rodrigues, and Marita writes to him next. But because there are several things she needs to mention, she first creates an outline file and types in the topics in random order:

Special order—300 BLS 210s

Start right away

Must meet delivery dates (quote them)

May have to work overtime

First date hardest to meet

Count—order enough to make 100—*today*

Then order 200 more

Count cartons—make more

Make a schedule

Now Marita scans the list and types a number in front of each topic (in the order she plans to cover the topics in her memo), and instructs the computer to rearrange the items into that order.

When Marita is ready to start writing, she keys in a command to depict the writing plan for an instruction letter in the upper half of the screen (see Figure 3-4).

For an instruction letter, two labels in the basic writing plan in Figure 3-1 are changed so that the four compartments become

- **Summary Statement,**
- **Reason** (which may include some Background),
- **Instruction Details** (which are the steps the reader has to follow), and
- **Closing Statement.**

Now Marita types a two-stroke command that shifts the writing plan to the upper-left quarter of the screen and places her outline beside it, in the upper-right quarter. Then, with the writing plan and outline in front of her, she types the letter shown in Figure 3-5. The following comments are cross-referenced to the circled numbers beside Marita's letter.

Ensure your reader understands why the instruction has to be followed

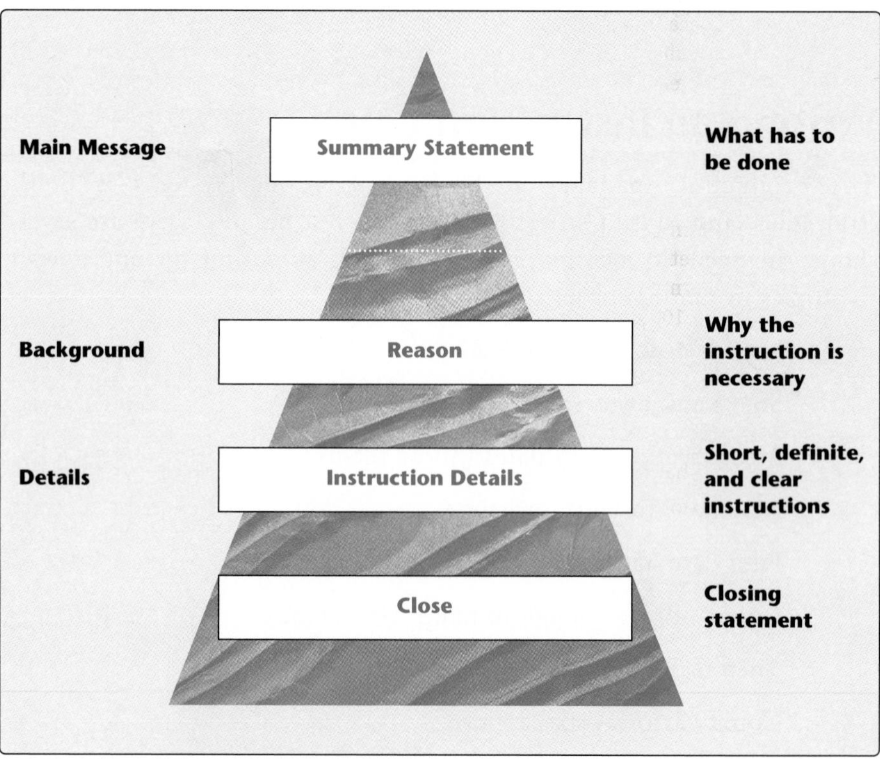

Figure 3-4 Writing plan for an instruction letter

Business Learning Systems Limited

Interdepartmental Memorandum

1	**To:**	Emilio Rodrigues Production Manager	**From:**	Marita Estavo Marketing Manager
	Date:	March 22, 2001	**Ref:**	Special Order for Tormont Inc, Montreal

2 We have just received a large order that is going to put considerable pressure on your department until May 7. The purchaser is Tormont Canada Inc of Montreal, and they are buying 300 BLS 210 Modular Interactive Learning Systems complete with the "ISM" 12-module Supervisory Management Software Program.

3 Delivery dates are extremely tight, which means we will have to gear up rapidly if we are to get the units to Tormont on time: 100 each on April 9, April 23, and May 7. (To secure the order, I have had to *guarantee* that we can deliver on these dates.)

Readers will follow instructions more readily when they understand the rationale

As the first 100 units have to be delivered in only 17 days, I suggest you take the following steps:

4

1. Count existing stocks of the system components.
2. Place orders today with suppliers for immediate delivery of sufficient numbers of each component to make up the initial 100 systems.
3. For each shipment, work out a schedule showing completion dates for parts acquisition, assembly, packing and shipping, and provide me with a copy.
4. Place follow-up orders with suppliers for delivery of the remaining 200 units of each system component.
5. Warn the system assemblers that they may have to work overtime to meet the assembly dates.
6. Warn the Packing and Shipping Department that they will need to make up 100 designer packing cartons one week in advance of each delivery date, and that they should be prepared to work overtime to get the units shipped on time.

Numbered steps denote sequence and provide a checklist

5 Please keep me informed of progress and particularly of any potential problems that may create a delay.

Marita

Figure 3-5 A memorandum containing instructions

Memorandums are far more common than letters for in-house communications. They are written just like letters, but their appearance and tone are less formal. The name "memorandum" does *not* mean a writer can take shortcuts and write incomplete sentences. (Marita could equally well have sent the message by email. She chose a memo because she felt a paper document would be visible and so carry more "weight." She also felt it would be natural for Emilio Rodrigues to want to place a check mark beside each item as he worked through the steps.)

The opening sentence is Marita's Summary Statement.

The second sentence and the next paragraph explain the Reason for the instructions. A person reading instructions will more readily carry out the steps if he or she knows why they are important.

The detailed instructions start here and continue through the six numbered steps. Note particularly that

- It is customary to precede a series of instructional steps with a brief lead-in line.
- Marita numbers the steps to indicate that their sequence is important (she does not use bullets, as I have used here).
- Each step starts with a verb written in the imperative mood. Action verbs like these help convey an impression of urgency and that the reader *must* perform the stated action. Coincidentally, action verbs also give the reader confidence in the writer as a conveyor of information.
- Each step is short. Concise instructional steps help the reader remember each step as a complete entity. They also prevent small details from being inadvertently missed, as they might be in a longer paragraph having several sentences.

Strong verbs establish a firm, definite tone

❺

This is the second draft of Marita's Closing Statement. In the first draft she also wrote, "This is a particularly important order, Emilio; our credibility is on the line!" But on rereading it during proofreading she felt

Emilio might think she was trying to tell him how to do his job, and so she decided to omit the sentence. A tone that may offend a reader can undo all the effective writing elsewhere in a letter or memorandum.

Conveying Information

The memorandum Marita writes to the company president announcing the Tormont sale could be called either an announcement or an information letter. Both follow the basic writing plan in Figure 3-1 (page 37):

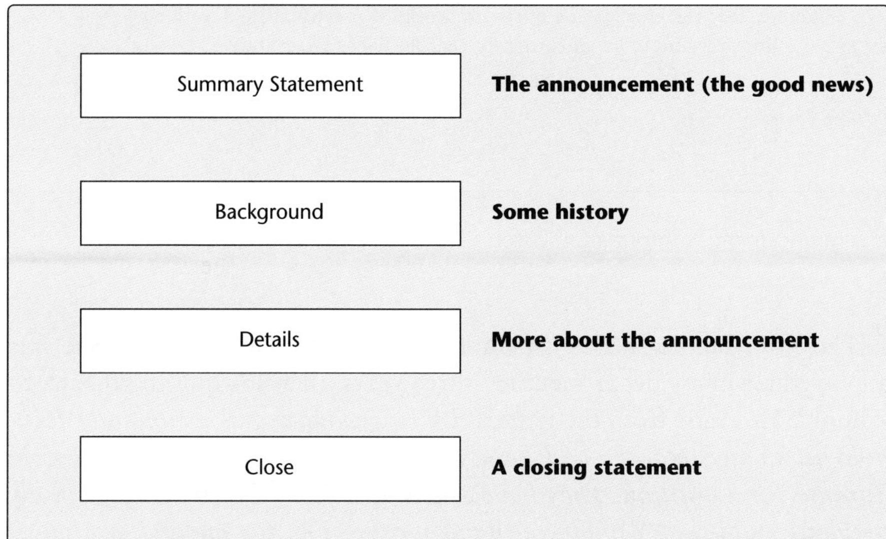

Never bury bad news. Put it right up front, as you would for good news.

Because the memorandum is short (see Figure 3-6), Marita combines the Summary Statement and Background into one paragraph, and the Details and the Closing Statement into another.

Writing a Personal Reference

When Emilio Rodrigues, with a letter in his hand, appears at Marita's door the following afternoon, she is immediately concerned that he has a problem with the Tormont order. He assures her that he has everything under control: "The monitors will be here tomorrow, and the CD-ROM disk drives on Wednesday. I've already started an assembly team cutting and terminating cables, and Todd is making up the cartons. I've gone out for quotes for shipping the systems to Montreal, and as soon as they're in—tomorrow, I expect—I'll make up a cost sheet and production plan."

"Good," Marita murmurs.

To: wilson_duluth@bls.com
From: m.estavo@bls.com
Date: March 22, 2001
Re: Big Sale of BLS 210 System

Sales representative Terry Wing telephoned this evening to inform me that he has closed a sale for 300 BLS 210 Modular Interactive Learning Systems. The purchaser is Tormont Canada Inc of Montreal, and delivery is to be completed in six weeks.

This major sale comprises both hardware and software, and so represents a $273 000 order. It is the culmination of several weeks of persistent field work on Terry's part. He is proving to be an extremely capable field representative.

Marita

Figure 3-6 An announcement or information letter

The letter Emilio carries is from Dana Paullsen. He explains, "She was an expediter in my department for three years, then she quit to go back to school." He reads from the letter: *"I'll be graduating as a computer technologist in two months and have applied to Macro Engineering Inc in Toronto for a position. They have asked for a letter of reference from my previous employer. Would you mind writing one for me and sending it directly to them?"*

Emilio lowers the letter. "People have always *phoned* for a reference before. I've never had to write one." In response, Marita turns to her computer and keys in a command. The writing plan shown in Figure 3-7 appears on screen.

Marita presses the "Prt Scr" key and the printer beside her desk whirs into action, printing a copy of the writing plan. She tears off the sheet and hands it to Emilio. "Take this with you," she suggests, and explains that a reference letter has only three writing compartments:

The Evidence must present facts so that your opinions will be well-founded

- A **Summary Statement**, in which Emilio should name the person and very briefly comment on his or her best qualities.
- An **Evidence** paragraph, in which he should describe the person's particular strengths both as an employee and as a person.
- A **Closing Statement**, in which he can, if he wishes, add a more personal touch to the letter, such as, "Please call me at 000-0000 if you would like more information about Dana," or "I can recommend Dana highly; it was a pleasure having her as a member of my department."

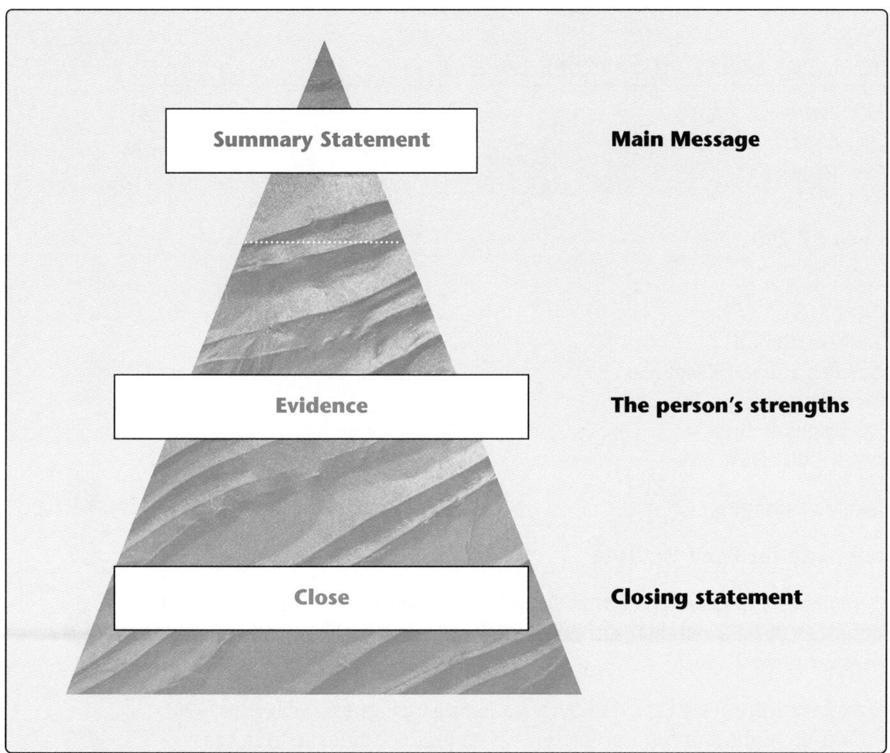

Figure 3-7 Writing plan for a reference letter

Back in his office beside the assembly area, Emilio starts to write the reference letter for Dana Paullsen. He prints it and revises it slightly. The letter he finally sends out is shown in Figure 3-8. Comments on the letter are also shown here (the number beside each comment is cross-referenced to a particular part of the letter).

Emilio feels that his reference will seem impersonal if he opens with the expression "To Whom It May Concern." He telephones Macro Engineering Inc in Toronto and asks for the name and title of the manager of human resources.

Always address the letter to a reader by name

A reference letter should have a subject line that states the name of the person for whom the reference is being written. This line helps the personnel department insert the letter into the appropriate applicant's file. The subject line should be set in boldface type and *not* underlined.

A reference letter must sound factual and sincere, or your opinions will not be accepted

Business Learning Systems Limited

200 Riverside
London ON N6J 1A8
www.bls.com

Tel: (519) 489-7240
Fax: (519) 489-7249

March 23, 2001

Frances Calhoun
Manager, Human Resources
Macro Engineering Inc
600 Deepdale Drive
Toronto ON M5W 4R9

Dear Ms Calhoun 1

Reference for Dana Paullsen 2

Throughout the three years that Dana Paullsen worked in my department I
found her to be a reliable, self-motivated employee with a consistently 3
pleasant disposition.

Dana joined Business Learning Systems Limited as an assembler in 1996,
but within eight months I promoted her to production expediter because 4
she demonstrated an ability to anticipate rather than react to material
shortages. As expediter she was responsible for ensuring that components
and materials were available for assembly at the right time and place, and
in sufficient quantities to meet production deadlines. She proved to be an 5
excellent organizer who worked equally well on her own or as part of a project team, and she was well liked and respected by other employees and
supervisors.

Dana was difficult to replace when she resigned in 1999 to enroll in 6
Computer Engineering Technology at Ryerson Polytechnic University. I wish
her well in her endeavors.

Sincerely

Emilio Rodrigues
Production Supervisor

Figure 3-8 A reference letter

This sentence is Emilio's Summary Statement.

Emilio's Evidence starts here. He feels that using Dana's first name reinforces the impression that he is well acquainted with Dana's work, and lessens any impression that he is writing only a "duty" reference.

The writer's "presence" should be felt to personalize a reference letter

As there is no connection between Dana's work at Business Learning Systems and her new vocation (computer engineering technology), Emilio draws particular attention to her self-motivation and organizational skills.

6

This information is Emilio's Closing Statement.

Writing a Transmittal Letter

Short Transmittal Letter

On March 27, Emilio Rodrigues signs a letter addressed to Tormont Canada Inc, pins it to a 110-page software user's handbook, slides them and a 3.5 inch disk into a padded envelope, and calls Federal Express. The letter is a transmittal letter (also known as a cover letter) and is shown in Figure 3-9.

A transmittal letter conveys a product or a document (a proposal, drawing, report, or handbook) from one person to another. Often a transmittal letter will contain no more than one or two sentences that

- identify the attachment(s), and
- refer to any previous correspondence or conversation about the attached item.

Longer Transmittal Letter

An expanded writing plan is used when a transmittal letter comments on the document or product it conveys. Glenda Freebach, for example, uses the longer writing plan shown in Figure 3-10 to offer her opinion about two drawings she is sending to MIC Insurance Corporation. Her letter is in Figure 3-11. The comments on page 51 refer to the circled numbers beside her letter.

A basic cover or transmittal letter simply moves the document from writer to reader

Business Learning Systems Limited

200 Riverside
London ON N6J 1A8
www.bls.com

Tel: (519) 489-7240
Fax: (519) 489-7249

April 3, 2001

Thérèse Vincennes
Training Supervisor
Tormont Canada Incorporated
1870 rue de Moulpied
Montreal QB H2R 8K3

Dear Thérèse

I am enclosing advance copies of the online and printed User Manual for the ISM Supervisory Management Software Program, as you requested in our telephone conversation of March 26. This will enable you to start working on your training plan before the first BLS 210 Modular Interactive Learning Systems are delivered on April 9.

Regards

Emilio Rodrigues

Emilio Rodrigues
Production Supervisor

enc: ISM User Manual; 3.5 inch disk

Figure 3-9 A short transmittal letter

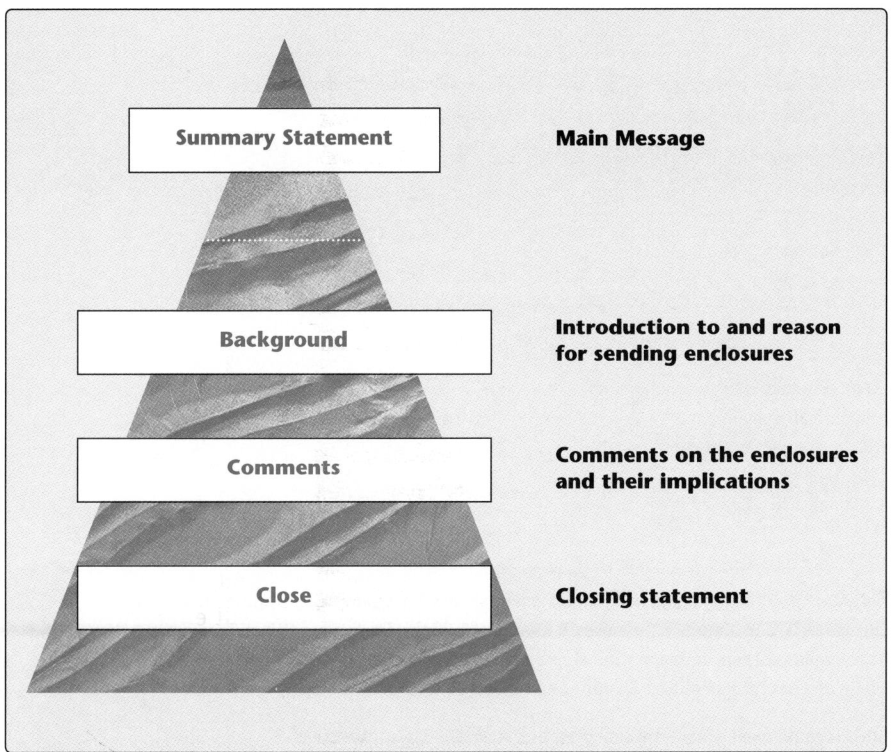

Figure 3-10 Writing plan for a longer transmittal letter

Glenda's two-sentence opening paragraph combines the Summary Statement and Background.

These three paragraphs contain Glenda's comments. She is correct to maintain her objectivity when describing the two plans (i.e. the reader should not be able to tell which plan she prefers).

A longer transmittal letter also comments on the document's content

In her Closing Statement Glenda implies that she is ready to offer an opinion if Glenn Yaremko (the person to whom she is writing) wants it.

A short transmittal letter that accompanies a report is often referred to as a cover letter. A long transmittal letter that comments on the report it accompanies is known as an executive summary. Both are described in Chapter 7 (pages 166 to 168).

FREEBACH & WOBURN
ENGINEERING CONSULTANTS
417 Cambridge Office Tower
Saint John NB E2L 2J7
Tel: (506) 648-1270

October 3, 2000

Glenn Yaremko
Branch Manager
MIC Insurance Corporation
1806 Western Inlet
Saint John NB E4R 2Y3

Dear Glenn

Here are two drawings depicting alternative layouts for your office equipment when you move MIC Insurance into suites 610 and 612 of the Cambridge Office Tower. I have prepared them following our September 12 discussion in your office, and the terms of reference specified in your September 15 letter. 1

Both layouts meet your requirements, but each has its advantages:

Follow an introductory sentence with a colon *only* if the sentence is complete . . .

- Plan A requires few structural alterations and will permit you to occupy the premises with only 10 days' notice. However, it offers a slightly awkward arrangement of the cubicles.
- Plan B offers a contemporary, open appearance and good traffic flow among the cubicles, but requires moderate structural alterations that will delay occupancy for six weeks and add $9000 to the cost of your move. 2

. . . and then start each bulleted entry with a capital letter

Please call me when you have considered the alternatives. I will be glad to discuss the pros and cons with you. 3

Sincerely

Glenda Freebach

Glenda Freebach, P. Eng

enc: 2 plans

Figure 3-11 A longer transmittal letter

TO SUM UP

Letters that are primarily informative follow a basic writing plan. They

- open with a short Summary Statement,
- provide brief Background details (enough to familiarize the reader with the situation),
- offer Facts (or Evidence) to amplify what has been said in the Summary Statement, and
- end with a brief Closing Statement.

If a sentence introducing a list is incomplete, omit the colon and do not capitalize the initial letter of each bulleted entry

EXERCISES

Exercise 3.1: Information Letter

You are employed by the PROVO chain of department stores and currently you are an assistant manager in the sports equipment department of the Gull Island branch, 15 kilometres from where you live. When you joined PROVO in June a little over two years ago, you had completed all but three subjects of a two-year Business Administration program at Milltown Community College. The deficiencies were Applied Statistics, Economics II, and Advanced Report Writing. (PROVO hired you because you had worked for them part-time during high school and between college terms, when you clearly demonstrated you had strong interpersonal communication skills and an above-average sales record.)

Just the same, PROVO inserted a condition into your terms of employment. "We will take you on as a permanent employee," personnel manager Dale Korchinsky explained, but with the provision that "you must make up all three deficiencies within three years—that will be one course a winter. If, after three years, you haven't cleared the deficiencies, you will be released. I'll write it in the letter accepting you as an employee."

Dale's letter was dated June 12, two years ago.

Today you receive a transcript from Milltown Community College announcing that you have achieved a B+ in Advanced Report Writing. The transcript also shows that you received a C in Applied Statistics on June 2 of last year and a C+ in Economics II on May 27 of this year. Attached to the transcript is a two-sentence letter from the college: "The attached transcript shows that you have completed the academic requirements for

Inform your employer that you have met your education requirements

a Diploma in Business Administration. We are happy to enclose your diploma."

Write an interoffice memorandum to the personnel department to inform them that you have met the requirements spelled out in Dale Korchinsky's letter. (He still is the personnel manager.) Attach your diploma and transcript. Ask for them to be returned and for copies to be placed in your personal file.

Exercise 3.2: **Instruction Letter**

Your friend Tania Young is a registered nurse at the local health sciences centre. She is also taking continuing education courses at the university at night. For a research project she has to write a comprehensive report that will become her major course assignment. So that she can do her writing at home, you lend her your laptop computer.

The next day Tania calls you: "Can you give me some instructions?" she asks. "Tell me how to switch your computer on and off, and how to get into and out of your word-processing program. The computers I am using in the computer lab at the university are always 'on.' And so are the ones in the hospital."

Tell a user how to operate a computer

From your knowledge of or experience with a personal laptop computer, write a memo to Tania in which you respond to her request. (Tania gives you a fax number at the hospital where you can send the instructions: 474-6134.) Include two warnings:

- Warn her not to carry the computer about when it's switched on (it's mighty dangerous for the hard disk, if you should trip or bump the computer).
- Also remind her that your laptop has a peculiar quirk: if you move the mouse while it's switching on or closing down, the mouse will freeze and you can't get out of the computer or do anything! (You've talked to your local supplier about this, but they can't suggest a remedy; the problem is peculiar to your computer.) The only remedy, you have discovered, is to disconnect the battery and then reconnect it. But that means moving the computer about while it's switched on. The alternative is to disconnect the power cord and let the battery run down, which takes about three to four hours.

Now write the memo.

Exercise 3.3: **Announcement**

You are employed by a small stationery and office supplies company known as OffStat Independent Office Supplies Ltd. In an era when few independent office supply companies have survived the immense competition from chain stores such as Staples and Office Depot, OffStat has continued to be successful by stressing a strong *service* element in its marketing of paper products, pens, file systems, etc. As well as having a store and showroom at 34 Goldstar Road, OffStat also has a mobile store in a large van that is driven to its customers' sites.

The company is small: Joe and Wendy Raphael are the owners. Martine Carlson is the company's Marketing and Product Consultant, Dave Williston drives the van and makes direct contact with OffStat's customers, twin sisters Janice and Jane Pervensey are the in-store salespeople, Meta Danon is the warehouseperson, and you are the orders clerk. You divide your time between taking orders by telephone, maintaining stock control, and ordering replacement stock when supplies grow low. You have been doing this for three years.

Today Wendy Raphael comes to you and says: "Martine Carlson has decided to take early retirement and move back to Waverley to look after her aging parents. This means we have to find a new Marketing and Product Consultant and, because you have shown an apt knowledge for the stationery supplies business, we have decided to promote you to that position."

You are to move up to a new position . . .

You are both pleased and nervous. You know that over the 14 years Martine has been Marketing and Product Consultant she has developed an excellent relationship with the company's customers, and this has been one of the reasons the company has stayed so successful. At Wendy's suggestion, you and Martine go out for lunch and discuss what the job entails.

"There are two aspects to the job," Martine says: "Finding new customers and calling on our existing customers to find out what they need and then have Dave deliver the supplies. These are the customers who rarely come into the store but depend on me—and now it will be you—to come in and sometimes even anticipate what they need." She explains that one of the primary products OffStat sells is the "Week-a-Page" business diary and appointment control planner, which OffStat imports from Australia and holds the sole licence for your province. "I keep a log of the type of diary each person has, and when they will need replacement pages, and make sure they have them at least one month in advance. I don't send them automatically; rather, I phone or drop in to see them, and check whether they want to continue with the same type of diary, and then two days later Dave delivers the new pages to insert. Often, it's at that visit or during the phone call, that I identify other supplies they need."

You know all about the Week-a-Page planner and use a particular version yourself to control stock and anticipate potential shortages.

"I'm leaving next week," Martine says. "It's all quite sudden, so I haven't had time to call or visit all our customers. Here are two lists: List

. . . but there are problems.

A contains the names of those I have visited, so they know I'm leaving but don't know who is taking my place (I didn't know it would be you when I talked to them). List B contains the names of those I have not had time to call or visit, and now won't have time. You will have to tell them you are taking over from me." With each list she gives you a file for each customer, which details the customer's buying habits and favored products.

Part 1

Write a letter to the customers in List A—those who know Martine is leaving—to announce you are the new Marketing and Product Consultant. Tell them briefly about your experience in stationery and office supplies, and your knowledge of their company. The first letter you write is to Connie Duprez, who runs a small business known as "Duprez Report and Proposal Writing Services" at Suite 410, 33 Manchester Road. She has three employees, and she and they provide specialized services to small companies needing good-looking reports and proposals produced quickly. The major supplies she buys are paper, binders, and computer printer cartridges.

Part 2

It's now ten days later, and Martine has left OffStat. Write a letter to the customers in List B—those who don't know Martine has left—to announce you are the new Marketing and Product Consultant. Tell them briefly about your experience in the office and stationery supplies business, and your knowledge of their company. The first letter you write is to Frank Charlesbois, who is an independent architect operating from his home at 515 Falaise Avenue. He occasionally employs junior architects under contract. The major supplies he buys are high-quality letterhead paper (Classic Laid, mainly), colored pens and pencils, large binders, heavy-duty hollow rolls for transporting and mailing drawings, and computer printer cartridges.

Exercise 3.4: Summary of a Conversation

You have been Marketing and Product Consultant for OffStat Independent Office Supplies Ltd for three months (for more information see Exercise 3.3). Today you receive a telephone call that evolves into a four-person conference call. The four callers are

- Valerie Leopold, Sales Manager for Avantek Products Inc in Philadelphia, Pennsylvania (email: *vleopold@avantek.com*),
- Amrat Sarindar, Avantek Products Inc's Canadian distributor, in Mississauga, Ontario (email: *amrat_sarindar@fulcrum.on.ca*),
- Morley Derwent, Avantek's area sales representative in Des Moines, Iowa (email: *mderwent@aventek.com*), and
- yourself (email: *[your_name]@offstat.org)*.

The only person you know in the loop is Amrat Sarindar. He is a wholesale distributor of numerous stationery and office supply products, and you have met him twice in the past two years, when he has been on sales trips, and have emailed and telephoned him at least once a month, concerning products you need. Amrat starts the teleconference at 1:30 p.m.

"Hi," he says, and you exchange greetings. "Avantek Products Inc in Philadelphia have come out with an excellent new product," Amrat continues, "and I want to test-market it in Canada. Your area would be an excellent test ground because you have numerous customers of the type the product is particularly designed for."

You ask what the product is.

"It's a one-stop inventory control system," he says. "It's called 'Incontrol' and it has experienced excellent sales in the US where it is now being marketed." Amrat says he has Valerie Leopold, the Sales Manager for Avantek, on hold, and introduces her into the conversation.

A new product for you to market . . .

"Incontrol is unique," says Valerie, "because it lets you maintain both a computer record and a paper record of stock, using a coded data entry system. There is none other like it on the market. With other systems you either maintain a paper inventory or a computer-based inventory, and their appearance differs markedly. With Incontrol the appearance, and the entries you make, are the same for both systems."

"I've got Morley Derwent on the line, too," Amrat intervenes, and he introduces Morley to you. Morley and Valerie, who know each other, exchange greetings.

Morley says: "I started a test market in the Des Moines area six months ago, just like Amrat is asking you to do. I tried it with 10 customers and within two months I was getting orders from other customers *before* we were officially marketing Incontrol. The test people were so pleased with it they talked about it to their business associates. Now I have 44 customers using it, and orders keep rolling in, mostly by word-of-mouth referrals rather than my having to make sales calls."

"This is what I would like you to do," Amrat says to you. "We'll send you a dozen sets of Incontrol at no charge, for you to give to customers you feel would gain most from it. Then after three months we will ask you to have each customer complete a questionnaire about Incontrol and how well it works for them."

"Do the customers keep the product, after the three months?" you ask.

"Definitely!" Valerie answers. "What's more, we'll guarantee to provide them with free product updates for a further two years."

"You can tell them that, when you ask them to test Incontrol," Amrat adds.

. . . and for your customers to field test

Morley makes a suggestion: "Keep one set of Incontrol for yourself," he says to you. "I did, and it helped me enormously when I talked to customers. What's more, I quickly discovered how efficient it is!"

"How much does it cost?" you ask.

Valerie says: "In the US it retails for $199.50. As the local distributor you get a 33.3% discount."

Amrat adds: "In Canada it will retail for $259.50, with the same discount."

"What does that include?" you ask.

Valerie says: "A one-year supply of the paper products, plus a CD-ROM of the software."

You agree to test-market it for them.

There are many details to remember

"Great!" says Valerie. "I'll courier 12 sets of Incontrol to Amrat tomorrow."

"I'll ship them to you within 24 hours of receiving them," Amrat says.

"Where does the evaluation form—the questionnaire—come from?" you ask.

"From me," says Valerie. "I'll fax a copy to Amrat, so he can modify it for the Canadian market, and he will send you a dozen copies within two months."

"It would be useful," you say, "if I could have some idea of the kind of user for whom Incontrol would be most valuable."

"I can help you there," says Morley. "I'll send you a profile of the customers who are using it. In fact I'll send you two: a list of the 10 customers who test-marketed Incontrol, and a list of the other customers who have bought it."

Amrat asks if anyone has any questions and then says to you: "I'd like you to have the products in the test market users' hands by two weeks from today, and to have them fill in the questionnaires 13 weeks (that's three months) from today."

You agree, and the teleconference ends.

To confirm that you fully understand who will do what, and when, you write a summary of the conversation and email it to the four telephone callers.

Exercise 3.5: Information and Instruction

You are a shift supervisor at the Westside High Gear Truck and Car Rental outlet in your city. HGTCR does not have an on-airport rental booth, so the Westside outlet, which is the one closest to the airport, picks up and delivers renters from and to the airport. Recently, HGTCR has rented three spaces at the airport for customers returning their cars or trucks to drop off their vehicles without coming into the Westside office.

(See Exercises 5.2 and 5.3 in Chapter 5 for more information about the arrangements.)

Branch manager Corinne Wasalyshyn comes to you and says: "Write a friendly form letter we can print and give copies to renters, to tell them where and how to drop off their vehicle at the airport." Here is some information you will require:

- From your city or town, renters would normally drive east toward the airport access road, travelling along Willesden Road, and then they need to turn south onto Lancaster Road, which brings them right up to the airport terminal (after 300 metres it becomes a one-way road). It's best to keep in the left lane, and remind the renters to keep an eye out for the overhead "Rental Car Return" signs and follow them until they reach lot 87N (which is where HGTCR's parking spaces are), all the time looking for a sign beside the left lane (it will be on their left) which says "87N" in big letters, and of course they have to turn left into the lot *just before* they reach the sign, and park in any one of the three spaces marked HG1, HG2, or HG3.
- On the rental agreement the renter will need to mark down three things: the odometer reading, the amount of gas in the tank (it should be full, unless the renter wants to pay for HGTCR to fill it, which'll cost them an extra $15!), and the time they drop off the car (we trust they will be honest here!). Then the renter needs to be reminded to *lock the car* and drop the keys and the rental agreement into the box which we have placed behind the 87N sign mentioned earlier, which is on the west side of the lot.

Information for car rental users

Make it a friendly letter and let it show that HGTCR is providing a special service for its customers.

Exercise 3.6: Transmittal Letter

You own a small company specializing in designing "very user friendly" accounting software for small business owners.

Today you receive a call from Martin Gervin in Medicine Hat, Alberta. "Can you help me?" he pleads. "We've had a fire here and all the software you sold me has been burned. I have back-up disks with all the data I've accumulated in a safe deposit box, but I've no way to access the data without the original program. I didn't take the precaution to store a copy."

You tell Martin that you will send him duplicates.

From your files you discover that over the past seven years Martin has bought six of your programs and their updates. You can find five of the programs on a CD-ROM. The sixth program you cannot find. Your records show that the program was called "Apeggio" and that there had been little demand for it. Apparently you dropped it from your list and deleted it from the hard disk.

Write a transmittal letter to accompany the CD-ROM

You dig out your list of Alberta customers and find that Sheelagh Freyer in Calgary also bought the program at about the same time that Martin did. You call her and explain the problem. "I remember that program," Sheelagh says, "but I don't use it any more. I'll look for it, though, because I'm sure I haven't discarded it. Tell your customer to phone me."

Write an email to Martin Gervin. Tell him you are sending all but one of the programs he needs on a CD-ROM, that you do not have "Apeggio," and that he should email Sheelagh. Also say that if Sheelagh cannot find it he should email you back. Sheelagh's email address is *s.freyer@ab.simpatico.ca*. Martin's email address is *martin_gervin@hotmail.com*.

Exercise 3.7: **Confirmation Letter**

You are a member of the Mid-Town Society of Business Administrators (MSBA) and one of three members who together form a program committee. The Society meets in a private room of the Norlander Inn at 5 p.m. on the first Thursday of every month from October to May. The procedure is always the same: at 5 p.m. the bar opens; at 5:30 the members sit on both sides of a long table and the chairperson (who this year is Janet Eliason) holds a business meeting; at 6 p.m. a three-course dinner is served; at 6:45 p.m. the guest speaker is introduced and addresses the meeting; and at 7:30 p.m. the meeting wraps up.

The three members of the program committee take turns arranging for speakers, which is usually done several months in advance of the actual speaking dates. Yesterday (January 24) you telephoned Sonja Haarstrup, president of Haarstrup Electronics Inc, whose small manufacturing company has had considerable success selling its products in China, a very difficult market to break into and establish a presence. You asked her if she would be willing to speak to the Society on the first Thursday in May, and after asking some questions she agreed. You told her you will meet her in the hotel lobby at 5 p.m.

Persuade a respected person to be a speaker

"To how many people will I be speaking?" Ms Haarstrup asked.

"Between 25 and 35," you replied.

"And for how long do you expect me to speak?"

"About 45 minutes," you told her. "Is there any special equipment you will need?"

"Ah, yes," she said. "I will need an LCD projector and a VCR. I'll bring my own laptop computer."

You said that both will be arranged, and then you asked, "Do you have a title for your talk I can use in the announcement I'll be sending to members?"

Ms Haarstrup replied, "Call it 'Strategies for Selling Canadian Products in China'."

At lunchtime today you met with the two other members of the program committee, and they agreed that Sonja Haarstrup would be a good choice.

Write a letter to Sonja Haarstrup to confirm the arrangements. Thank her for agreeing to speak, tell her that the Society members are eager to hear her topic, and repeat the essential details. Date your letter January 25. (Haarstrup Electronics' address is 2720 Aberdeen Avenue, in your city.)

Exercise 3.8: **Announcement**

Prepare a meeting announcement

You are a member of the program committee of the MSBA (see Exercise 3.7 for details) and it is now March 20. Write a memo-form announcement to all MSBA members, informing them of the date, time, and location of the May meeting and identifying who the speaker will be. (Your memo will be duplicated and a copy will be mailed to each member.) You may include additional details of your own about Sonja Haarstrup and her company, the need to establish connections with China, the problems manufacturers experience establishing a presence there, and the essential need to learn and understand the Chinese business culture.

Exercise 3.9: **Thank You Letter**

It's now May 28 and you are writing a letter to Sonja Haarstrup to thank her for speaking to the MSBA. For details about her talk, see Exercise 3.7. Here is some information you may want to use to write your letter:

Thank the speaker

- 34 MSBA members attended the meeting.
- Sonja's talk lasted 47 minutes.
- Her coverage of her experience in adapting to the Chinese business culture was particularly informative (and often humorous). Her videotape also provided a valuable insight into doing business there.
- The question period lasted another 18 minutes. (Even then the questions had to be cut off because it was 7:50 p.m. and the contract with the hotel stipulates that the MSBA will vacate the room by 8:00 p.m.)
- Four members approached you after the talk and congratulated you on your choice of speaker.
- Three more have telephoned you (one the same evening, two this morning) to comment that the meeting was a real success.
- Even retired member Dan Polandor, who has dozed during every previous speaker's talk, remained wide awake throughout.

Exercise 3.10: **An Information Letter**

You are the administrative assistant to Dana Wing, president of Midtown Furniture House. On the 4th and 5th of next month, the store is to hold a big sale. Today Dana tells you that previous customers are to be invited to a special preview of the sale items the night before the sale starts. "It will be from 7 to 10 p.m.," she explains, "on the 3rd of the month."

Inform customers of a special offer

She tells you to write a letter informing regular customers they are personally invited to attend. "We'll use mail-merge," she adds, "so everyone will get a personally addressed letter." Discount prices for the sale will range from 10 to 40% off the regular price, depending on the product. "For the specially invited customers," Dana says, "we will also reduce each item a further 5%, just for that one evening."

Write the letter, with Dana's signature at the bottom. The address of Midtown Furniture House is 210 Decatur Boulevard of your city or town. Address the first letter to Glenda Farrelli at Suite 807, 1400 Winchester Street. Include imaginary yet realistic postal codes for both addresses.

WEBLINKS

How to Write Business Letters that Get Results
www.smartbiz.com/sbs/arts/bly48.htm
Robert W. Bly, president of the Center for Technical Communication, provides writers with valuable advice about writing correspondence. He discusses how to use the AIDA formula—Attention, Interest, Demand, and Action—which he describes as a "simple formula [that] lets you cut through jargon and messy language to create straightforward writing that works."

Memos
www.rpi.edu/dept/llc/writecenter/
Rensselaer Polytechnic Institute's Writing Center offers suggestions about writing effective memos. Select "rtf" at the top of the page, then select the file entitled "memo.rtf" to view the document.

Business Letters: Accentuating the Positives
owl.english.purdue.edu/Files/92.html
Positive business letters often elicit a better response than do those with a negative focus. This site teaches you how to focus on the positives in your business correspondence.

Persuasive Letters and Memorandums

chapter 4

Stefan can see that Scott is angry. It shows in the fierce set of Scott's jaw and the determined way he marches into the cafeteria, brushing past people he normally would stand aside for. He throws himself into a chair across from Stefan and smacks two typed pages onto the table between them. "Silly old fool!" he grunts. Stefan looks up questioningly.

"Charles Withnair!" Scott explains. (Withnair is Manager of Administration Services and Scott and Stefan's boss.) "I can't decide if he's just slow on the uptake or if he's done it on purpose!" Scott fumes, pushing a sheet of paper toward Stefan. "I ask to go to a conference . . . " he continues, and then shrugs. "Read it!"

> To: Charles_Withnair@multind.com
> From: Scott_Chornysse@multind.com
> Date: October 17, 2000
> Re: Conference on Office Networking
>
> Do you remember last month, when we were talking about the need for better integration between the computers in our different offices, and you commented on the lack of good information on office networking?
>
> Well, take a look at the attachment! It describes a conference on "Networking in the New Century." It's only five weeks away, and in Canada too!
>
> I thought I should tell you right away, so the company can take advantage of airline discounts by booking 30 days in advance.
>
> Can I go ahead and make reservations?
>
> Scott

Stefan looks up from the memo. "So? You want to go to the conference?"

"That's not what old Withers thinks!" Scott groans. He pushes the second piece of paper toward Stefan.

Stefan reads for a moment, then starts to laugh. In a reply email, Mr. Withnair has written:

To: Scott_Chornysse@multind.com
From: Charles_Withnair@multind.com
Date: October 19, 2000
Re: Registration - Networking Conference

Scott's request is misunderstood

On October 17 Scott_Chornysse wrote:
>I thought I should tell you right away, so the company can take
>advantage of airline discounts by booking 30 days in advance.
>Can I go ahead and make reservations?
>Scott
<
That's good news indeed, Scott, and sharp of you to notice
the conference is scheduled. I wouldn't want to miss it.

Phone in a registration for me, will you? And book me to fly there
on November 20 and return on the 24th.

C. Withnair

"It's not funny!" Scott groans, but the corners of his mouth have turned up slightly.

"Well, you didn't make it entirely clear that *you* want to go!" Stefan replies.

"Of course I did!" Scott retorts. "Otherwise I wouldn't have written to Withers about it, now would I?"

"Withers seems to think you would," Stefan answers. "What are you going to do about it?"

"Nothing, I guess," Scott shrugs. "It's too late now."

IN THIS CHAPTER

A persuasive letter expects the reader to act or react

You will learn how to plan and write letters that will persuade readers to agree to a request or react to a suggestion. Specifically, you will learn how to write letters that

- request approval,
- make a suggestion,
- complain about a product or service,
- claim an adjustment,
- request settlement of an unpaid account, and
- advertise a product or service.

Writing a Request

"When you wanted to go to that business communication conference in Vancouver," Scott asks as they walk back to their office, "you got approval. What did you do that was so different?"

"Got off to a better start, mostly," Stefan replies, sitting at his desk and pulling open a drawer. He lifts out a file folder, extracts two sheets of paper from it, and lays one (containing the diagram in Figure 4-1) in front of Scott. "I followed this plan," he says.

Stefan explains that a request letter has four parts:

Stefan states his request right up front

- A **Summary Statement** states briefly what you are asking for.
- A **Reason** explains why your request is important or valid (the Reason compartment replaces the Background compartment of an informative letter). Sometimes the Summary Statement and Reason are combined into a single paragraph.
- The **Details,** the major part of the letter, describe what the request entails, what is to be gained if your request is granted, and what the cost will be, both financial and as a burden on people and facilities.

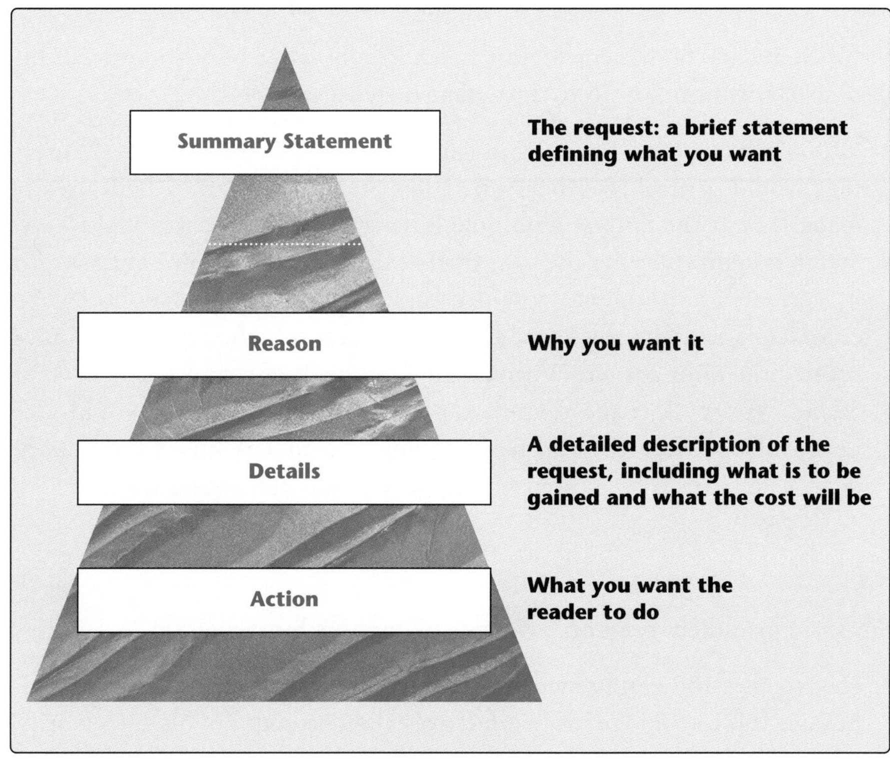

Figure 4-1 Writing plan for a request letter

- An **Action Statement** identifies what you want the reader to do after he or she has read your request. The Action compartment replaces the Closing Statement of the informative letter in Figure 3-1.

The label "Action" reminds you to tell the reader what you expect him or her to do

The major difference between the writing plans for an informative letter and a persuasive letter is the ending of the letter: an informative letter ends with a simple Closing Statement that sums up the outcome or result of the event being described; a persuasive letter ends with an Action Statement that identifies what action has to be taken.

Stefan lays the second sheet of paper in front of Scott. "This is the request memorandum I wrote to Mr Withnair," he says. "You can see how the parts fit the writing plan." He has written a memorandum (see Figure 4-2) rather than an email, for three reasons: he wanted his manager to have a visible document in his hands, to refer to and write on; he would be creating a table within it, which might not travel well electronically; and he needed to attach the brochure. The circled numbers along the left correspond to the numbered comments below.

In his Summary Statement Stefan states briefly what he wants to do, his Reason for wanting to do it, and what the cost will be.

If you don't like putting the cost in paragraph 1, try, "The cost is within our travel budget."

- "I don't like putting the cost up front like that," Scott remarks. "Surely that would turn old Withers off?" But Stefan says no: "I had already made it clear the dollars would be buying something worthwhile."
- Stefan is right: burying the cost further down in the memo, almost as if it were an afterthought, would create the impression that he lacked confidence and already knew the price was too high. This would have opened the door for Mr Withnair to deny his request.
- Stefan writes "I request your approval" rather than "I would like approval" because the former is strong and makes him sound confident. The latter is weak and would have made him sound unsure.

Stefan also could have written, "May I have your approval . . . "

2

Stefan immediately presents evidence to support his request.

- He attaches the conference brochure because it describes the comprehensive topic coverage more effectively than he could in his own words, which Mr Withnair might view as only Stefan's opinion.
- Because Mr Withnair may be overwhelmed or distracted by all the information in the brochure, Stefan lists the topics most likely to convince Mr Withnair that he should attend.

Interoffice Memorandum

To:	C M Withnair, Manager Administrative Services	**Date:**	August 16, 2000
From:	Stefan Peloquin	**Subject:**	Request to Attend Conference

1 I request your approval to attend the Pacific Rim Conference on Corporate Communication, which will address many questions on off-shore marketing that we are concerned about. The conference will be held in Vancouver from October 2 to 4, 2000. The cost will be $1470, which includes conference registration, travel, accommodation, and incidental expenses.

Stefan's request is clear, coherent, and complete

2 The enclosed folder lists the numerous topics that will be addressed. As we are sched-
3 uled to start marketing to China in 2001, I will particularly attend the following sessions:

4C - The Do's and Don'ts of Trans-Pacific Communication
4 7A - Holding Meetings with Asian Peoples
11A - Cultural Differences and Their Influence on Business Letter Writing
12C - The Importance of Graphics in International Instruction Manuals

The keynote luncheon speaker on Tuesday, October 3 is Kum Loo Kwong, president of International Hong Kong Bank. His topic is especially significant: "Conducting Business in Hong Kong After Four Years Under the New Regime."

5 As the conference covers the monthly department meeting to be held on October 2, I have arranged for Scott Chornysse to complete and forward my September 30 report to you. He is familiar with the process (we handle one another's reports during summer vacations), and before I leave for Vancouver I will document all transactions up to and including September 29.

The cost breakdown will be

	Conference registration*	$385
	Air fare*	525
6	Accommodation (3 nights @ $130/night)	390
	Per diem expenses (4 days @ $30/day)	120
	Airport transfers, etc	50
	Total	$1470

* Assuming discount for early registration and reservation.

7 May I have your response by August 25, so that I may take advantage of the discounts?

Stefan

enc: Conference brochure

Figure 4-2 A request memorandum

"Would," "could," and "should" are weak, wishy-washy words

"I used 'will' rather than 'would'," Stefan explains, "because I felt the conference was important and I *expected* to get approval."

- Again Stefan is right: because he was convinced that he should go to the conference, he wrote much more strongly and confidently than he would have if he had been less sure.

These are the "gains." Rather than try to explain what he expects to gain from attending these sessions (for then he would be offering an opinion, which again might weaken his case), Stefan lets the facts speak for themselves.

These are the non-financial costs. Stefan not only identifies them but indicates how he would handle any problems that might arise from his attending the conference.

Quoting a breakdown of estimated dollar costs shows that Stefan has looked at all the details and implies that he is taking his request seriously. (It also answers his manager's question: "How did you reach that figure of $1470?")

By quoting a "reply by" date in his Action Statement, Stefan prompts Mr Withnair to respond quickly.

Writing a Suggestion

A *suggestion* offers an idea; a *proposal* develops the idea in depth

The writing compartments for a suggestion are almost identical to those for a request, as shown in Figure 4-3. For example, when Fergus Halprin writes a brief email to his supervisor, Darwin Kemp, offering to look into the feasibility of introducing shifts to reduce line-ups at the company's lunch counter (see Figure 4-4), he is advancing an idea for further investigation. If Darwin nods his head and says: "Good idea! Look into it and get back to me with more details, then I'll take your idea to management,"

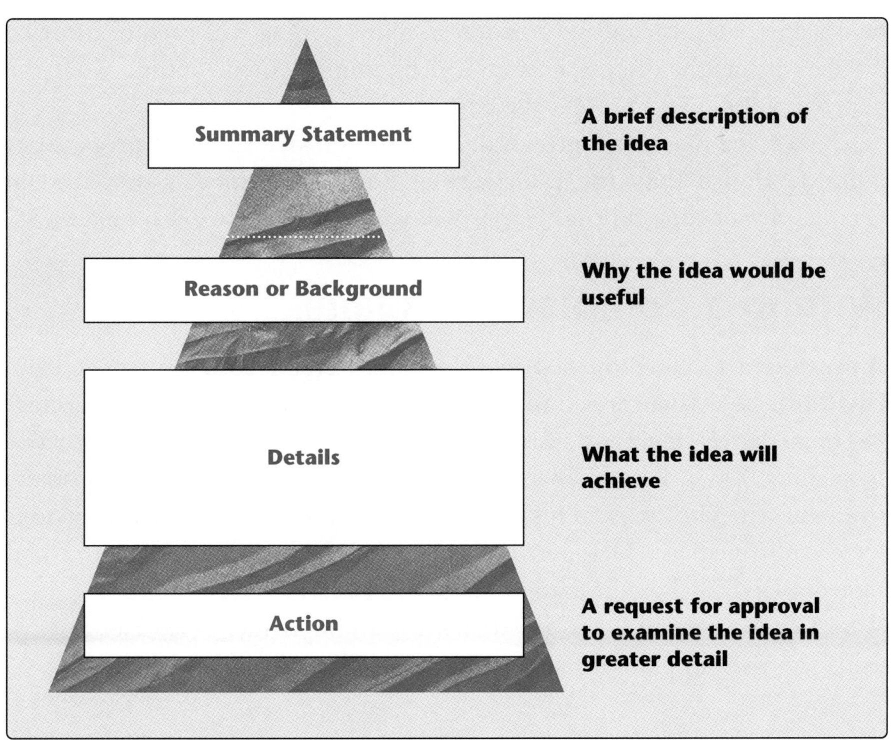

Figure 4-3 Writing plan for a suggestion

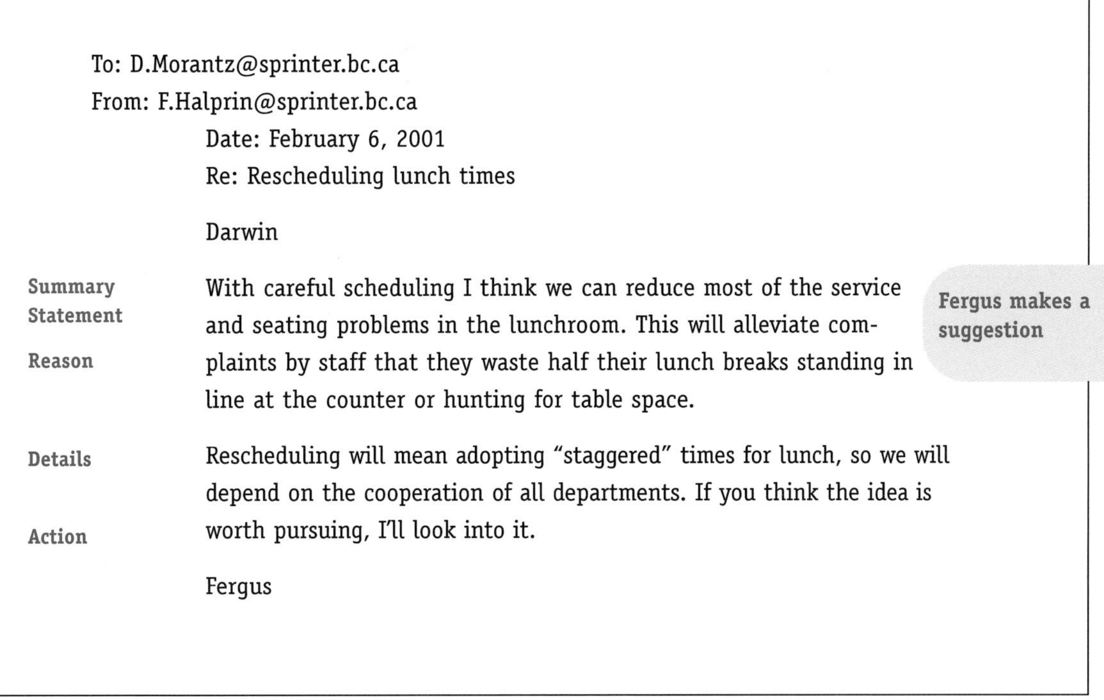

To: D.Morantz@sprinter.bc.ca
From: F.Halprin@sprinter.bc.ca
Date: February 6, 2001
Re: Rescheduling lunch times

Darwin

Summary Statement / Reason — With careful scheduling I think we can reduce most of the service and seating problems in the lunchroom. This will alleviate complaints by staff that they waste half their lunch breaks standing in line at the counter or hunting for table space.

Details / Action — Rescheduling will mean adopting "staggered" times for lunch, so we will depend on the cooperation of all departments. If you think the idea is worth pursuing, I'll look into it.

Fergus

Figure 4-4 An informal suggestion

he is asking Fergus to write a proposal. Now Fergus will need to describe his idea in depth, discuss how it will be implemented, outline what the benefits will be, and present the cost.

The writing plan for a proposal, even an informal in-house proposal, is more developed than for a suggestion. Proposal writing is described in Chapter 6. For the proposal Fergus will write, see Figure 6-1 on page 138.

Writing a Complaint or Claim

When Kevin O'Hare opened his November credit card statement from DiviCard, he was surprised to find it was much higher than he expected. He immediately felt that a single entry for $847.60 looked particularly suspicious. Kevin uses his personal DiviCard for the occasional business trip, and when he checked his expense account for October his suspicions were confirmed: on October 27 he had lunched with a client and had signed a DiviCard credit card voucher for $84.76.

Kevin seeks an adjustment

So Kevin wrote to DiviCard to ask for an adjustment (see Figure 4-5), using the writing plan in Figure 4-6 to organize his information.

This is Kevin's **Summary Statement.**

These are the **Background** details. Kevin has written them in point form because they are easier to access than if he had written them as a single paragraph:

> My account No. is 4109 4562 3378 0113; the statement date is November 20, 2000; the entry is No. 107005641; the entry date is October 27, 2000; and the entry amount is $847.60.

These are the **Complaint Details**, i.e. what happened.

This is Kevin's **Action** statement, in which he states clearly what he wants done.

Kevin O'Hare
635 Oxbridge Street
Winnipeg MB R3M 3J2

December 4, 2000

Customer Service Manager
DiviCard Inc
PO Box 2820 Station M
Toronto ON M5W 1X6

Dear Customer Service Manager

Re: DiviCard Account No. 4109 4562 3378 0113

1 There is an error on my November DiviCard statement that I am asking you to correct before you issue my December statement.

2 The following details apply:

- Statement date: November 20, 2000.
- Entry No.: 107005641.
- Entry date: October 27, 2000.
- Entry amount: $847.60.

Use bullets to list several discrete points

3 On October 27 I dined at Luigi's Italian Specialties restaurant in Calgary, Alberta, and signed a DiviCard credit card voucher for $84.76, a copy of which is attached. Apparently, when transcribing this voucher into your system, a decimal-point error occurred.

4 Please credit my account with $762.84, which is the difference between the amount I signed for on the voucher and the amount entered into my account. Concurrently, please also cancel any interest charges that may have been incurred.

Sincerely

Kevin O'Hare

Kevin O'Hare
enc

Figure 4-5 A complaint letter

How to register a complaint . . .

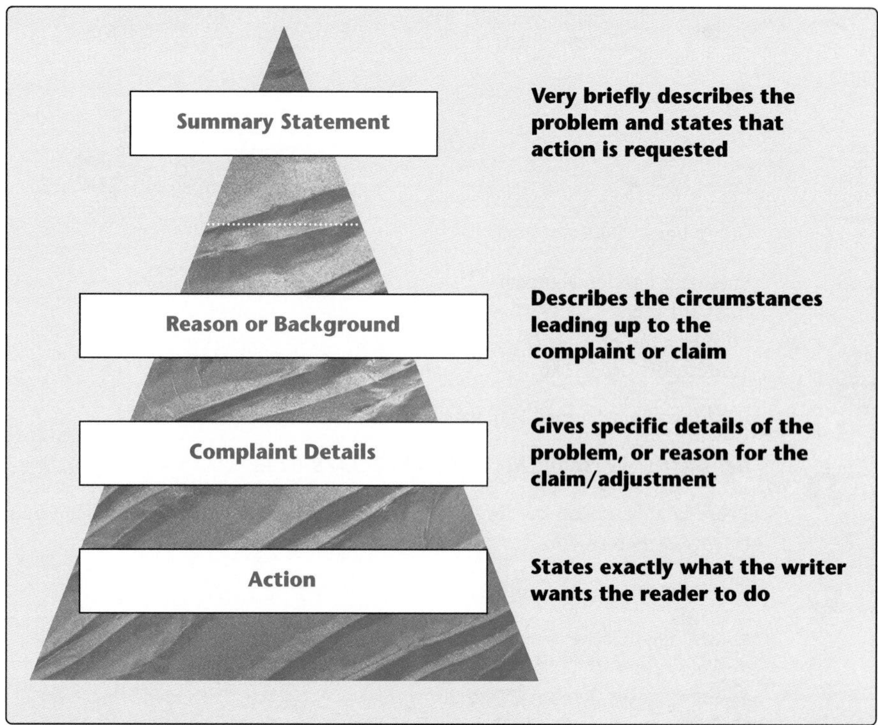

Figure 4-6 Writing plan for a complaint or claim letter

Responding to a Complaint

Lawrence Burchynski recognizes that a customer who sends him a complaint expects a speedy answer. So, when he receives a complaint from Ailsa Brooking that one of his cleaning crews has been doing less-than-satisfactory work, he phones her immediately to say he will look into the problem, takes steps to remedy it, and then writes to Ailsa to describe the action he has taken. His letter is in Figure 4-7, and the writing plan he used is Figure 4-8.

Lawrence's letter is significant on three counts:

Immediately acknowledge the problem and state what action you will take

- He has remembered that a Summary Statement for a response to a complaint or claim must do two things:
  1. It must acknowledge and, if applicable, apologize for the problem.
  2. It must state what will be done to resolve the problem.

  Most writers remember to apologize, but many forget the second part.

Avoid over-apologizing

- He apologizes only once. Some writers apologize at the start of their letter, and then, in their closing remarks, reduce the sincerity of the first apology by saying "I must apologize *again* . . . ." (Writers who have to express appreciation in a letter often make the same mistake, saying "thank you" both at the start and at the end of the letter.)

SUPERIOR BUILDING MAINTENANCE COMPANY
Suite 1311–202 Sylvan Avenue
Westmacott ON N4J 2B3

July 20, 2000

Ailsa Brooking
Office Manager
Oviedo Business Accountants
2728 Laredo Street
Westmacott ON N4H 1A8

Dear Ms Brooking

I was very sorry to read in your letter of July 18 that my crews have been providing you with less-than-satisfactory cleaning services. I will correct the situation immediately.

Recent expansion of our business has resulted in our hiring many new cleaners, some of whom obviously have not been performing at the level we expect. To correct the problem I will assign a senior supervisor to your building from July 23, with specific instructions to check that the problems you describe do not occur again.

Thank you for informing me of the difficulties and for giving me time to remedy them. I will telephone you again on July 31 to check that our cleaning service is meeting your expectations.

Regards

Lawrence Burchynski

Lawrence Burchynski

Summary Statement and Reference

Reason

Action 1

Closing Statement
Action 2

Figure 4-7 A letter responding to a complaint

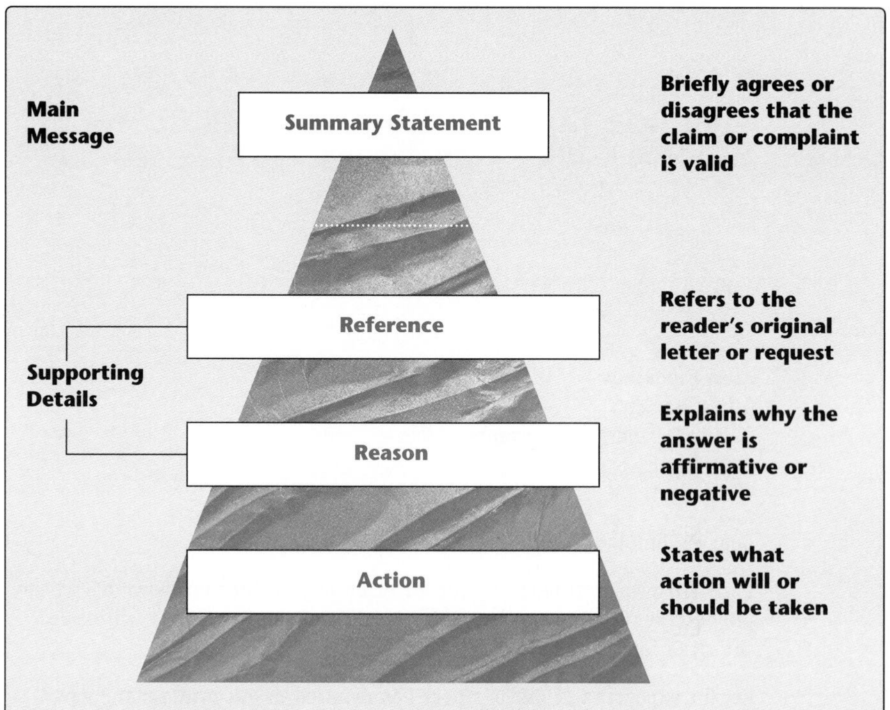

Figure 4-8 Writing plan for responding to a complaint or claim

. . . and how to reply

- Interestingly, he offers *two* Action Statements, one in the middle and one at the end of his letter. (Normally there is only one, right at the end of the letter.)

It's simpler to respond to a complaint when you are agreeing with a customer than when you have to tell the person that their complaint is not justified, and that you cannot agree to their request for an adjustment. Then your explanation (your **Reason** for not agreeing to the request) has to be more detailed. The tone of your letter must be firm yet remain pleasant, which can be difficult to achieve. The following excerpt from a letter written by a department store customer service manager provides an example:

	Dear Mr and Ms Albany
Summary Statement:	I regret that I cannot approve the return of your Irish Damask Linen red and green tablecloth and napkin set, or refund the purchase cost of $82.95, as requested in your letter of January
Reference:	13, 2001. This is the set you purchased on December 19, 2000, and attempted to return on January 3, 2001.
Reason:	At Provo Department Stores our policy is to cheerfully accept returned goods and to make refunds, *providing the goods are*

in their original condition (i.e. in the same state as when purchased). We determined that the two tablecloths and eight napkins comprising the set you bought had been laundered since you purchased them, which makes them ineligible for return or refund. Two identification tags, one pinned to a corner of the larger tablecloth, and one pinned to a napkin, enabled us to trace the laundering to Quality Launderers and Dry Cleaners at 350 McPhail Avenue. They in turn were able to trace the laundering to December 28, 2000, which was after you bought the goods.

Saying "no" to a complainant is not easy

Action: Consequently I am returning the Irish Damask Linen set to you, and hope that you are able to find good use for it in future years.

Sincerely

Timothy Williams
Customer Service Manager

Writing Collection Letters

Marianne Courtenay claims that the most difficult letters she has to write are collection letters. (Marianne is chief accountant at Winston Furniture Wholesalers and she is speaking to Phil Standahl, a junior accountant she hired three months ago.) "You have to be so careful not to upset customers," she explains, "or they'll take their business elsewhere and *still* owe us money!"

At the very moment when a company feels it should lean on a delinquent customer, she continues, it has to back off and be nice. "Going through the four stages of the collection sequence takes time, and only in the very last letter can you come right out and say, "Pay up, or take the consequences." Up to that moment the whole objective is to try to extract payment—or at least partial payment—without alienating the customer."

Collection letters demand careful, sensitive writing

The focus of each letter in the collection sequence is essentially the same: to point out that payment is overdue and encourage the delinquent customer to reply and, ideally, attach a cheque. Yet there are subtle differences in tone as the letters progress through the sequence:

- Letter 1 gently reminds the customer that the account is overdue.
- Letter 2 enquires if a problem is preventing the customer from paying the account and expresses the creditor's willingness to help.
- Letter 3 appeals to the customer to settle the account.
- Letter 4 demands payment and threatens legal action.

The tone must make the writer sound firm but approachable

The writing plan for a collection letter is short, and the same plan is used for all four letters (see Figure 4-9).

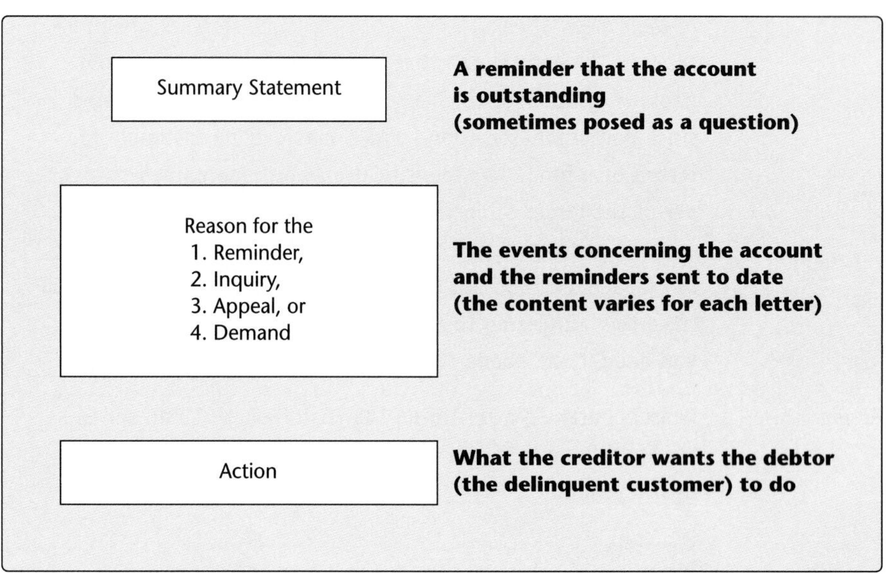

Figure 4-9 The same writing plan is used for each stage of the collection letter sequence

Reminder Stage

1. Just a gentle prod

Marianne pulls four letters from a file folder on her desk and holds one out to Phil. "Here's the first letter of a collection sequence," she says, "one in which we had to go all the way."

Phil reads the letter in Figure 4-10. "How did Mr Severin reply?" he asks.

"He didn't," Marianne explains. "That's the problem with collection letters: you rarely get a reply. Debtors are so embarrassed, they just put the letters aside. Often they don't even open them." Marianne says that getting debtors to respond is a major step in the right direction, because then she can help them work out a payment schedule that fits their resources. "It's much better to get a partial payment than no payment at all."

Inquiry Stage

2. An offer to help

Marianne lays a second letter in front of Phil (see Figure 4-11 on page 78). "In the inquiry stage you ask the customer if there is any way you can help. You want to lure the customer into replying, so you can jointly work out a repayment schedule."

"Did Mr Severin write to you?" Phil asks. "Or call?"

Marianne shakes her head.

Winston Furniture Wholesalers

3 Futon Place
Halifax NS B3R 1J6
Tel: (902) 455-1278
Fax: (902) 465-3492

January 25, 2001

Donald M Severin
Manager
The Home House
144 Putnam Road
Truro NS B2Z 4L8

Dear Mr Severin

My records show that in past years The Home House has always paid its accounts promptly, so I was particularly surprised to note that your account is now overdue. Clearly this is an oversight, and I thought you would appreciate a reminder.

Summary Statement

Your account currently stands at $5487.60, comprising furniture shipments on our invoices number B2213 of August 28 and B2649 of October 6, 2000.

Reason

May I look forward to receiving your cheque by return post? If your cheque has already been mailed, please accept my thanks and disregard this letter.

Action

Sincerely

Marianne Courtenay

Marianne G Courtenay
Chief Accountant

Figure 4-10 The first letter in a collection sequence

Appeal Stage

3. Please: we need your cash

"Now we really have to get down to business," Marianne announces, placing a third letter addressed to The Home House in front of Phil (see Figure 4-12 on page 79). "In the third stage you have to appeal to the debtor's sense of fair play and to his or her integrity. It's the last chance you have before you demand payment." As an afterthought she adds, "You'll notice my tone has become more businesslike."

"And there was still no reply?" Phil inquires.

"Nothing!"

Winston Furniture Wholesalers

3 Futon Place
Halifax NS B3R 1J6
Tel: (902) 455-1278
Fax: (902) 465-3492

February 22, 2001

Dear Mr Severin

Summary Statement

I was disappointed that you were unable to respond to my letter of January 25, in which I drew your attention to The Home House's outstanding account. Would it help if you were to make monthly payments for the time being?

Reason

I am concerned because the delay is likely to affect your previously sound credit rating. Any further delay will also mean I have to start charging interest on your outstanding balance of $5487.60.

Action

Could you drop me a line or, better still, call me at 238-0690, extension 106, so that we can discuss how I can arrange a repayment schedule that will suit you best?

Sincerely

Marianne Courtenay

Chief Accountant

Figure 4-11 Marianne's second collection letter

Demand Stage

4. Pay up, or else!

Marianne pushes the fourth letter toward Phil (Figure 4-13 on page 80). "This is the moment," she announces, "when you take off your gloves and tell the debtor you really mean business. And whatever action you say you intend to take, you *must* be prepared to carry it through. It's no good threatening to take the debtor to court, and then not doing so. Word soon gets around that you're a soft touch."

"Well, what happened?" asks Phil. "You make it sound like a mystery story!"

At last: a cheque!

Marianne laughs. "Oh, he paid up all right. Mr Severin came round to see me personally on April 26, cheque in hand."

3 Futon Place
Halifax NS B3R 1J6
Tel: (902) 455-1278
Fax: (902) 465-3492

March 22, 2001

Dear Mr Severin

Although you have received two letters from me about your overdue account, I have not yet heard from you. As we are dependent on maintaining a satisfactory cash flow to pay our suppliers, we in turn need to receive payment from our customers. Can you help us overcome this dilemma?

Summary Statement

Since October 6, 2000, your account has had a debit balance of $5487.60 (plus accrued interest, which so far I have deferred in anticipation of your cheque).

Reason

Please send your payment by April 5 so that I need not apply interest and you can maintain your credit rating with us.

Action

Sincerely

Marianne Courtenay

Chief Accountant

Figure 4-12 The third collection letter

"Did he say why there was a delay?"

"Oh, they'd had a cash-flow problem, which started in the winter and lasted right into April." Marianne explains that Mr Severin had been embarrassed by the whole affair. She laughs. "I sort of rapped him over the knuckles—he's really a nice guy—and told him next time to come and see me *early*. I can accommodate a customer who keeps me in the picture, but I can do nothing for a customer who hides his face."

Winston Furniture Wholesalers

3 Futon Place
Halifax NS B3R 1J6
Tel: (902) 455-1278
Fax: (902) 465-3492

April 19, 2001

Dear Mr Severin

Re: Outstanding Account of $5569.92

Summary Statement

I'm sorry, but unless we receive your cheque by May 3, 2001, we will start legal proceedings against The Home House to collect the $5569.92 overdue.

Reason

Your account has stood at $5487.60 since October 6, 2000. Although I have written three times since January 25, you have neither replied to my letters nor paid even a portion of the outstanding amount. As you are a long-standing customer, I deferred charging interest against your account until March 22, 2001. Interest is now being calculated at 1.5% per month from that date, and the outstanding balance quoted above reflects the first month's interest charge.

Action

I am reminding you that you have until May 3, 2001, to pay the account in full. If we have not received your cheque by then, I will instruct our lawyer to proceed.

Sincerely

Marianne Courtenay

Chief Accountant

Figure 4-13 The final collection letter

Writing Sales Letters

"Sales letters are a special case," Marita Estavo explains to Paula Roscoe, a new sales representative who graduated last June from Norton Community College. (Marita is marketing manager for Business Learning Systems of London, Ontario; see Chapter 3.) "They are the only letters in which you *intentionally* bury part of the main message—the price—and push it to about two thirds of the way down into the letter." Marita turns to the computer beside her desk and taps two keys. The writing plan shown in Figure 4-14 pops up on the video screen.

"You'll notice that the first four compartments of the writing plan are essentially the same as those for a normal persuasive letter," Marita continues.

"But they tend to contain a lot more information. In fact, there is a lot more to writing a sales letter than just working your way through the compartments." Marita explains that a sales letter must not only capture a reader's attention in the Summary Statement, but also hold the reader's interest all the way through. "Sales letters are longer than those you and I are accustomed to writing," she tells Paula. "You have to provide enough information to coerce the reader into *wanting* to buy, or at least to respond."

Sales letters demand imagination and creativity

Marita places a letter in front of Paula (see Figure 4-15 on page 83). "This came in yesterday's mail," she says. "Notice how each of its five paragraphs matches one of the five parts of a sales letter on my video screen." (They are printed in the "Writing Pattern" column to the left of the pyramid in Figure 4-14.)

Paula reaches across to her desk and pulls an envelope out of her purse. "This sales letter arrived last week," she says, handing the letter to Marita. "It's from my brother in Calgary."

"Mmmm . . . yes," Marita murmurs as she reads. "You can still identify the five parts, although they're not watertight compartments as they are in Vicki Wendrell's letter. But there is no reason why they have to be."

Two letters, two approaches

Paula invites Marita to number the parts beside the letter. Marita does so and the result is shown in Figure 4-16 on page 85. The following five numbered sections discuss how the parts have been used to create the two sample letters.

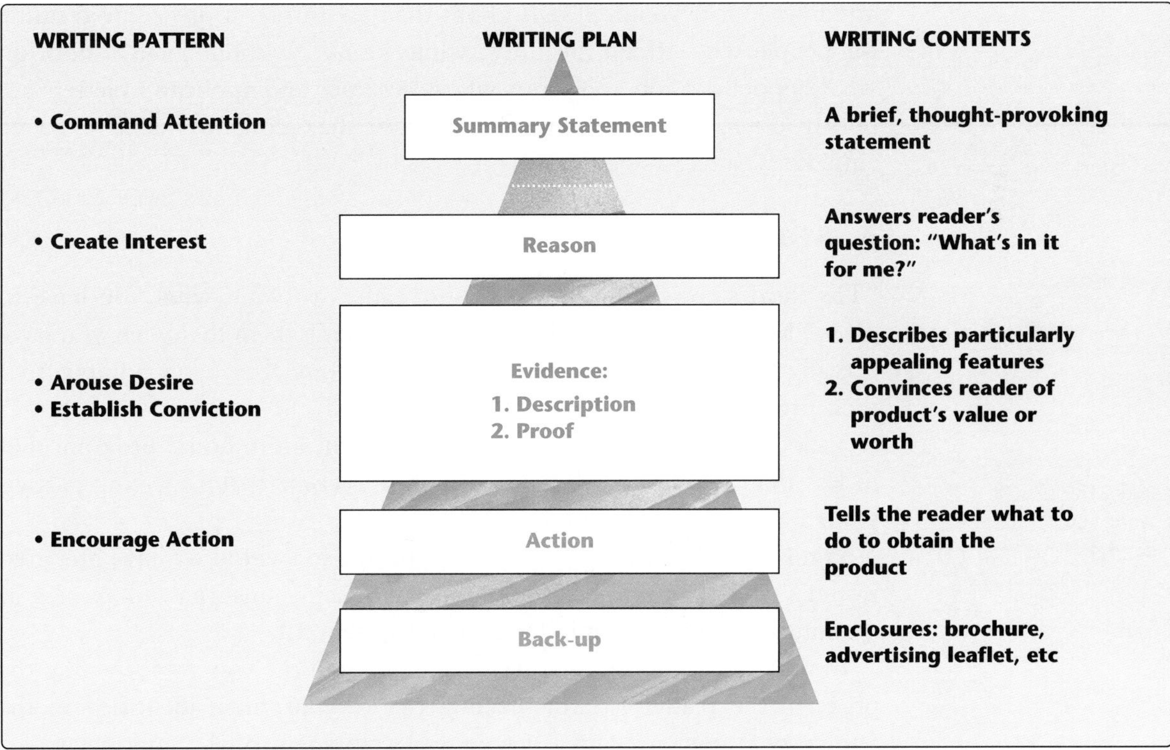

Figure 4-14 Writing plan for a sales letter

1. Command Attention

"The Summary Statement is the most difficult part of a sales letter to write," Marita says. "You have to grab your reader's attention by appealing to his or her emotions or logic. And you can't hope to write a good attention-grabber if you don't identify clearly who your audience is." She points out that both writers have clearly identified their audience and both appeal to the readers' emotions. In Figure 4-15 Vicki Wendrell addresses managers and supervisors who have experienced the frustration of attending lengthy, unproductive, and seemingly directionless business meetings. In Figure 4-16 Frank Nykoluk addresses individuals who have experienced applying for a job and then not being called in for an interview.

Grab and hold your reader's attention

The key to writing an effective opening statement for a sales letter is to identify a factor of particular concern to most readers, and to draw attention to an aspect they may not yet know but will want to know more about. "Your intention should be to make them *want* to know more," Marita adds. "You have to draw them into reading the next paragraph."

2. Create Interest

Having appealed to the readers' emotions, now you have to build their interest by offering at least one reason why they should continue paying attention. Vicki Wendrell tells about the new thrust in providing training for people who attend meetings, while Frank Nykoluk focuses both on what happens to job applicants whose resumes and application letters are poorly done, and on what his company has done to identify where employers' interests lie.

3. Arouse Desire

"The third step is to encourage your readers to want what you have to offer," Marita explains. "This means convincing them that what you have is really worthwhile. But concentrate on only one or two key points rather than fire a full volley of information at them."

Make the reader *want* your product or service

Vicki Wendrell writes, " . . . you can mount an in-house program that in less than one hour will help your staff become better meeting participants." (Figure 4-15, item 3.)

Frank Nykoluk writes: " . . . job applicants for whom we have prepared resumes and application letters are experiencing unsurpassed success at the interviews they attend." (Figure 4-16, item 3.)

In only one sentence each writer has pointed the way to correcting the problem the reader is experiencing, the very problem identified in the Summary Statement. This continuing development of the same theme—a theme to which the reader can personally relate—is an essential component of an effective sales letter.

Mentor Training Limited
316 St Mary's Road, Winnipeg MB R2H 1J8
Tel: (204) 233-6049 Fax: (204) 233-5622

February 13, 2001

Marita T Estavo
Marketing Manager
Business Learning Systems
200 Riverside
London ON N6J 1A8

Dear Ms Estavo

1 If you're lucky, you attend office meetings that are well focused and get a lot done in a minimum of time. If you're not so lucky, you sometimes have to attend meetings that seem rudderless, achieve little, and go on for far too long.

2 Most people think that poorly run office meetings are the chairperson's fault, but their assumption is only partly correct. Even the most experienced chairpersons cannot run effective meetings if they share the table with inefficient meeting participants. The problem is that until recently almost all training in how to conduct business meetings has been directed at managers and supervisors, the people who chair them. Little if any training has been given to the far greater number who attend meetings.

3 I said "until recently" because now you can mount an in-house program that in less than one hour will help your staff become better meeting participants. "Six Around a Table!" demonstrates how to prepare information for presentation, focus listeners' attention on key points, ask and answer questions, use visuals to enhance your words, and know when to speak and when not to.

4 The key to the program's success is a 24-minute dramatized videotape that shows a meeting in progress and depicts what happens when some people participate efficiently while others do not. The videotape is accompanied by a seminar leader's handbook that describes how to orchestrate a fast-paced interactive training session that conveys all the essential information in only 23 minutes. The cost is $395, which includes 20 copies of a specially prepared viewers' booklet titled *Steps to More Efficient Business Meetings.*

5 Write, telephone, or fax me today for preview copies of the videotape and the two booklets. Then judge for yourself how you can use the seminar materials to improve office meetings at Business Learning Systems.

Sincerely

Vicki Wendrell

Vicki Wendrell
Program Specialist

The writing compartments are clearly defined in Vicki's letter

Figure 4-15 A sales letter directed to business readers in a moderate-to-large organization

4. Establish Conviction

Present facts to prove your claims

Readers almost automatically question advertisers' claims. Therefore, Vicki Wendrell and Frank Nykoluk must immediately offer *evidence* that the desire-arousing statements they have just made are facts, not opinions. At item 4, Vicki describes the seminar materials that are available for teaching "meeting effectiveness" in-house. Frank quotes the results of a study that shows his clients achieve a far higher interview success rate than the average. Frank then arouses reader desire even further by stating, "We will groom you to present a superior image . . . ."

Hold cost information until late in your letter

Not until this stage—when you have said all you can to convince the reader to buy your product—should you mention price. "And even then you should try to reduce the impact of the dollar figure," Marita suggests. "Place it in a longish sentence, preferably with some other information so that the cost does not stand out too prominently."

Both sales letters in Figures 4-15 and 4-16 offer good evidence and mention the cost successfully (in the last sentence of point 4).

5. Encourage Action

Now you want your reader to send for more information, ask to see a sample, or—best of all—to order the product. You must use strong, active verbs to close your sales letter:

- "*Write, telephone,* or *fax* me today . . . " writes Vicki, " . . . then *judge* for yourself . . . ."
- "*Complete* the enclosed postage-paid inquiry card, or *call* me . . . " writes Frank, " . . . then *bring* a list . . . ."

Here are four additional factors that contribute to effective sales letters:

1. If you are enclosing a product leaflet or a brochure, mention it late in the letter (ideally, as evidence to support the "Establish Conviction" section).
2. Avoid weak statements such as

Avoid wishy-washy words

> *If you would like* more information . . .
> *I know you will find* ABC of value . . .
> *We hope* that when you have read . . .

3. Avoid using unsupported adjectives and adverbs such as

> Chieftain Software is *undeniably* faster than . . .
> You will *particularly* appreciate . . .

4. Be consistently objective, offering facts rather than opinions.

Personal Communication Services
Suite 1411–333 Seventh Ave SW, Calgary AB T2P 2Z1
Tel: (403) 668-7712

January 17, 2001

Peter J Roscoe
1650–2715 Avenue SE
Calgary AB T2B 0A2

Dear Peter

1 Recent research shows that on average only 25% of people who apply for a particular job are invited to attend an interview. Can you afford to be one of the 75% who are eliminated during the pre-interview stage?

2 Employers draw up their interview lists based on the written documentation provided by each applicant. If an application letter and resume fail to convince them that an applicant is worth interviewing, that person's name is not listed. Sometimes, extremely well-qualified applicants are eliminated because they have not presented themselves well on paper.

3 At Personal Communication Services we have studied the key factors that catch an employer's attention. Now, job applicants for whom we have prepared resumes and application letters are experiencing unsurpassed success at the interviews they attend. For example, from September to November 2000, we prepared job application documents for and counselled 237 clients, of whom

- 120 (over 50%!) were interviewed by the first company they approached.
- 78 (33%) were offered employment following their first interview.

4 Their remarkable success was achieved because we provide interview counselling as well as resume preparation. We will groom you to present a superior image of yourself, both on paper and in person. And, Peter, you will be surprised at how little it costs: our rates start at only $65 for an expertly prepared resume.

5 Complete the enclosed postage-paid inquiry card, or call me at 668-7712 to set up an appointment. Then bring a list of your previous employment history and details of your education with you. I will give you free initial advice and an estimate, all without obligation.

I look forward to meeting you.

Best wishes

Frank T Nykoluk
Senior Consultant
Personal Communication Services

Although the writing compartments are less easy to define in Frank's letter, the sales sequence is still present

Frank plants the ball firmly in the reader's hands

Figure 4-16 A sales letter directed to the general public (particularly professionals or paraprofessionals)

Know your product

"The key to writing effective sales letters," Marita finishes, "is to be personally convinced of the value of the product or service before you write. Then you can let your enthusiasm spill over into your writing. It's when you're not really convinced a product is all it's cracked up to be that you tend to write overblown, adjective-laden sentences and paragraphs."

TO SUM UP

In persuasive letters you expect your reader to act or react (reply) in response to your communication. A well-planned persuasive letter

- opens with a brief statement that summarizes the situation and identifies generally what you want the reader to do,
- continues with background information and a detailed description of the situation, and
- closes with a specific request for action

Your letter must command your reader's attention in the first sentence and then hold your reader's interest all the way through to the closing sentence.

Sales letters tend to be longer and to quote more facts than other persuasive letters.

EXERCISES

Exercise 4.1: Complaint

On Monday 12th December you booked flights for yourself and a friend to fly to Disney World. Your flights were from your home town or city to Atlanta, Georgia, where you would have to change planes to fly from Atlanta to Orlando. (You had wanted to get a direct flight to Orlando, but all the discount seats had been sold). Details:

Feb 8	Home city to Atlanta	Flight 1984	Depart 16:10	Arrive 20:55
	Atlanta to Orlando	Flight 1428	Depart 21:20	Arrive 22:33
Feb 22	Orlando to Atlanta	Flight 1415	Depart 09:10	Arrive 10:26
	Atlanta to home city	Flight 1863	Depart 13:00	Arrive 17:10

You booked direct with Remick Airlines, and spoke to agent Louise Fournier. She said you had to confirm the tickets within seven days, and told you to quote file R233078 when you called back.

On Friday 16th December you phoned Remick Airlines and spoke to Douglas Wiens. You gave him the file number and told him you were confirming the flights.

"OK," he said. "You leave for Orlando on February 8th, and you return on the 22nd. Right?"

Arrangements for flights seemed fine . . .

You agreed that it was. He asked if you would accept an E-ticket, and you agreed to that too.

Your confirmation and itinerary arrived by mail on December 23, just in time for you to gift-wrap it for your friend.

Now it's February 8 and you and your friend are at your home airport, standing at the check-in counter. The agent checks your baggage, assigns you seats, and hands your boarding passes to you. You glance at yours and say: "No, this can't be right. We're flying into Orlando today, not tomorrow!"

"No," says the agent. "You will be night-stopping in Atlanta and taking the 06:30 flight tomorrow morning."

"But that's not what I booked," you complain. "When I booked the agent said we connect to a flight to Orlando half an hour after we arrive in Atlanta."

"That's unlikely," the agent replies. "Twenty-five minutes is not considered sufficient time to change terminals in Atlanta."

You argue, but to no avail, the agent (whose name is Rita Winspear) cannot change the flights for you; the system won't let her do it. "But I'll tell you what," she says. "I'll put you on the wait list for Flight 1428. It's showing just one seat available right now, but there may be more by the time you get there."

Of course, there weren't. You and your friend ran from the arrival gate to the underground interconnection train, and from it to the departure gate for Flight 1428, and got there with three minutes to spare. But the aircraft was full and already pulling away from the gate.

It's two days later and you are sitting beside the pool of the hotel in Disney World, a pad of paper on your knees, writing a complaint to Remick Airlines and asking for a refund. Here are some additional details you may need:

. . . until you started to travel!

- Remick Airlines head office address is Suite 2700, 2820 Maltby Avenue in Toronto, M5G 1L7.
- The flight you took from Atlanta to Orlando was No. 1436. It departed Atlanta at 06:30 and arrived in Orlando at 07:42.
- You stayed at the Sunset Inn, just outside the Atlanta airport, where your room cost you $106.82US (including tax). Use the current exchange rate between US and Canadian dollars to convert the hotel room cost to Canadian dollars.

Strong communication skills are the first step toward promotion

- You insert your home address at the top of your letter.
- The E-ticket number was 1-776-3384-8.
- You are writing to complain that the change of flights was made by Remick Airlines between the time you booked and the time you received your itinerary, and that the airline did not inform you of the change. (The revised flight *was* listed on the itinerary, however, but you did not notice it in your hurry to gift-wrap it!)
- You are claiming the cost of the hotel in Atlanta, plus a charge (of your choice) for being inconvenienced.

Exercise 4.2: **Claim**

After graduating from college three years ago, you started a small accounting and administrative services business, working from your home, where you have taken two rooms at the back of the house and converted them into offices. For a long time you managed with an old desk and chair, and a home-made computer table. Last week, however, when you were buying some computer supplies at Berwell Office Supplies, you saw a computer desk that really would suit you. And it was marked down 20% as a "special sale" item. So you bought it (for $559.95 plus tax) and a high-backed computer chair on rollers ($159.95 plus tax). You also paid an extra $25 to have the desk and chair delivered.

Two days ago Marion Movers and Shippers carried the three pieces (desk, hutch, and chair) through the house and into your office, and that evening you proceeded to set up the desk, mount the hutch, take the cover off the chair, and move your computer, printer, scanner, and monitor into position. It was then that you noticed there was a long scratch running along the left side of the desktop, which you were certain was not there when you examined the desk in the store. So you called Berwell Office Supplies and spoke to the person who sold the piece to you. He agreed he did not see any damage when you bought it.

Who damaged the desk: the supplier or the shipper?

"But if you want an adjustment, you'll have to speak to the Sales Manager," he continued. You asked for the manager's name.

"That's Frank Wheatstone," he said, "but he's out of town right now, until next week. I suggest you write to him and say what you want done."

Write to the Sales Manager. Tell him what you have found and ask for Berwell Office Supplies to . . . (well, you decide what action you would like him to take: Repairs? Full replacement? A further reduction off the purchase price—another 15%, maybe?)

Here is some additional information you may need:

- The shipment was made on Berwell's Invoice No. 2324A.
- You paid for the goods with Visa No. 4511 2333 0106 7786.
- Your address is 1444 Craig Street in your town or city.

- The salesperson was Mark Favori.
- The delivery people were Marion Movers and Shippers of 406 Perimeter Road and are regularly hired by Berwell Office Products to make deliveries. The driver's name was Jim; you didn't catch his assistant's name.

Exercise 4.3: **Response to a Claim**

You are Sales Manager Frank Wheatstone's administrative assistant at Berwell Office Supplies. Today Frank received a letter from Dana Matzjieski, who bought a desk and chair from the store exactly one week ago, and is complaining that a scratch on the desk's left upper surface was not there when she bought it. (For details, see Exercise 4.2.) She is asking for Frank to replace the desk.

Part 1

Frank brings the letter to you and says: "We can't replace it: it's not company policy; and anyway we don't have another one like it. It's an older model. Tell her we'll either repair it free of charge or she can have another 10% off the purchase price. That's the best I can do."

Write the letter. Work out what 10% off the purchase price would be. Dana's address is 313 Beaver Dam Road in your town.

Part 2

The supplier says "No. Not us."

Frank brings the letter to you and says: "No way! I'm not replacing it or paying for any repair work. That particular desk was in the shop for a long time. Anything could have happened to it. That's why we marked it down 20%. It could even have been done by the delivery people. (You can tell her to write to them, too!)"

You talk to the salesperson (Mark Favori), who pulls the sales tag out of a drawer. "It was sold as an 'as is' product, he says. She has no claim."

You go back to the original invoice and note that the words "As is" were not typed or written onto it. "Never you mind," says Mark, "it was there when she examined the desk. I can vouch for that."

Write to Dana Matzjieski and tell her the company will take no action.

Exercise 4.4: **Request**

You have worked for nearly two years as a sales clerk, shelf stocker, etc, in the Red Star convenience store. It's an independently held store owned by Georges and Maria Popondopolos. Gradually, over time, you have established a reputation with Georges and Maria as a confident, capable worker who has a nice way with customers and who sorts out and deals with problems without always telephoning the owners for help.

You live with your partner Chris, who works as a shift worker for Multiple Industries, producing products for the defence industry. The problem is that with your variable shifts, and Chris's variable shifts, there are days and sometimes weeks when you "virtually wave at one another" as one arrives home just as the other leaves for work. Chris's shifts change from 8 a.m. to 4 p.m. for five days, and then 4 p.m. to midnight for the next five days, and then midnight to 8 a.m. for the next five days.

In discussions with Multiple Industries, Chris has arranged to work a moderately stable schedule: day shift (8 a.m. to 4 p.m.) during odd-numbered months (January, March, etc) and night shift (midnight to 8 a.m.) during even-numbered months (February, April, etc).

Ask for a change in your work schedule

Now you would like to make a similar arrangement with your employer, where there are three shifts a day (it's a 24-hour per day store): 7–3; 3–11; 11–7. Currently you work the morning shift, from 7 a.m. to 3 p.m.—you have been doing this for eight months—and have been given the responsibility to keep the books (the accounts), and to make the bank deposit each day at 3:00 p.m., on your way home. You would like to work similar hours to those Chris has obtained. You both want this. ("If we had a baby, it would be a different story," Chris quips. "We'd probably *want* different shifts so we wouldn't have to hire a baby sitter!")

Write a memo to your employer requesting that they accept a change in shift for you. (You know they are not going to be happy about this, because they have come to depend on you as the daytime "supervisor and bookkeeper.")

Exercise 4.5: **Request**

Your claim to work evening shifts and day shifts that mesh with your partner Chris's shifts (see Exercise 4.4) has been successful. You still do the accounts for one month, and have trained Candace to do them on the months you work the night shift (the store owners were not too happy with this arrangement, but they have accepted it). But on the months you do the night shift, a problem has arisen.

In the apartment block where you live—you and Chris have a main floor apartment—twice a week you are wakened by considerable noise: the employees of the company that cuts the grass once a week in the summer and clears snow with a snow-blower after each snowfall in the winter, come marching past your window between 10 a.m. and noon, waking both of you. Two days later, the garbage removal truck roars up to the garbage container 6 metres from your window, and noisily lifts it high into the air and tips its contents into the truck.

Ask for more peaceful sleep times

Twice you have phoned the grass cutting/snow removal company (Sunshine Services Ltd) and have asked them to cut grass and remove snow after 3 p.m. Both times they agreed, and for two days the arrangement worked. But each time on the third day they were back to the same schedule. You also phoned the garbage removal people and asked for a late-afternoon garbage removal, and they, too agreed, but it worked only for a couple of days.

Now you decide to *write* to the two companies and ask them again. These are the addresses:

- Sunshine Services Ltd, 440 Ebby Street (owner/manager: Francine Busch).
- Inner City Garbage Removal Company, 800 Purity Lane (manager for your area: Don Carlos).

Your address is: Suite 106, Bentall Apartments, 230 Western Avenue.

Exercise 4.6: **Request**

You are employed by the City of Montrose Hospital, where you have dual responsibilities as a library clerk and medical records technician. You also are a member of the Provincial Association of Medical Records Technicians (PAMRT). In this morning's mail you receive a folder from PAMRT advertising a two-day conference and seminar to be held in the resort centre of Waverley, 327 kilometres from Montrose, on the third Thursday and Friday of next month. You want to go.

You glean the following details from the folder:

Ask to attend a conference and seminar

- The conference is to be held at the Venture Inn South in Waverley.
- Day 1 is the annual conference of PAMRT, which includes three parts:

    1. The annual general meeting (AGM).
    2. Professional development sessions on combatting stress in a high-pressure work environment, developing strong interpersonal communication skills, and keeping abreast of new strategies in electronic documentation.
    3. A formal luncheon with Mildred Holdenrath, president of the International Association of Medical Records Technicians (with headquarters in New York), as keynote speaker. Her topic will be "The Increasing Importance of Documentation in the Burgeoning Health Industries."

- Day 2 is a special limited-attendance seminar on storing records in a digital library, and the technique's applicability to the health service industries. It is titled "Digital Storage of Medical Documents."
- The registration fees are $105 for Day 1 and $165 for Day 2. (The fees increase by $20 per day for registrations received after the last day of this month.)

- There is unlimited space for attendance on Day 1 (about 175 members are expected), but only 20 members can be accommodated for Day 2.
- You can sign up for Day 1 only, or Day 1 and Day 2, but not for Day 2 only.
- Hotel accommodation (conference rate) is $115 per person per night.
- The sessions run from 9 a.m. to 5 p.m. each day.
- There is a wine and cheese "ice breaker" reception on Wednesday evening (the evening prior to Day 1), from 7:30 to 9:30 p.m.

Factors to consider

You also consider these other factors:

- If you drive your own car, you are entitled to claim 28 cents per kilometre.
- The bus fare is $92.50 one way, $165 return.
- There is only one bus each way per day:

Leave:	*Arrive:*
Waverley 8:30 a.m.	Montrose 12:45 p.m.
Montrose 1:30 a.m.	Waverley 5:45 p.m.

- There is no rail or air connection.
- Pamela Rudnicki and Chris Hinton (both are hospital staff) went to last year's conference in Kettering and reported that it was well worth attending (Pamela was particularly enthusiastic). Montrose Hospital covered all their expenses.
- You applied to go last year, but you were turned down. (There was money for only two to attend, and both Pamela and Chris have more seniority.)
- You can arrange for Pamela to switch work shifts with you (she is agreeable), but you need to make the arrangements no later than seven work days from today (which is the day that next month's work schedules are finalized).
- If others from the hospital are approved to attend the conference, you would be willing to take them in your car (so far, you have been unable to identify anyone else who is interested).

Write a memo requesting attendance at both the conference and the seminar. Address it to Rita Shirling, your hospital's director of administration. Remember that you need an answer soon, so you can get your name in early to the seminar/conference committee and be guaranteed a seat as one of the 20 who will attend Day 2.

Exercise 4.7: **Request**

You are Marketing and Product Consultant for OffStat Independent Office Supplies Ltd, which is owned by Joe and Wendy Raphael (for more information, see Exercise 3.3 on page 54). Your primary responsibility is to keep in touch with customers, to ensure you provide the office supplies they need.

In talking to customers recently, you have had several requests that OffStat should supply European-size paper.

"It's known as 'A4'," says Marvin Harcourt, a business consultant, when you visit him. "It's used in the UK and all over Europe. Australia and New Zealand, too. In fact, North Americans are about the only users of 8.5 × 11 inch paper."

"What's the difference?" you ask.

"Not a lot," Marvin explains. "A4 paper is slightly longer and slightly narrower than the 8.5 × 11 inch paper we use." He pulls out a letter from a consultant in the UK and lays it on top of a letter he has written.

You measure the difference. "It's 17 mm longer," you say.

Marvin pulls out a file folder: "You'll find A4 paper is *exactly* the same length as this file folder: 296 mm."

European paper sizes differ from North American

"But it's 6 mm narrower than 8.5 × 11 inch paper," you add.

"A4 is exactly 209 mm wide. 8.5 × 11 inch paper is 215 mm wide."

"But why would you want to use A4 paper?" you ask.

"For compatibility. I work with international companies all over. If I'm providing information for a joint proposal being prepared, say, in Germany, I could send my sections to them on the correct-size paper. They wouldn't have to reprint it onto their paper."

When you visit Rebecca Gerbrandt later in the same week, she offers a similar opinion. (Rebecca is an architect, working for an international firm.) "If I type my stuff up on 8.5 × 11 inch paper, I can never get it looking long enough on the page when they print from my disk in Europe. If I try to make it longer, my printer says I am printing outside the boundaries of the paper. If I had A4 paper to print on, I could set my word-processor to type for A4 length paper and there would be no problem. But if I set the word-processor for A4, and print on 8.5 × 11 paper . . . well, the printer just won't do it."

In addition to Marvin and Rebecca, you also get requests for A4 paper from Ginny Friedrich, who is co-owner of Friedrich and Goldstein, Chartered Accountants, and from Robert Wendell, who is a lawyer with Manders, Wendell and Schumacher. They tell you they would like to have plain white paper in two qualities: Classic Laid for proposals and 24 lb bond for ordinary work. "It would be useful to have some pads of writing paper, too," adds Robert Wendell, "for when I'm working with international clients. When I travel to Australia and New Zealand, the first thing I do on arriving is go to a stationery store. Usually I bring some pads back with me, but they are heavy and I never seem to be able to carry enough."

"You don't need to change the 9 × 4 envelope size," Ginny Friedrich says. "But you would need to get some slightly longer page-size envelopes, instead of the 9 × 12 inch ones we use now."

"Do you think we could start a trend in Canada, to adopt A4 size?" you suggest.

"No way! The paper industry wouldn't hear of it. It would be much too expensive to change over."

Ask for permission to stock European size paper

Write a memo to Joe and Wendy Raphael, suggesting you bring in a limited supply of European-size paper and envelopes. Describe what kind and the quantities you think would be sufficient. (You recognize that buying in the comparatively small quantities you would need will be more expensive than buying at the price you usually pay for bulk orders you currently place with the wholesalers.) Suggest that you could be developing a niche market, which could bring in orders from customers you currently don't have. And you're sure the chain stores don't stock European-size paper; there wouldn't be enough demand for their high-volume approach to stationery marketing.

Exercise 4.8: **Proposal**

Maria Cantafio is president and general manager of Deli-Fare Limited, a small chain of eat-in/take-out restaurants open from 10 a.m. to 6 p.m. Monday to Friday at key locations in the business districts of major cities. You are Ms Cantafio's assistant manager. Deli-Fare has three local restaurants and another 18 operated by franchisees in other cities. Several more franchise arrangements are pending. The restaurants do a roaring trade serving homemade sandwiches, quiches, soups, and salads to businesspeople each lunch hour (all the tables in the restaurants are fully occupied from 11:15 a.m. to 2:45 p.m.).

Over the past 18 months the take-out segment of the business has grown significantly, ever since you persuaded Ms Cantafio to install a fax machine at each location so businesses could fax in their orders. At that time you wrote:

Your original proposal

> We could preprint order forms and leave them with current and potential customers, and ask them to enter their requirements (quantities and time required) on the form and then send it to us by fax. There would be no more errors in writing down telephone orders (which seems to happen too often), no more disagreement about the price, and no more frustrated customers (or missed orders!) because our two telephone lines are both busy during peak order times . . .

Today you have an even better idea: to establish a Web page with a combined menu and order form built into it, so that businesses can send their lunch orders to Deli-Fare via the Internet. Doing this will mean establishing a Web domain. The restaurant will not have to buy a computer: it already uses one to document orders, for both pick-up and dine-in customers. And you have already checked whether it has spare slots for a memory card (it has) and a modem.

Part 1

Write a memo to Maria Cantafio, proposing that Deli-Fare offers a Web-based electronic lunch-ordering service. You will have to include the following factors in your proposal:

Propose setting up a Web page

- The cost of the memory card and modem will be $325.
- Subscribing to Octagon Express—a local Internet provider—will cost $50 for the hook up, then $19.95 per month thereafter.
- You will probably need an additional "dedicated" telephone line, for connecting the modem, at a cost of $35 for the initial hook up, and then $15.90 per month rental thereafter. (Although it can be done, it would be impractical to hook up the computer and the fax machine to the same line.)
- The cost to list a Web page would be $5.00 per month. There would be no cost for designing it, because you could do that on your home computer.
- The cost to prepare, print, and mail 330 copies of a letter announcing the new service to local businesses would be $275 for preparing and printing the letter and $158.70 for mailing it.

Part 2

Write the letter announcing the new service to local businesses. Tell them that until now they have been able to phone or fax their orders, but from the 1st of next month they will be able to email their lunch orders. Your address will be **www.delifare.mancom.ca**. This announcement is a sales letter, so be sure it grabs readers' attention.

Exercise 4.9: Collection

Erik Vanderhoof was immediately noticed when he strode into Words and Disks Unlimited. He was unusually tall, had a bushy red beard that tumbled over the top two buttons of a striped bush shirt, and wore blue jeans with knee-high, rust-colored leather boots. He prowled along the shelves, picking up books as he went, and eventually dumped them on the order desk at the back of the store.

Deal with a demanding customer

"Will you take a purchase order?" he barked. You replied that occasionally the bookstore did.

"Well . . . do you or don't you?" he insisted. You murmured that you would fetch Ms Fennymore, the owner.

She examined the purchase order. "What kind of consulting do you do?" Ms Fennymore asked.

"Business consulting. All over. Particularly in the north, for people going into business for themselves."

"You live in the north yourself?"

"That's what it says," he replied laconically, pointing to the top of the purchase order on which this address was printed:

Erik J Vanderhoof
Business Consultant
Box 1848
Leaf Rapids MB R0B 1W0

"All right," Ms Fennymore nodded to you. "Mr Vanderhoof can have a $300 line of credit."

You listed his purchases on a sales slip (No. B1043) and he copied the titles onto his purchase order (No. 0002):

The customer's purchase

1. Random House II Unabridged Dictionary		$115.95
2. Business Management Principles and Practices—JF Ryder (Dover Press)		37.50
3. Writing Proposals that Sell—Baker and Carlson (Lakeshore Books)		28.95
4. Monitoring Human Behaviour—VJ Samson (Cardigan Bay Books)		33.60
5. Compact Disk Series CD-1211: Introduction to Business Psychology		57.95
	GST @ 7%	19.18
	Total	**$293.13**

He signed both the sales slip and the purchase order, picked up the books, and marched out to a dilapidated truck.

His visit to the bookstore occurred on May 3. On May 31 you mailed him an invoice (No. 1788). On June 30 Ms Fennymore asked you to write Mr Vanderhoof a reminder letter. There was no reply, so on July 31 you launched into the remainder of the collection sequence. ("I should have been more suspicious," Ms Fennymore confided to you, "when I saw the purchase order was only number two. A dead giveaway, really!")

Write *one* of the following letters:

Write a collection letter

a. Reminder Letter (June 30)
b. Inquiry Letter (July 31)
c. Appeal Letter (August 31)
d. Demand Letter (September 30)

The address of Words and Disks Unlimited is Unit 13, Keewatin Mall, 2800 Miners Trail (of your city or town).

Exercise 4.10: **Sales**

You are enrolled in year one of a three-year course, and you need a job for the summer. Jobs are scarce, and in any case you would rather work for yourself than someone else. You decide to offer a home and yard maintenance service for homeowners in your city while they are on vacation. You target a particular area of your city and decide to drop personally addressed letters into the homeowners' mailboxes. You plan to write a sales letter and print multiple copies, but will handwrite each homeowner's name at the top of the letter (you will get the names from the city directory).

You also write down some of the services you could offer, such as

- mowing and watering the lawn,
- weeding the garden,
- collecting the mail,
- washing the windows (inside and out),
- feeding, walking, and looking after pets,
- watering the plants,
- putting the garbage out, to create a "lived in" look,
- checking automatic light timers,
- painting, and
- driving homeowners to and from the airport.

Write a sales letter offering home maintenance services

You work out fees for various duties and services, and for combinations of services. You also make a note of some of the reasons for giving a home a "lived in" look, which will be your main selling point. Give your service a suitable company name, then write the sales letter. *Note: You may include other services, in addition to those in the list, that you feel you could offer.*

WEBLINKS

Strategies for Writing Persuasive Letters
www.wuacc.edu:80/services/zzcwwctr/persuasive-ltrs.wm.txt
This step-by-step guide covers the purpose of the persuasive letter, prewriting questions for the writer, writing strategies, and revision tips. Examples are included.

10 Easy Ways to Write More Effective Letters

www.smartbiz.com/sbs/arts/dir5.htm

A concise site with 10 tips for writing effective letters, like delivering your main message early and using plain language.

Sales Letters—Four Point Action Closing

owl.english.purdue.edu/Files/93.html

This site discusses how to write the most important part of a sales letter—the closing.

Informal and Semiformal Business Reports

chapter 5

Candace Dannaire walks up the eight brass-edged steps to the mezzanine at Mansask Insurance Corporation and perches herself on the corner of Stewart Frohlig's desk. For nearly four years she has shared the cramped space on the mezzanine with three other insurance adjusters, but now Candace has been promoted to supervisor of client services and yesterday she moved into a cubicle in room A107 on the main floor.

"It's still here," she moans, waving a hand toward her now empty desk across the narrow aisle. "The people from Building Services were supposed to move my computer down for me early this morning."

Stewart leaps to his feet. "I can fix that for you!" he says. Already he is pushing the monitor to the back of the computer's upper surface and laying the keyboard horizontally in front of it.

"I thought all heavy equipment had to be moved by Building Services," Candace starts to say, but Stewart interrupts her.

"Nothing to it! Just down the stairs and 20 metres along the passage." His hand is on the power cord, still plugged into a wall socket. "Have you locked the hard disk drive?"

"I pressed 'Control,' 'Alt,' and 'Break,' if that's what you mean."

"Right!" Stewart pulls the plug out of the socket, folds the cord double, and lays it across the computer top between the keyboard and monitor. "Here we go, then."

He wraps his arms around the three pieces and lifts them up. "Follow me," he instructs Candace, and strides clumsily to the end of the room.

"Be careful of the . . . ," Candace starts to warn him. She has seen the end of the power cord slide off the computer and fall to the floor between Stewart's feet.

At that moment Stewart stubs the toe of his left foot against the protruding metal of the top step. Simultaneously, the power cord wraps itself around his right ankle. He stumbles, lunges against the wall on his right, and then he and the computer tumble down the eight steps.

Scenario for an accident

"Oh, no!" Candace yelps, and scurries after him. "Are you all right, Stewart?" she gasps, bending over his sprawled body.

"Ugh," he grunts, opening his eyes and peering at the glass from the shattered monitor lying around him and the computer angled crazily against the wall. "I guess your computer's had it," he murmurs, his right hand prodding his left shoulder, "and I think I've broken something."

Now the incident has to be documented

"You'll have to write a report," branch manager Lorna Friedrichs tells Candace one hour later. "I gather you're the only person who saw what happened?"

Candace nods.

"In fact," Lorna continues, "you'll have to write two reports: one for the Workers Compensation Board, and one for me—for the record."

IN THIS CHAPTER

You will learn how to use the writer's pyramid to organize short informal reports, all of which will be informative and some of which also will be persuasive. Specifically, you will learn how to plan and write reports that describe

- an incident that has occurred,
- progress of a job,
- completion of a project,
- an assignment involving travel, and
- the results of an investigation.

Incident Report

Candace Dannaire's report describing Stewart Frohlig's accident is brief and complete (see Figure 5-2 on page 102). She wrote it using the writing plan in Figure 5-1.

Incident reports may be widely read

You may ask why Candace provides so many details in the Background when she is writing a report from herself to her manager, who knows who Stewart Frohlig is, and where his and Candace's offices are. However, Candace is aware that reports are often distributed more widely than business correspondence. She knows, for example, that if a staff member or a customer is injured on Mansask's premises, within 24 hours the branch has to fax a copy of an incident report to head office in Toronto. If Candace omits pertinent details, head office will undoubtedly ask for them. By anticipating and then answering the questions head office is likely to ask, she reduces the amount of future interoffice communication.

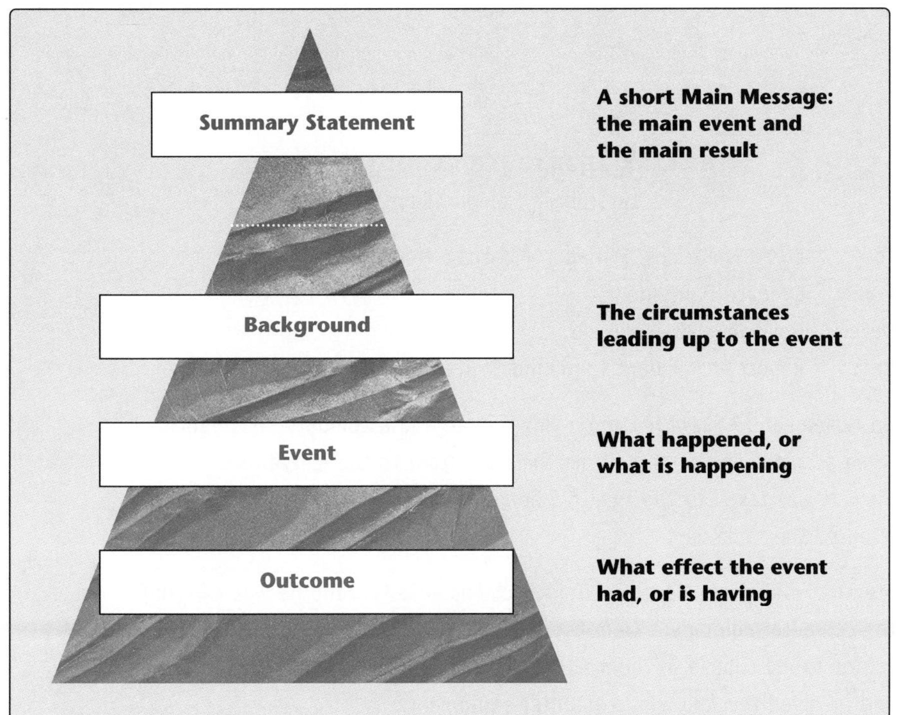

Figure 5-1 Writing plan for an incident report

An incident report most often is a "tell" document

When Candace had to write a report for the first time—some three years ago—she visualized a formal document with a stiff cover and a plastic binding. She has since learned that most reports are prepared as letters or interoffice memorandums, and that only long formal reports and proposals are wrapped within a jacket or cover. Candace has also discovered that the basic writing plan for business letters shown in Figure 3-1 and repeated below can readily be applied to short reports.

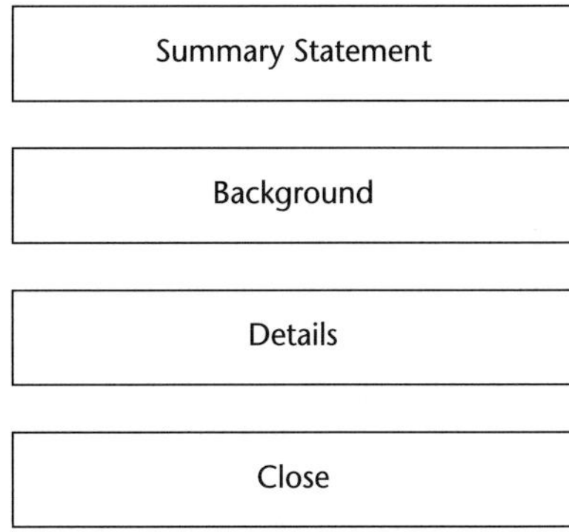

Summary Statement

Background

Put *all* the situation details in the Background to create a simpler, tidier description of the Event

Event

Outcome

Mansask Insurance Corporation

Interoffice Memorandum

To: Lorna Friedrichs, Manager, Montrose Branch
From: Candace Dannaire
Date: November 20, 2000
Ref: Report of Accident Involving Stewart Frohlig

Summary Statement

On November 19 Stewart Frohlig was injured and a computer was damaged in an accident on the steps from the main floor to the mezzanine. Stewart was taken to the Health Sciences Centre for treatment and was released the same day.

Background

Stewart Frohlig is a Montrose Branch claims adjuster, and he was carrying the computer equipment from the insurance adjuster's room on the mezzanine to my cubicle in room A107. The incident occurred at 3:15 p.m. and involved the following computer equipment:

- Nabuchi computer ES2, Serial No. 8271665
- Nabuchi keyboard KB3, Serial No. 1164718
- Calypso monitor 300, Serial No. M45107

Put all the situation details in the Background to create a simpler, tidier description of the Event

Event

As Stewart approached the top step, one end of the computer power cord slipped from its stowage and fell to the floor, twisting around Stewart's right foot. He tripped and fell down the eight steps.

Outcome

Stewart incurred a fractured shoulder blade and contusions to the left side of his head. The computer was badly dented but may be repairable. The monitor and keyboard were damaged beyond repair.

C.D.

Figure 5-2 Candace Dannaire's incident report

The compartments are relabelled slightly or expanded to suit the purpose of each report. Those for an incident report, for example, are **Summary Statement, Background, Event,** and **Outcome** (see Figure 5-1). Those for a progress report and job completion report, however, each have an additional compartment: a job completion report, for example, is labelled **Summary Statement, Background, Highlights, Exceptions,** and **Outcome.** This informal labelling helps remove much of the awe some beginning report writers feel when they first sit down to write.

Job Progress Report

Informal labelling of the pyramid's compartments is particularly apparent in the writing plan for a job progress report (see Figure 5-3), in which the Facts and Events compartment is divided into **Past Work** and **Present Work,** and the Outcome compartment is relabelled **Future Work.** This arrrangement separates the information into three parcels, with each written in a different tense:

Document what work you have done, what you are doing now, and what work you plan to do

1. Work done so far (past tense)
2. Work being done now (present tense)
3. Work still to be done (future tense)

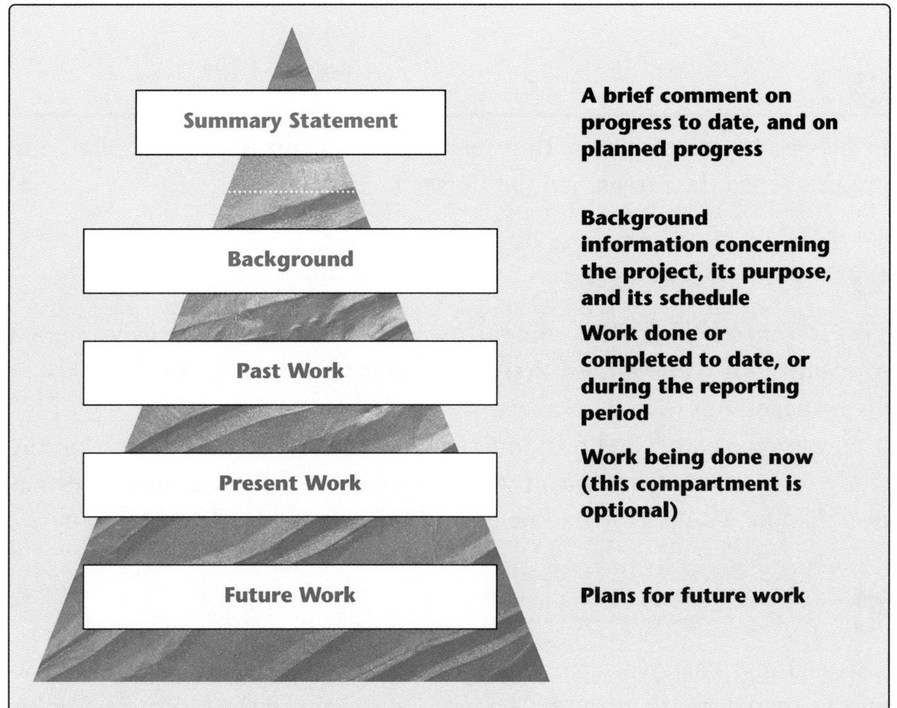

A progress report has five compartments

Figure 5-3 Writing plan for a job progress report

Jack Hallman leans out of the teller's cage and beckons to Tom Kirfauver. (Jack is a new employee at Fairview Credit Union, and a recent graduate of a two-year accounting course.) "You left this in the cage," he says, handing Tom a memo. "It's your report. I hope you don't mind, but I read it."

"Be my guest!" Tom says.

"I don't understand why you would write a progress report to Lynn for such a short job," Jack continues. "I mean, you'll be finished in six weeks and you see her every day. You can just tell her how the job is going."

"True," Tom replies, "but most managers like to have more than just an oral report. It gives them much greater confidence in you, as the person who is carrying out the project or study, if they can *read* that you have everything under control."

After a moment Tom adds thoughtfully, "But, you know, writing a progress report is more than just an exercise. It makes me stop and take a look at what I've done, to examine my data and see where I'm heading."

"Is this the only progress report you'll write for this job?" Jack asks.

"Yes, I should think so, unless something goes radically wrong and I'm delayed even further. On a large project I'd probably write a progress report once a month, but it wouldn't be worth it for a short-term project like this."

Tom's progress report is shown in Figure 5-4, with the five circled numbers beside it identifying the five report-writing compartments he used to construct it.

In his Summary Statement Tom mentions his main findings to date and predicts when the project will be finished.

Identify and then target your reader(s)

This is Tom's Background compartment, but before writing it he paused to identify his reader(s). At first he thought he would be writing only to his manager, but then he realized she probably would send a copy of his progress report to Credit Union Central, since they had asked for the study to be done. Consequently, he inserted more Background information than he would have had he been writing solely for Lynn Mahaffey.

This is Tom's Past Work, in which he describes what he has achieved so far (and concurrently provides evidence to support what he has said in his Summary Statement).

Fairview Credit Union

Interoffice Memorandum

To: Lynn Mahaffey, Manager **From:** Tom Kirfauver

Date: March 13, 2001 **Subject:** Survey of Long-Term Members

1 I have examined approximately half of the long-term members' records and so far have found that less than 45% use the credit union's banking services. The estimated completion date for my research is now April 20, two weeks later than originally planned.

2 The study was requested by Credit Union Central, which, in a letter dated January 5, 2001, recommended that Fairview C.U. should encourage more long-term members to use the C.U.'s banking and related financial services. (Long-term members are those who joined the credit union movement in the 1960s and 1970s, when the C.U.'s primary role was to provide low-interest loans to members from funds invested by other members.) As information on long-term members cannot readily be accessed from the computer, I was to visually inspect the individual files of current members who joined Fairview C.U. before 1984, which was the year banking services were first introduced.

3 I started the project on January 28, first separating the 1200 files into four batches of about 300 files each. I planned to spend two weeks inspecting each batch, but after six weeks had been able to examine the files of only 670 active members—those who joined Fairview C.U. between 1957 and 1972. My examination to date shows that only 281 (42%) use our banking and related financial services.

The Past . . .

4 Currently, I am examining the files of 343 members who joined Fairview C.U. between 1972 and 1976. Progress is slower than planned because there are 15% more files to inspect than anticipated, and this week I am acting as relief cashier in the teller's cage.

. . . the Present . . .

5 I plan to complete the third batch of files by April 2, and to examine files in the fourth batch (members who joined the C.U. from 1976 to 1984) between April 3 and 20.

. . . and the Future

Tom

Figure 5-4 A job progress report

Under Present Work Tom outlines and comments on the work he is tackling now.

Under Future Work (which is also the Outcome compartment) Tom describes when he will complete the Present Work, do the next batch, and complete the project. Note that he quotes exact dates, which adds credibility to his predictions.

Job Completion Report

Six weeks later Tom sits at his computer terminal, typing in a report. Jack strolls up and peers at the screen over Tom's shoulder.

A job completion report may be the last in a series of progress reports

"It's a job completion report," Tom explains. "It's rather like a final progress report. You tell the reader that the job is complete and add a few comments about any noteworthy events or achievements, such as obtaining an even better result than expected, finishing the job on or ahead of schedule, or coming in under budget."

Jack peers at the screen. "It looks just like the progress report you wrote before," he says.

"It starts like one," Tom explains, "but you plan the middle differently." Tom types in an instruction and the writing plan for a job completion report appears on his screen (see Figure 5-5). The report's five compartments are described below:

- The **Summary Statement** states whether the report writer has achieved what he or she set out to do.
- The **Background** establishes why the project was undertaken and what the main objectives were.
- The **Job Highlights** describe the main results and sometimes discuss trends they seem to indicate.
- The **Exceptions** describe any deviation from the original plan or objective, and discuss why the exceptions occurred and what effect they had on the project. (If there are no exceptions, this compartment may be omitted.)
- The **Outcome** offers a final comment about the project and may predict whether further work needs to be done.

The Exceptions compartment describes variances from the project plan

Tom's completion report is shown in Figure 5-6 on page 108.

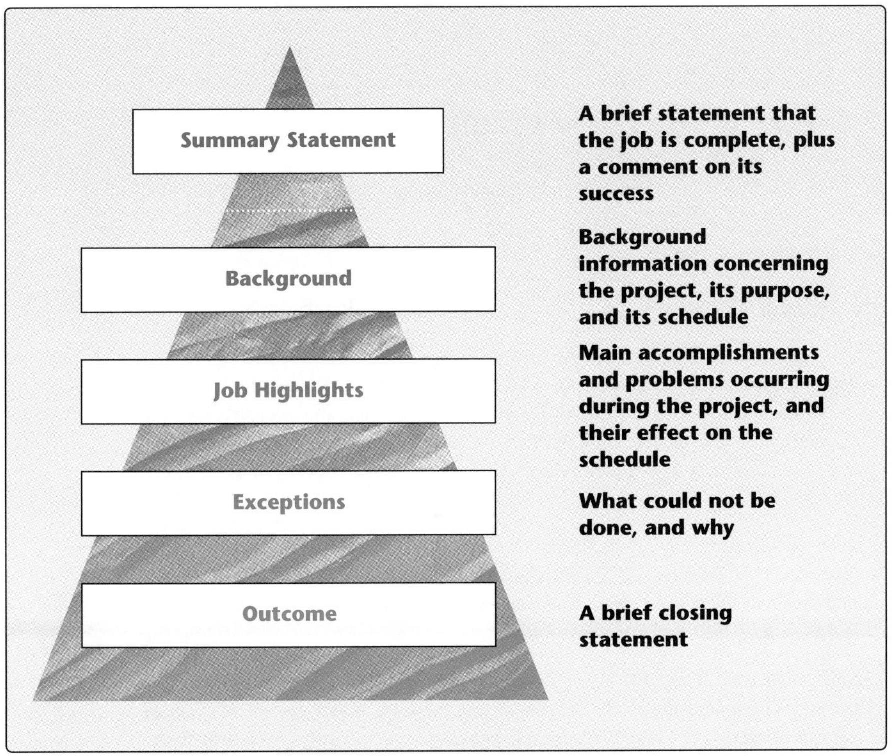

Figure 5-5 Writing plan for a job completion report

Travel Report

Describe where you went and what you did

A travel report (also known as a trip report or field trip report) describes a task you have undertaken away from your normal place of work. You may have crossed the city to see a desktop publishing demonstration, driven to a neighboring town to examine the circumstances affecting a fire insurance claim, or flown to another city to negotiate a contract with a supplier. In each case, on your return you will be expected to write a travel report. You will have to describe what you did and did not accomplish, outline what still needs to be done, and comment on the results of your travel assignment.

The writing plan for a travel report (see Figure 5-7 on page 109) is similar to the writing plan for an incident report. It has four main writing compartments:

- A **Summary Statement** says briefly what you did while you were away, and what the result was.
- A **Background** section describes who was involved, where you went, why you went there, and when you left and returned.

Fairview Credit Union

Interoffice Memorandum

To:	Lynn Mahaffey, Manager	**From:**	Tom Kirfauver
Date:	April 20, 2001	**Subject:**	Results of Survey of 1957–1984 Members

Summary Statement

A physical inspection of members' records shows that slightly less than half the members who joined Fairview Credit Union from 1957 to 1984, and who still maintain an active account with us, use the Credit Union's banking and associated financial services. The remaining 54% use Fairview C.U. solely to make deposits and/or take out loans.

Background

My study was prompted by Credit Union Central's letter of January 5, 2001, which recommended that Fairview C.U. encourage long-term members to use the Society's banking services. I was to examine the records of members who enrolled in Fairview C.U. between May 1957 and December 1984.

Highlights

I examined the records of 1304 active members, of whom 596 currently use our banking services. Closer scrutiny of the records shows, however, that members who joined the Society between 1957 and 1970 use our banking services considerably less than those who joined after 1970:

Period (Year Member Joined C.U.)	*Total Current Members for Period*	*Number Using Banking Services*	*Number Not Using Banking Services*
1957–1961	307	83 (27%)	224
1962–1969	363	127 (35%)	236
1970–1973	296	166 (56%)	130
1974–1977	338	220 (65%)	118
Total:	1304	596 (46%)	708

Exceptions

I was unable to examine members' records for the years 1978 and 1979. In 1980, Credit Union Central audited our books for the three-year period 1977 to 1980. The records were returned on November 27, 1980, but not stored in sequence with the previous records and I was unable to locate them. I tried accessing the database, but the format used at the time made this a tedious process and with your agreement I discontinued the search. However, the table shows an increasing trend, from which I predict that 70% of members who joined the C.U. in 1978 and 1979 currently use our banking services.

Outcome

The attached list documents all current members who joined Fairview C.U. from 1957 to 1977, together with their account number(s) and computer access codes.

Tom

Figure 5-6 A job completion report

- A **Travel Activities** section describes the work you did. It's best to subdivide it into three subsections:

  1. *Planned Work Done.* This is the work you set out to do, and did. It becomes the major part of your report, in which you identify the main events and results. You also describe any problems affecting the work, how you overcame or adjusted for them, and what effect they had on your task. Whenever possible refer to a task specification, and so keep this part short.

  Keep it brief: attach a work plan

  2. *Unplanned Work Done.* Here you describe any work that was not part of your assignment but unexpectedly became part of your travel activity. It may be something you notice needs to be done, or a task someone at your destination asks you to do. (For example, you may travel from Montreal to London, Ontario, to advise a client on the cost and time required to translate a product service manual into French. While you are there the client shows you a product brochure that has been translated by someone else, and you notice that it contains errors. At the client's request you remain an extra day to correct it.)

  Now bring in all the details

  3. *Planned Work Not Done.* In this section you describe any work that was part of your assignment but that you were unable to do.

  Include details here, too

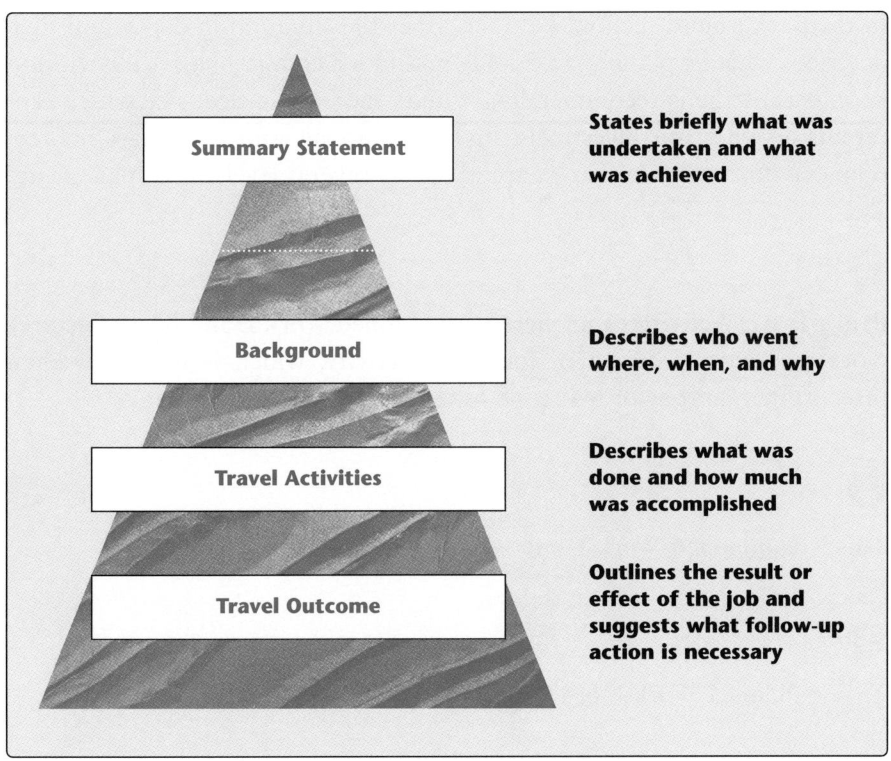

Figure 5-7 Writing plan for a travel report

You have to describe why the work could not be done and, if appropriate, suggest when and by whom it should be completed.

(*Note:* The sequence in which you report the Unplanned Work Done and Planned Work Not Done is interchangeable. You have to decide whether you prefer to keep the Planned Work sections adjacent to one another, or have the Planned Work Not Done section immediately before the Outcome section.)

- An **Outcome** section completes the report. You may offer a closing comment about your assignment and perhaps recommend any further action that you think needs to be taken.

Paul Williston's travel report in Figure 5-8 follows this arrangement of information (refer to the circled numbers beside his report).

This is Paul's **Summary Statement,** in which he briefly identifies the problem and states what action the company needs to take.

2

A comprehensive description of the circumstances helps "set the scene" for what is to follow

In the **Background** section, Paul describes the situation in depth and then describes what he planned to do. He provides a comprehensive description here, because he is recommending a hefty increase in fleet size which represents a significant investment for the company, and recognizes his recommendation will have to be approved by several levels of management.

Paul's **Travel Activities** start here with **Planned Work Done.** The table provides a *visual* prediction of increased activity, which is far better than three subparagraphs of text (one for each exploration company).

This is **Unplanned Work Done.**

This is **Planned Work Not Done.**

High Gear Truck and Car Rentals

Interoffice Memorandum

To: Darren Schofeld
From: Paul Williston
Date: January 20, 2001
Ref: Need to Increase Alberta Fleet

1 If we are to maintain our market share of truck rentals in Alberta for the coming spring and summer, we will have to build our Alberta truck fleet up to 372 vehicles by April 1, 2001. This will be an increase of 168 vehicles, compared to the 204 vehicles we had in April 2000.

2 On January 7 Fern Whitmore, the area superintendent for Alberta, telephoned to say that she had heard from several corporate truck renters that they expected a "significant" increase in activity in Alberta, starting in the second quarter and extending into the late fall. Fern suggested that HGTCR should anticipate the extra truck rental business that will accrue from this increased activity and plan to bring in additional stock. I flew to Calgary, Edmonton, and Fort MacMurray from January 14 to 17 to assess the volume of vehicles we will require.

My plan was to visit HGTCR's primary renters in the oil exploration and pipeline construction industries, and in the forest firefighting sector, to identify the extent of their anticipated increase in truck rentals.

This sequence *must* be replicated in the descriptions further down in the report

3 In April 2000 we leased 146 trucks to the oil exploration industry. To identify trends for April 2001, I met with the management of three key players in oil exploration to whom we rent trucks. Our discussions showed the following:

Client	*April 2000 rentals*	*April 2001 projection*	*Increase (units)*	*Increase (%)*
Whitmar Explorations	18	25	7	39
Tar Sands Corporation	27	33	6	22
True North Oil Sands Inc	44	75	31	70
Total/average	**89**	**133**	**44**	**49**

As the mood throughout the oil exploration industry in Alberta is highly optimistic, I suggest that we increase our truck rental expectations for this sector by 49%. Our total rentals to the oil exploration companies in the second quarter of 2000 was 132 vehicles. For 2001, I predict rentals for the same industry will increase by 65 to 197 trucks.

Figure 5-8 A travel, or field trip, report

The second sector I visited was the Nor-West Pipeline construction company, which is building parallel oil and gas pipelines from Fort MacMurray to Chicago, with a spur to Philadelphia. Pipeline construction started in March 2000 and will continue through to November 2001. During the second quarter of 2000, when the company was gearing up, we rented 87 trucks to them, and these trucks are still out on rental. In the spring of 2001, Nor-West expects to increase construction activity, and its number of installation crews, by 54%. Consequently, I suggest we also should anticipate a 54% increase in truck rentals for this sector, which will represent an increase of 50 units for a total of 137 vehicles.

4 An additional sector, which we have serviced only once before—in 1995—is the film industry. I met with the Business Development Bureau in Edmonton on January 16, and they informed me that three film companies are planning to shoot major films in Alberta, starting in mid-April 2001. Two of these companies are from Hollywood (Sony and MCA); the third is from Europe (Ariel Film Limitée). The names of the films, and the players, are secret.

A prediction needs to show on what evidence it is based

From our experience in renting trucks to film production crews in Ontario, Manitoba, and British Columbia, I expect there will be a demand for 68 trucks total for the three shoots. As our market share of new industry rentals normally averages 37%, this should translate into 25 vehicles for HGTCR.

5 I was unable to obtain a commitment from the Province of Alberta forest firefighting department. Most members of the department take their vacation in midwinter, consequently the department was understaffed. I doubt, however, whether there will be an increase in this particular sector.

In addition to the oil exploration, pipeline construction, and firefighting industries, at any given moment in the first quarter of 2000 HGTCR rented an average of 112 trucks to 59 smaller companies. Given the optimistic business mood in the province, I predict we can expect these smaller rentals to increase by approximately 25%, or 28 vehicles, in the second quarter of 2001.

6 To summarize, I recommend that our fleet of trucks in Alberta should be increased by 168 vehicles by April 1, 2001, with the vehicles being allocated as follows:

Oil exploration industry:	65
Pipeline construction:	50
Film production:	25
Miscellaneous:	28

Paul Williston

Figure 5-8 A travel report, or field trip report (*continued*)

6

In his **Outcome** (which in this case becomes an **Action** statement), Paul recommends what needs to be done and summarizes how he anticipates the increased number of trucks will be distributed.

Conference Report

A conference report also is a travel report

An employer may approve an employee's attendance at a conference, course, or seminar—and pay the employee's expenses—for several reasons:

1. To keep the company abreast of changes in the field in which it operates.
2. To provide professional development for the employee.
3. To be a convenient reward for good performance.
4. To promote better employee morale.

If your employer sends you to a conference or course, when you return you will be expected to describe how you have benefited. Your employer will want to know (not necessarily in this order)

- what you gained or learned,
- how what you have learned can be applied to the company's operations,
- whether the company got good value for its money, and
- whether the company should send other employees to future events on the same or a similar topic.

When should you write a travel report? Start by making notes *during* the conference or seminar

Initially your manager may ask you to describe the conference or course informally over a cup of coffee. But he or she will also expect you to provide a written report of your experience.

Figure 5-9 shows that the writing plan for a conference report is essentially the same as that for a travel report. The chief difference lies in the Travel Activities compartment, which is relabelled **Conference Details** and covers two main areas of activity:

1. Scheduled (conference program) events you attended, and what you particularly learned from them.
2. Unscheduled events, such as personal discussions with the speakers or other attendees at lunch or similar social occasions from which you learned informally what they are doing in their work and of new methods or techniques they are using.

Betty Mahler's report on an educational seminar she attended is in Figure 5-10 on page 115, with the following numbers keyed to the circled numbers beside her report.

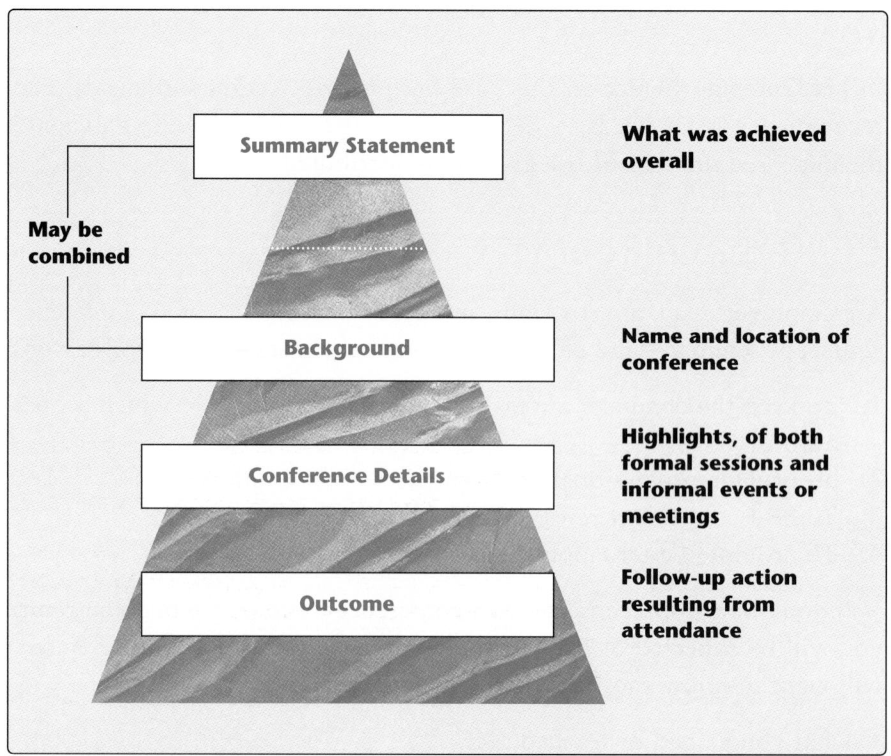

Figure 5-9 Writing plan for reporting attendance at a conference, seminar, course, or meeting

Write the full report as you travel home, while ideas are still fresh

❶

The Summary Statement identifies where Betty went, whether her attendance was worthwhile, and whether anything needs to be done as a result of her participation.

❷

The Background describes *who went where, why,* and *when.* As Betty has already identified the seminar, she does not need to do so again.

❸

The Conference Details start here, with the Scheduled Events that Betty attended. The events may be just one paragraph or several paragraphs, depending on how much Betty has to report.

Fairview Credit Union

Interoffice Memorandum

To:	Lynn Mahaffey, Manager	**From:**	Betty Mahler
Date:	May 8, 2001	**Subject:**	Report on "Meetings" Seminar

1 I have just attended a particularly useful one-day seminar on running and participating in meetings, and have tentatively arranged for a shortened version to be held for Fairview C.U. staff in September.

2 The seminar was presented by Professional Training Resources Inc (PTR) of Cambridge, Ontario, and held at Credit Union Central's training rooms on May 6. The participants were managers and assistant managers from the 20 credit unions affiliated with C.U. Central.

3 The morning was divided into two $1\frac{1}{4}$-hour sessions: the first focused on what a chairperson should do to run an effective meeting; the second concentrated on what individual meeting participants should do when they have to present information at a meeting. Both sessions included a 24-minute videotape: for chairpersons, John Cleese's *Meetings Bloody Meetings*; for participants, PTR Video Production's *6 Around a Table: Taking Part in Office Meetings*.

In the afternoon the seminar participants were broken into two groups, with each group preparing for and participating in a scenario-driven meeting. While one group took part in its meeting, the members of the other group critiqued the participants on a one-to-one basis.

4 During lunch I asked Marilyn Duvall—PTR's course leader—whether we could rent the *6 Around a Table* videotape to show to our staff (see the attached brochure). She suggested that the staff would benefit more if she were to come in and run the videotape as part of a one-hour seminar, during which she would discuss key points with them. She quoted $95 to rent the videotape alone, and $225 for the combined seminar/videotape session.

5 I have made a provisional booking for Ms Duvall to present a one-hour session on September 10, with a specific time to be determined later. If you approve, I will confirm the booking.

Betty

enc

Figure 5-10 A report on seminar attendance

The Conference Details continue with the Unscheduled Events, which in Betty's case conveniently lead into the Outcome.

The Outcome suggests what specific action needs to be taken (if there is any follow-up action).

Problem Investigation Report

Vernon Shreeba, who is Assistant Project Administrator at LaVerendry Insurance Corporation, has been trying to find a larger training room. Eighteen months ago LaVerendry Insurance amalgamated with Robinson Assurance Ltd, and since then the company has occupied all available space within the Morton-Hampshire Securities Building. The existing conference room doubles as a training room, but has become clearly unsuitable for the larger groups, particularly of marketing representatives, who attend training sessions.

An investigation report may be just a short memorandum, a letter, or a bound document

Marsha Rollins, who is Manager of Human Resources, assigned Vernon to seek out space the company could rent on an occasional basis. To write a short report of his findings, he used the writing plan in Figure 5-11.

Anticipating readers' questions means writing according to a plan. For a short problem-solution report, the plan in Figure 5-11 is ideal. The major difference between this plan and previous writing plans is that the **Project Details** compartment is opened up into five subcompartments:

1. *Approach*. Here you describe how you tackled the situation or problem you investigated (i.e. what you did).
2. *Findings*. These are the facts you discovered that identify the cause of the problem or difficult situation (i.e. what you found out).
3. *Criteria*. Here you establish the objectives that any method for correcting the problem or improving the situation must meet (i.e. you have to identify what needs to be achieved). The position of this step may vary: it can be part of the Approach, follow the Findings, or it can appear between the Ideas and the Evaluation.
4. *Ideas*. These are the alternative ways in which the problem can be remedied or the situation can be improved (i.e. what can be done).
5. *Evaluation*. Now you examine each of the alternatives to identify how effectively it meets the objectives established at step 3 (i.e. for each ask: "How well will it work?").

The criteria help you retain your objectivity

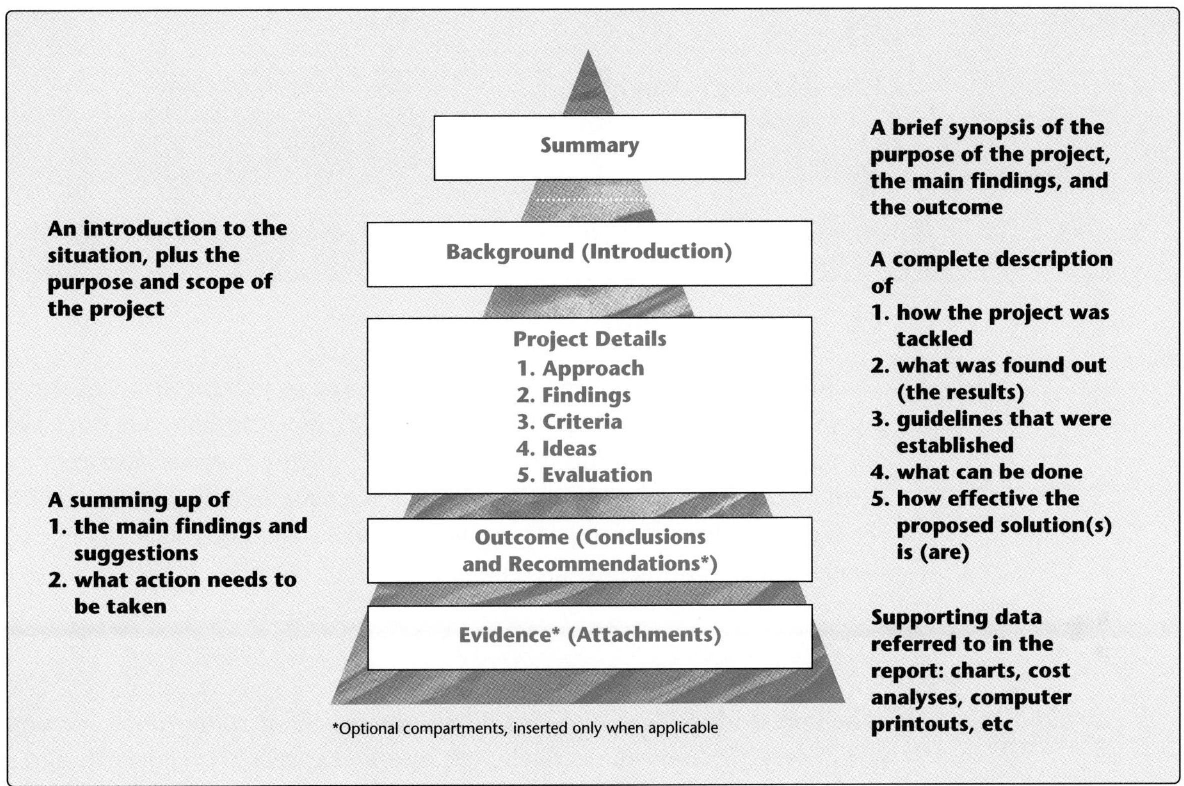

Figure 5-11 Writing plan for a short investigation report

There may also be an additional (final) compartment for detailed supporting information such as drawings, specifications, cost analyses, and computer printouts, which are referred to as attachments (if part of a letter-form report) or appendices (if part of a semiformal or formal report).

Vernon's report is shown in Figure 5-12 on page 119, with comments listed below.

This is Vernon's **Summary Statement**, in which he identifies what Marsha Rollins most wants to know: that he has found a solution to the problem, and has provided a price.

In the **Background**, Vernon describes the circumstances leading up to his investigation. He realizes Marsha knows these facts, but he also recognizes that other managers may not.

3

This is Vernon's **Approach** . . .

4

. . . and these are his **Criteria**.

The **Ideas** section starts here. Vernon has chosen to present his ideas starting with the least suitable and ending with the most suitable. He does not tell his readers he is doing this, but it will quickly become apparent to them. (The alternative is to start with the most suitable idea and end with the least suitable. Each report writer comparing methods or ideas has to decide which approach to take.)

6

Choose the *objective* approach if you are not sure whether to sound objective or subjective

When presenting Ideas, you can do so *objectively* or *subjectively*. Vernon has chosen to do so subjectively, because he expects his readers to agree with his recommendation. (For more advice about writing an objective vs a subjective comparative analysis, see page 175.)

7

This is the **Evaluation**, in which Vernon draws the reader's attention to the key conclusions.

8

Vernon has chosen to write an **Action Statement** rather than just an Outcome, because he believes firmly that the company should use the over-budget option. Note that he correctly writes a confident "I recommend . . ." rather than a wishy-washy "It is recommended that . . .".

The writing plan in Figure 5-11 can be used for almost all reports that examine a problem that needs to be corrected or a situation that should be improved:

- If the problem has already been remedied, then the report identifies the problem, describes how it was investigated and corrected, and outlines the results.

LaVerendry Insurance Corporation

Interoffice Memorandum

To:	Marsha Rollins, Manager Human Resources	**Date:**	March 16, 2001
From:	Vernon Shreeba, Assistant Project Administrator	**Ref:**	Identifying Satellite Training Facilities

1 I have found three training rooms that could serve as overflow for courses requiring larger attendance than is available in our conference room. The cost will range from $180 to $600 per month, depending on the location, convenience, and quality of equipment.

2 Training at L.I.C. has traditionally been held in conference room B, which can accommodate 10 around the boardroom table. For short training courses for only a few individuals this has been sufficient, although having course participants sit around a table, rather than at individual tables facing the front of the room, has been only partly satisfactory. However, since L.I.C. amalgamated with Robinson Assurance 18 months ago, there has been a considerable increase in sales staff, and a greater need to hold larger group training sessions with up to 25 participants.

Last month we used a hotel room for a marketing course, but it proved expensive and inconvenient (see my report of February 14). Consequently, I was asked by Marsha Rollins to investigate whether other training facilities would be available locally on an ad hoc basis, probably for up to four days per month.

Set the scene . . .

3 I visited eight companies and two community centres that could accommodate us. Only two, however, meet all of our requirements, which are

4
- the ability to accommodate up to 25 participants sitting two to a table, with space for the participants to set up their portable computers and sufficient electrical outlets,
- a reasonably professional setting,
- four days availability per month, and
- a maximum cost of $125 a day, for a tentative budget of $500 a month.

. . . establish the requirements, and . . .

I will also describe a third organization because, although using its training room would exceed our budget, it offers significant other advantages.

Figure 5-12 A short investigation report

. . . show how well they are being met

5 **Westside Community Centre.** The least expensive of the three sites is the meeting room at Westside Community Centre, 1.3 km from our office. It is available almost every day until 6 p.m., because it's used only at night during the week. The cost is only $45 per day, which is well within our budget, but the low price is offset by the rather sparse surroundings, uncarpeted floor, and very basic tables and chairs. There are sufficient electrical outlets on the side walls, but we would have to provide extension cables and bring our own projection equipment, VCR, and monitor.

6 **Central Post Office.** The post office, which is only 0.8 km from our office, has a training room in the basement of the building. Its rental cost at $100 a day would be comfortably within budget. The post office manager says on average the room is used twice a week, which means it would be available for up to 12 days a month. The room was set up originally to train users of automatic mail sorting machines, so there are electrical outlets beside each table. The floor is carpeted, the room is well-lit, and the tables can accommodate two people with ample work space for each person. It has an overhead projector and screen, but does not have an LCD projector or VCR and monitor.

Present the pros and cons *without* overtly showing your bias

Management Accounting Association. The most convenient of the three locations is the training centre of the Management Accounting Association, on the second floor of the Morton-Hampshire Securities Building, where we also are located. However, its cost at $150 a day would be $100 a month above budget (assuming we use their facilities four times a month), and the room is available only from Monday through Thursday, because the M.A.A. runs its courses on Fridays and Saturdays. It is equipped with a ceiling-mounted LCD projector, VCR and monitor, overhead projector, and electrical outlets at each table, so we would not have to take in our own projection equipment. The tables are long and each can accommodate three people.

7 To select the most suitable training centre means balancing cost, convenience, and achieving a professional setting:

- From a cost viewpoint, Westside Community Centre offers the greatest advantage, with the Post Office also falling within budget.
- For convenience, the Management Accounting Association clearly offers the greatest advantage.
- For a professional setting, again the Management Accounting Association offers the greatest advantage, with the Post Office offering a moderately professional setting.

8 I recommend that, if the tentative budget can be increased by 20% to $600 a month, we select the Management Accounting Association training room. If the budget cannot be increased, then I recommend the Post Office training room.

Vernon Shreeba

Figure 5-12 A short investigation report (*continued*)

- If the problem or situation has only been studied, then the report identifies the problem, describes what is causing it and what steps can be taken to resolve it, and then recommends what should be done.

The former becomes a "tell" report; the latter becomes a "sell" report because its purpose is to convince the reader to take or approve the most appropriate action. The report may be only one or two pages, as Vernon Shreeba's report is, or it may become a multi-page document as described in Chapter 6.

An investigation report that recommends corrective action is a "sell" document

TO SUM UP

Although there appear to be several report shapes for describing different situations, in effect all short informal reports are structured the same way. Each has

- a Summary (a synopsis of the report's main features),
- a Background (events leading up to the situation),
- the Full Details (all the facts and events), and
- an Outcome (the result[s]).

In longer reports the Details section is often divided into subcompartments, each describing a separate aspect, such as "Approach," "Work Done," "Findings," and "Analysis."

Short reports may be written as email messages, memorandums, letters and, occasionally for longer reports, in semiformal report format.

EXERCISES

Exercise 5.1: Incident Report

It was 9:55 in the evening when the hose-and-bucket car-washing facilities at the small Westside outlet of High Gear Truck and Auto Rentals Ltd caused you a problem. You were working alone, and just about to close the office for the night, when a bright red Mazda turned into the entrance to the lot with squealing tires and headlights flashing. You recognized the car as one of your fleet. The driver gunned the engine and made a sharp turn so he could pull up dramatically in front of the office door. Or so he thought. But he hadn't reckoned with the water on the lot, which had spilled over from the tiny hand-operated car-wash bay beside the office

An aggressive customer creates a problem

and now had frozen onto the pavement. Rather than turn, the Mazda spun into a green Toyota parked beside the building. *Your* Toyota!

"What's all that ice doing here?" the driver shouted at you as he climbed out of the red car. "It hasn't rained! Or snowed!"

You wanted to tell him that he was driving incautiously, but instead you described how the car wash overflowed.

"Well, don't expect *my* insurance to cover all of this," he was still shouting as he pointed to the damaged cars. "It's your company's fault!"

Deal with an awkward customer

You explained that High Gear's insurance would cover the damage to the red car, but that the green car was another matter because it was a private car. (You had already taken a quick look at the rental agreement and had seen he had not taken out collision or third party insurance. And from a brief examination of the caved-in left-front quarter of your Toyota you reckoned the repairs would cost close to $3000.)

"We'll have to report the accident to the police," you say. "Damage is more than than $1000."

"That's your problem," he replies. "You just keep my name out of it. I don't even live here."

"I have to," you start to say. "I really don't have a choice . . . ."

"Let's get the rental agreement closed off," he interrupts, pushing the folder across the counter at you. "I've got a plane to catch."

Two hours later, the police have come and taken your report. Your irate, irrational customer left before they arrived and now is on a flight to Denver. Now you are writing a report of the incident for Corinne Wasalyshyn, your branch manager, with a copy to Fern Whitmore, High Gear's area superintendent. In the morning you will have to call your insurance company and inform them of the damage to your Toyota.

Here is some additional information you may need for your report to Corinne:

1. The rental contract was No. 14682CA.
2. The driver was Fred G Lawton, #210-1880 Derwent Drive, Denver, Colorado.
3. The Mazda was a current year 787, licence number DWA 610, with 917 kilometres on the odometer when the driver brought it in.
4. Your car is a two-year-old Toyota Tercel, licence number 778 OBA, with 21 826 kilometres on its odometer.
5. Your car's insurance contract number is 119462133, with Mansask Insurance Corporation.

Exercise 5.2: **Trip Report**

You are manager of the Westside outlet of High Gear Truck and Auto Rentals Ltd. As yours is the closest outlet to the airport (a distance of six kilometres), you run a shuttle van to pick up and drop off customers.

Fern Whitmore, superintendent of operations at High Gear's head office in your city, asks you to investigate the feasibility of opening a car rental booth alongside the big names (Avis, Budget, Hertz, etc) at the airport. "It's the only way we're going to increase the number of airport contracts we sign with fly-in customers," she adds.

You drive out to the airport and talk to Winston Talbot, the airport manager.

"Yes, we do have space," he says, "beside the Tilden booth. But you'll find it's a fairly expensive proposition for a relatively small leasing outfit like yours. We charge $2000 per year for the booth space, plus 10% of each leasing agreement you sign."

"We could live with that," you say.

"Ah! But there are conditions! You have to staff the booth from 6 a.m. every day, regardless of whether you're expecting any fly-in business, and you have to keep it open until the very last flight of the day has arrived, no matter how late it is. And then you have to pay $43 per month for each stall you rent out in the parking lot, and you have to have a *minimum* of 20 stalls. On top of that you have to set up and staff a service centre beside the stalls."

So that's why the big name companies charge so much more than we do, you think.

"I'm sorry if that puts a booth out of your company's reach," Winston adds. "But it's the same deal at every airport across Canada."

Research the feasibility of an airport car rental operation

On the way back to your car you walk around the car rental parking area. At the north end of the parking lot, across from the exit ramp, you notice a small, triangular-shaped piece of paved asphalt that clearly is not being used by anyone. "Hmmm . . . " you murmur to yourself. "There's enough space here for parking three cars, maybe even four . . . ."

You walk back to the Administration Building, knock on Winston Talbot's door, and describe what you have in mind. He pulls out a map.

"That's lot 87N," he says. "Nobody wants it. It's too small and too far removed from the other parking stalls."

"What would it cost?" you ask.

"The same as the others: $43 per stall per month."

As you drive home you consider the possibilities. Clearly, renting a booth, with its attendant costs, is out of reach. You calculate that High Gear would have to keep two people on duty (one in the booth and one in the service centre) for close to 18 hours a day. That's 36 hours total, which at an approximate hourly rate of between $8 and $10 would require over $300 in wages alone per day. And High Gear would still have to build a booth and a service centre.

But creating three spaces on lot 87N might work. It would give High Gear an edge over other small car rental companies that operate off the airport property. "I don't think we would be able to let passengers pick up their vehicles there, because of the rental documentation that has to be done," you think, "but they certainly could drop their vehicles off. All we'd have to do is provide a box for depositing the key." You reckon it would cost about $700 to paint three parking stall marks on the asphalt and to put up a sign for High Gear parking.

Write your findings and recommendation as a trip report to Fern Whitmore.

Exercise 5.3: **Progress Report**

It's April 28th, three days before the May 1st opening date for the High Gear Truck and Car Rental (HGTCR) drop-off point at your local airport, and it has been raining all day. The drop-off point has room for three vehicles in Lot 87N, a triangular lot at the north end of the parking lot (see Exercise 5.2 for more details). Three things have to be done before the lot is ready for use by HGTCR customers:

1. White lines and stall numbers have to be painted on the lot:

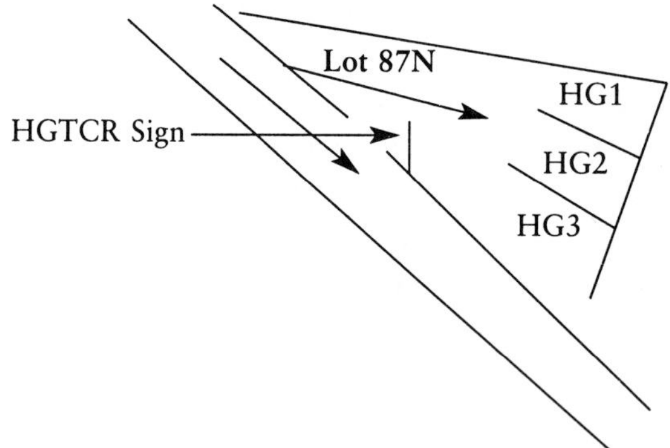

2. A sign has to be erected indicating it is HGTCR's lot:

Lot 87N
High Gear Truck and Car Rentals Ltd

Rental Vehicle Drop-off Point

3. A box for return of keys and rental agreements, plus instructions, has to be placed on the rear of the sign.

You drive out to the airport to check on progress, and find that lines have been painted on the asphalt but the lot numbers have not, the last line on the sign says: *Rental Vehical Drop-off Point*, and the key drop-off box has not been placed on the reverse side of the sign.

You call the asphalt painter (McArthur Road Markings Inc), who says he had difficulty finding the right size of stencil for the letters and numbers. Jim McArthur says: "I've got the stencils now, but I've got to wait for a dry day. I should be able to do it tomorrow, if the weather forecast is right."

You also call the sign painter, Carol Wesserman, and ask when the box is going to be put in place. "On the 30th," she says. "I'm just waiting for the lettering to dry on it." You tell her to check the spelling very carefully, and to correct the error on the sign she has already put up.

Write your progress report as an email to Corrinne Wasalyshyn, the Westside HGTCR manager, with a copy to Fern Whitmore, the area superintendent.

Exercise 5.4: **Problem Report**

Now it's May 31st and the High Gear Truck and Car Rental drop-off lot 87N at your local airport has been operation for a full month. The problems identified on April 28th were rectified in time for the opening on May 1st (see Exercise 5.3). But the month hasn't gone by without some problems. For example, six vehicle renters telephoned on different days to say the lot was full, and you had to instruct them to put their vehicle in public parking and to leave the car keys and rental agreement in the glove compartment. Then HGTCR had to pay the parking charges when you picked up the vehicles. Each time you checked lot 87N and found non-HGTCR vehicles parked in it. On each vehicle you placed a warning note under the windshield-wiper blade saying they were parked on private property.

On May 25th you called Waybright's Towing Service and arranged for them to tow away unauthorized vehicles. "How will we know when a vehicle is illegally parked?" Harry Waybright asked, and you told him there would be a circular HGTCR sticker on the bottom left corner of the rear window of authorized vehicles. Any other vehicles would be illegally parked. Waybright said one of his drivers would pass the lot every 90 minutes during the day, to check for illegally parked vehicles ("We do it for other rental companies, so there will be no charge for that," he added. You agreed to a start-up charge of $165 plus GST for Waybright to install a warning sign to non-HGTCR renters. "After that," Harry Waybright said, “we make our money from the people we tow away. There will be no charge to you.”

Write a problem report as a memo to Corinne Wasalyshyn, HGTCR’s Westside manager, with a copy to Fern Whitmore, HGTCR’s area superintendent.

Exercise 5.5: Field Trip/Project Completion Report

Assume that today is May 11 and that you are a junior consultant with the local branch of Windermere Business Consultants (WBC), a firm with its head office in Vancouver and branches across Canada. WBC has been contracted by the owners of Mini-Copyshops, whose main office also is in Vancouver, to carry out unannounced annual miniature audits of the Mini-Copyshops across the country. Apart from that, each Mini-Copyshop runs its business entirely independently, and is accountable only to the local owner for its operation.

Background for an audit check

All materials and supplies for the Mini-Copyshops are ordered in bulk by the head office once every four months and shipped directly by the suppliers to the individual Mini-Copyshops. The intent of the annual audit is to check that the supplies are being accounted for accurately and used appropriately. (It was discovered three years ago that two of the Mini-Copyshop owners were buying large quantities of the paper at the very low bulk price achieved by head office, and selling the paper locally at just under retail price, with a markup of approximately 30%. The audits were inaugurated to prevent this from happening.)

On May 4 your branch of WBC received a directive from the WBC head office to conduct an unannounced audit at Mini-Copyshop No. 78, in your local community. Audit Directive 447 listed the following information:

Information from last year’s audit (April 28):

The status one year ago

Supplies:

Paper:	8.5 × 11 in. white	16 200
	8.5 × 11 in. color	3 100
	8.5 × 14 in. white	13 300
	8.5 × 14 in. color	500
	17 × 11 in. white	500

Copier Toner Cartridges:	Black	9
	Color	4

Copier counter readings:

Unit No. 1 (728A)	2 135 875
Unit No. 2 (1447)	1 476 118
Unit No. 3 (1550RG)	3 188 764

Shipments of supplies since April 28:

Item supplied	*September 4*	*December 17*	*April 4*
Paper:			
8.5 × 11 in. white	30 000	40 000	40 000
8.5 × 11 in. color	2 000	3 000	3 000
8.5 × 14 in. white	8 000	5 000	7 000
8.5 × 14 in. color	1 000	1 000	—
17 × 11 in. white	2 000	—	2 000
Copier toner cartridges:			
Black	1 doz	2 doz	1 doz
Color	1/2 doz	1/2 doz	—

Today (May 11) you call on Mini-Copyshop No. 78 at 4:45 p.m. and are greeted by shop owner Jessica Boyd. (You choose 15 minutes before shop closing time, so that you do not interrupt business while doing your stock count.)

"I wondered when you might be coming," Jessica says. "You're a bit later than last year."

Audits often are unannounced and so unexpected

"We try not to be predictable," you reply. "It could be February next time!"

She puts a "Closed" sign on the door and you start taking inventory. Your first step is to take copier counter readings:

No. 1:	2 135 875
No. 2:	1 514 591
No. 3.	3 263 093

Next you count the stocks of paper:

Paper:	8.5 × 11 in. white		11 800
	8.5 × 11 in. color		5 500
	8.5 × 14 in. white		8 700
	8.5 × 14 in. color		1 300
	17 × 11 in. white		600
Copier Toner Cartridges:		Black	20
		Color	10

Jessica comes to you with three packs of paper, which are stained and crinkled. "These got damaged when a water pipe broke," she says. "There are 500 in each pack."

"How many do you think are wasted in a year?" you ask. "I mean sheets of paper that are thrown out because they are damaged and never go through the printer." And you ask her not to include the three packs that were water-damaged.

This event becomes an exception

"Oh, about six or seven hundred, I guess," Jessica says.

You ask to see the sales slips for the past three months, which is a routine part of the audit.

"I'm sorry, I can't give them to you," Jessica says. "I sent them over to the company accountant last week, to do the annual tax return. It will be a month before I get them back."

You decide that if there is a discrepancy between the readings and the consumption, you will need to see them; but if there is no discrepancy, then it won't be necessary. As this is a regular part of the audit, you must include a comment about your decision in your report.

Now you are back in your office calculating the number of items used, to compare them against the stock in hand.

You write your report as a memo addressed to Gary Lagimodiere, who is the audit manager at head office in Vancouver, with a copy to Winona Taverner, who is manager of the local branch of Windermere Business Consultants (i.e. your personal manager), and another copy to Jessica Boyd.

Exercise 5.6: **Travel Report/Investigation Report**

"I want you to go to our distribution centre in Kimberley," Bill Korton tells you over the phone. "Come down to my office and I'll give you the details." Bill is distribution manager at Meridian Wholesalers, a multiple-branch firm with its head office in your city. You are his expediter, which means you chase problems and keep products moving as they come in from the manufacturers, are stored, and then are shipped to the retailers who order them.

Dual-purpose travel means *two* reports

"Officially you'll be going to Kimberley to examine an order of Scandinavian teak lamps that have been damaged during shipment," Bill says when you walk in. "I want you to meet the insurance adjuster and determine how many can be written off. But unofficially I want you to find out why handling costs are so much higher at Kimberley than they are at any of our other distribution centres. You're to tell *no one* your real reason for going there, not even Cal Wozny, the branch manager. I would go myself, but it would be obvious I'm checking up on something more than damaged lamps."

You like Cal Wozny from the moment you meet him, and you quickly discover why the staff at Kimberley think so highly of him. He is very much a "people person." He knows every employee on a first-name basis, yet he is firm and definite in identifying what he wants done. Cal is about 50. He does not have much hair, and what there is has turned silvery grey, yet it suits him: the silver fuzz above his round face creates an immediate impression of amiability.

Mansask Insurance Corporation's insurance adjuster in Kimberley is Penny Bernstein. When she arrives at Meridian Wholesaler's warehouse you show her a copy of the shipping waybill (No. HO2371), which identifies that 24 Danish Dektar teak lamps were shipped from Meridian's head office to the Kimberley branch on the 27th of last month. They were transported in a truck owned by D and A All-Purpose Carriers, and were listed as being worth $174.50 each (the total value of the shipment was $4188.00).

You and Penny walk through the warehouse, which is stacked from floor to ceiling with merchandise (you have never seen so much stock!), until you come to the lamps stacked in a corner. You start to sort through them.

Information for the damage report

"From what I can see, 15 of the lamps are totally beyond repair, and three are completely undamaged," Penny observes. "Do you agree?" You nod.

"And six more are only partly damaged, but individually they are probably not worth repairing . . . " (you nod again) " . . . but I suggest they could be taken apart and their undamaged parts reassembled to form three complete lamps."

You examine the lamps and find that this is true.

"Then Mansask Insurance Corporation will reimburse you for the loss of 18 lamps," Penny announces. "I'll write you a letter confirming this."

That evening Cal Wozny takes you out to dinner and you discover even more what a gentle, kindly person he is. You also discover why the Kimberley branch's overhead costs are so high.

"For 16 years I've been running the Kimberley warehouse," Cal says as the two of you sip piping-hot clam chowder, "and I know nearly every retailer by name. Around Kimberley, retailers have come to rely on us. They know that when they place an order with Meridian Wholesalers we'll deliver the very next day. They never have to wait. They never have to be bothered with goods being back-ordered for weeks on end. From experience, I know their business patterns and can anticipate when they're getting ready to place the next order. So I order goods in advance, ready for when their purchase orders start to roll in."

So that's why the warehouse is stacked high with products! you muse. And then you ask out loud, "But what happens if an order doesn't come in? What do you do with all that extra stock?"

"Oh, it goes," he replies with a smile. "It always does. Someone else orders it. It may take a month or two, but it does go."

"Surely that's an awful lot of cash to tie up in stationary stock," you observe.

"A small price to pay for keeping our customers happy, for encouraging them to come back," Cal enthuses. "You'll come to realize that the wholesale business is built on having satisfied customers who place repeat orders. And spread the word!"

The problem of high costs unfolds

For the moment you let the matter drop. But later you casually ask Cal if he is using the 4Tell computer software head office sent out last year. "You simply type in the details of every sale over the last five years—the date, the quantity, and the item code—and then the software predicts when you need to place the next order to restock your shelves. And as each further sale is made, you enter it into the computer and the software automatically adjusts its predictions."

"Very nice," Cal agrees, "but a computer doesn't think. It doesn't know when we have an early winter or spring, and it can't allow for a sudden surge of orders, as I can."

"You can even enter that sort of information," you try to explain, but it is clear that Cal isn't really listening, or doesn't want to hear. Nevertheless, you are appalled at the immense amount of working capital tied up in what you consider to be needless overstocking. You have to look no further to discover why the operating costs at the Kimberley warehouse are so high.

Before you drive home the following day, Cal introduces you to Connie Nieumeyer, his assistant manager. While the three of you are chatting, Cal is called away and you have a few moments to talk to Connie alone.

"You carry an immense stock," you venture, gesturing toward the warehouse. "With such a volume, wouldn't you find a computer stock control program helpful?"

"Well, yes, I suppose so," Connie murmurs noncommittally.

"The company owns some good programs," you suggest. "I could send you a copy, if you like . . . ."

"Do you mean 4Tell?"

"Uh-huh."

"We have a copy."

"But you don't use it."

"Cal prefers the way we do things now."

You wait. After a moment Connie continues, a little hesitantly. "I . . . I took a look at the program. I could see it would work . . . in a different setting."

You decide not to pursue the subject any further. You have already sensed that Connie is interested in 4Tell, but is too loyal to Cal to say any more.

People problems are difficult to describe

Later, back in your home office, you are writing your travel report. In fact, you realize you really have two reports to write: one about the insurance on the damaged lamps and one about the overstocked warehouse. But what are you to say, or even suggest? Clearly Cal Wozny is the problem, but you know for certain that he will not readily abandon his personal method of stock control. You feel that Connie Nieumeyer is capable—and possibly even eager—to try using 4Tell (you saw an active personal computer in her office, but none in Cal's); maybe the system could be instituted through her. But what of Cal's self-esteem? Should he be transferred to another office or even retired early? These thoughts whirl around in your head as you settle down to write. What a difficult situation!

Here is some additional data you may need to write your report(s):

- Kimberley is 370 kilometres from your head office.
- You drove there in your own car on Wednesday of last week (work out the real date).
- You drove home on Friday.
- You stayed at the Overlander Motel for two nights.
- You have used 4Tell extensively and are impressed by the 90% to 92% accuracy of its predictions.
- Bill Korton tells you, "Be sure to write CONFIDENTIAL in capital letters at the top of any report or attachment in which you write anything about Cal Wozny."

You write the report describing the insurance claim as an email message to Bill Korton. You write the second report as a confidential interoffice memorandum.

Exercise 5.7: **Conference Report**

On Air Canada's flight 519 from Chicago on the first leg of your journey home, you adjust your meal tray in front of you and plop a writing pad onto it. "Not a bad moment to start writing my report," you think to yourself, "while the events of the conference I have just attended are fresh in my mind."

Today is the 17th of the current month. You left home on the 13th and spent the 14th to 16th inclusive at the AlFresco Inn in Chicago, Illinois, which was the site of this year's "Office Methods and Practices" conference. Your employer sent you there because a full day was being devoted to workshops and presentations on word-processing practices, followed by a half-day panel focusing on developing in-house training programs. (You are supervisor of administrative services at the head office of Mead-Baxter Corporation.)

Part 1

Of the formal program, two presentations particularly appealed to you: a two-hour workshop titled "Designing Macros for Instant Setting of Keystroke Parameters" and three papers presented in a session titled "Outlining at a Computer Terminal." The workshop was presented on the 14th by Carla Renneslaere, manager of corporate communications for the Renn-Will group of consultants in Toronto. Carla handed out 20 pages of printed notes to each participant.

Write a conference report

The three papers were *Evaluation of Commercially Available Outlining Software*, presented by Dr Marvin T Sprecht, head of the language and linguistics department of Laronde University, *Brainstorm Your Outlines!* by Magda Horowicz, president of Computer Innovations in Toledo, Ohio, and *Killing the Urge to Press the PRINT Key: Working Without Hard Copy*, by Nona K Robertson. (The program did not identify Nona's affiliation. When you asked her, she said she had just started working out of her home as a private writing consultant in St. Paul, Minnesota.)

Dr Sprecht and Nona Robertson handed out copies of the papers they presented, which you plan to attach to your conference report. You asked Magda Horowicz for a copy of her paper, but she admitted, "I haven't finished writing it, but I'll send you a copy in about a month if you'll leave me your name and address" (which you did).

Write your conference report as an interoffice memorandum addressed to Lawrence Warrenton, manager of administration. Assume that you attach the conference program, Carla's notes, and the two papers to your report (you should give each an identification number and refer to it within your report). Assume that you plan to keep other conference literature and manufacturers' catalogues at your desk and will invite readers of your report to borrow them from you. Also assume that the Air Canada flight you are taking from Chicago will land at Toronto, and that you will make appropriate flight connections from that city.

Overall, you feel the conference was worth attending because you are bringing some very useful ideas home with you.

Part 2

Although the formal presentations were interesting, you also gained much from the equipment displays, which ranged from computer supplies to desktop publishing equipment. A display that particularly interested you was a demonstration of software for creating multimedia training courses on the Web. It was titled "Design8," and carried a subtitle: "If It Moves—Web It!" (You realize later that *Design8* is a subtle way to say Designate—which in this instance means to assign training steps into designated modules of instruction.)

Design8 sales representative Marla Bridges gives you some descriptive literature and then demonstrates some of the techniques embedded into the software. "Too many people think you can simply take an instruction manual or an existing training course and type it directly onto pages for displaying on the Web," Marla explains. "That's not true."

She points out that the software will help a program developer shape a course so that it is a good learning experience. She explains several unique factors built into *Design8* that will help users create the right effect. For example:

1. It helps the user create a mixture of media (online text, illustrations, and tests; video inserts; audio emphasis).
2. It provides an *interactive* learning experience at least every fourth screen, to hold the user's interest.
3. It helps users develop *short* learning modules. ("Long courses are too overpowering," Marla says. "Users give up too easily.")
4. It recommends access to a live instructor, and shows how to implement it.
5. It builds in remedial learning loops that correct the user's incorrect understanding. The loops neither repeat the previous learning word-for-word, nor tell the reader he or she is wrong. ("Users simply think the loop is part of the course; they are never made to feel they are dummies!" Carla adds.)

Carla peers at your name tag. "We'll be doing demonstrations across Canada next month," she says, opening up her diary. "In fact, we'll be in your area from the 17th to the 21st." She suggests you book an appointment for a *Design8* salesperson to come into your offices and demonstrate what can be done.

"To get a thorough feel for what Design8 can do, you need a good two-and-a-half to three hours," she adds, and suggests you round up a number of people within the company to attend.

You explain that you will have to get approval from company management.

"Sure," she says. "I'll write a tentative appointment in my book. There's no obligation. After you get back, email me to either confirm or cancel the booking."

You choose an appropriate date and she writes it down. She also gives you her business card, which she staples to the brochure. In fact, she gives you a duplicate copy of the card and the brochure. "So you can circulate one, and keep one yourself."

Now you are back in your office. Write a memo to Lawrence Warrenton, manager of administration, recommending that he approve holding the demonstration and that several other members of the company should attend.

Write a recommendation report

WEBLINKS

Progress Reports

www.io.com/~hcexres/tcm1603/acchtml/progrep.html

This page deals with the purpose, timing, format, and organization of progress reports. A revision checklist alerts the reader of specific problems to avoid. An example of a progress report can be downloaded.

Style Exercises

www.nmsu.edu/techprof/materials/style/style.htm

The readability of a report can be much clearer if the writer uses a clear, concise writing style. Complete the exercises at this site to improve your writing style.

Technical Reports

www.io.com/~hcexres/tcm1603/acchtml/techreps.html

Here you will find examples of technical reports, discussion of different types of reports, and questions to consider when writing a technical report.

Semiformal Business Proposals

chapter 6

It's just four days into the new year when Hannah Petrie opens a brown kraft envelope that arrived in the morning's mail. She reads it and then immediately reaches for the telephone.

"Sandi," she says. "Come on over. And bring Dave with you. I've got something interesting to show you."

Hannah, Sandi, and Dave are co-owners of "The Proving Ground," a small company that provides investigative business consulting services. They all attended the same central Ontario business college and, upon graduation 18 months ago, set up The Proving Ground as a joint venture. They have managed to find sufficient work to keep the business afloat, but no job has been particularly spectacular.

"Are you ready for some late-night work?" Hannah asks when Sandi and Dave walk into her office.

They look questioningly at her as she holds up a two-page letter and waves it in front of them. "It's an RFP," she explains. "A 'Request for Proposal.' It's from Skin Care Unlimited in Mississauga. They're asking for a proposal to carry out a blind study on a new suntan lotion they've made." Hannah reads from the letter: "*Your proposal and, if you are the successful bidder, your study and report, will have to be carried out quickly because we plan to use the results in our spring marketing campaign. That means your proposal must be in our hands by January 11. We will inform the successful bidder by January 20 and we will need your report by February 15.*"

Good news with which to start the new year!

"We're not the only people who will be bidding, then?" Dave asks.

"No," Sandi says. "They said: 'If you are the successful bidder.' There will be others."

"So, what we've got to do is work out what it will cost, and tell them that."

"No, much more," Hannah says. "They'll expect us to describe exactly how we plan to carry out the study. They'll judge us on that as well as our price."

"So, even if we are the lowest bidder, it doesn't necessarily mean we get the contract?" Dave asks.

"Right! We need to convince Skin Care Unlimited that we know exactly what we will be doing and fully understand the difficulties and intricacies of the project. A well-written and substantiated proposal will demonstrate that."

IN THIS CHAPTER

You will learn how to plan and write proposals that will convince readers of your company's capability to carry out a specific task, or for the need to implement a change or to purchase new equipment or system. Specifically you will learn how to

- select an existing writing plan that will present your information in a coherent sequence, or adapt an existing writing plan so that it better fits your needs,
- assign your information to the appropriate parts of the writing plan,
- organize your information in each part so that it develops a persuasive argument, and
- write in a confident style that will convince readers of the validity of the points you make.

Hannah, Sandi, and Dave start jotting down factors they need to consider for the proposal they will have to write. For example:

Identify what you need to discuss *before* you start planning or writing

- They will need to hire people on whom to test the various sunscreens.
- Some of the people should have fair skin and some should be slightly darker skinned.
- Because it's January, Hannah suggests they should take the participants to a winter vacation spot, most likely in the Caribbean. "I *like* that idea!" Sandi agrees.
- Although it would be much less expensive to use tanning beds in a suntan parlor, they consider it would be too slow and would result in less-controlled conditions because each bed, depending on the quality and newness of the lamps, tends to give different levels of exposure. ("I know," says Hannah. "I tried it one winter and learned to *ask* for a particular bed which had newer lamps.")

- Dave suggests they also carry out washability tests of the lotions on clothing. "Not every proposer will think of that," he adds. "It will insert an additional factor into our proposal, and it won't add much to the cost."
- "Then maybe we should also include UVB tests," says Sandi. "We'd have to send samples out to a lab for that. We don't have the equipment."

"Okay," says Dave. "But how do we pull it all together?"

Hannah lifts a slim textbook from the shelf behind her desk.[1] "I'd like you to look at Chapter 5," she says. "It presents several designs for different types of proposals. One of them should fit what we need, or can be adapted to our needs."

Hannah points out that there are four main writing plans, and they fall into two general categories:

Proposals come in many forms; four are described here

1. Proposals in which only one solution or plan is offered.
2. Proposals in which alternative solutions or plans are offered, and their relative merits are discussed.

Both types of proposal follow the "pyramid" approach and have essentially the same overall structure:

- A **Summary**, which describes very briefly what is being proposed. It may include the total cost.
- **Background** information, which describes the circumstances leading up to the proposal being written.
- A **Details** section that describes what will be done, how it will be done, and what results are expected. This is the main part of the proposal and its depth of detail depends on the situation. Generally, this section is shorter in single-solution proposals than in multiple-solution proposals.
- An **Action Statement** that asks for a decision or requests approval for the proposer to go ahead with the plan.
- **Attachments** or **Appendices** that contain detailed evidence, such as a cost analysis or a computer printout, to support what is said in the Details section.

Proposals Offering a Single Solution or Plan

A single-solution proposal can be as simple as a memorandum from a supervisor to a manager, suggesting that the company ask the contractor providing cafeteria services to extend the lunch-hour to accommodate the

[1]Ron Blicq and Lisa Moretto, *Get to the Point!* (Scarborough, Ontario: Prentice Hall Canada Inc, 2000).

A single-solution proposal offers no alternatives

increase in staff caused by many new hirings, or it could be a detailed proposal for integrating two departments or finding new rental accommodation for an expanding business.

Writing a Short Informal Proposal

Fergus Halprin's brief email in Chapter 4, in which he suggests to his manager, Darwin Morantz, that the company reschedule the lunch times for staff, became an informal proposal when Darwin suggested he investigate further and prepare his idea for presentation to management. The writing plan he used for his informal proposal is shown in Figure 6-1.

For Fergus's proposal, the parts of the writing plan would contain the following information:

These notes form an easy writing outline to follow

Summary: A request to increase the cafeteria contractor's time on site, plus a suggestion for staggered lunch hours.

Background: The problem of staff standing in line at the cafeteria for 15 to 20 minutes, with attendant personal irritation and reduction in morale.

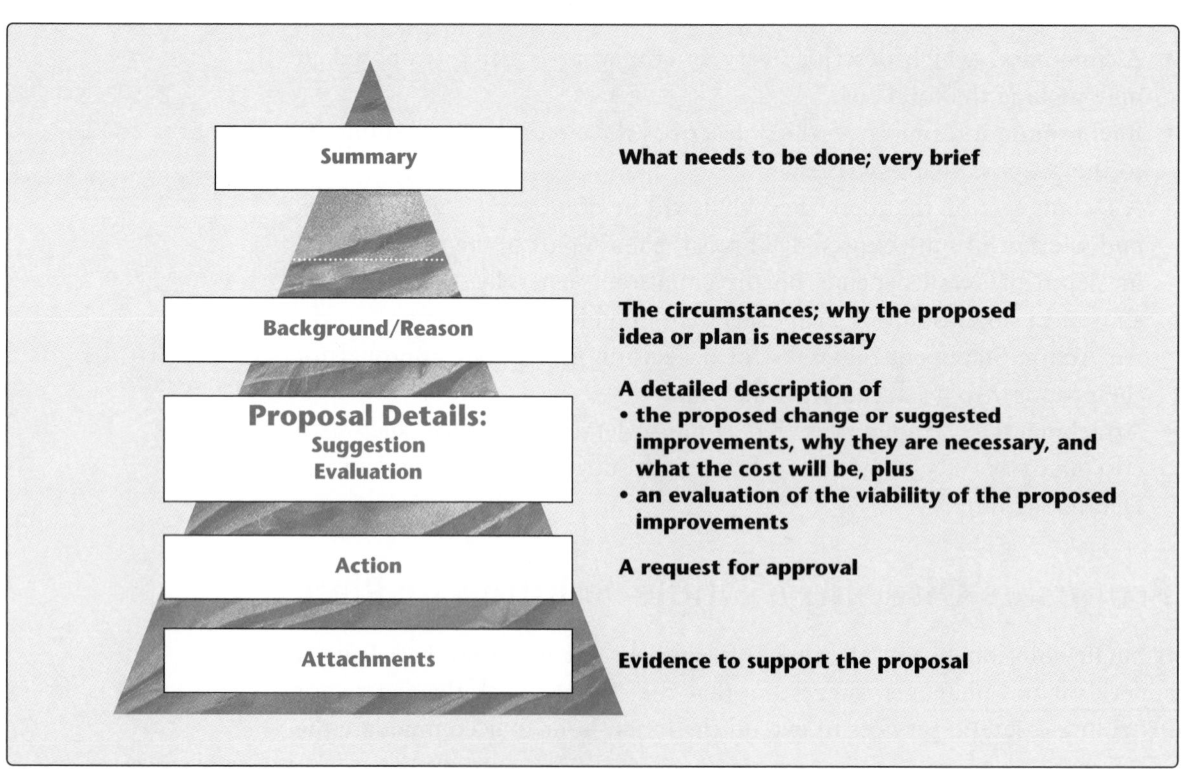

Figure 6-1 Writing plan for an informal single-solution proposal

Details: *Suggestion:* His plan to have the contractor be present for 45 minutes longer each day, at a cost of $xxx, and for different departments to be scheduled for lunch at different times.

Evaluation: The effect this will have; which departments will experience a change in their lunch time; how special arrangements will be made for departments that cannot close down completely, by scheduling certain people to have lunch at certain times; how problems will be dealt with; how cost will be absorbed; how much morale will be improved.

Action: A firm request for approval to go ahead with the plan.

Attachments: Scheduling plan; cost breakdown, including a quotation from the contractor.

Kimmy Soong also used this writing plan for a proposal to her supervisor, in which she outlined an alternative method for shrinkwrapping the company's baked products. In her memo (see Figure 6-2) she describes how the new procedure will be put into effect, the advantages that will accrue, the changes that will be implemented, and the effect upon sales and cost. The notes below are keyed to the different parts of her memo proposal.

Answer the questions "what?", "how?", and "why" to establish the proposal's validity

This is Kimmy's **Summary Statement**, in which she not only says what she will do but also identifies that there will be advantages (increased sales) and disadvantages (increased cost).

In the **Background/Reason** compartment, Kimmy establishes the validity of her proposal by commenting on public opinion (background) and two of the main advantages to be gained if her plan is implemented.

The **Details** start here and continue into the next two paragraphs. They start with the **Suggestion** by describing the two shrinkwrap products.

Keeping an informal proposal short (here, just one page), and yet complete, encourages the reader to say "yes"

Memorandum

To:	Leila Carstairs Production Manager	**From:**	Kimmy Soong, Supervisor Production Control
Date:	May 26, 2000	**Ref:**	Proposal to Change to Biodegradable Shrinkwrap

1 I propose that we switch to biodegradable shrinkwrap for our baked goods when the current supply of non-biodegradable shrinkwrap is exhausted. The cost will be 8% higher, but the sales department considers that the change will increase sales sufficiently to offset the cost.

2 Now is just the right time to make the change. The southern Ontario public is becoming increasingly sensitive to the combined problems of finding new landfill sites and filling them with plastic-based bags and products that never decompose. If we were to advertise that we are switching to a biodegradable shrinkwrap because it is more ecologically sound, we would be seen to have lined up with public opinion. Coincidentally, we would be changing to a Canadian-made product.

3 The non-biodegradable shrinkwrap we currently use is "Clarifilm," an imported film distributed by O-Z Distributors of Hamilton, Ontario. The biodegradable shrinkwrap I am proposing is "Ecowrap," which is manufactured and distributed by Filmwrap Ontario Limited of Mississauga. Ecowrap starts to decompose 30 days after use, which is at least two weeks beyond the "best before" date of any of our baked goods.

By describing possible problems, Kimmy anticipates "Yes, but . . . " reactions

4 I have tested a sample of Ecowrap on the Otto Mk IIIC wrapping machine and found only minor adjustments were necessary: mainly the tension required to feed the film from its roll into the machine's pick-up rollers, and the need to make a −1.4°C adjustment in the temperature of the heat sealer. Neither change affects operation.

Mark Hamilton, in the sales department, has drawn up a draft newspaper and flyer advertisement, which he will release on the day we start using Ecowrap. He predicts that the increased cost to wrap each product package (which I estimate will average $0.0047) will be offset by the increased sales generated through public awareness.

5 I propose that we use Ecowrap on a trial basis for the balance of 2000. May I have your approval to place my next order for shrinkwrap with Filmwrap Ontario Limited?

Kimmy S

Figure 6-2 A letter-form proposal (prepared as a memorandum because it is for in-house use)

In her **Evaluation**, Kimmy describes both the physical testing (in paragraph 4), how she has worked with the Marketing Department to introduce a sales campaign at the same time that the company will start using the new shrinkwrap (paragraph 5), and how although there will be an increased cost it will not be a problem (also in paragraph 5).

This is the **Action Statement**, in which she clearly *asks* the Production Manager to respond positively. She uses a strong closing statement in the active voice (she writes: "I propose . . .") rather than in the softer, weaker passive voice (i.e. "It is requested that . . .").

By demonstrating that she has examined all aspects of the suggestion, and closing with a firm, definite request, Kimmy has provided strong evidence to encourage the Production Manager to approve her proposal.

Writing a Longer, Semiformal Proposal

The writing plan for a longer, in-depth semiformal proposal is essentially the same as for an informal proposal, although the Details compartment is expanded to include more subheadings (see Figure 6-3).

A semiformal proposal like this is used when one company (such as a consultant) is proposing to another company (such as a client) that a particular course of action be taken. The proposal may be initiated by the proposing company, or it may be prepared in response to a request from a client. The Request for Proposal (RFP) in some cases is a letter that states in general terms what is required, such as that sent to The Proving Ground by Skin Care Unlimited. In other cases it may be a detailed specification that describes exactly what is to be done and how the proposal is to be prepared.

An RFP often establishes how your proposal is to be presented

Example of a Single-Solution Proposal

The next part of this chapter contains the single-solution semiformal proposal that The Proving Ground submitted in response to Skin Care Unlimited's RFP. Figure 6-4 (page 143) contains the cover letter and Figure 6-5 (pages 147–153) contains the proposal. Comments on both are listed below.

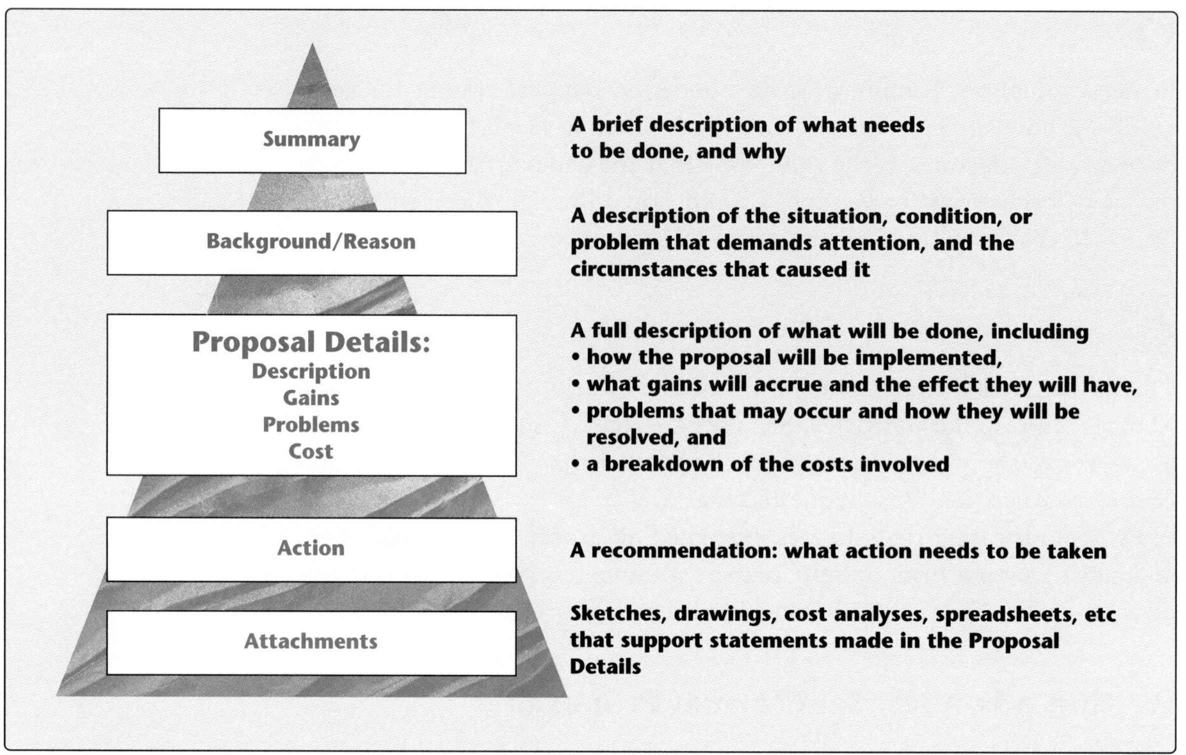

Figure 6-3 Writing plan for an in-depth single-solution semiformal proposal

A more detailed plan for a single-solution proposal

Comments on Cover Letter

Hannah's cover letter draws attention to the most important element of The Proving Ground's proposal: that they are going to provide the results to the client several days in advance of the requested delivery date. This may become a significant factor when Skin Care Unlimited evaluates all the proposals they receive.

Use an executive summary to focus readers' attention on concerns you have addressed

Consequently, Hannah's letter in effect becomes an executive summary, as described on page 166 of Chapter 7.

Although the proposal was written by Sandi McPherson, Hannah wrote the cover letter, partly because the Request for Proposal was addressed to her and partly because she is The Proving Ground's senior executive.

Comments on Proposal

The comments that follow are keyed by number to the appropriate sections of the proposal.

The Proving Ground
1011 – 240 Menzies Street
Burlington ON L7G 4V3
(416) 317 2216

January 9, 2001

Rachel Maguire
Marketing Manager
Skin Care Unlimited
310 Benjamin Street
Mississauga ON M5W 1X3

Dear Ms Maguire

I am enclosing our proposal to test Skin Care Unlimited's new sunscreen "Whisper" against six other brands of sunscreen, as requested in your Request for Proposal of January 3, 2001.

As the attached proposal shows, we recognize your need to have the results of the tests early so that they can be used in Skin Care Unlimited's spring marketing campaign. Consequently, we plan to provide the results to you well in advance of your requested delivery date of February 15:

1. Preliminary results: on February 5, 2001
2. Final report: on February 9, 2001

In addition to the requested tests of direct exposure to sun, we are also offering the option to select from further tests, such as imperviousness to seawater, washability from clothing, and UVA/UVB resistance. Our cost for providing the services will range from $26 325 to $31 780 (plus GST), depending on the range of tests you select.

Please call Sandi McPherson at (416) 317 2216, extension 324, if you need more information or have questions.

Sincerely

Hannah Petrie

Hannah Petrie
President

Separating the delivery dates from the main text, and indenting them, draws the reader's eye to particularly important information

Figure 6-4 The cover letter for the proposal in Figure 6-5

Sandi McPherson has used elements of information design to create a proposal that is visually appealing. She does this by using two simple tables as templates and inserting information into the appropriate compartments. The first table comprises two equal-size compartments bearing the names of the client and Sandi's company.

This is the **Summary**, in which Sandi briefly describes what her primary reader (Rachel Maguire of Skin Care Unlimited) most wants to know: what will be done; the completion date for the project, which Sandi shows is several days *earlier* than the date stipulated by the client; and the total price. To draw the reader's eyes to the Summary, Sandi centres this section of the text and indents it 15 mm from each side.

The **Background/Reason** starts here. It refers to the guidelines identified in the client's Request for Proposal (RFP) and the strict requirements regarding delivery dates.

The second table also starts here and continues for the remainder of the report. This template has two columns:

Information Design techniques shape a proposal for maximum effect

- The left-hand column is 2 inches (50 mm) wide and contains only headings, which are set in Times New Roman 13 pt bold.
- The right-hand column is 4 inches (100 mm) wide and contains the text, which is set in Times New Roman 12 pt. To make the text even more readable, Sandi insets two blank lines between text paragraphs each time she inserts a new heading.

Although this paragraph contains a new heading beside it, it is still part of the **Background/Reason.**

Sandi closes this section by stating that the client will provide the test samples, to ensure there is no misunderstanding later.

7

The **Proposal Details** start here and continue almost to the end of the proposal. The first compartment within the Proposal Details—labelled **Description** in the writing plan—also is the largest subcompartment within the proposal. It starts with a brief overview of how The Proving Ground plans to evaluate the sunscreen products.

8

Sandi has assigned a separate heading to this topic, and placed it at the start of the tests, to demonstrate to the client that The Proving Ground recognizes the client's request that the testing be conducted "blind."

The **Description** of all the tests starts with an overview of what the following paragraphs contain. This is similar to the summary statement at the start of a document and shows that smaller pyramids can be nested within larger pyramids.

Each test is described separately, for two reasons: to indicate to the client that The Proving Ground has examined the project requirements in depth; and to allow the client to select just certain tests, if she prefers.

Sandi states directly that the UVA and UVB testing will be subcontracted. This is better than saying *Because we do not have the specialized equipment to perform UVA and UVB tests, we will subcontract these tests to . . .*, which might create the impression that The Proving Ground has certain deficiencies that need to be considered before awarding them a contract.

Ensure "negative" aspects are presented in a positive manner

This short section is the **Gains** subcompartment. In this proposal it becomes a major selling point, which Sandi hopes will encourage Skin Care Unlimited to select The Proving Ground rather than one of the other companies submitting proposals. She recognizes that when proposal content is similar, the choice usually depends on price. She anticipates that, by promising to deliver the results several days earlier than specified by the RFP, Skin Care Unlimited will identify it as a significant factor when making their decision. The detailed schedule in the attachment is particularly helpful, in that it demonstrates that The Proving Ground has "done its homework." This is much better than simply saying: "We will deliver the results five days early."

This is the **Problems** subcompartment. A good proposal writer will always anticipate that the reader may bring up objections, who mentally may say something like: "Yes, I hear what you are saying, but have you considered . . .?" (This is known as the "Yes . . . but" syndrome.) So Sandi has identified two factors that the client may question, and has dealt effectively with both of them.

Address problems positively; don't try to conceal them

By showing the client *how* the company will deal with potential problems, The Proving Ground demonstrates that their consultants think proactively rather than reactively. This gives the reader additional confidence in the proposal.

This is the **Cost** subcompartment. By providing a breakdown of the cost for each test, Sandi enables the client to be selective and perhaps identify only those tests she feels are essential.

There is no compartment in the writing plan for inserting information about the proposing company. Sandi chooses to insert it at the end of the Project Details.

Sandi has chosen to change the **Action Statement** at the foot of the writing plan in Figure 6-2 into an **Outcome**. Her reason: the Action Statement will be written in the cover letter.

This is the only **Attachment**. If there had been more than one attachment, this one would have been labelled Attachment 1.

The Proving Ground

1 ### Proposal to Test Sunscreen Products

Prepared for **Skin Care Unlimited** Mississauga • Ontario	Prepared by **The Proving Ground** Burlington • Ontario

2 We are proposing to evaluate the effectiveness of Skin Care Unlimited's sunscreen product *Whisper*, and to compare it against six competitive products. Our evaluation will comprise six tests:

- Direct protection from sunburn,
- Comfortableness on the skin,
- Water resistance,
- Ease of removal from the skin,
- Ease of removal from clothing, and
- Protection from UVA and UVB rays.

This is the proposal's Summary, although it's not labelled as such

The evaluation will be completed by February 5, and we will submit our report on February 9, 2001. Our fee for evaluating and analyzing the sunscreen products will be between $26 325 and $31 780 plus GST, depending on the range of tests selected by Skin Care Unlimited.

3 **Introduction**

4 This proposal has been prepared in response to a January 3, 2001, Request for Proposal (RFP) originated by Rachel Maguire, Marketing Manager of Skin Care Unlimited. The RFP identified the tests to be performed and the time frame within which a proposal must be submitted (no later than January 11) and the date the successful bidder must file its report (no later than February 15, 2001). Meeting this schedule is essential if Skin Care Unlimited is to incorporate the results of the tests into its spring marketing campaign.

1

Figure 6-5 A semiformal proposal offering a single solution

This is a subtle table of contents, again not labelled as such

Proposal Plan The proposal covers the following: 5

- Our overall plan for carrying out the tests.
- Precautions we will take to conceal the identity of the products being tested.
- A detailed description of each test.
- Our plan for reporting the results.
- Our contingency plan for accommodating problems that may arise.
- A cost analysis.

Skin Care Unlimited will provide the samples of 6
Whisper and the six competitors' products.

Approach to the Study We will recruit six participants to be test models 7
and will fly them to the Caribbean to carry out the sun exposure tests. Simultaneously, one of our consultants in Burlington, Ontario, will carry out the clothing washability tests and arrange for evaluation of UVA and UVB protection.

We considered using local suntan parlors, but were constrained by the limited time that the models would be permitted to be exposed to the lamps, the varying quality of the lamps in different sunbeds, and the extent to which we would be able to maintain control over the tests.

The white space in the left column permits readers to pencil in notes

Concealing Product Identity Sunscreen products will be decanted into unmarked 8
containers and each container will be assigned an identifying code letter. We will then make a single list of the products and their identification codes and place it in a sealed envelope, which will be stored in a safety deposit box at a local bank. The bank will have instructions that the box cannot be opened until a specific date, which will be *after* the date we expect the tests and analyses will be complete.

2

Figure 6-5 A semiformal proposal offering a single solution (*continued*)

9 **Description of Individual Tests**

The Proving Ground's (TPG's) primary test will be to assess the effect that each sunscreen has in protecting the participants' skin from sunburn. Secondary tests will evaluate the "feel" of each sunscreen, its water resistance, and the ease with which it can be removed from the skin and clothing. A final test will determine the UVA and UVB protection provided by each sunscreen.

The start of an embedded pyramid: it summarizes what is to follow in this section of the proposal

10 **1. Testing for Sunburn Protection**

We will advertise for volunteers to participate in the tests, and will select three females and three males who can demonstrate that they have no residual tan from the previous summer. Within each group we will also select one with fair complexion, one with medium complexion, and one with slightly darker complexion. This will provide a spectrum over which to measure each sunscreen's protective ability. We will then fly the six participants and two TPG consultants to Nassau in the Bahamas.

Each participant will take part in two tests, to be held on separate days to prevent overexposure in any one day. The tests will be carried out on participants' backs and legs, using a specially designed clothing template with seven holes cut in it, one for applying each type of sunscreen.

The participants' backs and legs will be inspected three times to determine the effect each sunscreen has had: once immediately after each test, then six hours later, and again twelve hours later. Each time we will record the appearance and the sensitivity to touch of the participant's skin in the various sunscreen-protected areas.

2. Testing for "Feel"

This will be a subjective test. On a day when no sun-exposure tests are being held, we will ask each participant to rub the seven different sunscreens on

3

Figure 6-5 A semiformal proposal offering a single solution (*continued*)

their arms and legs to determine whether the sunscreen feels comfortable or oily or sticky. The on-site TPG consultants, who will be applying the sunscreens to the participants during the exposure tests, also will comment.

Headings and subheadings stand out, make it easy for reader to find specific information

3. Testing for Removal from Skin

Concurrently, the participants will be asked to wash the sunscreen from their arms, and to comment on how easily it washes off. Again, the TPG consultants will take part in this test, because when applying the sunscreens to the participants, they will have to wash the previous sunscreen thoroughly from their hands to prevent it from contaminating the next sunscreen they apply.

4. Testing for Water Resistance

Waterproof capability will be tested at Nassau, on one of the days when sunscreen protection is not being measured. Participants will apply some of the sunscreen and then swim, both in salt water and in fresh water. We will then assess the extent to which the sunscreen has been eroded. These tests will be correlated with the results of test No. 3.

5. Testing for Removal from Clothing

We will carry out hand- and machine-wash tests of the seven sunscreens on cottons and nylon/lycra, to determine how well each can be removed from clothing.

Positive statement avoids saying "We don't have the necessary facilities"

6. Testing for UVA & UVB Protection

We have arranged with EnviroTest Labs Ltd of Guelph, Ontario, to evaluate UVA and UVB protection capability of all seven sunscreen products. The names of the products and their manufacturers will not be revealed to EnviroTest Labs. 11

Advantage of the Proposed Approach

The primary advantage in following the steps described in our proposal is that we can guarantee to provide definitive, thorough tests results well in advance of the prescribed date (see the project sched- 12

4

Figure 6-5 A semiformal proposal offering a single solution (*continued*)

ule in the attachment to this proposal). We propose to inform Skin Care Unlimited of the results in two ways:

1. By couriering a short letter summarizing the key results on February 5, 10 days before the completion date stipulated by the RFP.
2. By providing a formal report describing the results in detail on February 9, 2001, five days before the completion date stipulated by the RFP.

13 **Anticipating Potential Problems**

We have identified two potential problems, one concerning inclement weather interfering with the sun exposure tests and the other concerning possible lawsuits being instituted by participants who, in the future, develop medical conditions they try to attribute to the tests.

Expect the reader to say "Yes, but, have you thought of . . . ?" . . .

1. Protection Against Inclement Weather

We require two sunny days to complete the tests. As insurance against overcast conditions, the program will provide four complete days in Nassau (the Nassau Tourist Board claims that in late January and early February we can expect 23 sunny days per month). As further insurance, we will be prepared to create a fifth day by changing the early morning return departure time planned for February 1 to an evening departure, and have negotiated a nominal eight-person last-minute change fee with the airline if we need to exercise this option.

2. Protection Against Lawsuits

We will inform the participants of the limited length of exposure and ask them, before they accept the assignment, to sign a waiver absolving Skin Care Unlimited and The Proving Ground of any responsibility for accident or future medical problems.

. . . by anticipating and answering questions the client may ask

5

Figure 6-5 A semiformal proposal offering a single solution (*continued*)

Project Costs

14 The Proving Ground's fee for evaluating the efficacy of seven sunscreen products for Skin Care Unlimited will be $31 780, plus GST. The fee will cover five main activities:

Offering a price breakdown permits the client to choose specific services

1.	Tests for sunburn protection:	$26 325
2.	Tests for removability from skin:	320
3.	Tests for removability from clothing (i.e. washability):	1 205
4.	Tests for UVA and UVB protection:	1 675
5.	Analysis of test results and preparation of a definitive report:	2 255

About The Proving Ground

15 The Proving Ground was formed in May 1999 with a mandate to provide cost-effective professional investigative and evaluative services for Canadian and US businesses. Typical projects include, among many,

- identifying a new office location for Arbutus Engineering Consultants Ltd, Toronto, Ontario,
- conducting a comparative analysis of accounting software for the Canadian Association of Small Business Owners,
- comparing the cost of travel by airline, coach, and rail, for the province of Ontario, and
- assessing the impact of higher registration fees on students' choice of college, for the Board of Regents, Kanata Community College.

Toot your own horn: provide specific facts rather than adjective-laden opinions

We enclose a brochure providing further details about our company and services.

To Sum Up . . .

16 We propose offering Skin Care Unlimited a thorough evaluation of *Whisper* and six competing sunscreen products, and will provide the results of the study five days in advance of the prescribed completion date.

Sandi McPherson

Senior Consultant
The Proving Ground
January 9, 2001

6

Figure 6-5 A semiformal proposal offering a single solution (*continued*)

Attachment

17

Schedule for Implementing Sunscreen Product Tests

Activity	*Date (2001)*
Receipt of contract	January 20
Recruit participants	January 22–24
Obtain and code sunscreen samples	January 23–25
Fly participants to Nassau, Bahamas	January 27
Tests for sun protection	January 28–31*
Tests for washability from clothing	January 28–31
Tests for UVA/UVB protection	January 28–February 1
Fly participants from Nassau to Toronto	February 1, 10 a.m.*
Correlate and analyse results	February 2–3
Obtain code identification from bank	February 5, 10 a.m.
Courier preliminary report to Skin Care Unlimited	February 5, 3 p.m.
Write definitive report	February 5–8
Courier final report to Skin Care Unlimited	February 9

*If necessary, February 1 will be a fifth testing day at Nassau and the participants will return on an evening flight.

A detailed attachment supports statements made in proposal narrative

7

Figure 6-5 A semiformal proposal offering a single solution (*continued*)

Show the reader you are providing a comprehensive analysis

Proposals Offering Alternative Solutions or Plans

Proposals offering alternative solutions give the reader two or more choices and then recommend which choice the writer feels is the best solution to a problem or most suitable method for improving a situation. They can be presented as a relatively short informal proposal or as a longer, more fully developed semiformal proposal. In both cases they present the reader with a comparative analysis of the alternatives (for more information turn to "Conducting a Comparative Analysis" on page 175 of Chapter 7).

Writing an Informal Proposal

Alternative solutions help readers feel they have options. . .

The writing plan for an informal proposal that offers alternatives is shown in Figure 6-6. The figure shows that, in the Proposal Details, you first identify your objectives and establish your criteria for selecting the recommended alternative. You then present the recommended alternative but *do not* evaluate it at this point: you simply present its key features. Next, you present any alternatives that you feel the reader may question or ask about. Again, you do not yet evaluate these alternatives.

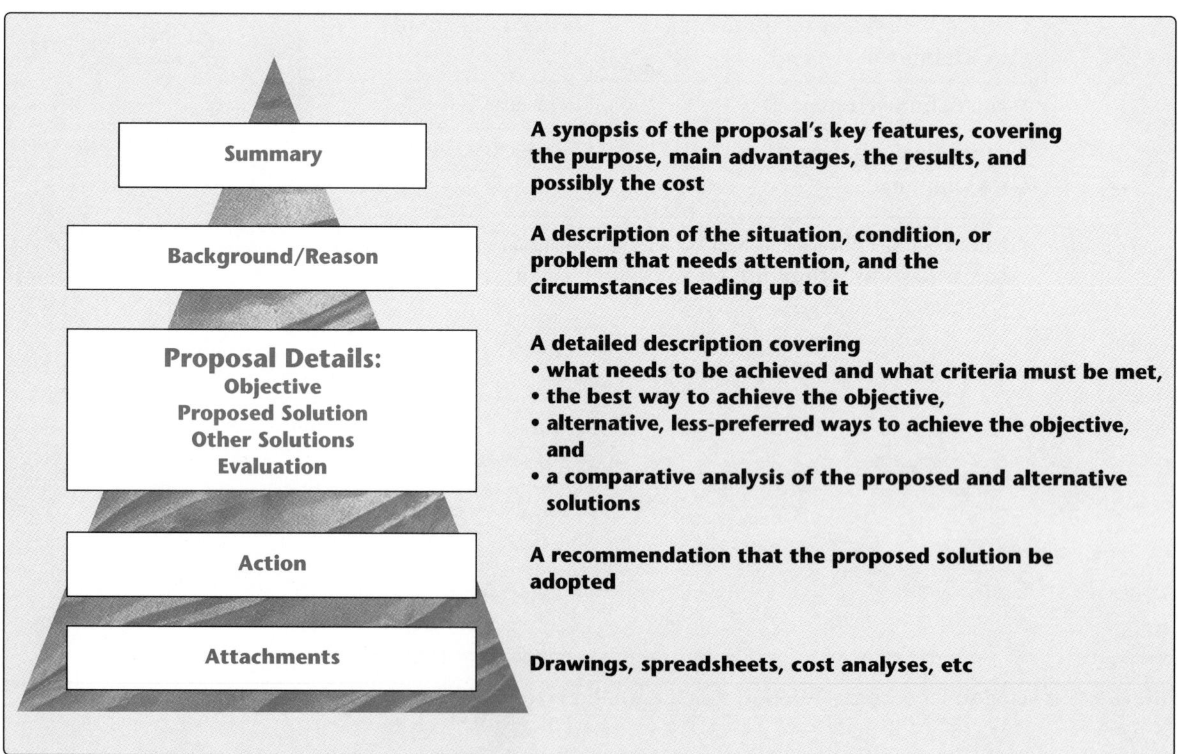

Summary
A synopsis of the proposal's key features, covering the purpose, main advantages, the results, and possibly the cost
Background/Reason
A description of the situation, condition, or problem that needs attention, and the circumstances leading up to it
Proposal Details:
Objective
Proposed Solution
Other Solutions
Evaluation
A detailed description covering
• what needs to be achieved and what criteria must be met,
• the best way to achieve the objective,
• alternative, less-preferred ways to achieve the objective, and
• a comparative analysis of the proposed and alternative solutions
Action
A recommendation that the proposed solution be adopted
Attachments
Drawings, spreadsheets, cost analyses, etc

Figure 6-6 Writing plan for a semiformal proposal offering alternative solutions

Evaluation of the alternatives becomes a separate section, in which you compare each alternative against the criteria you established earlier, as part of the objectives.

Finally, you close with an Action Statement, in which you recommend that the proposed alternative be selected.

Writing a Semiformal Proposal

The writing plan for a semiformal proposal that offers alternatives is shown in Figure 6-7. Often, a semiformal proposal like this is written in response to a client's request, in which the client asks for a proposal identifying the best way to do something, to improve a situation, or to remedy a problem. The writer then describes in detail the recommended solution or plan, and then identifies possible alternatives the reader should be aware of or may want to consider.

This writing plan creates a much more comprehensive proposal than that for an informal multiple-alternative proposal.

. . . and feel confident you have examined all possibilities

The **Proposal Details** section starts by establishing how you will carry out the study (your plan), and the objectives you will establish for the project. This shows the reader that you have a firm grasp of the situation and any con-

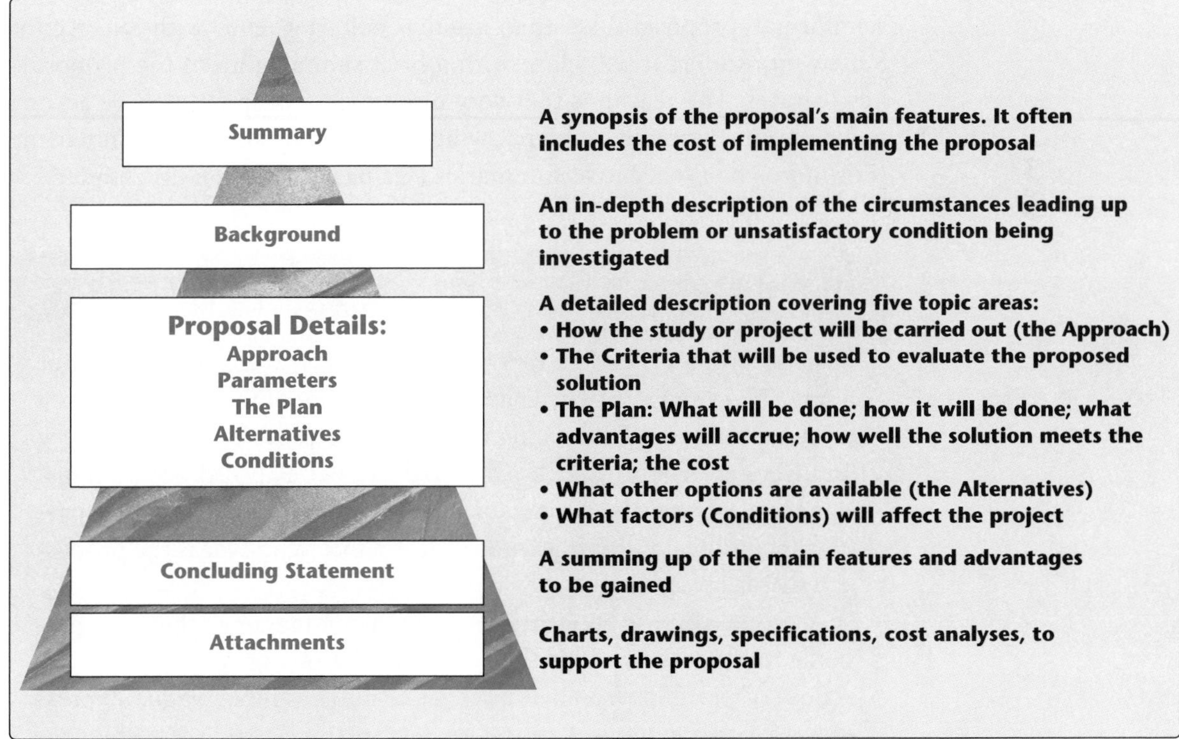

Figure 6-7 Writing plan for a comprehensive proposal offering alternative solutions

straints that apply. Then, under the heading **Parameters**, you establish the criteria you will use to measure the suitability of each alternative you will offer.

The Plan provides a detailed analysis of the proposed solution or plan being offered. Unlike the informal proposal, however, it also evaluates the solution, comparing it against the criteria established under the Parameters section. How this is done is shown in Figure 7-4 and its accompanying narrative (see pages 175–176 in Chapter 7.)

The **Alternatives** section describes other solutions or ways the same objectives can be achieved, but which the writer feels are less suitable. The writer evaluates each solution before describing the next alternative.

Establish conditions now to prevent problems later

The **Conditions** provide information concerning constraints, time limitations, and responsibilities of each party involved.

Two other factors may be introduced at this point in the narrative, depending on the situation:

- The cost of implementing the proposal. Cost details may appear here or in the cover letter/executive summary.
- Information about the proposing company and its capabilities. Such information is inserted if the proposing company is not well known by the client for whom the report is being prepared.

In contrast to the writing plans for previous proposals, an in-depth semiformal proposal like this usually will not end with an **Action Statement**. Rather, it will close with a brief summing up of the proposal's key features. The reason is that very often such a proposal will be accompanied by an executive summary, which will contain the Action Statement. (For more about executive summaries, see pages 166–168 in Chapter 7.)

TO SUM UP

Business proposals can be of varying length and complexity. The four writing plans shown in this chapter are examples of the various forms a proposal can take. The writing compartments provide examples of the arrangement of a proposal's parts, and can be relabelled or additional compartments may be inserted. The arrangement of the parts of a proposal contribute much to a reader's acceptance of the ideas the proposal writer is presenting.

A proposal must be written in convincing language that will persuade its readers to adopt the recommendations or take appropriate action. There is no room for weak, wishy-washy, or vague expressions, for they will weaken the readers' readiness to accept the proposal's recommendations.

EXERCISES

Most of the exercises at the end of Chapter 6 require you to obtain information from local sources outside your school or college. These exercises may be undertaken individually or as group projects: your instructor will inform you how each is to be tackled.

Exercise 6.1: **Planning a Conference**

For this exercise we want you to assume that you are a member of the Student Council at the college, university, or school you are attending. At a Council meeting held last Thursday, the Council members voted to propose to the College Administration that the college should hold a conference to discuss one of the topics listed below (your instructor or professor will inform you which topic you are to propose). The conference is to be a joint venture between the Student Council and the College Administration. You were elected to chair a small committee that will prepare the proposal.

Plan for a collaborative effort involving college students and administration

"But what do you write?" you asked. "How do I know what is appropriate to put in the proposal?"

"No problem," said Greg Kowalchuk, who is President of the Student Council. "You just answer six questions: *Who?*, *Why?*, *Where?*, *When?*, *What?* and *How?*"

The ensuing discussion identified the following points that should be articulated in the proposal:

1. **Who?**
   - Who is to coordinate/run the conference?
   - Who will be interested in attending?
   - Who will be invited to speak? (Should we invite specific speakers or post a "Call for Papers" and select speakers from those who respond?)
   - Who will be responsible for incurring the cost if there is a loss?
2. **Why?**
   - Why should the conference be held?
   - Why is the topic of importance?
   - Why is it necessary to address this topic?

Answering these six questions quickly establishes whether the idea is viable

3. **Where?**
   - Where should the conference be held?
     - — On college property?
     - — At a hotel?
     - — Elsewhere?

4. **When?**
   - When should the conference be held?
   - When will be most suitable from the College's viewpoint?
   - When will be most suitable from the Student Council's viewpoint?
   - When will be most suitable from the potential participants' viewpoint?

5. **What?**
   - What will be the primary focus of the conference?
   - What will be related but subsidiary topics?
   - What will be established as a minimum attendance for the conference to proceed?

Many proposals suggest *what* should be done; the really good proposals also examine *how* it will be done

6. **How?**
   - How will the conference be implemented? (Who will do what?)
   - How will it be advertised/marketed?
   - How will it be funded?
   - How will we obtain "seed money"?
   - How much should we charge each participant?
   - How will any surplus be distributed?

This is only a partial list of questions. You are expected to identify more questions that need to be answered.

Suggested Topics:

1. The need to address more interpersonal and human relations topics into each curriculum, in addition to the core subjects.
2. Coping with the steadily increasing cost of student fees, and the impact that each increase is having on registration.
3. Strategies for marketing students to potential employers: how to increase employers' awareness of the value inherent in hiring college graduates.

Exercise 6.2: Proposal to Buy Replacement Portable Computers

You are employed as an administrative assistant in the local branch of Kleyton and Johnston Insurance Services Limited, a company that sells personal life, property, and commercial insurance. The branch has 12 sales staff, each of whom has a portable computer containing software they use to calculate rates and to write their sales reports.

It's time to consider buying new technology

The 12 computers are identical and are 3 years and 5 months old. Recently, the sales staff have been complaining to branch manager Corinne Mahoney that their computers have insufficient memory, are too slow, and are unable to work with much of the new insurance software programs coming onto the market.

Corinne is sympathetic and asks you to research what new portable computers are available, what software they can handle, and what they will cost. You are then to write a proposal that she can send to the head office for approval to purchase replacement computers.

To undertake this project, you will first need to identify what portable computers were being sold three and a half years ago, and to document their principle features, such as memory size, speed, hard disk size, weight, and dimensions. I suggest you select one portable computer from that era and describe it as the model currently being used by the sales staff.

What were portable computers like $3\frac{1}{2}$ years ago?

Your next step will be to identify what features the new portable computer ideally should have, such as memory (RAM), hard disk size, internal or external 3.5 inch floppy disk drive and CD-ROM, built-in modem, large screen, and physical size and weight.

When they heard that you are preparing a proposal, three of the sales staff emailed you to say they want the lightest possible computer to carry around. Another group—four in all—indicated they want a minimum 13.3 inch LCD screen.

I suggest you identify more than one portable computer, obtain a specification sheet for each, and then conduct a comparative analysis to see which best meets the needs of the staff.

Corinne does not give you a budget. "But try to see what kind of price you can get for a computer that will meet most of our needs," she adds. "If a provider knows we will be buying 12, they probably will come up with a better deal."

So . . . do your investigation and then write your proposal.

Exercise 6.3: Proposing a "Graduation Event"

Assume that you are in your final year at your college, university, or school, and that at the end of the year you will be one of many students who will be graduating. You and three other students have been appointed by the Student Council to form a "Graduation Planning Committee" with the mandate to: "Propose an event that will become a significant feature of this year's graduation ceremonies, and will be remembered in future years as unique, unusual, and memorable."

You are instructed by the Council that you must document your plan in a proposal to the Student Council, and must obtain approval from the Council before you can put your plan into effect.

You will need to tackle the project in three steps:

1. Brainstorm ideas for the event, which may comprise an activity, entertainment, or ???? (whatever you can think of). Remember: you have to ensure your plan is unique.

2. Determine the cost, viability, and practicability of the event you are proposing.
3. Write the proposal.

To plan the proposal you will first need to address a series of questions, such as these:

Big plans for the day you graduate: but will anyone come?

- Why will the event be unique, unusual, and memorable?
- Why will students want to participate in it, or attend it? (Whether they participate or attend will depend on the type of event you choose.)
- Will it be practical and feasible to implement?
- What will the cost be?
- Will the Student Council have to bear the whole cost, or will students pay part of the cost? (Or will the college possibly bear part of the cost?)
- If students have to pay part of the cost, will that deter them from participating?
- Who will organize and run the event?
- Where and when will it be held?
- Will the college be likely to approve the event?
- If the event is to be held on college property, how will you get the College Administration to approve it?
- What impact will the event have on maintaining college security?

When writing your proposal, remember to anticipate and deal with other questions your readers may ask. Your primary readers will be the members of the Student Council; however, there may be secondary readers such as the College Administration and the head of the college security department.

Exercise 6.4: Proposal for More Parking Space

You are employed by Mercantile Shippers and Importers. The office is on the ground floor of the Tarquin Building, located at the southwest corner of the junction of Martin Avenue and Rory Street in your town (see Figure 6-8). The company has seen phenomenal growth over the past two years, and is expecting to hire another 10 employees over the next eight months.

Researching more parking space for office staff

Parking has always been a problem. You have been employed by Mercantile for 15 months and you still do not have a parking space. Neither have 11 other employees. Most of the time you take a bus to work, which is inconvenient because you live in the suburbs and have to change buses twice; the result: a 50-minute journey. When you do bring your car it costs you $8.00 a day at a public parking building at the southwest corner of Sharpe Avenue and Marjorie Street.

Currently there are 40 parking spaces immediately west of the Tarquin

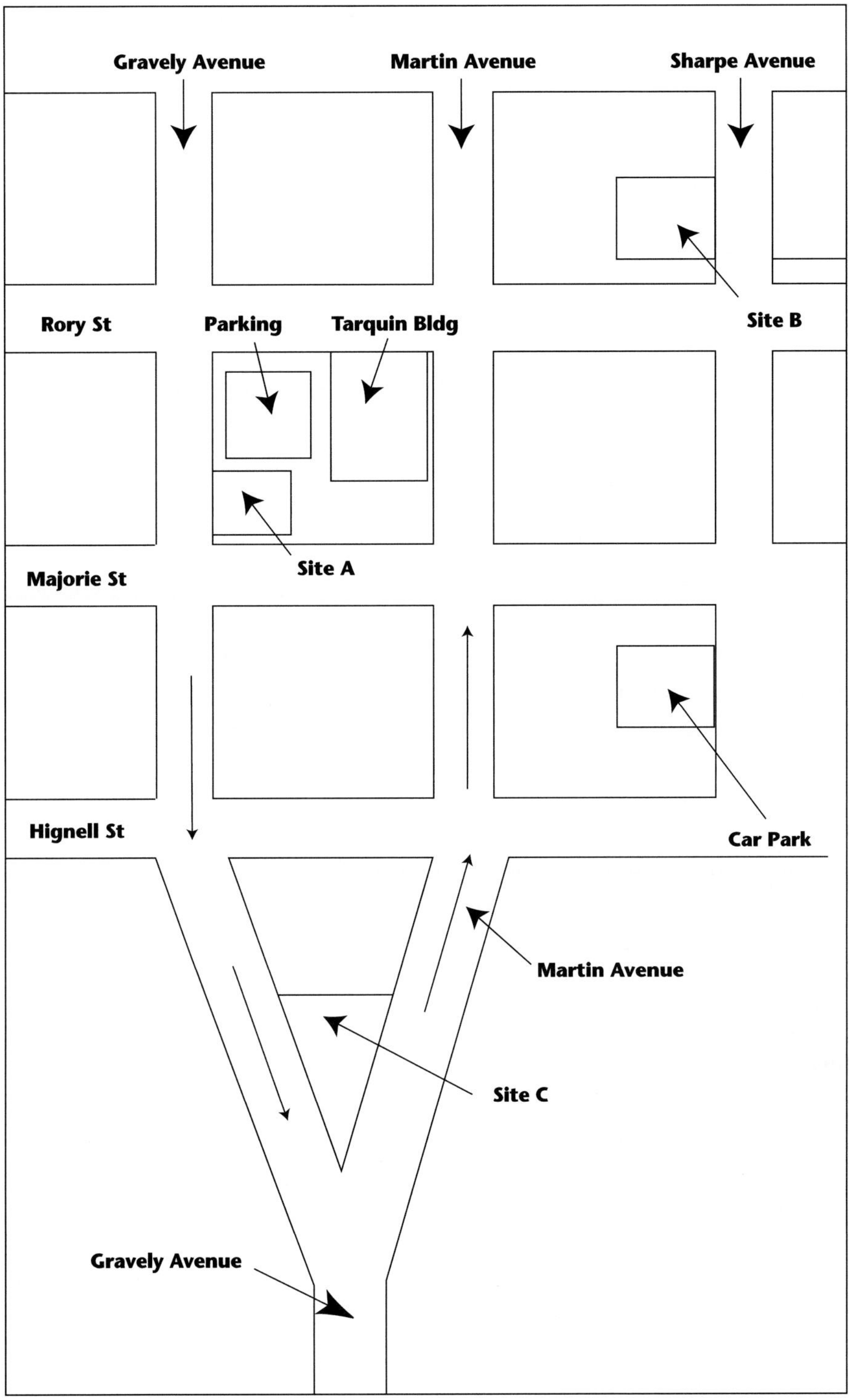

Which parking space will most appeal to staff?

Figure 6-8 Locations of alternative parking space

Building, which are used by the building's occupants. Of these, 18 are occupied by Mercantile staff and 22 are rented to other building occupants. These rental spaces are owned by Federated Insurance, which also owns the Tarquin Building and is a principal occupant. Staff who are lucky enough to have a parking space pay $65 per month for the privilege.

Over the past five weeks you have been quietly searching for alternative parking for Mercantile employees. You have found three possibilities:

Site A

- Within the same city block as the Tarquin Building (at northeast corner of Gravely Avenue and Marjorie Street).
- Site of a small, single-story warehouse, currently being demolished.
- The lot will be asphalted in 10 days.
- Entrance is from Gravely Avenue, travelling south.
- There will be space for 16 cars.
- Owned by Grange-Lindt Developers.
- Rent will be $85 per space per month.

Site B

Three alternatives, with three different conditions

- At northwest corner of Sharpe Avenue and Rory Street.
- Only one block from Tarquin Building.
- Already is a parking lot, with space rented to employees of MidWest Manufacturers and other local companies.
- Lot has 40 spaces; 15 are occupied by MidWest employees.
- MidWest Manufacturers is moving out to the suburbs in six weeks.
- Current rent is $45 per space per month; will go up to $55 in six weeks.
- Lot is owned by MidWest Manufacturers, who want to lease the 15 rental spaces their employees will soon vacate.
- They'll sign a one-year rental agreement, renewable annually unless lot is sold.

Site C

- Triangular lot at junction of Gravely Avenue and Martin Avenue.
- 2.5 blocks from Tarquin Building.
- Lot is owned by Kelvin Properties.
- Was site of Harry's Diner, which closed eight months ago when Harry died and a buyer couldn't be found.
- Shack-type building in very bad condition; it's now derelict and is scheduled to be removed in two weeks.
- Jack Kelvin is keen to rent the lot: he will sign a three-year contract at $600 per month.
- You make a sketch of the lot: it could hold 20 vehicles.
- Entry is from left-hand northbound lane of Martin Avenue, shortly

after it separates from Gravely Avenue.

- Renter will have to surface the lot. You get prices from local contractors:
  — Gravel surface: $2200
  — Asphalt surface: $5500
  You calculate a monthly cost per parking space, including amortizing the surfacing over the first 36 months. (You have to decide whether it should be gravel or asphalt.)

This morning you mention briefly to Karla Vipond, who is Manager of Operations (and your boss), that you think you have found additional parking spaces. You tell her there are several choices.

Now write up your findings

"Write me a proposal," she says, "and I'll take it to the executive meeting next month."

Because there are three sites, you will need to establish criteria for an "ideal" site, and include a comparative analysis in your proposal.

WEBLINKS

Proposals
www.io.com/~hcexres/tcm1603/acchtml/props.html
This document is part of an online course at Austin Community College. It describes types of proposals, their organization and format, and the common sections in a proposal. Several samples of proposals and a revision checklist are included.

Improving Your Style
www.uoguelph.ca/csrc/writing/style.htm
Improve your writing style at the University of Guelph Online Writing Centre by learning how to eliminate the passive voice, clean up errors, and think about overall tone.

The Fog Index
www.wtn.org/jan96/writestu.htm
Check the readability and level of your proposals through the steps outlined at this site on the Fog Index.

chapter 7

The Formal Report

Division manager Tim Higgins whistles when he reads the fourth letter in his morning mail, then he reaches for the telephone and punches in three numbers.

"Dave Kosty here."

"Dave, it's Tim. Can you come down for a minute? There's something I want to show you."

As soon as Dave steps into the office Tim announces, "I've just heard from the Quonset Corporation. They like your proposal."

"Great," Dave says, as he sits on the other side of Tim's desk, "but will they buy?"

"There's a good chance," Tim replies. "They want you to conduct a detailed study. They're thinking of installing 220 terminals."

"Two hundred and twenty!" Dave is surprised.

"Uh-huh," Tim murmurs. "Listen to this." He reads from the letter: "*We want to know the purchase price, predicted effect on sales, length of time to install, amount of operator training required, and total cost recovery time.*" Tim glances up at Dave. "Sounds promising!"

Dave nods thoughtfully. "They've really thought it through."

"But there's a catch: they want your report by the 29th. That's only ten days."

"Ten days!" Dave explodes. "Out of the question!"

"What are you working on now?"

"The proposal for Walston Oil."

"Can Sharon do it?"

"Yes, but . . . " Dave raises his arms in a shrug.

"Then hand it over. You'll have to drop everything."

"But ten days!"

Tim hands him the letter. "If that's what the client wants . . . ." He shrugs, as if to add, "then we have no choice."

"Well," Dave groans, "there goes the weekend!"

Tim agrees. "You'll have to pull out all the stops on this one. Give it the full treatment."

"Formal" refers to the report's appearance

"You mean write a formal report?"

Tim nods.

"I'm going to need some help."

"Oh, a formal report is not as formidable as it sounds," Tim reassures him. "After all, it has the same parts as a short report. They're just longer and the whole report is dressed up a bit more."

IN THIS CHAPTER

You will learn how to plan, write, assemble, and present a full formal report that will create a confident, persuasive impression. Specifically, you will learn how to

- develop a writing plan that arranges your information in a logical sequence,
- assign your information to the appropriate parts of the writing plan,
- organize the information within each part to create a cohesive, coherent narrative,
- extract the essential details to form an informative summary or abstract,
- develop a list of references or a bibliography,
- create appendices that support and expand on the details in the body of the report,
- compile all the report parts into an impressive-looking document, and
- write a cover letter or executive summary to accompany the report.

Writing a formal report demands careful attention to detail

Tim Higgins is right: the words "formal report" may convey the impression of a heavy, formidable document, yet in effect a formal report is similar to a medium-length semiformal investigation report. The main difference lies in its appearance and language. Where a semiformal report is more often a letter or memorandum with its collection of pages bound by a single staple, a formal report has a title page and clearly defined sections, each often starting on a fresh page, and the whole report is bound within a cover or jacket. Additionally, where an informal or semiformal report frequently is written in the first person (particularly "I," which is natural for a letter or memorandum), a formal report more often is written in the third person and, if it uses the first person at all, usually sticks to the plural "we."

The Report's Parts

A formal report normally has six primary information-bearing parts (shown in **bold** letters in the following list) and four subsidiary parts (shown in regular letters), in this sequence:

This is the traditional arrangement of report parts

Cover

Title Page

Summary (or **Abstract**)

Table of Contents

Introduction

Discussion

Conclusions

Recommendations

List of References (or Bibliography)

Appendices

Usually the report is preceded by a cover letter or executive summary, with either serving as a means for transmitting the report from one person or organization to another.

This sequence is known as the traditional arrangement of report parts and is illustrated in Figure 7-1. Guidelines for writing these parts and a complete formal report (titled "Evaluating the Effectiveness of Selected Canadian-Made Sunscreen Products," which starts on page 193) are provided on the following pages.

Cover Letter/Executive Summary

A cover letter is also known as a transmittal letter

A cover letter is used to move a formal report from originator to receiver. It is paper-clipped or stapled to the outside of the report's cover. Most cover letters simply state that the report is attached, describe its purpose, and identify on whose authority the project was undertaken, like this:

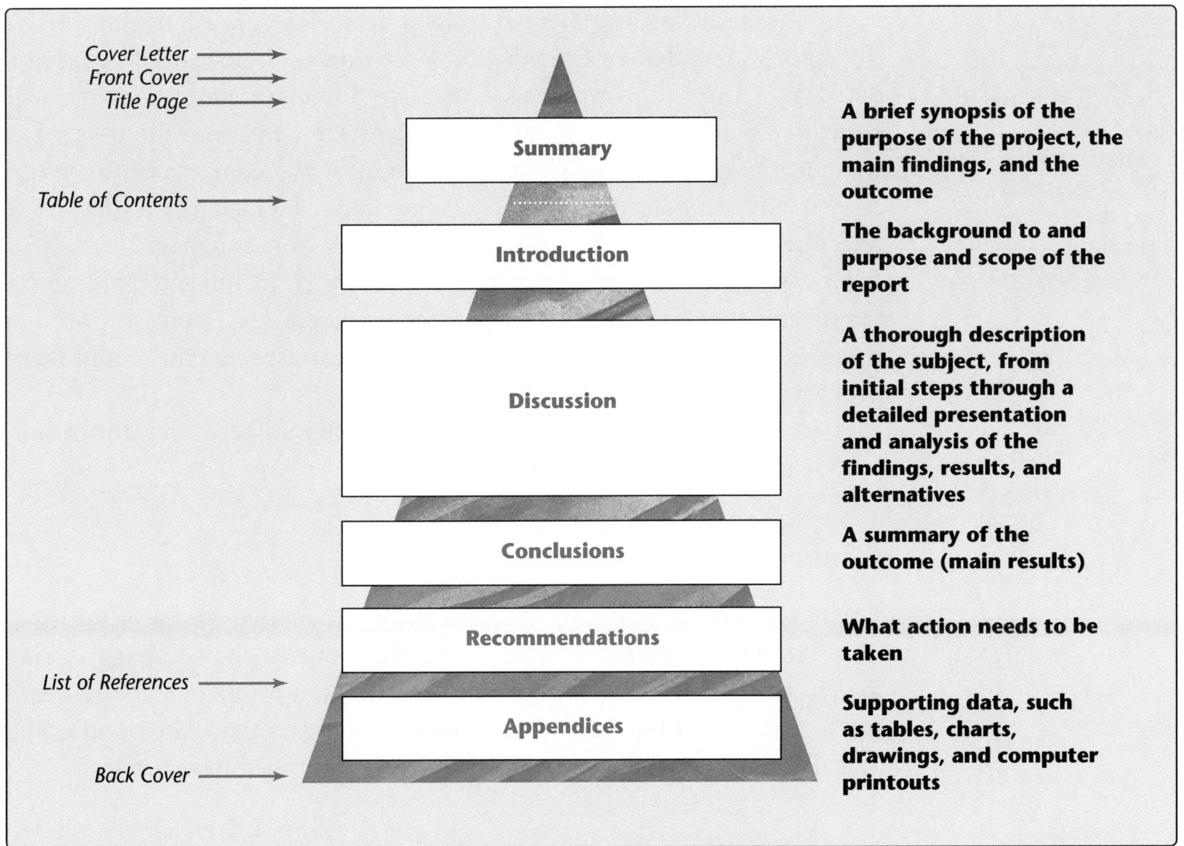

Figure 7-1 The writing plan for a formal report (traditional arrangement)

Dear Ms Pradahr

I enclose two copies of our report No. 2001/3, "Measuring the Effectiveness of the ConAir Invisible Antitheft System," as requested in your January 31, 2001 letter authorizing the project.

Please call me if you have any questions after you have read the report.

Regards

Janice Timmerman

If a cover letter also comments on or draws attention to specific information in the report, it becomes an Executive Summary. Its intent then is to inform the executive to whom it is addressed of certain features in the report that may not be readily apparent but could have important implications. When an Executive Summary conveys private, confidential, or financially sensitive information, the executive can remove it before circulating the report to other staff members. This is the traditional and most-used type of Executive Summary (see example on page 192).

The addressee often will remove the executive summary before circulating the report

A *traditional executive summary* draws attention to sensitive or confidential issues. An *integrated executive summary* summarizes the report's highlights

An alternative arrangement is to include an Executive Summary *inside* the report, immediately after the Table of Contents. Instead of being prepared as a letter, however, this Executive Summary simply has the title **Executive Summary** centred at the head of the page, and the text starts two lines below the title. The text summarizes the contents of the whole report, and may be two or three pages long. (When this is done, the Executive Summary often replaces the normal short summary.)

However, because this Executive Summary is an integral part of the report and therefore visible to everyone who receives a copy, it does *not* comment on confidential, financial, or political aspects that would be of primary interest to executives.

A report with an integral Executive Summary still requires a transmittal document such as a cover letter.

Cover (or Jacket)

The report's cover normally contains only one or two pieces of information: the title of the report and, often, the name of the company issuing the report. The title is set in bold letters and often printed on colored card stock. Sometimes the title is superimposed on a drawing or photograph that illustrates a product or a special aspect described in the report.

Title Page

The cover sets the mood; the title page establishes reader confidence

The title page follows immediately after the cover page and contains four pieces of information:

1. The report title (always exactly the same as on the cover page).
2. The name of the organization for which the report has been prepared, and sometimes the name of the person to whom it is directed.
3. The name of the organization issuing the report with, sometimes, the name of the person who wrote it.
4. The date the report is issued.

To create an effective title page, centre each piece of information between the left and right margins. Also space the information vertically with the title about 4.5 cm (2 inches) below the top of the page and about 4 cm (1 3/4 inches) between each entry, so that the date is about 4.5 cm to 5.5 cm above the bottom of the page. This spacing is illustrated on page 193.

Selecting an informative title is particularly important, so that readers will understand what the report is about and simultaneously be encouraged to read further. For example, a title such as

Offshore Surcharges

would create little interest. A better title would be

Surcharges on Offshore Shipments

but even it might make a reader wonder if the report contained only a list of the charges. Still better, because both more clearly define the report's scope, are

Assessment of Surcharges on Offshore Shipments

or

The Effect of Surcharges on Offshore Shipments

Summary (or Abstract)

The Summary is generally recognized as the most important page of a formal report, yet it can be the most difficult to write. It should catch readers' attention and encourage them to read the whole report. Consequently, it is placed right up front, immediately after the title page but before the table of contents.

A Summary must be short—no more than two or three paragraphs, even for a long report—yet it must cover all the key points presented within the report. It must also be coherent and written in simple language that anyone picking up the report will understand. And, although it is placed at the front of the report, it should be written last, after you have written all the information-bearing parts of the report (so you can draw on them to extract the key points).

Let the Summary sell your ideas and encourage the reader to dig further into the report

When writing a Summary, keep these six guidelines in mind:

- Assign the Summary a complete page to itself, and centre it horizontally and vertically on the page.
- Widen the margins on both sides and create an equal amount of space at the top and bottom of the page (see the Summary preceding the formal report on page 194).
- Centre the title "Summary" three lines above the first line of text.
- Check that the Summary has three, and sometimes four, parts that
  - — state the purpose of the study, project, or investigation,
  - — describe the main highlights,
  - — state the outcome or result, and
  - — suggest what action (if any) needs to be taken.

Tell readers right away what they most need to know

- Ensure that the Summary is informative and provides facts rather than just says the facts are there. For example:

  An Uninformative Summary
  An investigation has identified three ways to resolve delays in delivery of internal mail, one of which can be implemented economically and is recommended.

- Such a statement gives readers very little information on which to assess whether they want to read the report. Here is a better, more informative example:

  An Informative Summary
  Delays in delivery of internal mail can be resolved in one of three ways: by hiring a second mail clerk; by installing a laser mail coding system; or by contracting out the internal mail collection and delivery system. Hiring a second mail clerk is the most economical method, and is recommended.

- Centre the page number in lower-case roman numerals at the foot of the page.

For an example of an effective Summary, turn to page 194.

Table of Contents

The T of C demonstrates how well you have developed your information

A table of contents (T of C) not only helps readers find specific parts of the report, but also shows them the scope of the report and how its author has organized the information. To form the T of C, copy the headings in the report, using exactly the same words. (Your word processing program should be able to identify and store the entries for the T of C as you type. It then automatically compiles the headings into a draft T of C that you can view on screen or print out.) Here are some additional guidelines:

- Copy all but the most minor subheadings.
- Indent the major headings five spaces to the right of the left margin.
- Indent subheadings a further five spaces to the right, and sub-subheadings a further 10 spaces to the right, so that the different heading levels will be apparent to readers.
- Against each heading list the page number on which the heading appears. Set these page numbers in arabic numerals (except for the Summary page) as a column on the right side of the page, indented roughly five spaces (0.5 to 0.8 cm) from the left margin.
- Below the T of C, list the appendices with their identification letters and full titles, e.g.:

  A - Cost of Proposed Renovations

- Omit page numbers for appendix entries.
- Centre the heading "Table of Contents" or "Contents" two or three lines above the first entry. Similarly, centre the title "Appendices" three lines below the last T of C entry and two lines above the first appendix entry.
- Centre the report page number in lower-case roman numerals at the foot of each T of C page

A typical T of C is shown on page 195.

Introduction

The Introduction starts the narrative sections of the report and prepares readers for the detailed discussion that follows. It provides them with three pieces of information:

1. The Background to the project, study, situation, assignment, or events being reported. It describes the circumstances leading up to whatever work has been done, and may refer to previous studies or reports on the same topic.
2. The Purpose of the project, study, or assignment, and on whose authority it was undertaken.
3. The Scope of the work, which describes the extent of the study or project and defines its parameters.

Don't assume that readers have read the Summary; start afresh

These three parts need not be presented in this order, and may be interwoven rather than treated as separate items. A typical Introduction appears on page 196, as part of the formal report evaluating the effectiveness of sunscreen products.

Follow these guidelines when writing the Introduction:

- Start it on a fresh page and centre the title "Introduction" at the top.
- Centre the page number—it will be "1"—at the foot of the page, and let the number stand alone (that is, do not place it within brackets or insert a dash on either side of the number).
- If the Introduction finishes before the end of the page, decide whether the Discussion will continue on the same page or start on a fresh page, bearing in mind that
  — if the Discussion starts on the same page as the Introduction, the Conclusions and Recommendations should follow immediately after the end of the Discussion (i.e. they should *not* start on a new page), or
  — if the Introduction has a page (or pages) to itself, the Conclusions and Recommendations should start on a fresh page.

Present the Introduction and Conclusions in parallel form

In the formal report later in this chapter, the Discussion starts immediately after the Introduction (see page 196).

Discussion

Because every report addresses a different topic, the suggestions presented here can offer only a general plan for writing the Discussion. As a report writer, you will have to adapt the suggestions to your particular situation. Figure 7-2 shows that the Discussion is like a three-part story in which you

Do more than simply present the facts; *discuss* them

- outline your approach,
- describe what you did or found out, and
- discuss the results.

For example, Dick Johannsen has been evaluating delivery vans to determine the best purchase for the company's eight field service technicians. Now he is getting ready to write his report, so he types a brief outline of the points he will cover in the Discussion (see Figure 7-3).

By typing brief notes like these, Dick develops a basic writing plan that helps him write coherently and logically. In particular, he knows that management wants him to do more than just parade his findings in front of them: they want him to *analyse* the findings so they can more readily reach a decision.

In some reports—such as Dick's—the three parts of the Discussion can be identified clearly. In others they are present but are not so readily apparent. This is particularly true of the Approach section of the Discussion.

Positioning the Approach. Sometimes there may be similarities between part of the Introduction (particularly the Scope) and the start of the Discussion (particularly the Approach). For example, you may establish a study's terms of reference in the Scope, only to find that you also planned

A formal report does not seem nearly as formidable when separated into three logical compartments

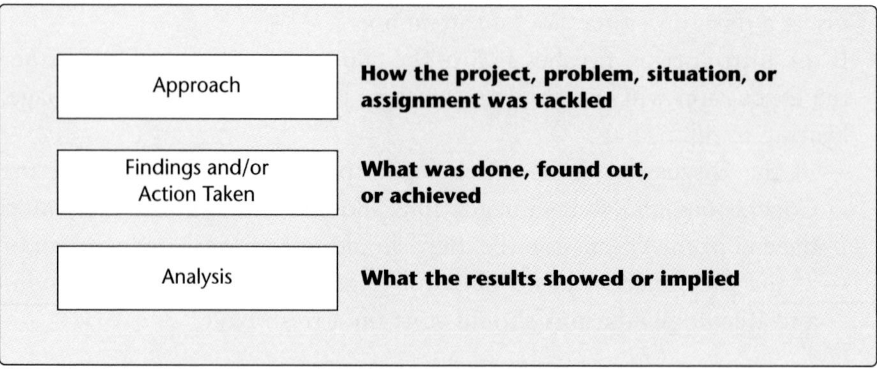

Figure 7-2 The Discussion has three main writing compartments

Discussion Outline

Approach

I will outline the steps I planned to take:

- Determine how much the company is willing to spend, what the vans will have to carry, and the technicians' special requirements.
- Identify which vans, from the range of vans available, seem to fit the company's needs.
- Establish which van is most suitable.

Findings

I will describe what I did:

- Talked to management and technicians to establish criteria for selecting the vans.
- Obtained van specifications from dealers.
- Identified which vans met the criteria.

Analysis

I will discuss my results:

- Identify the most important criteria (those that most influence the selection).
- Compare individual vans against the criteria.
- Identify which van best meets the company's needs.

Figure 7-3 Dick Johannsen's writing plan

to do that in the Approach. If this occurs, simply omit the terms of reference in the Discussion.

Organizing the Findings. The sequence in which you present your Findings will depend on the subject you are describing. For instance:

You can develop your information in three ways:

- **In chronological order**

- If you are describing the effect of a series of actions (such as the installation of a new computer network, the interruptions while it was being installed, and the delays created while staff were being trained), most likely you will present your information chronologically, in the order in which the events occurred.

- **As a concept**

- If you are describing an idea, or several ideas, you will most likely present your information in concept order; that is, you will present your ideas in the best sequence to persuade the reader that the information is important and your recommendations should be acted upon. For example, Karen Schmidt has studied job sharing in other companies and hopes to persuade her management to institute a job-sharing program. However, she knows that her management is only marginally partial to the idea, so in her report she first establishes what the company can gain by becoming involved in job sharing, and then describes the job-sharing programs she has studied.

• In subject order

• If you are evaluating equipment or conducting a comparative analysis (such as Dick Johannsen's evaluation of vans), you will probably present your Findings in subject order; that is, you will group the topics into evaluation compartments. Dick, for example, would group the vans either by their names or by his evaluation criteria:

Use subject order to evaluate different ideas, methods, or products

Item Grouping	***Evaluation Grouping***
Minivan:	Purchase Price:
Purchase price	Minivan
Operating cost	Maxivan
Interior space	Careervan
Size of access door	Utilivan
Maxivan:	Operating Cost:
Purchase price	Minivan
Operating cost	Maxivan
Interior space	Careervan
Size of access door	Utilivan
(etc)	(etc)

When introducing each main topic (e.g. Minivan or Purchase Price), Dick should follow the initial heading with a brief paragraph that establishes why the van is included or the topic is important. For example, for Item Grouping he would write:

The Minivan

The Minivan was included in the evaluation because of its low purchase price, low operating cost, and well-established record for reliability.

1. ***Purchase Price.*** The Minvan sells for a base price of $24 500, which includes all the desired options except automatic transmission and a roof rack. These options would cost an additional $1300, bringing the price up to $25 800.

Maintain objectivity by establishing criteria, then comparing each product against the criteria

For Evaluation Grouping he would write:

Purchase Price

The capital budget established for purchasing eight vans is $208 000, or a maximum of $26 000 per van.

1. ***Minivan.*** The Minivan's base price is $24 500, which means it is priced well inside the prescribed budget. However, as the base price does not include automatic transmission or a roof rack, a further $1300 has to be added for a total price of $25 800 per van.

Conducting a Comparative Analysis. A comparative analysis, such as Dick Johannsen's evaluation of vans, may be presented either objectively or subjectively, as illustrated in Figure 7-4. In a primarily **objective** analysis, as depicted by the left-hand column in Figure 7-4, you present *facts*:

1. Introduce the products, plans, processes, or services you will be evaluating, and identify why you chose them.
2. Describe each product, etc, you are evaluating *without* offering any opinion about it or commenting on its suitability. Ideally, list the items in a descending (i.e. best to worst) or ascending (worst to best) order.
3. Establish, and prove, the criteria you will use to assess the suitability of the products, plans, processes, or services.
4. Compare each product, etc, against the criteria. (*Never* compare products, etc, against each other: that's the fastest way to write a confusing report!) Now you can allow some subjectivity to creep into your narrative: your readers will expect to "hear your voice," to feel your presence as you analyse the data.
5. Draw your conclusions and make your recommendation.

Now you can let your presence be felt!

In a primarily **subjective** analysis (see the right-hand column in Figure 7-4), you still present facts but you also discuss them:

1. Introduce the products, plans, processes, or services you will be evaluating, and identify why you chose them.
2. Establish, and prove, the criteria you will use to measure the products, etc, you plan to evaluate. (Establishing the criteria *before* describing the products, etc, is the first major difference between a subjective and an objective analysis.)
3. Describe each product, plan, process, or service, this time also commenting on its suitability by comparing it against the criteria. (Offering opinions *during* the descriptions is the second major difference between a subjective and an objective analysis.) Again, list the items in best-to-worst or worst-to-best sequence.
4. Draw your conclusions and make your recommendation.

In the subjective approach there is no need to have a separate evaluation section following the product descriptions, because an analysis of each product, plan, process, or service has been integrated with each description at point 3.

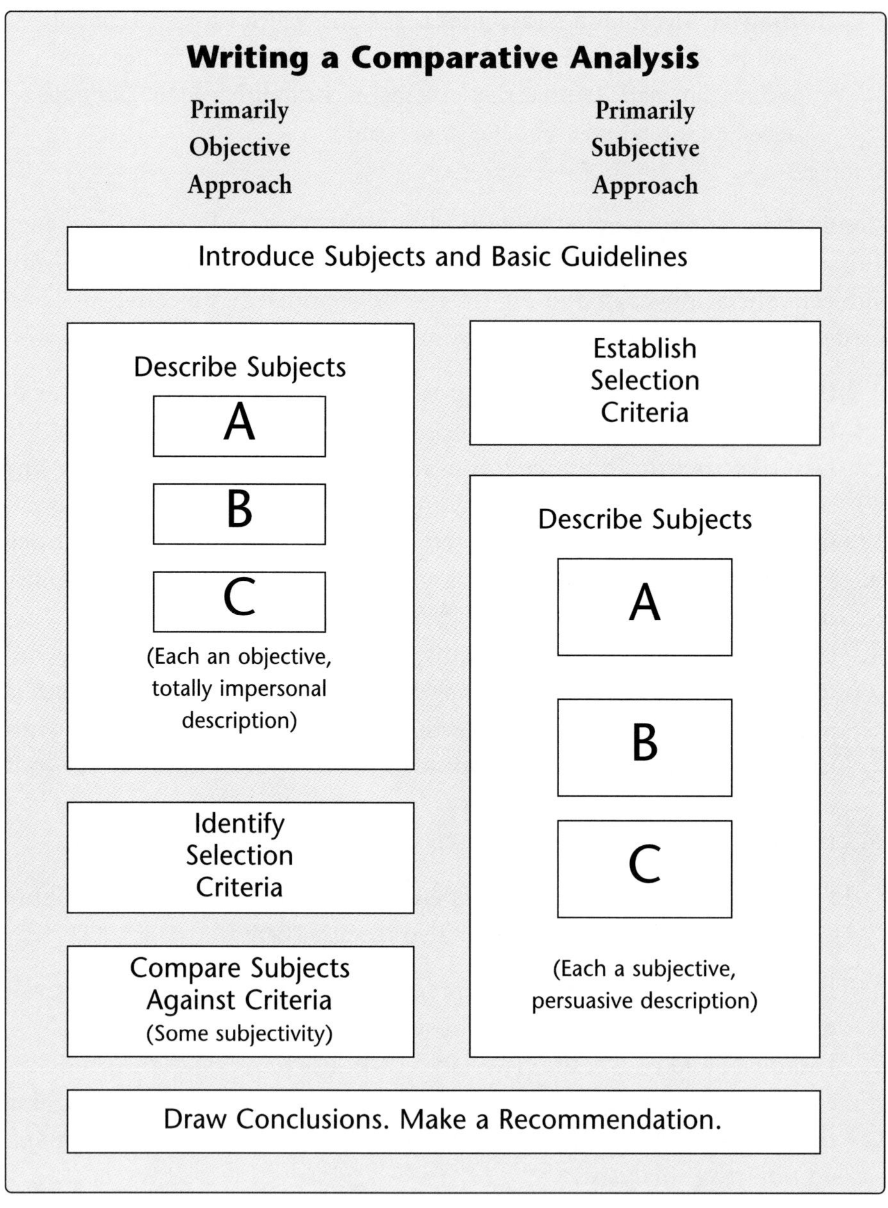

Figure 7-4 Alternative methods for writing a comparative analysis

Organizing the Sections. You can structure each section of the Discussion as an internal mini-report by arranging each section so that it follows its own miniature Introduction-Discussion-Conclusions format (see Figure 7-5):

1. Open with a brief paragraph or even just one or two sentences that tell readers what the section is about and what they can expect to find within it. For example:

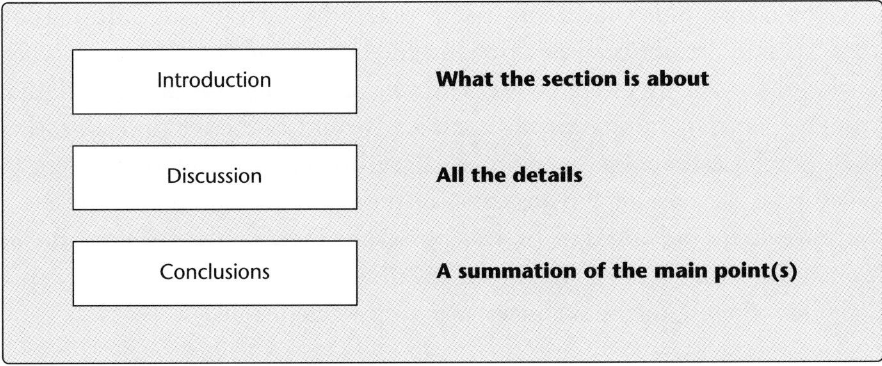

Figure 7-5 Use an Introduction-Discussion-Conclusions arrangement to organize each section of the report

> **Broadening the Scope of the Project**
>
> Further examination of the company's list of job classifications showed that several additional positions would be suitable for job sharing. These comprised . . .

2. Continue with the full development of the section. For the above example, the sentences that follow should identify the positions and explain why each would be suitable for job sharing.
3. Close the section with a brief summation of the key points, or the outcome:

> The 38 employees holding these positions were approached and seven agreed to try job sharing.

Avoid using the expression "in conclusion" or "I conclude" in the closing section of a mini-report. Reserve such expressions for the true Conclusions at the end of the whole report.

Nesting pyramids within pyramids is essential in a long report

Conclusions

You may ask: "Why do I need to draw conclusions, when the Analysis section of the Discussion seems already to have done that?"

Keep in mind that while the Conclusions *do* repeat some of the information in the earlier parts of the report, this duplication is intentional. Some readers—particularly busy executives—will read the Introduction and then immediately turn to the Conclusions (to discover the main outcome) and the Recommendations (to identify what needs to be done). Then they decide whether they need to read the whole report or will send it to one of their staff for a detailed reading.

Conclusions must never surprise a reader by introducing information that has not already been described in the Discussion. For example, when Dick Johannsen investigated vans for his company, he discovered that from a financial standpoint the company would do better to lease rather than purchase the vans outright. Because his terms of reference were to investigate the cost of *buying* vans, in the Discussion he had to insert a section on the advantages of leasing. Only then could he state in his Conclusions that leasing was more advantageous.

Follow these guidelines for writing your Conclusions:

Conclusions sum up the major findings and ideas presented in the Discussion

- Keep them short.
- Check that they answer or respond to the objectives established in the Introduction.
- State the primary conclusion first, and follow it with subordinate conclusions in decreasing order of importance.
- If there is only one conclusion, write it as a single paragraph.
- If there are two or more conclusions, use subparagraphs.
- *Never* advocate action (i.e. never say what should be done); save that for the Recommendations.

Recommendations

Recommendations *must* advocate action and, like the Conclusions, must never introduce new information. Use these guidelines for writing Recommendations:

Never write a wishy-washy recommendation

- Keep them short.
- Make them strong: use the active voice and personal pronouns:

  I recommend that the company install a networked personal computer in each division manager's office.

- Avoid using the unassertive passive voice and unidentified writer:

  It is recommended that a networked personal computer be installed in each division manager's office.

- State the primary recommendation first, and follow it with subsidiary recommendations.
- When making a personal recommendation, use the personal pronoun "I." When making a company recommendation, or if you are representing more than one person, use the plural "we."
- Check that the Recommendations evolve naturally from the Conclusions and the Discussion.

Conclusions and Recommendations are sometimes referred to jointly as a Terminal Summary

- If there is more than one recommendation, use a separate subparagraph for each recommendation.

List of References

A list of references identifies the sources from which data has been obtained during a study or investigation. These sources need to be listed in the report that evolves from the study, for four reasons:

Use source references to prove your facts

1. To demonstrate the validity of the data mentioned in the report.
2. To help readers find the information, if they want to refer to the original source.
3. To acknowledge the writer or speaker as the originator of the information.
4. To prevent you from being accused of plagiarism.

If Shirley Curzon writes, "Only 38% of children in Saskatchewan have access to approved day care centres," her readers are likely to sit up and say: *How do you know that? Did you go out and count them?* If Shirley has done some original research and determined these figures herself, she should say so in her report. But if she obtained the data from a private or Government of Saskatchewan report, she must identify it as her source.

Shirley can list her data sources in three ways:

1. In a numbered list, known as a list of references, placed at the end of her report.
2. In an alphabetical list, known as a bibliography, also placed at the end of her report.
3. As a footnote, entered at the foot of the page on which the data is mentioned.

A list of references is the most commonly used method for business reports; a bibliography is used primarily in scientific and academic reports; footnotes, although occasionally still seen in some documents, are rarely used in modern business reports.

Typographical errors and misspelled names or document titles are *not* acceptable

Regardless of which source-referencing method you use, *you must be accurate*. If you misspell an author's name or a document's title, your readers will have difficulty identifying and ordering that document. This situation will be particularly true if you are conducting a library search using a computer "browse" program. If you use a manual card search system, you will probably rationalize that, if the name Bertrand Jurgens is spelled incorrectly in a reference at the end of a report, it is probably the Bertram Jorgen listed on the library's index card. But a computer is less accommodating and is likely to display the message *Author name not found* if the name does not exactly match the computerized records.

Building a List of References (Endnotes)

In business reports, a list of references is more common than a bibliography

As a report writer you are responsible for recording sources in a recognizable manner, adopting the style guidelines of an authority such as the Modern Languages Association (MLA), the Canadian Press (CP), or The University of Chicago Press, which uses the Chicago Manual (CM) style. The guidelines printed here tell you what details you need to record and suggest a style most commonly used in Canadian business reports. Remember, however, that there are many opinions on the correct way to list references, so before writing your first report check with your employer that the system you propose is acceptable.

Book by One Author. Copy the following information from the book and list it in this order:

Author's name
Book title (set in italics)
Publisher details (enclose this part within brackets):
  City of publication (followed by a colon)
  Publisher's name
  Copyright date (the most recent copyright date)
The page number on which the specific information you are referring to begins (list only the starting page)

For example:

1. Renée Larivière, *Finding Venture Capital for Young Entrepreneurs* (Montreal, Québec: Favori Publishers Inc, 1999), p 17.

Book by Two Authors. Insert the authors' names in the order they are listed in the book; all other information remains the same:

Insert punctuation and brackets exactly as shown

2. Marrianne G Arsenault and Wilhelm V Buchmeier, *Managing Job-Sharing in the 21st Century* (Halifax, Nova Scotia: The Treadmill Press, 2000), p 145.

Book by Three or More Authors. Insert only the first author's name and follow it with the words "and others" (the Latin expression *et al.* is no longer used):

3. Franklin Woodhaus and others, *Seniors: Canada's Primary Market for the Twenty-first Century* (Winnipeg, Manitoba: Prairie Publishers' Press, 2001), p 203.

Book as a Subsequent Edition. If a book is a second, third or fourth edition, as often is the case with textbooks, insert the edition number immediately after the book title. Abbreviate the edition number to 2nd, 3rd, etc, and "edition" to "Edn" but do not underline or set the abbreviated words in italics. To refer to the third edition of this book, and this page, you would write:

4. Ron Blicq, *Communicating at Work: Creating Messages that Get Results*, 3rd Edn (Don Mills, Ontario: Prentice Hall Canada Inc, 2001), p 181.

Book with Multiple Authors and an Editor. When a book is a compendium of articles or essays, each written by a different author, two rules apply:

- If you refer to the book generally (possibly to the preface written by the editor), then identify the editor as the primary name in your listing and insert "ed" (for editor) after his or her name:

5. Frances M Spivak, ed, *Trans-Pacific Marketing* (Vancouver, British Columbia: Bonus Books Ltd, 2000), p 3.

Inserting a period after a person's initials or after the "p" of page number is optional

- If you refer to one of the articles or chapters written by one of the contributing authors, you will need more detailed information:

  Author's name (or authors' names, if more than one)
  Article or chapter title (place it within quotation marks)
  Book title (set it in italics)
  Editor's name (insert "ed" in front of the name)
  Publisher details:
    City of publication (followed by a colon)
    Publisher's name
    Copyright date (the most recent)
  Page number on which article or chapter starts

For example:

6. Wing L Matsubara and Dennis M Engstrom, "Communication Between Business Peoples of the Pacific Rim," *Trans-Pacific Marketing*, ed Frances M Spivak (Vancouver, British Columbia: Bonus Books Ltd, 2000), p 156.

"ed" means "editor" or "edited by"; "Edn" means "edition"

Some Comments and Rules for Referencing Books. In the six references listed above, notice that

- Commas are used consistently to separate the author identification and the book title (i.e. the book identification).
- The entries are numbered, in the same sequence that they are referred to in the report narrative.
- The left-hand edge of each entry is set as a solid block (i.e. each line is indented the same amount from the left margin).

- The sequence in which the parts of each entry are presented is mandatory, as are these conventions:
  —Set the book title in italics (or underline it if you are writing by hand).
  —Place quotation marks around an internal title.
  —Place brackets around the publisher identification.
  —Insert a colon between the city of publication and the publisher's name.
  —Quote only the first page number of a source reference.

Magazine or Journal Article. The guidelines for source-referencing a magazine or journal article are similar to those for a book. Copy the following information from the magazine and list it in this order:

Author's name (or authors' names)
Title of the article (place quotation marks around it)
Magazine or journal title (set it in italics)
Volume and issue number
Month or date of issue
Page number on which article starts

In handwritten or typewritten reports, underline the title

Here is an example:

7. Sudir Saha, "The Four P's of Personnel Management," *The Human Resource*, 6:4, September 2000, p 15.

Additional Guidelines for Referencing Magazine and Journal Articles. Here are some additional guidelines:

- List authors' names exactly as you would for a book.
- If no author's name is shown at the top of an article, start the entry with the title of the article (in quotation marks).
- Omit the words "Vol." and "Issue No." Simply insert the two numbers, one on either side of a colon: 21:7.
- Write the issue date exactly as it is written in the magazine or journal.
- Omit the magazine or journal editor's name.

Business Report. For a report, copy the following information in this order:

Author's name (or authors' names)
Title of the report (set it in italics)
Report number (if the report has one)
Name of organization issuing the report
City and province (or US state) of issuing organization
Date of report
Page number in report from which information has been derived (list only the first page). This item is optional.

The report written by David Horoschuk at the end of this chapter would be listed like this:

8. David Horoschuk, *Evaluating the Effectiveness of Selected Canadian-Made Sun Protection Products*, The Proving Ground, Burlington, Ontario, February 5, 2001.

If the author of the report is not identified, start the entry with the report title.

Electronic Documents. An electronic storage medium often is used to store, in a very compact form, lengthy documents and information that have been published elsewhere. The medium may be CD-ROM, a 3.5 inch disk, or magnetic tape, in which case it is continually accessible, or it may be online, such as on a Web page or the Internet, in which case its presence may be only transitory and there is no guarantee it will continue to be accessible. For that reason, you need to record not only the electronic source of the item, but also its original identification (i.e. as a book, journal article, newsletter, etc):

Electronic documents and messages can be listed too

author's name (if an author is identified),
title of excerpt (place quotation marks around it)
title of publication (*set it in italics*)
name of electronic medium (e.g. CD-ROM, disk, magnetic tape), and
city of publication
name of publisher } (of the electronic medium, set within brackets)
date of publication

For example:

9. Thomas L Warren, "Cultural Influences on International Communication" in *ISTC Golden Opportunities Anniversary CD*. CD-ROM (Letchworth, Herts, UK: The Institute of Scientific & Technical Communicators, August 1998).

If the information is presented *only* on a Web page (i.e. there is no printed equivalent), the entry should contain

Web identification is set within angle brackets

author's name (if an author is identified),
title of the specific piece of information (within quotation marks),
title of the "document" (*in italics*)
the date the information was entered (day [numeral], month [spelled out], year [numeral]), and
the Web identification <within angle brackets>.

For example:

10. J James Conklin, "How to Write Proposals That Win!" in *TCI 99: The Fourth Annual Technical Communication Institute.* 19 January 1999 <http://www.umanitoba.ca/faculties/con_ed/partners/tci>.

If the information has also been published elsewhere (in print form), then the entry should contain

the full printed identification (for a book, article, paper, etc),
the date the information was entered on the Web site (day, month year), and
the Web identification <within angle brackets>.

For example:

11. "Are You Drowning in Email?" in *RGI News*, No. 3, Fall 1998. 2 February 1999 <http://www.rgi-intl.com>.

Even conversations can be referenced as information sources . . .

Letter or Conversation. Communications between individuals—by letter, memorandum, telephone, fax, face-to-face, or email—are all referenced in roughly the same way. In each case, record the information in this order:

Originator details:
- Writer's or speaker's name
- Writer's or speaker's company or organization
- City and province/state of company or organization
- Type of communication (i.e. letter, memo, fax, email, conversation)

Receiver's identification:
- Reader's or listener's name (most often you, as the writer of the report)
- Reader's or listener's company or organization
- City and province/state of company or organization

The date (that the communication took place)

Here is a reference entry for correspondence:

12. Phyllis Horton, Sarrandon Business Consultants, Prince Albert, Saskatchewan, letter to Michelle Desaulniers, Marketing Canada Incorporated, Hull, Quebec, May 18, 2000.

Here is a reference to an email:

13. Karla D Devinney, "Re: Selecting a Conference Site," in email to Marilyn Peters, 21 February 2001.

And this is an entry for a conversation:

14. Peter Quon, Quon-Lee Manufacturing Company Ltd, Burnaby, British Columbia, in conversation with Dennis Piper, Craven Electronics Centre, Vancouver, British Columbia, January 5, 2001.

A Speech or Conference Paper. If you are referring to something said by a speaker at a meeting or conference, record the following:

. . . and so can oral presentations

Speaker's name
Title of speech or conference paper (set it in italics)
Name of organization holding the meeting or conference
City and province/state where the meeting or conference was held
The date the presentation occurred

An entry for a speech would look like this:

15 Julie Fisher, *Looking to the Future: Where Does Technical Communication Go From Here?*, speaking at the Ideas to Communication conference, Melbourne, Australia, November 13, 1999.

Repeated References to the Same Document. If, in your report, you refer to the same document more than once, but to a different page each time, you need to insert the full reference entry only once. For the second and subsequent references to the same document, simply state the author's surname (or authors' surnames) and the new page number, like this:

16. Matsubara and Engstrom, p 211.

Use a shorter form to reference the same source more than once

If you have listed more than one publication by the same author, you may need to identify which one you are referring to in a subsequent entry that lists only the author's name. To do this, insert the year the publication was issued (in parentheses) immediately after the author's name:

17. Larivière (1999), p 218.

(Note that the once-popular expressions *ibid.* and *op. cit.* are no longer used in multiple-document referencing.)

Drawing Attention to the Source Reference. The report narrative must draw attention to every entry in the list of references. To do so, insert a superscript (raised) number into the text, immediately after quoting, alluding to, or mentioning information drawn from another writer or speaker. The superscript number identifies the entry in the list of references. For example:

Create textual cross-references

Only 38% of children in Saskatchewan have access to approved day care centres.[3]

If you are unable to print superscript characters, place the reference number within brackets:

A report from the University of Alberta (4) states . . .

Creating a Bibliography

A bibliography performs the same function as a list of references, with one major difference:

- In a list of references you list *only* those documents that are directly related to the report, and refer to all of them within the report.
- In a bibliography you list as many documents as you feel are generally related to the subject and may prove of interest to the report reader, and you do not have to refer to all of them within the report.

The information contained in a bibliographical entry is essentially the same as that in a list of references, but the method of presentation differs. The differences are identified by the following guidelines and illustrated in Figure 7-6.

First-named authors' surnames determine the bibliography sequence

- List the individual bibliographical entries in alphabetical order, using the surname of each first-named author to determine the sequence. For example, in Figure 7-6 *Arsenault* is listed first, *Quon* is in the middle, and *Woodhaus* is at the end. If the author's name is not shown on the document, use the first letter in the document's title to determine the document's alphabetical position.
- Omit entry numbers.

Only the first-named author's name is reversed

- Reverse the order of the first-named author in each entry, so that the author's surname appears first (for example, Janet B Frelinn becomes Frelinn, Janet B) but do *not* reverse the order of the second author (see the first entry in Figure 7-6).
- Carry the first line of each bibliography entry about 1 cm or 5 keystroke spaces to the left, so that it stands out from the subsequent lines of the entry:

> Finnisterre, Jack B. "Methods of Reducing Overhead to Increase Product
>   Competitiveness in a North American Free Trade Environment."
>   *Small Business Owners' Review*, 15:2, February 2001.

- Insert a period to separate the three main compartments of each entry for a book, report, or journal:
  - — One immediately after the author's name (or authors' names).
  - — One immediately after the document title (book or report title, or article title if a magazine).

  The previous entry for Jack Finnisterre shows how these periods are positioned.

BIBLIOGRAPHY

Arsenault, Marrianne G, and Wilhelm V Buchmeier. *Managing Job-Sharing in the 21st Century*. Halifax, Nova Scotia: The Treadmill Press, 2000.

Conklin, J James. "How to Write Proposals That Win!" *The Fourth Annual Technical Communication Institute*. 19 January 1999. <http://www.umanitoba.ca/faculties/con_ed/partners/tci>.

Devinney, Karla D. "Re: Selecting a Conference Site." Email to Marilyn Peters. 21 February 2001.

Fisher, Julie. *Looking to the Future: Where Does Technical Communication Go From Here?* Ideas to Communication conference, Melbourne, Australia. November 13, 1999.

Horoschuk, David. *Evaluating the Effectiveness of Selected Canadian-Made Sun Protection Products.* Report: The Proving Ground, Burlington, Ontario. February 5, 2001.

Horton, Phyllis, Sarrandon Business Consultants, Prince Albert, Saskatchewan. Letter to Michelle Desaulniers, Marketing Canada Incorporated, Hull, Quebec. May 18, 2000.

Matsubara, Wing L, and Dennis M Engstrom. "Communication Between Business Peoples of the Pacific Rim." *Trans-Pacific Marketing*, ed Frances M Spivak. Vancouver, British Columbia: Bonus Books Ltd, 2000.

Quon, Peter, Quon-Lee Manufacturing Company Ltd, Burnaby, BC. Conversation with Dennis Piper, Craven Electronics Centre, Vancouver, British Columbia, January 5, 2001.

Saha, Sudir. "The Four P's of Personnel Management." *The Human Resource*, 6:4, September 2000.

Spivak, Frances M, ed. *Trans-Pacific Marketing*. Vancouver, BC: Bonus Books Ltd, 1997.

Woodhaus, Franklin, and others. *Seniors: Canada's Primary Market for the Twenty-first Century*. Winnipeg, Manitoba: Prairie Publishers' Press, 2001.

Hanging indents enable easy identification of alphabetical sequence

Each entry has three distinct parts, separated by periods

Figure 7-6 A bibliography formed from some of the references quoted as examples on the previous pages

- For a book, do not insert brackets around the publisher's identification (i.e. the city, publisher's name, and copyright date).
- Omit the page number of all entries except those in which only an illustration or a short item in a major work is being referenced.

Because bibliography entries are not numbered, a way has to be found to refer to those that support statements made in the body of the report. To do this, insert a bracketed entry containing the author's surname (or authors' surnames) and the appropriate page number into the report narrative. For example:

Textual cross-references are more detailed for bibliography entries

A report from the University of Alberta (Winoski, p 22) states that . . .

If two publications by the same author are listed in the bibliography, insert the year of the appropriate publication immediately after the author's name:

A report from the University of Alberta (Winoski, 2001, p 22) states that . . .

Forming Footnotes

Footnotes are used only occasionally today, since most business report writers find them more awkward to use than endnotes. When they are used, the following guidelines apply:

- Insert footnotes at the bottom of the page, reducing the length of the typing area to make space for them. See the foot of this page for an example.[1]
- Insert a consecutive superscript number ([1, 2, 3] etc, as in the line above), at the appropriate place in the narrative, and always on the same page as the footnote.
- Arrange the information in exactly the same way that you would for an endnote (i.e. an entry in a list of references).
- Indent the first line of the footnote to the right, 1 cm for handwriting or five characters or spaces for typing (see the example at the foot of this page).
- Superscript the footnote number, do not place a period after it, and set it immediately in front of the first letter in the footnote.
- To refer to the same document more than once, write it in full the first time and then insert only the author's surname (or authors' surnames) and the new page number each subsequent time.[2]

Footnotes can be awkward to arrange on the page

---

[1]Carolyn G Wicks and Dennis Alferton, *Computer Literacy in Business* (Edmonton, Alberta: The Business Bookshelf, 2000), p 86.

[2]Wicks and Alferton, p 144.

Appendix

The appendix provides a storage area for drawings, graphs, test results, detailed calculations, computer printouts, and miscellaneous documents such as a manufacturer's catalogue, brochure, or product specifications. The individual pages or whole documents are inserted at the back of the report, rather than in the Discussion, to prevent them from impeding reading continuity.

The following guidelines apply to preparing and presenting appendices:

- Ensure that every document in the appendix *contributes* to the report and *is referred to* in the Introduction or Discussion. (Never create an appendix so that it becomes merely a storage area for a piece of information that may be of only marginal interest.)
- Insert the appendices in the order in which you refer to them in the report. If you refer first to a graph, label it Appendix A; if you refer next to a pension calculation table, label it Appendix B. (Label appendices alphabetically, not numerically.)
- Centre the appendix identification at the top of the first page of the appendix, immediately above the appendix title. For example:

Appendix D

Comparison of Insurance Claims: 2000 to 2001

- Restate the appendix identification on each subsequent page of the appendix, either at the top right by inserting App D so that the "D" is flush with the right margin, or as part of the page number, as in D-2, D-3, D-4, etc.
- If there is only one appendix, simply title the page Appendix (do not assign an appendix identification letter).
- Number the appendix page numbers in one of two ways:
  1. Treat each appendix as a stand-alone document, and number its pages starting at "1" (the preferred method).
  2. Treat the appendices as part of the whole report. For example, if the last narrative page of the report is 16, label the first page of Appendix A as "17" and continue to number the pages consecutively through all the appendices.

Appendices provide evidence to support what you say in the report

Each appendix is a separate, stand-alone document

Sample Formal Report

The formal report in Figure 7-9, pages 193 to 206, was prepared by Dave Horoschuk, a senior consultant with The Proving Ground of Burlington,

Client authorizes study, describes project background, and establishes guidelines

Skin Care Unlimited
310 Benjamin Street
Mississauga ON M5W 1X3

January 17, 2001

Hannah Petrie
President
The Proving Ground
1011 - 240 Menzies Street
Burlington ON L7G 4V3

Dear Ms Petrie

We accept your proposal of January 9 to undertake tests on our new sunscreen *Whisper* and six other Canadian sunscreens, as defined in our Request for Proposal dated January 3, 2001.

The tests are to comprise the following:
- Direct protection against sunburn.
- Comfortableness on and ease of removal from the skin.
- Ease of removal from clothing.
- Water resistance.

We decline your proposal to conduct UVA and UVB tests, since this was done during development of the sunscreen.

The total cost of the project will be $29 525, plus 7% GST.

The results of your tests are to be delivered in preliminary form on February 5, and in final form—as a formal report—on February 9, 2001.

Please acknowledge your acceptance of this order by email to
r.maguire@skincare.com
no later than January 20, 2001. I look forward to receiving the results of your tests.

Sincerely

Rachel Maguire

Rachel Maguire
Marketing Manager
Skin Care Unlimited

Figure 7-7 The letter authorizing sunscreen testing

Ontario. Three of The Proving Ground's consultants have evaluated the quality of seven sunscreen products for Skin Care Unlimited in Mississauga, Ontario, whose letter authorizing them to do the work is shown in Figure 7-7. The following sections comment on the cover letter and the report.

Comments on the Cover Letter

David Horoschuk wrote and identified himself as the author of the report, although Hannah Petrie, as president of the company, signed the cover letter in Figure 7-8. This is similar to the arrangement for the cover letter preceding the proposal written by Sandi McPherson in Chapter 6.

Hannah's cover letter does more than simply say: "Here is our report." Instead, in the letter she draws readers' attention to the key results that will be of most importance to them. This is the information that Skin Care Unlimited most wants to hear. In that sense, the cover letter says essentially the same as in the report's Summary. Yet the cover letter does not fall within the guidelines for an executive summary, because it does not touch on aspects that perhaps caution the reader or point to side issues that may evolve. For comparison, see Hannah Petrie's cover letter/executive summary accompanying the technical proposal in Figure 6-4 on page 143 of Chapter 6.

Client engages independent consultant to conduct an objective study

Comments on the Report

The title page identifies the topic of the report, states for whom the report has been prepared and who prepared it, and lists the date.

Although the report objectively evaluates seven sunscreen products, the Summary concentrates only on the qualities of *Whisper*. In doing so, Dave recognizes that the reader wants an immediate answer to the question: "How good is *our* product?"

The Summary is short and informative. Dave has drawn the information for it primarily from the Conclusions on page 8 of the report.

The Table of Contents clearly shows the logical approach The Proving Ground has taken: i.e. *Preparation, Testing, Evaluating.*

(Comments on the Report continue on page 207)

This cover letter summarizes key outcomes rather than acts solely as a transmittal document

The Proving Ground
1011 – 240 Menzies Street
Burlington ON L7G 4V3
(416) 317 2216

February 8, 2001

Rachel Maguire
Marketing Manager
Skin Care Unlimited
310 Benjamin Street
Mississauga ON M5W 1X3

Dear Ms Maguire

We have completed our evaluation of sunscreen proposals, as requested in your letter of January 17, 2001, and enclose three copies of our report describing the tests and our evaluation of the results. The report is titled "Evaluating the Effectiveness of Selected Canadian-Made Sunscreen Products."

As I mentioned in my preliminary report emailed to you on February 5, Skin Care Unlimited's new sunscreen *Whisper* was ranked as the best sun-protection product among the seven we tested. It is easy to apply and is very waterproof. From the point of view of ease of washing from the skin or from clothing, it was classified as "moderately easy."

We appreciated having the opportunity to carry out this interesting project for you. If you have questions evolving from the report, please call me or Dave Horoschuk at (416) 317 2216, extension 327.

Sincerely

Hannah Petrie

Hannah Petrie
President
The Proving Ground

Figure 7-8 The cover letter accompanying the report in Figure 7-9

The Proving Ground
1011 – 240 Menzies Street
Burlington ON L7G 4V3
(416) 317 2216

1

Evaluating the Effectiveness of Selected Canadian-Made Sunscreen Products

The title page must create a professional image

Prepared for
Rachel Maguire
Marketing Manager
Skin Care Unlimited
Mississauga ON

Prepared by
David Horoschuk
Senior Consultant
The Proving Ground

February 5, 2001

Figure 7-9 A formal report written by a consultant

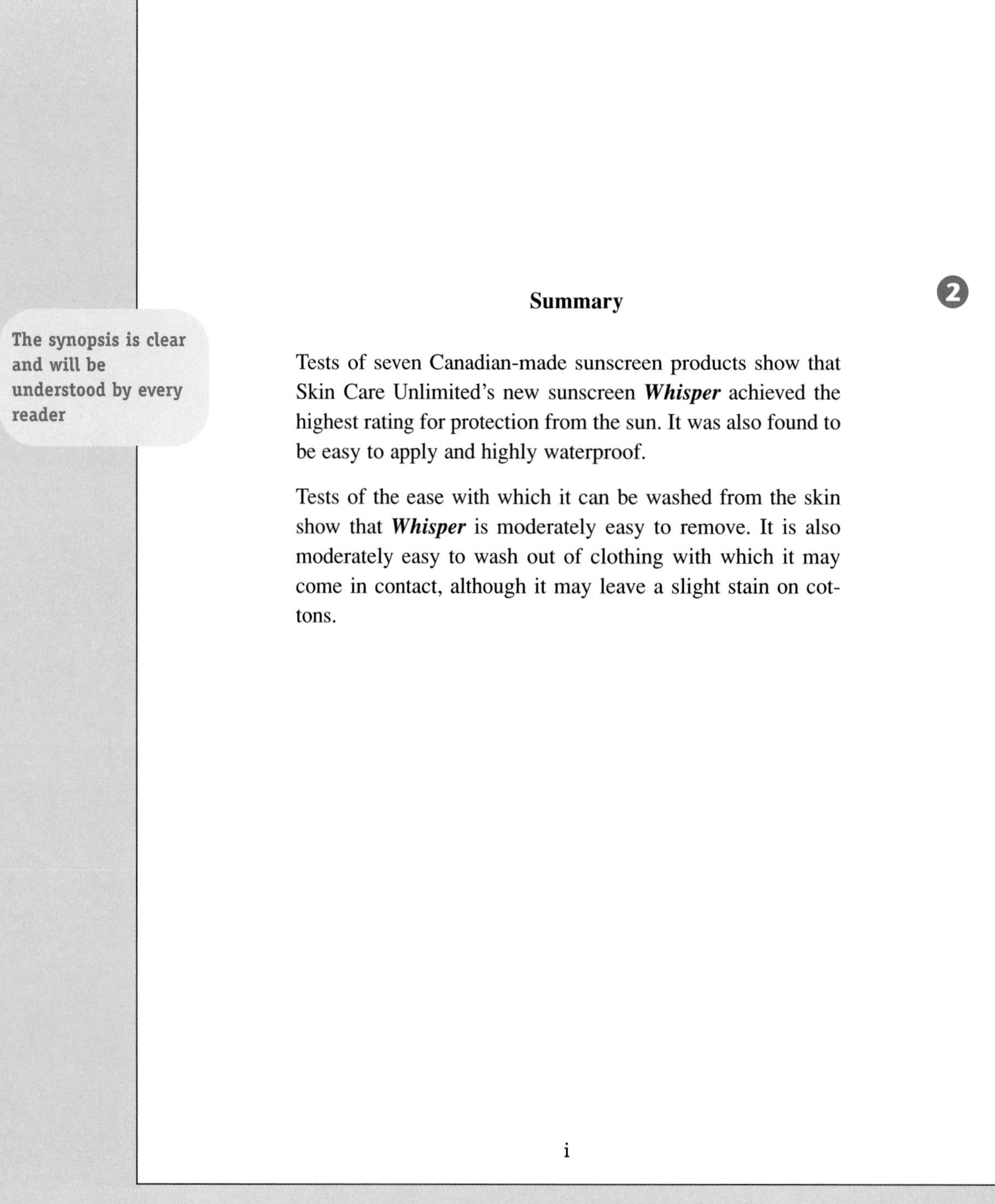

2

Summary

The synopsis is clear and will be understood by every reader

Tests of seven Canadian-made sunscreen products show that Skin Care Unlimited's new sunscreen ***Whisper*** achieved the highest rating for protection from the sun. It was also found to be easy to apply and highly waterproof.

Tests of the ease with which it can be washed from the skin show that ***Whisper*** is moderately easy to remove. It is also moderately easy to wash out of clothing with which it may come in contact, although it may leave a slight stain on cottons.

i

Figure 7-9 A formal report written by a consultant (*continued*)

Contents

ii

The T of C demonstrates the report's organization and comprehensiveness

Figure 7-9 A formal report written by a consultant (*continued*)

Evaluating the Effectiveness of Selected Canadian-Made Sunscreen Products

The Introduction establishes the purpose . . .

INTRODUCTION

Skin Care Unlimited of Mississauga, Ontario, has developed a new brand of sunscreen called *Whisper* which will be marketed in Canada starting in the early summer of 2001. Before launching a marketing program for the new product, Skin Care Unlimited wants to test the sunscreen's efficacy and to compare it with competing sunscreen products also manufactured in Canada. 4

In a letter dated January 17, 2001, Rachel Maguire, Marketing Manager for Skin Care Unlimited, authorized The Proving Ground (TPG) to carry out five tests:

1. Direct protection from the sun's rays.
2. Comfortableness on the skin.
3. Ease of removal from the skin.
4. Water resistance.
5. Ease of removal from clothing.

. . . describes the background . . .

The tests were to be conducted "blind" on *Whisper* and six competing sunscreens. Skin Care Unlimited would supply samples of the seven products.

. . . and identifies constraints

The tests were to be completed and this report submitted no later than February 9, 2001.

PREPARING FOR THE TESTS

Preparation for the tests involved concealing the identity of the sunscreens, selecting participants (models), and purchasing swimwear and body-masks that would provide apertures for applying the different sunscreens on the participants' torsos. 5

Concealing the Identity of the Sunscreens

To ensure that the identity of each sunscreen would be unknown throughout the tests, we instructed a TPG staff member who was not connected with the project to decant the seven sunscreens into unmarked containers and to label the containers from A through G. She then listed the sunscreens, cross-referenced them to the seven letters, and deposited the list in the Toronto-Dominion Bank in Burlington, Ontario, with instructions that the list was not to be released until 10 a.m. on February 5. 6

1

Figure 7-9 A formal report written by a consultant (*continued*)

Selecting the Participants

7 We recruited six participants to be test models—three males and three females—and within each group selected one person with a fair complexion, one with a medium complexion, and one with a darker complexion. From each we obtained assurance that they carried no residual tan from the previous summer and that they would be available for the five days of testing. As a term of employment, each participant was required to sign a waiver absolving Skin Care Unlimited and The Proving Ground of any responsibility for accident or future medical problems.

A careful, detailed description of preparatory steps . . .

Purchasing Sun-Exposure Clothing

8 To ensure maximum exposure for the backs and legs, for the female participants we purchased one-piece swimsuits with low-cut backs. For male participants we chose European-style swimbriefs. For both groups we also purchased two-piece track suits to be worn when the tests were not being performed, and a light hat to be worn at all times.

For additional protection we purchased form-fitting T-shirts that would not slide about, and in the back of each T-shirt cut eight 6-cm diameter round holes (see Figure 1), one hole for each sunscreen and one as a control in which no sunscreen would be applied.

. . . sets the scene for the test descriptions that follow

9

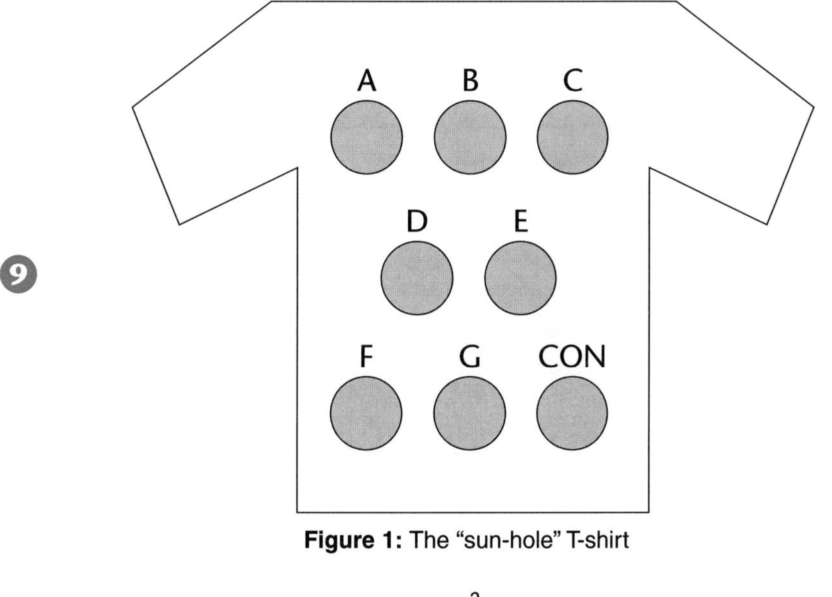

Figure 1: The "sun-hole" T-shirt

2

Figure 7-9 A formal report written by a consultant (*continued*)

The top of an embedded pyramid, covering this and the next page

Conducting the Tests

The tests were carried out in two locations: 10

- In Nassau, in the Bahamas, to test sun protection, product "feel," ease of application to and removal from the skin, and resistance to water.
- In our lab in Burlington, Ontario, to test the ease with which sunscreen that had contaminated clothing could be washed out.

Testing for Sun Protection

11 The participants and two TPG consultants flew to Nassau in the Bahamas on January 27 and returned on February 1. On arrival at the hotel the participants were instructed to remain indoors for the remainder of the day, and for the following days to keep their bodies covered with the track suits when they were outside, except when they were participating in the tests.

The First Set of Tests 12

The first tests were held on the morning of January 28. The participants wore their swimsuits, with the sun-hole T-shirt over the upper half of their body, a track suit bottom covering their legs, and hats.

In this section: a comfortable mix of predominantly active voice and some passive voice

13 The two TPG consultants applied the sunscreens onto the participants' backs, rubbing each sunscreen into the appropriately lettered hole in the T-shirts. To avoid one sunscreen affecting the results of another, the consultants applied sunscreen A to all six backs, then washed their hands thoroughly and applied sunscreen B to all six backs, and so on. The consultants also made notes of how easily each sunscreen could be applied, and asked the participants to comment on how each sunscreen felt on the skin.

The participants were then asked to lie face down, with their legs and the backs of their necks and heads covered, for 2.5 hours.

Immediately after the exposure test, the participants removed their T-shirts so that the consultants could note the color of the skin in each hole, touch the skin to check for skin tenderness, and record the results.

The participants were then encouraged to swim for 15 minutes, after which the consultants checked whether the sunscreen was still present or had partly or fully washed off.

3

Figure 7-9 A formal report written by a consultant (*continued*)

The consultants checked the participants' skin color and tenderness twice more, once after six hours and again after twelve hours, and recorded the results.

The Second Set of Tests

The weather forecast was for continuing fine weather over the next three to four days, so the second set of tests was deferred until the third day. This avoided exposing the participants to too much sun too quickly.

On day three the participants again wore their swimwear but covered the upper half of their bodies with track suits. The consultants applied five strips of half-inch medical tape horizontally to the back of the participants' legs, from the swimsuit down to the knee, spacing the strips 5 cm apart to create eight horizontal open spaces for applying the sunscreens, with an identifying letter for each space marked on the medical tape.

These details help validate the results to be presented later

They then applied sunscreen to the appropriate spaces and instructed the participants to lie face down for 2.5 hours with their backs and the lower half of their legs covered. As in test one, they noted skin color and tenderness immediately after exposure, and again after 6 and 12 hours.

After the first check the participants washed the sunscreen off each others' legs and noted whether each sunscreen was easy or difficult to remove.

The two TPG consultants tabulated the results overnight and the following morning faxed them to the TPG office in Burlington.

Testing for Washabililty from Clothing

Concurrently, a TPG consultant in Burlington tested the ease with which the sunscreens could be washed out of clothing. Tests were conducted twice and on two sets of materials: nylon/lycra and cotton. Each of the different sunscreens was rubbed into four separate pieces of cloth: two into nylon/lycra and two into cotton.

1. In the first test, the consultant hand washed two complete sets of materials, using a light detergent, and recorded whether the sunscreens were easy or difficult to remove. After the pieces of cloth were dry, they were inspected to determine whether any of the sunscreens had left a stain.
2. In the second test, the consultant repeated the process on fresh pieces of cloth, but this time machine washed them using a moderate detergent.

To maintain objectivity, the writer refers to himself in the third person

4

Figure 7-9 A formal report written by a consultant (*continued*)

EVALUATING THE RESULTS

The following evaluation was carried out before the identity of the sunscreens was known. We are identifying the sunscreens here to facilitate reading: 

Readers will want this information, so it's better to place it here than in an appendix

Table 1: Identification of Sunscreens and Manufacturers

Code	***Product Name***	***Type***	***Manufacturer***
A	**Coral Sun**	White Liquid	Western Chemical Co. Calgary, Alberta
B	**Mahoganee**	Brown cream	Winspear Limited Toronto, Ontario
C	**Mellow Tan**	Tan-colored oil	The Mellow Corporation Winnipeg, Manitoba
D	**Formula 0-7**	Clear gel	Pitt Pharmaceuticals Peterborough, Ontario
E	**Whisper**	Beige creamy oil	Skin Care Unlimited Mississauga, Ontario
F	**Protec Sun**	Clear oil	Waters & Smithson Ltd Halifax, Nova Scotia
G	**Flavelle**	Pink creamy oil	Flavelle Ltée Montreal, Québec

Exposure to Sun

When evaluating the different sunscreens' performance, we considered three factors to be most important: the sunscreen's ability to create a light tan *without* reddening the skin or causing a burn and, particularly, without causing skin tenderness. 

The control—that is, the area of skin on which no sunscreen was applied—produced the following results:

- For participants with a fair complexion, considerable reddening of the skin and severe tenderness.
- For participants with a medium complexion, red skin with moderate tenderness.
- For participants with a dark complexion, pink skin with mild tenderness.

5

Figure 7-9 A formal report written by a consultant (*continued*)

 Although all sunscreens provided some protection, only three met all of our criteria. These were *Whisper* (E), *Flavelle* (G), and *Mellow Tan* (C):

- ***Whisper*** caused only a mild reddening of the skin on participants with fair complexions (and even then only for the first few hours after exposure). No participants experienced skin tenderness and all showed a light tan after 12 hours.
- ***Flavelle*** came a close second with almost identical results, except that participants with darker complexions showed no evidence of having gained a tan.
- ***Mellow Tan*** also had similar results, except that participants with fair complexions experienced an initial light pinkness of the skin with some mild tenderness.

The four remaining sunscreens failed to meet one or more of our criteria. The results are documented in Appendix A.

Ease of Application

With the exception of *Formula 0-7*, all sunscreens were easy to apply. *Formula 0-7* is a rather thick gel that needs some work to spread and rub into the skin. For complete details, see Appendix B.

Every appendix must be referred to in the report narrative

Feel on the Skin

 Three sunscreens were rated as "smooth and comfortable." These were *Mellow Tan*, *Whisper*, and *Protec Sun*. The participants rated the remainder as "feeling mildly to moderately sticky."

Washability from Skin

Our tests indicate that, although there are exceptions, there is generally a reverse correlation between a sunscreen's "waterproofness" and the ease with which it can be washed off the skin. For example:

- *Coral Sun* and *Mellow Tan* are easy to wash off the skin but have the lowest waterproof rating, and
- *Mahoganee*, *Formula 0-7*, *Whisper*, and *Flavelle* are moderately easy to difficult to wash off the skin but have the highest waterproof rating.

6

Figure 7-9 A formal report written by a consultant (*continued*)

Washability from Clothing

Washing synthetics such as nylon and lycra, and a natural fibre (cotton), shows that

- no cottons and very few synthetic materials could be washed satisfactorily by hand, and
- most cottons and synthetics could be washed satisfactorily by machine, but there were exceptions:
  - — *Mahoganee* left stains on both cottons and synthetics.
  - — *Mellow Tan, Whisper,* and *Flavelle* left stains only on cottons.

Complete details are shown in Appendix C.

OVERALL ANALYSIS OF THE SUNSCREENS' EFFECTIVENESS

A. ***Coral Sun*** provides moderate sun protection for people with medium or dark complexions, but creates pinkness and some tenderness on the skin of people with fair complexions. It is easy to apply, feels mildly sticky, is easy to wash off the skin and clothing, but is not very waterproof.

Thumbnail sketches of each product, culled from data in the appendices

B. ***Mahoganee*** provides moderate sun protection for people with medium or dark complexions, but poor protection for people with light complexions. It is only moderately easy to apply and wash off the skin, but is highly waterproof. It is difficult to wash off clothing and tends to leave a stain.

C. ***Mellow Tan*** provides good sun protection for all complexions. It is very easy to apply to and wash off the skin, feels smooth and comfortable, but has low waterproof capability. It is moderately easy to wash out of synthetic clothing but difficult to wash out of cottons, on which it may leave a stain.

D. ***Formula 0-7*** provides poor to only moderate sun protection for people with fair and medium complexions, but is good for people with darker complexions. It is difficult to apply, feels somewhat sticky on the skin, and is difficult to wash off. However, it is highly waterproof. It is easy to wash out of clothing and does not leave a stain.

E. ***Whisper*** provides excellent protection from the sun for all complexions. It is easy to apply, has a smooth, comfortable feel, is only moderately easy to wash off the skin, and is highly waterproof. It is only moderately easy to wash out of clothing and may leave a stain on cottons.

7

Figure 7-9 A formal report written by a consultant (*continued*)

F. ***Protec Sun*** provides moderate sun protection for people with medium or darker complexions, but only low protection for people with fair complexions. It is easy to apply, has a smooth, comfortable feel on the skin, and is moderately waterproof and moderately easy to wash off. It is also easy to wash out of clothing and does not leave a stain.

G. ***Flavelle*** provides excellent protection from the sun for all complexions. It is easy to apply, leaves a slightly sticky feeling on the skin, is highly waterproof, but is difficult to wash off. It is also difficult to wash out of clothing and may stain cottons.

20 **CONCLUSIONS**

Of the seven sunscreens tested, *Whisper* and *Flavelle* achieve the highest rating for protection from the sun. Both are easy to apply and are highly waterproof, so will not easily wash off when users swim or perspire.

21

If a sunscreen is highly waterproof, it can be difficult to wash off the skin or out of clothing with which it may come in contact. In this regard, *Whisper* washes out moderately easily, whereas *Flavelle* is difficult to wash out. Both sunscreens may leave a slight stain on cottons.

Conclusions sum up the outcomes; they must never surprise readers by introducing new information

8

Figure 7-9 A formal report written by a consultant (*continued*)

24

Appendix A
Protection from Sun Afforded by Sunscreens

Sunscreen/ Complexion	*Immediate Effect*	*Effect After 6 Hours*	*Effect After 12 hours*	*Skin Tender?*
A. Coral Sun				
Light	Pink	Pink	Pink	Moderate
Medium	Light tan	Medium tan	Medium tan	Mild
Dark	No change	Light tan	Light tan	No
B. Mahoganee				
Light	Red	Pink	Pink	Moderate
Medium	Pink	Light tan	Light tan	Mild
Dark	Light tan	Light tan	Light tan	No
C. Mellow Tan				
Light	Pink	Pink	Light tan	Mild
Medium	Light tan	Light tan	Light tan	No
Dark	No change	Light tan	Light tan	No
D. Formula 0-7				
Light	Red	Dark pink	Pink	Moderate
Medium	Pink	Pink	Pink	Mild
Dark	Light tan	Light tan	Light tan	No
E. Whisper				
Light	Pink	Light pink	Light tan	No
Medium	No change	Light tan	Light tan	No
Dark	No change	Light tan	Light tan	No
F. Protec Sun				
Light	Pink	Pink	Pink	Moderate
Medium	Light pink	Pink	Pink	Moderate
Dark	No change	Light pink	Light pink	No
G. Flavelle				
Light	Light pink	Light tan	Moderate tan	No
Medium	No change	No change	Light tan	No
Dark	No change	No change	No change	No
Control				
Light	Red	Very red	Red	Yes, very
Medium	Red	Red	Dark pink	Moderate
Dark	Dark pink	Pink	Light tan	Mild

The appendices were prepared first, then used to help the writer organize the report

Figure 7-9 A formal report written by a consultant (*continued*)

Appendix B
Sunscreens' Effect on the Skin

Sunscreen	*Ease of Application*	*Feel on Skin*	*Ease of Removal*	*How Waterproof?*
A. Coral Sun	Easy	Mildly sticky	Easy	Low
B. Mahoganee	Moderate	Slight skin tension	Moderate	High
C. Mellow Tan	Easy	Smooth, comfortable	Easy	Low
D. Formula 0-7	Difficult	Moderately sticky	Moderate	High
E. Whisper	Easy	Smooth, comfortable	Moderate	High
F. Protec Sun	Easy	Smooth, comfortable	Moderate	Moderate
G. Flavelle	Easy	Slightly sticky	Difficult	High

These comments are subjective, based on testers' opinions

Figure 7-9 A formal report written by a consultant (*continued*)

Appendix C
Sunscreens' Washability from Clothing

Sunscreen	*Type of Material*	*Remove with Hand Wash?*	*Remove with Machine Wash?*	*Does it Leave a Stain?*
A. Coral Sun	Synthetic	Only partly	Yes	No
	Cotton	No	Yes	No
B. Mahoganee	Synthetic	No	Only partly	Slight stain
	Cotton	No	No	Yes
C. Mellow Tan	Synthetic	Only partly	Yes	No
	Cotton	No	No	Slight stain
D. Formula 0-7	Synthetic	Yes	Yes	No
	Cotton	Yes	Yes	No
E. Whisper	Synthetic	No	Yes	No
	Cotton	No	Only partly	Slight stain
F. Protec Sun	Synthetic	Yes	Yes	No
	Cotton	Yes	Yes	No
G. Flavelle	Synthetic	Only partly	Yes	No
	Cotton	No	Only partly	Slight stain

To have referred to products only by their code letters would have made the results difficult to comprehend

Figure 7-9 A formal report written by a consultant (*continued*)

An Introduction should cover three main topics: Background, Purpose, and Scope. Dave's *Background* is in paragraph 1, his *Purpose* is in the introductory sentence of paragraph 2, and the *Scope* is in the remainder of the Introduction. Although it was easy for Dave to cover the topics in this natural sequence, it is not always necessary to do so; indeed, the three parts can overlap.

An Introduction often lists some of the criteria established in the letter of authorization

The Discussion starts here. This introductory paragraph neatly introduces the topics that will be covered in the first section of the Discussion. In doing so it acts like a miniature summary at the start of the section.

It's important to mention the topics *in the same order that they will be discussed in the following paragraphs*. Readers become confused when they read the ensuing development and find the topics are not presented in the expected sequence.

It's important to demonstrate early in the report how The Proving Ground concealed the identity of the products being evaluated. This helps underscore the objectivity of The Proving Ground's report.

In this and the following two paragraphs, Dave sets the scene for the tests to be described in the next section. Keeping the preparation and the test descriptions separate makes the tests much easier to read and understand.

It's acceptable to use the first person in formal reports, rather than try to seem totally uninvolved personally. However, for a formal report like this it's better to use the plural "we" rather than the singular "I."

❾

The illustration is probably unnecessary, because the description in the preceding paragraph was clear. Dave chose to include it so that the report would have a "lighter" appearance (that is, it would not be only pages of text).

Here is another introductory statement that acts like an opening Summary to this section (see also point 5).

Constructing "pyramids within pyramids" is an ideal way to carry a reader smoothly through a long document

This section briefly describes the circumstances leading up to the start of the tests. In effect, Dave has created a natural *Summary—Background—Details* structure to the testing section, as though it is an independent report. "Nesting" pyramids within the overall report pyramid is an effective way to organize a longer document.

Setting this heading in italics, yet retaining the same 12 pt font size used for the previous heading, identifies it clearly as a subheading.

Dave intentionally chose to use the active voice rather than the passive voice for most of his report. (He wrote: "The two TPG consultants applied the sunscreens. . ." rather than "The sunscreens were applied. . .".) However, in the next short paragraph he used the passive voice to insert some variety into his writing.

Although Dave personally carried out the washability tests on clothing, he correctly chose not to identify himself as having done so. He recognized that the client would be using the results of the tests to develop its marketing strategy, and that if its strategy is challenged the report on which it is based must appear as objective as possible.

To maintain that objectivity, in his first draft Dave identified the products only as A, B, C, etc, and then cross-referenced the letters to the real identities at the end of the report. However, when Hannah and Sandi read the draft they found it not only difficult to remember which product proved successful in which tests, but also rather dull, confusing reading. Consequently Dave brought the identification information forward and used the products' real names from then on. As report writers we sometimes have to balance the need for objectivity against the need for clarity.

When reporting an evaluation, it's important to establish the measurement criteria at the start of the section, as Dave has done here.

Here, the initial results are compared against the criteria, which starts preparing the reader for the conclusions that will be drawn at the end of the report.

In an alternative approach, Dave could have presented the results and evaluated them immediately after each test. For a less complex report it could be done successfully. But when five different factors are being evaluated, as they are here, it is clearer from the reader's point of view to separate them.

By this point the reader has seen the results for each test, and has obtained a general impression, but cannot easily identify how each sunscreen rates overall. This section pulls the results together and evaluates each sunscreen independently. It does *not* compare one sunscreen against another.

A writer *knows* the results before starting to write, but will not let that knowledge affect his or her objectivity

Dave's objectivity, and hence that of The Proving Ground, is maintained until this point. The Discussion section of the report has not indicated which sunscreen is best. The Conclusions do that.

The Conclusions do not compare the sunscreens against each other: they simply identify which are best and then show any limitations that exist for them. If any comparisons are to be made, that will be done by the client when preparing their marketing strategy.

22

I asked Dave why he had not included a Recommendation, which is the second part of the Outcome or Action Statement at the end of a report. He replied: "The client asked us to test and evaluate seven sunscreens.

They did not ask us to compare them or to recommend which is best. If they had, I would have written a Recommendation something like this:

> **Recommendation**
>
> We recommend that Skin Care Unlimited concentrates on *Whisper's* sun-protection capabilities in their advertising, and downplays that it is only moderately easy to wash off the skin and out of clothing, and may leave a stain on cottons.

If there had been references or a bibliography they would have been inserted here, immediately following the Conclusions and Recommendations.

The appendices provide the evidence to support the evaluation section. Each appendix is only a single page, so does not bear a page number.

Report Writing Sequence

A well-written report is rarely written straight through, from start to finish

When I asked Dave Horoschuk how he had tackled writing his report, he replied: "I wrote it backwards!"

He explained how he first assembled all the data from the sunscreen tests in the Bahamas and the washing tests in Burlington, and from it created the three appendices. Next he wrote three brief statements:

1. What The Proving Ground team set out to do (their purpose, criteria, and preparatory steps).
2. What they did (the steps they carried out as they conducted the tests).
3. What the results were and what an analysis of them revealed.

Then he filled in some headings between the three statements, which produced an outline similar to the Table of Contents on page ii of the report.

From the three appendices, Dave formed a composite table of all the results (a table he did not insert but used to gain an overall picture of each sunscreen). From this table he wrote the section titled "Overall Analysis of the Sunscreens' Effectiveness" (pages 7 and 8 of his report).

Then he stepped to the front of the Discussion and wrote the "Preparing for the Tests" section, and followed it with the "Conducting the Tests" section and the "Evaluating the Results" section, in that order.

"I realized at that point that I didn't have an Introduction," Dave said, "so I wrote it next. Then I wrote the Conclusions. That was easy to do once I had established what the purpose and scope were in the Introduction." Finally, he wrote the Summary, which he also found easy to do now that the full report had been written.

This apparently "backwards" way of writing is used by many experienced report writers. They claim that preparing the Appendices often provides the key for them to plan and write the Discussion, and that writing the Introduction, Conclusions, and Recommendations, and finally the Summary, is much easier when the shape and content of the report are known.

The Conclusions must evolve naturally from and answer questions posed in the Introduction

Writing in the First Person

Where he has used the first person, Dave used the plural "we" because he was reporting for his organization (The Proving Ground) rather than for himself. He has used the first person predominantly in the "Preparing for the Tests" and "Evaluating the Results" sections, but not at all in the Introduction or the "Conducting the Tests" and "Overall Analysis" sections. Neither has Dave used "I" or "we" in the Summary, even though it is often acceptable to use the first person there. Again, he wanted to ensure that a clearly objective tone was established right from the start.

An Alternative Format for a Formal Report

Not all readers will read a whole formal report. Some—particularly busy executives—tend to focus on only three pieces of information:

1. What the report writer set out to do or achieve.
2. What he or she actually did or found out.
3. What he or she suggests should be done.

They know they can find this information quickly (if the report has been constructed properly) by reading just four short parts: the Summary for a quick overview, and then the Introduction, Conclusions, and Recommendations for more details.

For such readers, many report writers now bring the Conclusions and Recommendations forward and insert them between the Introduction and the Discussion. This arrangement is shown in Figure 7-10.

Sometimes report writers can write their report in the traditional format and then simply shift the Conclusions and Recommendations forward. More often, however, they have to revise the report slightly, usually in four places:

Alternative format reinforces the pyramid approach . . .

- In the Conclusions and Recommendations, to ensure that they follow naturally from the Introduction that now immediately precedes them, and are clear to readers who have not yet read the Discussion.

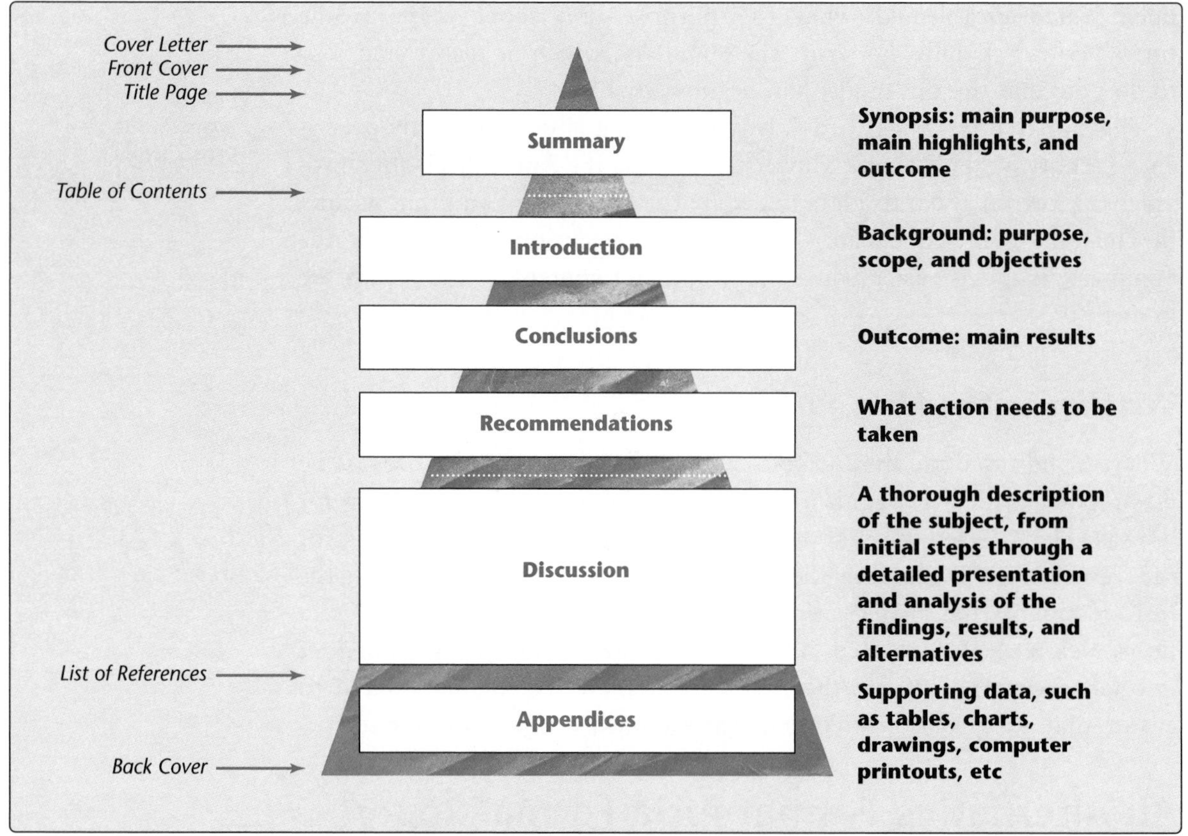

Figure 7-10 An alternative writing plan for a formal report

. . . but may require special attention to opening and closing of Discussion

- At the start of the Discussion, which may need a new introductory paragraph because the Introduction no longer immediately precedes it.
- At the end of the Discussion, which may need a new closing paragraph because the Conclusions no longer follow immediately after it.

If Dave Horoschuk had used the alternative format for his report, he would have inserted a little more information into the Conclusions to make them more understandable when read immediately after the Introduction. To see how the changes would improve continuity, read the Introduction on page 196 and then immediately read the revised Conclusions below.

Conclusions

Our tests show that, of the seven sunscreens tested, two achieved the highest rating for protection from the sun. One of these was Skin Care Unlimited's new sunscreen *Whisper*. It also was found to be easy to apply and highly waterproof, and so will not easily wash off when users swim or perspire.

We also determined that, if a sunscreen is highly waterproof, it can be difficult to wash off the skin or out of clothing with which it may come in contact. We found that *Whisper* washes off only moderately easily from both skin and clothing, and may leave a slight stain on cottons.

The chief difference between this Conclusion and the one in the original report is that there is no mention of *Flavelle*, the sunscreen the original report equates in quality with *Whisper*, because the reader has not yet read about the tests on this particular sunscreen. To include it would confuse the reader, who would think he or she has missed something.

Dave would not need to change the Discussion because the first and last paragraphs could stand well on their own, without an Introduction immediately before or Conclusions immediately after them.

The report format you choose depends on the circumstances

Is the alternative format better than the traditional format? Not at all. Both have their place and every report writer has to decide which format will better suit the subject matter and the intended audience. As a general rule, the alternative format may be better for very long reports, since the Conclusions and Recommendations are easier to find (they are not buried between the Discussion and Appendices). Similarly, the traditional format may be better for a report written for a primary reader who is not expecting or may not like the Conclusions the writer draws and the Recommendations he or she makes (hopefully, the reader will have read and understood the Discussion before encountering the Conclusions and Recommendations).

TO SUM UP

A formal report presents the results of a study, investigation, or evaluation. As its purpose often is to persuade readers to agree to a suggestion, invest in a service, purchase a product, or modify a method of operation, the report must convince them that the case the author is making is valid.

The report's appearance, organization, language, and tone all contribute to its quality, and consequently the image perceived by its readers. If readers are to be convinced that the writer has a strong case to make, they must sense they are holding a high-quality document from the moment they pick it up until the moment they read the last word.

EXERCISES

Exercise 7.1: Investigating New Office Space

"I want you to take a look at commercial rental space," Mr Charlebois tells you, "and identify three or four locations that would be suitable for our business."

Pierre Charlebois is general manager of Northwinds Investment and Loan Corporation (NILC). You are NILC's supervisor of office services. The building in which NILC now rents space has been sold and will be demolished to make room for a major hotel on the site. In any case, the space currently occupied by NILC is severely overcrowded, and as Mr Charlebois has mentioned more than once at executive meetings and repeats to you today, "Our address at 231 Main Street was all right when we were mainly in the land properties business, but now that we are predominantly a financial services organization we really could use a more prestigious address."

NILC needs more space and a prestigious location

You ask him how much floor space the company needs.

"Right now we occupy 1470 square metres for 187 staff," he replies, "but that's not nearly enough. We could easily use another 200 square metres right now, but even that will suffice for only a short while. If the company continues to expand as it has recently, I expect to hire an additional 40 staff over the next three years. I suggest you plan on it."

"What about rent?" you ask. "Can you give me a rough idea how much the company wants to pay?"

"Right now this space is costing us a little over \$12 000 a month, or \$8.25 per square metre. But that's cheaper than we'll get elsewhere." He suggests that \$18 000 a month sounds like a more realistic figure. He also suggests several other factors you should take into account:

- The location's accessibility, for staff travelling by car or bus.
- The amount of parking space available, and the price for parking. (Staff currently pay \$20 a month for parking and there are 55 parking stalls. Another 12 staff members are on a waiting list.)
- The local availability of amenities such as a restaurant and small shops such as a drugstore and grocery store.

From the local library you borrow a book titled *Staff and Space: A Case of Give and Take,* written by Kelvin V Lacuna and published by Dover Press of Vancouver in 2000. On page 33 Mr Lacuna writes, "A good rule of thumb in planning space is to allow nine square metres per staff member."

Using this statement as a guideline, you calculate that NILC needs 1683 square metres for its current 187 staff, but within three years will need 2043 square metres to allow for the additional 40 staff Mr Charlebois predicts he will hire.

By calling on real estate agents you identify and visit 11 possible locations, eight of which you examine only cursorily and quickly discard for various reasons (three have too little space, two are too expensive, one is in the second storey of a cold storage plant and has no windows, another is in a distant suburb served by only a single bus every 50 minutes, and the last is a building that is in worse condition than the building NILC currently occupies).

Carol Carruthers of Simkin Agencies takes you on a tour of the Rothesay building at 200 Broadway Avenue. "If you're looking for property on financial row," she comments as you step into a glass and stainless steel elevator, "this address is just right for you. There's the TD bank on your left, and the Royal and CIBC are on your right. The building is only six years old and most of the tenants are investment houses, insurance companies, and chartered accountants, with the occasional business consultant thrown in. And tenants seem to stay once they have moved in. The only reason we'll shortly have some space is that the people at Federal-Provincial Trust have built their own building farther down the avenue and have just started to move out."

You step off the elevator at the fifth floor and move through heavy glass doors into a sumptuous decor. The ceilings are high, the floor is covered with a deep pile carpet, and the layout is modern yet conservative. The whole impression is of a bright, sunny area with wide windows looking onto the tops of the trees that line Broadway Avenue—all ideal for a tenant seeking a prestigious environment.

Prestigious surroundings, however, are expensive

"How much space is there?" you ask.

"There are 1910 square metres."

"And the rent?"

"$10.50 per square metre: $20 055 per month."

"Parking?"

"In the basement."

"Seventy stalls?"

"More than that. But $55 per month."

Ouch! you silently murmur to yourself.

Some other features you note about 200 Broadway Avenue are that it is 0.5 kilometres from the city centre and is served by three major bus routes; there are four restaurants within 0.3 kilometres; and the lease will be for two years, after which the rent will be renegotiated.

The second building you feel has possibilities is at 3105 Grantham Avenue, in a suburb 6.5 kilometres from the city centre. The agent this time is Leslie Dietmann of Princeton Leasing, who explains: "Until four years ago this building was part of a major food chain, but was vacated when the chain built an even bigger store over on Carlton Avenue. It stood empty for two years, then Princeton Development Company converted it into a small shopping mall for prestige stores that suit the well-heeled clientele of Sylvan Heights on the other side of Grantham Avenue. At the same time Princeton decided to build a second floor above the mall as a business complex."

As you park in front of the building you realize the architect has created an interesting design. Outside, the building is covered with dark glass panels that create a fresh, modern appearance. Inside, the main floor tenants are specialty stores that, from the number of people in them, seem to be well frequented.

New, lots of space, but away from the city centre

The office complex can be approached only through a security-controlled entrance to a single pair of escalators, and clearly has been designed with the upscale business market in mind. There are light, airy open spaces, the floors are carpeted, and the ceilings contain a new style of recessed "egg crate" fluorescent lamps.

"You will be the first tenants," Leslie says hopefully. "The offices will be ready for occupancy in three weeks."

"How much space is there?" you ask.

"You'll have 3400 square metres."

"That's too big. We need only 2000 square metres."

"It can be subdivided," Leslie explains. "The architect designed it for up to 10 tenants, each taking one 340 square metre unit. But you can take as many units as you like. When we know how many are leased, then we'll put up the dividing walls."

"Could we rent, say, five units now," you ask, "and take a sixth in another two years?"

"You could, but you would be depending on space being available at the time. You would do better to take all the space you need right from the start."

"How much is the rent?"

"$9.50 per square metre."

You make a quick calculation: if NILC takes five units, that would be 1700 square metres for $16 150 a month. One more unit would provide 2040 square metres for $19 380 a month.

"How long is the lease?"

"Two years, automatically renewable, except for the rent. We give you a proposal four months in advance."

From the window you look out at the wide expanse of asphalt surrounding the building. "Parking is free?" you ask.

"Yes, unless you want a block heater plug. Then it's $30 a month. There are 50 stalls with plugs. We can put more in, if there's enough demand."

Your overall impression is that 3105 Grantham Avenue would be an ideal location for NILC, providing that management can accept being away from the business centre of the city, and that staff who travel by bus can accept the inconvenience of a single bus route out to a suburb (even though buses travel both ways along Grantham Avenue every eight minutes throughout the day).

As well as boutiques, the mall houses a nice little restaurant, a convenience store, and a chain drugstore. Other restaurants are 1.2 kilometres away, east on Grantham Avenue.

The third location you investigate in-depth also is the cheapest. It is only two thirds of a kilometre from your present location and near the now-closed railway station, in what was the commercial centre of the city back in the early 1900s.

The price is right, but is the location adequate?

"For many years the district was completely run-down," Rhonda Drohan explains as she drives you there (she is part-owner of Dro-Mar Properties, the agency handling the leasing arrangements for 45 Bullion Street). "Some of the buildings were torn down in the late 1940s and early 1950s, then the government stepped in and classed some of the buildings as Heritage Properties. Since then there have been gradual improvements. The city has given tax breaks to developers to encourage conversion of some of the buildings into business complexes, and others into residences."

"Like the old Barton warehouse?" you suggest.

"Right!"

In the office on the main floor, Rhonda shows you the building's plans and explains that because of the building's design and fire regulations most of the offices are fairly small. "They range from 360 to 1186 square metres," she adds.

"We need a little over two thousand," you say.

"Then you'll need two adjacent offices. We could cut a door between them."

Rhonda suggests taking the largest suite and combining it with one of the suites on either side. "Suite 306 is the only one left at 1186 square metres. On one side it has suite 304 at 410 square metres, and on the other side suite 308 at 934 square metres."

You make a calculation: "That would give us 1596 or 2120 square metres."

Rhonda agrees.

"And the rent would be . . . ?" you ask.

"Only $8.75 a square metre. It's low because the city wants to attract businesses to move here."

"How long is the lease?"

"Three years. Then we'd renegotiate."

"Will parking be a problem?"

In a city centre, parking can be a critical concern

"At the moment there is sufficient street parking. It could become tight later, as the building fills up, so we're building a 200-vehicle parkade one block away, at 36 Rory Street. It will be ready in two months."

"What will be the cost?"

"Long-term parking will be $40 a month."

The offices seem pleasant enough, even though they have brick walls, small, high windows, and very high ceilings with 0.4-metre square wooden beams running across them.

"This was a warehouse," Rhonda says, "which explains why the ceilings are so high. The city won't let us conceal the brick walls . . . "

"I like them," you interject. "They add a feeling of warmth!"

" . . . or the heavy wooden beams," Rhonda continues. "They are a far better fire risk than steel. Steel buckles when it gets too hot. These old beams only char, and very slowly at that." She points to the floors. "These are the original wood floorboards, which have been varnished and polished. You may place loose carpets on them, if you like, but not fitted carpets or tiles."

The nearest shops and restaurants, you learn, are on Main Street, one third of a kilometre away. And so are the buses, which are frequent.

"In about three months," Rhonda tells you, "The 'Little Baker' chain of family restaurants will be putting in a cafeteria on the main floor, to serve this and adjacent office buildings."

As Rhonda drops you at your office door, she adds, "If you do move into 45 Bullion Street, your company will be recognized as a supporter of Heritage Sites."

Now write your report!

Now you are preparing to write your investigation report. You like all three locations, so the choice is going to be difficult. You're going to have to balance cost against the need for a prestigious location, and also consider the convenience of employees. And Mr Charlebois will be expecting you to offer a recommendation as well as present all the details.

You meet briefly with Mr Charlebois and describe your findings. "Sounds excellent," he says. "I'd like you to write a formal report and to make 10 copies so that I can circulate it to the business partners."

Write the report and precede it with a memo-form cover letter or executive summary.

Exercise 7.2: **Researching Professional Presentation Equipment**

Two months after graduating from college you are hired as an administrative assistant by the local branch of Wilson, McGee, and Associates, an international firm of business consultants with offices across Canada and in the US, England, and Australia. The office in your home town, where you are employed, is the corporate head office. You work in the Public Affairs Department, where your manager is Lori Anderssen.

Yesterday, Lori asked you to research projectors for the business consultants to use when they make presentations to clients. "We need systems that are portable," she said, "and can be shipped easily when our consultants travel to clients' offices in cities around the world."

Lori handed you a piece of paper containing a list of factors that must be considered. The list was drawn up during the monthly management meeting one week ago today:

LCD Projectors: Requirements

1. Number of systems needed: 4.
2. Where the systems will be lodged:
   - Your office, and one system each at
   - White Plains, New York,
   - Melbourne, Australia, and
   - London, England.
3. Budget: $60 000 (Cdn $), which is to include GST and appropriate provincial tax.
4. Each system is to contain
   - LCD projector with computer and video input,
   - VCR (two for working with PAL videos and two for working with NTSC videos), *
   - small stereo loudspeakers, to be driven by LCD projector, with sufficient output for use with audiences of up to 75 people,
   - compatibility for working with PCs working in either Windows or Mac operating systems,
   - appropriate cabling,
   - plugs/transformers, etc, for use in Europe, Scandinavia, and Australia,
   - one-year manufacturer's warranty plus additional three years' extended warranty (optional), and
   - shipping cases.

* PAL video operating systems apply in Europe and Australia; NTSC in North America.

Find projection equipment that will create a positive, professional image

Lori also told you to recommend whether the company should continue to use Microsoft *PowerPoint*, which is included with the software programs in the company's PCs and portable computers, or should adopt an alternative Canadian-made projection software.

Lori said she needs a formal report, because copies have to go to executives in each of the named offices, as well as to the company's executive board in your home office.

You will have to visit or write to suppliers of projectors and multimedia projection systems to obtain information to carry out this project. Identify three or four suitable systems and then insert a comparative analysis into your report.

Exercise 7.3 **Evaluating Telephone Service Suppliers**

You are the Administrative Assistant to Marnie Halprin, who is president and owner of Pro-Mar Business Services Inc. Pro-Mar has a staff of 44, of whom 22 are business consultants, 13 are support staff, and 7 represent Pro-Mar in other cities.

Pro-Mar has 12 telephone lines at its home office, 11 of which are regular lines, and one is a dedicated line reserved solely for incoming "800" calls. Current billing with the local telephone company averages approximately $2850 a month. This is broken down into five cost centres:

- $180 is for equipment and line rental
- 39% of long distance (LD) calls are to points within Canada
- 34% of LD calls are to the US
- 19% are to other countries
- 8% are "800" calls.

Comparing telephone rates can be difficult—there are so many options

Yesterday, Marnie emailed this message to you:

> I'd like you to investigate alternative telephone suppliers to see if we are getting the best deal. In my mail I get numerous leaflets advertising the great rates offered by other suppliers. And at home I am hounded by salespeople who call at dinnertime to see if I want to change. I'd like you to prepare me a report—a formal report I can show the Associates—identifying whether we should stay with our present supplier.

For this exercise you will need to assume that Pro-Mar currently is using one of the local suppliers of telephone services. From this supplier you will need to obtain current business rates for the volume of calls Pro-Mar makes monthly. And then from alternative suppliers you will need to obtain quotes for similar volumes. Also you should determine whether there are limitations that would affect each service. When you have amassed your information, you will need to conduct a comparative analysis, to demonstrate which service supplier "offers the best deal," and then recommend whether Pro-Mar should stay with the current supplier or change to another. Now write your report.

WEBLINKS

Stages of Report Preparation

ltid.grc.nasa.gov/Publishing/editing/vidcover.htm

This NASA guide was written to make writing reports easier. Separate chapters deal with the stages of report preparation, report style, the introduction, concluding and supporting sections, and references.

Bibliography Style Handbook

www.english.uiuc.edu/cws/wworkshop/bibliostyles.htm

Part of the University of Illinois's Writer's Workshop, this site provides information about the bibliographic styles of the American Psychological Association (APA) and the Modern Languages Association (MLA).

The Shape of Business Letters and Reports

"When my secretary brings in the morning mail," Tina Mactiere explains, "I sort the letters and memos into two piles: those I must deal with immediately, and those that can wait until later in the day."

"Makes sense," George Dunn replies. "But how do you identify which you have to deal with first, if you don't read them?"

Tina is president and chief executive officer of a Toronto high-tech company known as Macro Engineering Inc, a position that demands considerable management expertise. George Dunn is the company's controller, which is the equivalent of chief accountant and office administrator combined.

"Several factors come into play," Tina explains. "Some letters and reports I recognize right away are bringing me information I'm waiting for, so I automatically put them in the 'do now' pile. And others come from people who through experience I have learned consistently send me important information, so their letters go in the same pile. But the remainder . . . " and Tina shrugs. "I judge them on their appearance."

"Their appearance?"

"It's a sixth sense, really," Tina replies, "something I've developed over the years."

She tells George that every piece of paper that crosses her desk sends her a subtle signal about the quality of the information it contains—before she reads a word! "It doesn't matter whether it's a letter, a memo, a report, a proposal, or a brochure. If it is carefully presented and well arranged on the page, if the print is crisp and dark, I gain an immediate image of an efficient, knowledgeable writer working for a well-organized company. So I put it into the 'do now' pile."

"And if you come across a letter that uses a non-standard format," George interjects, "or is untidily arranged and has faint print, do you visualize a sleepy, untidy individual working in a cluttered office, and so toss the letter into the 'do later' pile?"

"Right!"

IN THIS CHAPTER

You will learn how to design a document so that it creates an image of you, and the company you work for, as effective conveyors of information. Specifically, you will learn how to plan and present
- business letters and memorandums,
- fax and email messages, and
- research papers and semiformal business reports.

The first impression a reader gains is from a document's appearance

Full Block and Modified Block Letters

The full block letter format is most commonly used today

The two most common formats for Canadian business letters are known as the full block and the modified block. The main difference is that in full block letters *every* line of the letter starts at the left margin, whereas in modified block letters some lines are indented to the right. These methods are explained well by the writers of the two letters in Figures 8-1 on page 225 and 8-2 on page 227.

Rather than use preprinted letterhead, today many organizations have a custom-designed letterhead stored as a "macro" in their computer's memory, which individual writers insert with a couple of keystrokes as they write their letters and memos.

The two letters have been typed using different fonts. David Courtland's letter in Figure 8-1 is in a plain *sans serif* font known as Arial. Sherry Curtis's letter in Figure 8-2 is in a *serif* font known as Times New Roman. Both are set in 12 pt type. For more information on fonts and type sizes, see the section "Designing Information for Maximum Effect" in Chapter 13.

The circled numbers beside the two letters refer to the comments below, which describe the general guidelines for writing business correspondence in Canada.

Two items normally appear at the top of the letter: the date, which is always present, and a file reference, which is used only occasionally.

- Set the date against the left margin in a full block letter, and against the right margin in a modified block letter.
- File references are optional. If used, there may be two: yours and your reader's (for when you reply to a letter in which your correspondent has quoted a file reference). Set the file reference against the left margin; if there are two, set them single-spaced, one under the other.

As Sherry Curtis explains in her letter (Figure 8-2, paragraph 2), using punctuation in the inside address, salutation, complimentary close, and signature block is optional. A more traditional use of punctuation is shown in her letter; a more contemporary use is shown in David Courtland's letter in Figure 8-1 (you may also omit the period after *Mr* and *Ms*). If you do not know your reader's name, insert a title such as "Manager, Human Resources" or "Customer Service Manager," so that the mail clerk will know to whom he or she should direct your letter.

The city, province, and postal code are typed in a single line with one space between the city and province, and two spaces between the province and postal code, and *no* punctuation. The same guidelines apply when you write to a US address. The province or state is always two capital letters.

The salutation should *name* the reader. Follow these guidelines:

Inject a personal touch into your letters and memos

- Use the reader's first name in the salutation as early as possible in an exchange of correspondence. This establishes a friendly tone right from the start. The only exception should be in the first letter to a person you do not know, or for formal correspondence between organizations. When replying to a letter, gauge whether to use a person's first name in the salutation by seeing how the letter to you has been signed (for example, Sherry Curtis can tell immediately from David Courtland's signature and signature block in Figure 8-1 that he is inviting her to address him as "David").
- If you do not know what sex the person is, omit *Ms* or *Mr,* like this: *Dear S D Curtis.*
- If you do not know the addressee's name, address him or her by title: *Dear Personnel Manager* or *Dear Marketing Manager.*
- Never use a sexist salutation, such as *Gentlemen* or *Dear Sir,* or an impersonal salutation such as *Dear Sir or Madam* or *To Whom It May Concern.*
- Always address a woman as *Ms* rather than *Mrs* or *Miss*, unless in a previous letter she has signed her letter as *Mrs* or *Miss.*
- Insert a colon after the salutation if you are using more traditional punctuation in the inside address (see item 2); omit it if you are omitting all but essential punctuation from the inside address.

VANCOURT BUSINESS SYSTEMS INC
2 Sheppard Avenue East, Willowdale ON M2N 5Y7

1 April 5, 2001
File: 91-RGr-01

2 Sherry D Curtis
Specialist, Business Communication
The Roning Group Inc
Box 181 RPO Corydon
3 Winnipeg MB R3M 3S7

4 Dear Sherry

5 **Re: Correct Business Letter Format**

6 I would appreciate your evaluation of this letter as an example of our current business letter format. When we met at the Association of Business Communication conference in Montreal last February, you suggested I send you a sample and kindly offered to comment on it.

We adopted the full block format 12 years ago and have not deviated from it since. Three main features differentiate our full block format from other formats:

7
- Every line starts at the left margin, including the date, file reference (if used), subject line, and signature block.
- The first line of each paragraph is never indented (i.e. it also starts at the left margin).
- Most punctuation is omitted from the inside address and signature block (a feature we adopted only recently).

Could you also tell me whether, now that we prepare all our correspondence on a word processor, we should be justifying the right margin of our letters?

I enjoyed our conversation in Montreal and will value your comments and
8 suggestions.

Sincerely

9

10 David N Courtland
Chief Executive Officer

enc

Be consistent: insert punctuation or omit it throughout the letter

Bullets indicate sequence of points is not important

Figure 8-1 A letter written in full block format and printed in a sans serif type

Subject lines are optional: in a long letter, you would do better to insert one (David Courtland has used a subject line in Figure 8-1, but Sherry Curtis has not in Figure 8-2). Use these guidelines:

- Make the subject line informative. David's subject line in Figure 8-1 would have been much less informative if he had written only "Letter Formats."
- Insert *Re:*, *Ref:*, or *Subject:* at the start of the subject line, or omit the prefatory word altogether (its use is optional).
- In a full block letter start the subject line at the left margin. In a modified block letter, centre the subject line between the two margins.
- Set the subject line in **boldface type**.

6

Pay particular attention to the appearance of the letter

Business letters are typed single-spaced, with a double space between paragraphs. If the letter is short, centre the body of the letter vertically on the page by inserting additional blank lines between the date/reference and the first line of the inside address.

Subparagraphing is a useful way to show the subordination of ideas or to list several points. Each subparagraph should be preceded by a bullet (•) or a number (1, 2, 3) set against the left margin. Use these guidelines:

- Use a number if the reader is likely to reply to each of the points separately, so that he or she may refer to them by number, or if the number of items and their sequence is important.
- Use a bullet whenever the sequence or the numbering is unimportant (which often is the case).

Note the differences in punctuation of the indented paragraphs in Figures 8-1 and 8-2:

Guidelines for subparagraphing

- In Figure 8-1 each subparagraph is considered as a separate statement and so starts with a capital letter and ends with a period, and the lead-in line that introduces the subparagraphs ends with a colon.
- In Figure 8-2 each subparagraph is considered to be part of a series, and so starts with a lower-case letter and ends with a comma (except for the second-last sentence, which has "and" after the comma, and the very last sentence, which naturally ends with a period). Note that the lead-in line in this letter has no colon at the end of the line, and

The Roning Group Inc
Communication Consultants
PO Box 181 RPO Corydon
Winnipeg MB R3M 3S7

1 Your file: 91-RGr-01 April 12, 2001

2 David N. Courtland
Chief Executive Officer
Vancourt Business Systems Inc.
2 Sheppard Avenue East
3 Willowdale ON M2N 5Y7

4 Dear David:

Your April 5 letter is a good example of how the parts of a letter should be arranged to conform to the full block letter format.

I have just two comments to make: although omitting punctuation from the inside address, salutation, and signature block is prevalent in Europe, such punctuation is rarely
6 omitted in the United States (for this letter I am inserting the bare minimum that I use for U.S.-bound letters). And, although word processing makes it easy to justify the right margin, I do not recommend it for business correspondence.

For comparison, I am writing this letter in the more conservative and less-common format known as the modified block. The primary difference between the two formats is that in a modified block letter

- the date is moved to the right and ends flush with the right margin,
- 7 the subject line is centred between the two margins,
- the first line of each paragraph may be either started flush with the left margin or indented five spaces to the right (but whichever you use in a letter, be consistent), and
- the signature block is moved to the right, so that each line starts at the page centre-line.

As a general rule, the modified block format is ideal for personal letters and very informal business letters, whereas the full block format is better for regular business correspondence.

I hope you find the comparison useful. If you have more questions about either format, please write, fax, or email me at s.curtis@rgr.mb.ca.

Regards,

8 Sherry Curtis

9 Sherry D. Curtis
Specialist, Business Communications

A ragged (unjustified) right margin is preferred for modified block letters

Figure 8-2 A letter written in modified block format and printed in a serif type

that with a series arrangement like this each subparagraph contains only one sentence.

To determine whether you should insert or omit the colon at the end of the lead-in line, check whether the lead-in line could stand alone as a complete sentence. If it can, insert the colon. The lead-in line preceding the bullets in Figure 8-1 can stand alone; the lead-in line in Figure 8-2 cannot, so it is not followed by a colon.

The outdated *Yours truly, Yours very truly,* and *Yours faithfully* are rarely used in contemporary business correspondence. Most letter writers now use a single word: *Sincerely* or *Regards*. If you have inserted a colon after the salutation (see item 4), then insert a comma after the complimentary close. In a modified block letter (Figure 8-2), the complimentary close and signature block are moved to the right so that each line starts at the page centreline.

Introduce a personal touch with the complimentary close and your signature

The signature block gives the letter writer an opportunity to show how he or she wants to be addressed when the reader replies. If you want your reader to reply to you on a first name basis, type both your first and last names and insert your first name when you sign. If you write and sign a letter on behalf of another person, handwrite the word "for" in front of the other person's typed name:

Sincerely

Myra Harbrugge

for David N Courtland
Chief Executive Officer

"Enc" warns the reader to look for an enclosure in the envelope. If a copy of the letter will also be sent to a third person, the letters "cc" and the person's name are typed two lines below the last line of the signature block, starting at the left margin:

cc Ruth L Goodwin, V-P Administration

When you write letters that continue on a second or more pages, three additional guidelines apply:

- At the bottom of the first page type /2 . . . so that the third dot ends at the right margin:

/2 . . .

(Type /3 . . . , etc, for the third and subsequent pages.)

- At the top of the second page, starting at the left margin, type the addressee's name and the page number:

David N Courtland - page 2

Print the addressee's name in boldface type or italics.

- Insert headings to lighten the appearance of a long letter. Start each heading at the left margin, use lower-case letters (with the first letter of principal words capitalized) set in boldface type. Be sure your choice of headings is appropriate and conveys your overall approach to the subject. For example, Sherry Curtis conceivably could have inserted two headings in her letter in Figure 8-2:

Comment on Your Letter (before paragraph 2)

Comparison with Modified Block Letter (before paragraph 3)

Long letters need headings to lighten the heaviness of straight type

Interoffice Memorandums

An interoffice memorandum—or memo—is an informal letter sent between people who work for the same organization and who may be in the same office, in adjoining offices, in different buildings in the same city, or in different cities. Memos are seldom sent between people who work for different organizations.

Although memos are intentionally informal, as Tina Mactiere remarks in Figure 8-3, the label "informal" does not mean that memo writers have a licence to write snippets and sentence fragments. A memo is still a letter, although its circulation is limited to people in-house. Guidelines for writing interoffice memorandums are listed below, and are cross-referenced by circled numbers to the memo in Figure 8-3.

Memos require good sentence and paragraph construction, just as letters do

Although sometimes the company name and the words **Interoffice Memorandum** and **To**, **From**, **Date**, and **Subject** are preprinted on blank memorandum forms, more often they are stored as a macro in the computer's memory, ready for a writer to key in the names, date, and topic.

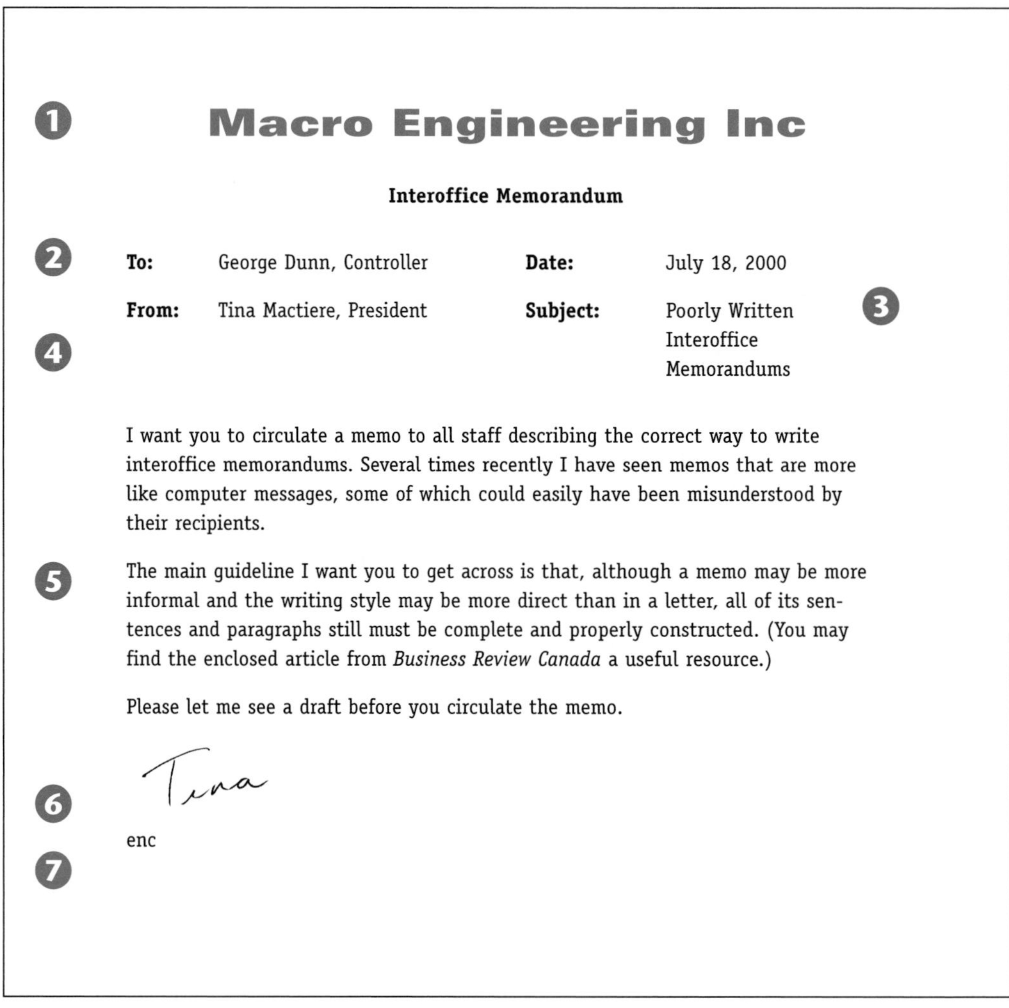

❶

Macro Engineering Inc

Interoffice Memorandum

❷ **To:** George Dunn, Controller **Date:** July 18, 2000

From: Tina Mactiere, President **Subject:** Poorly Written Interoffice Memorandums ❸

❹

I want you to circulate a memo to all staff describing the correct way to write interoffice memorandums. Several times recently I have seen memos that are more like computer messages, some of which could easily have been misunderstood by their recipients.

❺ The main guideline I want you to get across is that, although a memo may be more informal and the writing style may be more direct than in a letter, all of its sentences and paragraphs still must be complete and properly constructed. (You may find the enclosed article from *Business Review Canada* a useful resource.)

Please let me see a draft before you circulate the memo.

Tina

❻

enc

❼

Figure 8-3 An interoffice memorandum (The article referred to as an enclosure is not shown here.)

❷

Keep the names of people simple. Omit the prefixes *Mr* and *Ms*, and often the addressee's title.

❸

Make the subject line informative yet brief. If Tina Mactiere had written Memos, or even Interoffice Memorandums, as her subject line, she would not have been sufficiently informative.

4

Omit a salutation and a complimentary close.

Guidelines for memo writing

5

Never indent the first line of each paragraph.

6

Sign the memo with either your initials, first name, or full signature (initials are more common). Some memo writers insert their initials immediately after their name on the "From" line, rather than at the foot of the memo.

"Enc" means another document is attached to the memo. If copies of the memo are sent to additional readers, type the letters "cc" and the readers' names at the foot of the memo or immediately beneath the addressee's name at the top.

Fax Messages

Facsimile transmission (fax) is a means for sending prewritten messages by the telephone between one organization and another. The message may be a letter, memorandum, list, diagram, or illustration. It may be a preprinted document fed through a fax machine or an online document transmitted directly from a computer.

Letters sent by fax are delivered in *minutes*

The message normally is preceded by a cover sheet that gives details about the message that follows. A typical cover sheet is shown in Figure 8-4. The cover sheet is preprinted with the originating company's name, address, fax number, telephone number, and email address, or a macro containing the same information is stored in the computer. The originator has to fill in the following details:

- The name and fax number of the recipient.
- The name of the message originator.
- The date and time the message was originated.
- The number of pages making up the whole message. This entry is important because it tells the recipient the number of pages to look for (in case transmission is interrupted and only some of the pages are printed).

Fax transmittal cover letters have become short and simple

Mainstream Video Productions
316 St Vital Place, Winnipeg MB R2H 3J9
Tel: (204) 233 6049 Fax: (204) 233 5022

FAX

To: Kevin Cholander, Kolmedia Inc, Toronto

Fax No.: (416) 935 4471

From: Tanys Shadar, Mainstream Video, Winnipeg

Date: January 17, 2001

MESSAGE:

Kevin:

This is the cover sheet we will be using for all our fax messages. If the message is very short you may write or type it in this message square and the recipient will receive only the cover sheet. If the message is longer, prepare it on a separate sheet or sheets, and write or type a brief note here (optional).

This time I am enclosing two pages listing the fax numbers for all of our product suppliers.

Tanys

No. of pages (including this sheet): 3
If not all pages received, call (204) 233 6049

Figure 8-4 Cover sheet for a faxed document, with the attached sheets omitted

The message originator may also write a message in a space provided on the form (as has been done in the lower part of Figure 8-4).

Rather than prepare a separate cover page, and providing you do not need to write a brief note to accompany the document, you may write transmittal information on a stick-on slip and affix it to the top of the document. The slips may be purchased in 50-slip pads from most office stationery suppliers.

Electronic Mail

There is no designated shape for email, other than that dictated by the messaging system you use. There are, however, some guidelines for writing email, which are covered in Chapter 13 (see "Netiquette").

Messages sent by email are delivered in seconds

Semiformal Paper or Report

Some research papers and business reports need to be presented more formally than as a simple memorandum or letter, yet do not need a cover and the separate title, summary, and contents pages of the long formal report described in Chapter 7. For these special papers and reports, Figure 8-5 (on page 235) offers a middle-of-the-road semiformal design for the first page, a design also suitable for college term papers. The following suggestions are keyed to the circled numbers beside the sample paper.

Effective layout and appearance help convince readers to read the whole report

Position the title 6.5 cm below the top of the page. Use boldface upper- and lower-case letters and centre the title between the margins. If the title is long, use two lines with no space between the lines (printing conventions recommend keeping the second line shorter than the first line). Use 14 point type.

Start the author identification four lines below the title and centred between the margins. You may introduce the author with the words *Prepared by:* or simply *By:*, or you may omit the introductory line.

Insert the date either here or at the end of the paper or report. If you insert it here, centre it between the margins; if you insert it at the end of the paper, leave three blank lines after the last line of text and then type the date starting at the left margin.

4

Start the Abstract (or Summary) four lines below the author's name and title (and date of report, if included). Centre the word **Abstract** or **Summary** between the margins, using 12 point boldface type.

5

Abstracts or Summaries are sometimes set in italics

Keystroke the Abstract or Summary in a noticeably narrower column than the remainder of the paper. Indent it on both sides as described in Figure 8-5, and type it single-spaced.

Start the body of the paper or report four lines below the Abstract. Keystroke the first section heading (and all subsequent section headings) in boldface upper- and lower-case letters. Centre the headings between the margins.

Type the body of the paper or report using the full column width. Most research papers and reports are written with single line spacing, although occasionally a research paper—and particularly an academic research paper—is prepared with 1.5 or double line spacing. You may justify both margins or leave the right margin "ragged."

Set secondary headings within each section against the left margin and type them in boldface upper- and lower-case 12 point type.

The Words Within

Pay attention to the details

Creating the right appearance for a letter or report is only the first step. Many readers are equally influenced by misspelled words and carelessly constructed sentences. Rightly or wrongly, they feel that a person who has not taken care to look after the writing may not have paid enough attention to the information.

The message is clear: if you want readers to respond positively to your letters and reports, you have to pay attention to *every* aspect of their construction.

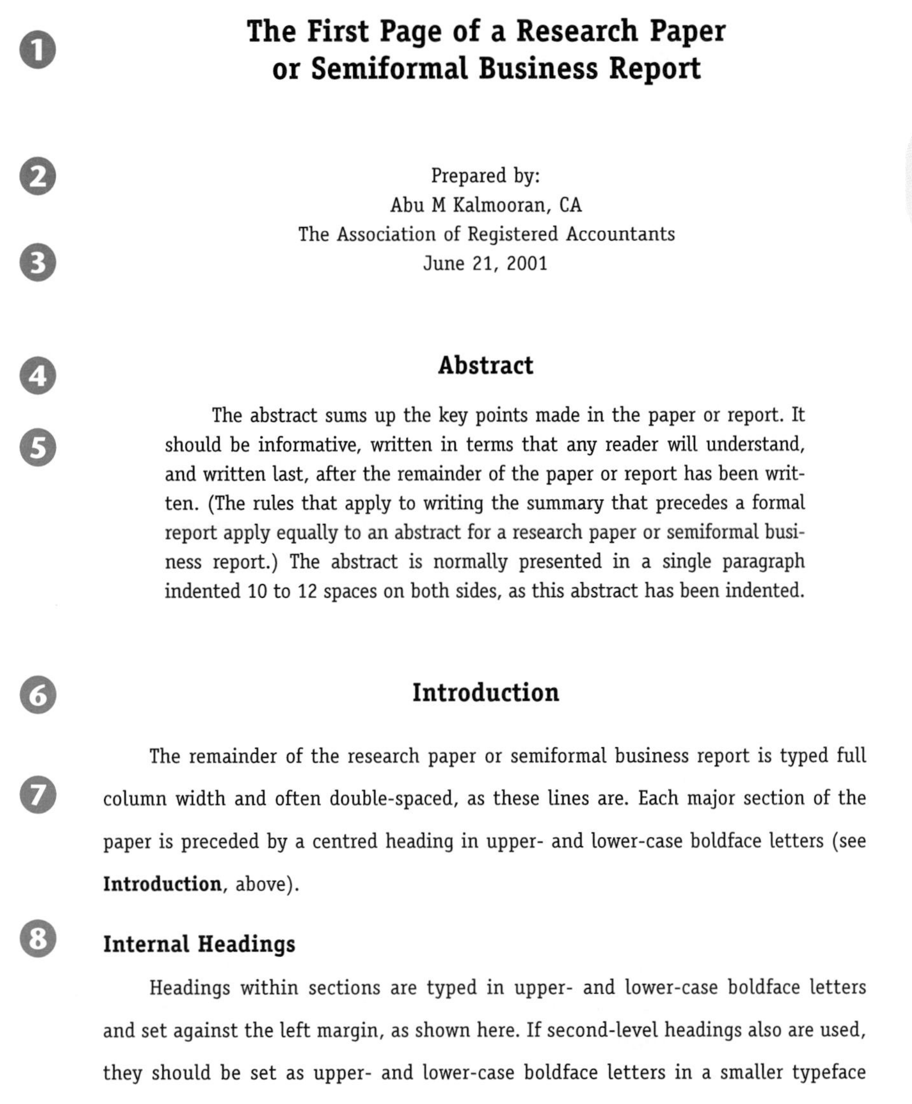

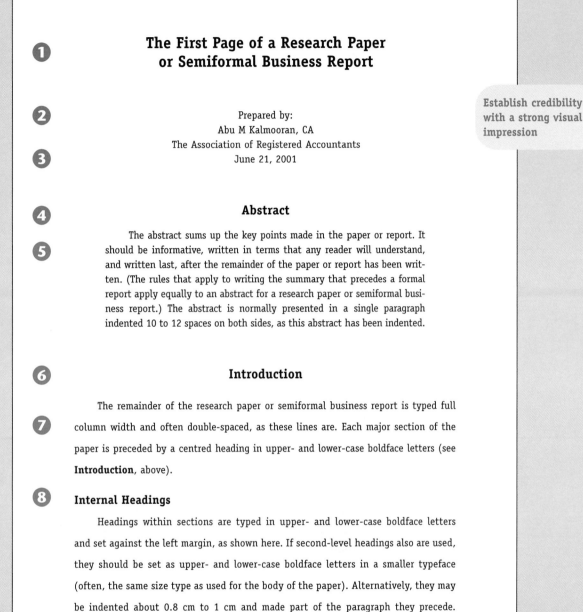

1 **The First Page of a Research Paper or Semiformal Business Report**

2 Prepared by:
Abu M Kalmooran, CA
The Association of Registered Accountants
3 June 21, 2001

4 **Abstract**

5 The abstract sums up the key points made in the paper or report. It should be informative, written in terms that any reader will understand, and written last, after the remainder of the paper or report has been written. (The rules that apply to writing the summary that precedes a formal report apply equally to an abstract for a research paper or semiformal business report.) The abstract is normally presented in a single paragraph indented 10 to 12 spaces on both sides, as this abstract has been indented.

6 **Introduction**

7 The remainder of the research paper or semiformal business report is typed full column width and often double-spaced, as these lines are. Each major section of the paper is preceded by a centred heading in upper- and lower-case boldface letters (see **Introduction**, above).

8 **Internal Headings**

Headings within sections are typed in upper- and lower-case boldface letters and set against the left margin, as shown here. If second-level headings also are used, they should be set as upper- and lower-case boldface letters in a smaller typeface (often, the same size type as used for the body of the paper). Alternatively, they may be indented about 0.8 cm to 1 cm and made part of the paragraph they precede.

1

Establish credibility with a strong visual impression

Figure 8-5 Page 1 of a research paper

TO SUM UP

When you present a letter, memorandum, or report to a reader, the reader's receptiveness is influenced first by the document's appearance. If the document is cleanly presented and well arranged on the page, the reader approaches your information with confidence. But if the appearance is sloppy, the reader approaches your information with some hesitation. The effect is subtle and subconscious.

WEBLINKS

Effective Letter Writing
www.csun.edu/~vcecn006/lettr.htm
This site discusses the lost art of letter writing and also includes tips for effective letter writing, such as how to format a business letter.

Memos
owl.english.purdue.edu/Files/99.html
This page will help you solve your memo-writing problems by discussing what a memo is, presenting some options for organizing memos, describing the parts of memos, and suggesting some hints that will make your memos more effective.

A Beginner's Guide to Effective Email
www.webfoot.com/advice/email.top.html?Yahoo
This useful guide includes an introduction to email and a discussion about why it differs from ordinary correspondence. Other sections describe email context, page layout, intonation, and gestures. Links to other sites about email are included.

Illustrating Business Reports

chapter 9

Lynn Mahaffey taps a fingertip on the report she is holding. "You've written an excellent analysis," she says to Sheena Dhalmi. "Good research, good information. It's all there!"

"Thank you," Sheena says quietly. It's true: she researched her data thoroughly and took care to document her facts coherently. Yet now Sheena is concerned, for she has detected a slight hesitation behind Lynn's words. (Sheena is a junior accountant for Fairview Credit Union, and Lynn is the branch manager.)

"All it needs is one or two illustrations," Lynn continues. "Just enough to draw readers' attention to the report's salient features."

"Ah, but I've done that," Sheena counters, on the defensive now. She flips over the pages of the report and points to a five-column table (see Table 9-1). "Here!"

"That table's fine," Lynn reassures her. "It supports your analysis very nicely. But it's not easy to read at a glance, not with all those numbers!"

"I didn't intend it to be read at a glance," Sheena explains. "It's there because I expect people will want to examine the numbers for themselves."

"Some people may," Lynn corrects her. "But not everyone at Credit Union Central will want to take the time. Many would prefer to scan a chart or graph that shows trends and variations rather than search for them among a lot of numbers." She pauses for a moment and then adds, "Look, I don't want you to change a word in your report, but I would like you to include an illustration that draws attention to the key factors you want your readers to grasp—the dip in sales caused by the recession in the early 1990s, for example."

"And the slowdown in 1995?" Sheena asks.

"You've got the idea!"

Table 9-1 Sheena's original table

Fairview Credit Union
Annual Sales of Travellers Cheques, 1991 to 2000
(in Equivalent Canadian Dollars)

Year	*US Dollars ($1000)*	*UK Pounds ($1000)*	*European Currencies* ($1000)*	*Asian Currencies ($1000)*	*Other Currencies** ($1000)*
1991	218.3	126.9	77.2	39.6	18.8
1992	226.0	139.8	95.1	55.7	20.6
1993	213.8	123.2	72.0	43.2	14.3
1994	218.6	133.6	81.3	61.0	17.2
1995	238.7	137.0	75.7	34.8	10.9
1996	245.4	152.5	88.2	36.3	16.7
1997	253.1	179.4	113.9	47.9	27.8
1998	259.8	213.3	147.1	79.1	43.2
1999	267.6	259.0	190.2	130.4	56.7
2000	278.9	316.2	250.1	208.6	73.5

* Includes Euro (only in 2000).

** Primarily S. America, S. Africa, and Iceland.

A table may be factual, but it may also be difficult to interpret

IN THIS CHAPTER

You will learn how to select and design illustrations that will complement your written reports. Specifically, you will learn how to

- select a particular drawing or chart to illustrate a specific situation,
- design a drawing or chart that can be readily understood and will support your written words,
- position illustrations so that they face or are adjacent to the information they relate to, and
- design illustrations for both print and oral presentations.

Computer-Designed Graphs and Charts

Computer graphics software makes illustrating easier

Constructing graphs and charts with a pencil and squared paper used to be a laborious process, but computer technology has simplified it. Software programs can now ask a report writer to key in the quantities of each function, view the completed graph, bar chart, or pie chart on screen, and then print a hard copy. The illustration is then inserted into the appropriate place in a report, the printed copy is used to make a slide or transparency, or a slide is made directly from the computer image.

The advantage is that you can make graphs and charts in only minutes, which gives you the opportunity to view a particular graphic and decide whether it conveys the appropriate information—a process that would take hours if you had to draw the graphic manually.

Then why is it necessary to have 20 pages in this book on how to construct graphs and charts? Because you need to know the guidelines for creating effective graphics, so you will be able to identify whether the software you have chosen will illustrate your report in an appropriate way.

A graphic has to help a reader understand facts or a concept quickly and easily. Consequently, it must be as simple as possible. Many software programs create very attractive two- and three-dimensional illustrations, often in multiple colors on a computer screen, which may look fine in a glossy magazine or daily newspaper but look out of place in a business report. Knowing the guidelines will help you plan effective illustrations to insert into your reports. Be guided by an old adage that says: "An illustration must help explain the narrative; the narrative must never have to explain an illustration."

Does your software do what you want it to do?

Graphs

Sheena converts the data in Table 9-1 into a graph (see Figure 9-1). She selects a graph for three reasons: there are two variables to consider (time and sales), a graph will show trends more readily than most other illustrations, and most readers will be familiar with graphs. She chooses to portray only the four most significant currency groups in the table, and to omit the "Other Currencies" group because it is small and fragmented.

Let a graph or chart illustrate key points

Sheena takes care to devise an illustration that not only provides good information but also creates a visual image that clearly supports her text. To do so, she conforms to three general and five specific guidelines.

General Guidelines for Constructing Graphs

1. A graph is a visual way of showing how one factor affects another—in Sheena's report, how the advance of time affected the sales of travellers cheques. These factors are known as the independent variable and the dependent variable. The independent variable—time, in Sheena's graph—is not affected by the dependent variable. The dependent variable—sales, in Sheena's graph—*is* affected by the independent variable (in other words, time *affects* sales). Other examples are

One variable is always dependent on the other

Independent Variable		*Dependent Variable*
Automobile speed	*affects*	Fuel consumption
Equipment noise	*affects*	Staff productivity
Freezer temperature	*affects*	Food storage life

Either the vertical or horizontal axis of a graph may be the independent variable, depending on the information being portrayed.

Limit the number of curves

2. The lines within a graph are known as curves, and there should be no more than four curves within a graph, or three if the curves intersect more than once. (Sheena chose to omit the "Other Currencies" column in Table 9-1, to limit the number of curves.)
3. In a simple graph all the curves may be solid lines of the same weight. In a more complex graph the appearance of the curves may differ so that each can be readily identified (e.g. a solid line, a series of dashes, a series of dots, as shown in Figure 9-1). Colored lines should rarely be used to differentiate between curves, because if copies of the report are printed later they are likely to be all one color (usually black) and the differences will no longer be apparent.

A graph can depict two continuous variables

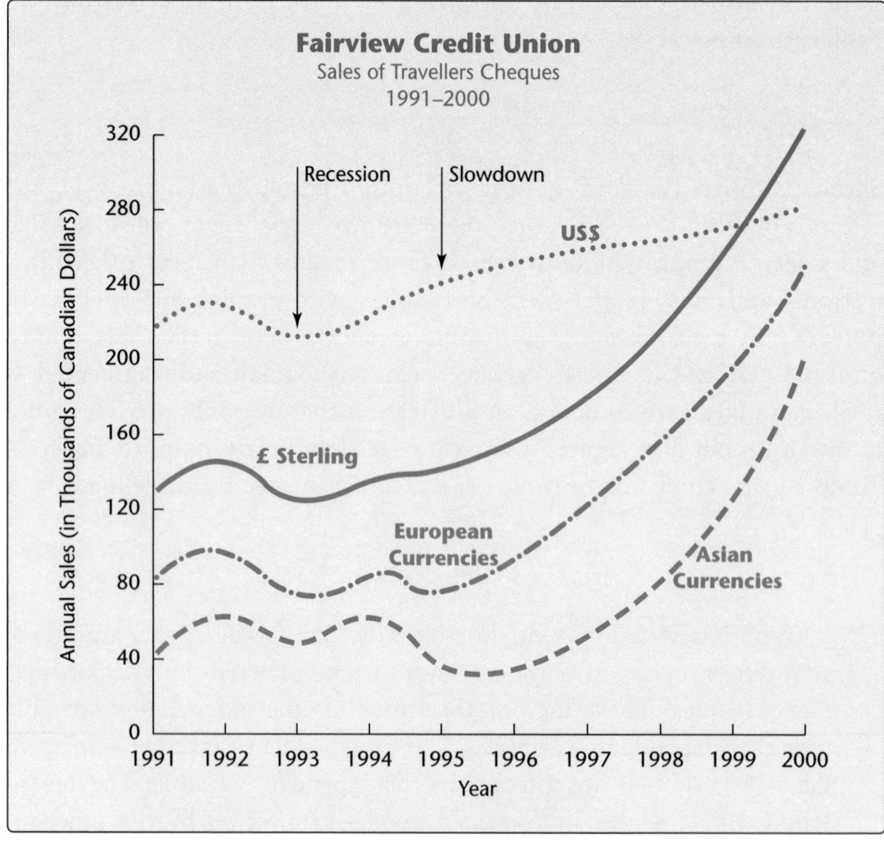

Figure 9-1 A graph with four curves

Specific Guidelines for Constructing Graphs

1. Label each curve, and keep the letters *horizontal* (never slope the letters by placing them along the curve like a river name on a map).
2. Apply the horizontal rule to all lettering on and surrounding the graph, with one exception: the title of the vertical axis. Align its letters so that they run parallel to the vertical axis, as Sheena has done in Figure 9-1.
3. Delete the plot points used to construct the curves and, unless readers will want to extract exact readings from the illustration (which is unlikely), smooth the curves out just enough so they flow smoothly. (Plot points are the individual positions marked on the graph paper or entered on the screen to design a curve, through which a line is drawn to form the curve.)

Some software programs automatically insert plot points; you may choose to accept or remove them

4. Select scales along the vertical and horizontal axes so that the curves portray the data correctly:

   - Fill the available space. Sheena positions the curves correctly in Figure 9-1, but the person who designed the graph in Figure 9-2(a) positioned them awkwardly so that there is too much white space on one side and at the bottom. The vertical axis should start at 2 rather than 0 hours.
   - Create the correct image. Figure 9-2(b) shows a curve illustrating the time it takes for an automobile body to cool after it leaves the paint-drying oven. At first the temperature drops rapidly, and then the body cools more slowly as it gradually approaches the ambient (room) temperature. Figures 9-2(c) and (d) show the effects of poorly chosen vertical and horizontal axes. Both are technically accurate, yet the shortened vertical axis of graph (c) creates the visual impression that the automobile body cools only slowly, while the cramped horizontal axis of graph (d) seems to show that the temperature plummets until almost the very last moment. As a visual aid, neither correctly supports the data it represents.

Ensure the dimensions of your graph depict the correct effect

5. Keep the background clear of all but essential lettering, and insert grid lines only if the reader is expected to extract data from the graph. The grid lines may be drawn in, as in graph (e), or implied, as in graph (f).

Keep the graph clean and simple

Pie Charts

Before showing her graph to Lynn, Sheena decides to make a second illustration in which she will compare the dollar value of travellers cheques purchased for each currency category in 1991 with those purchased in 2000. This comparison, she feels, will indicate the shift in travel destinations that occurred over the past decade.

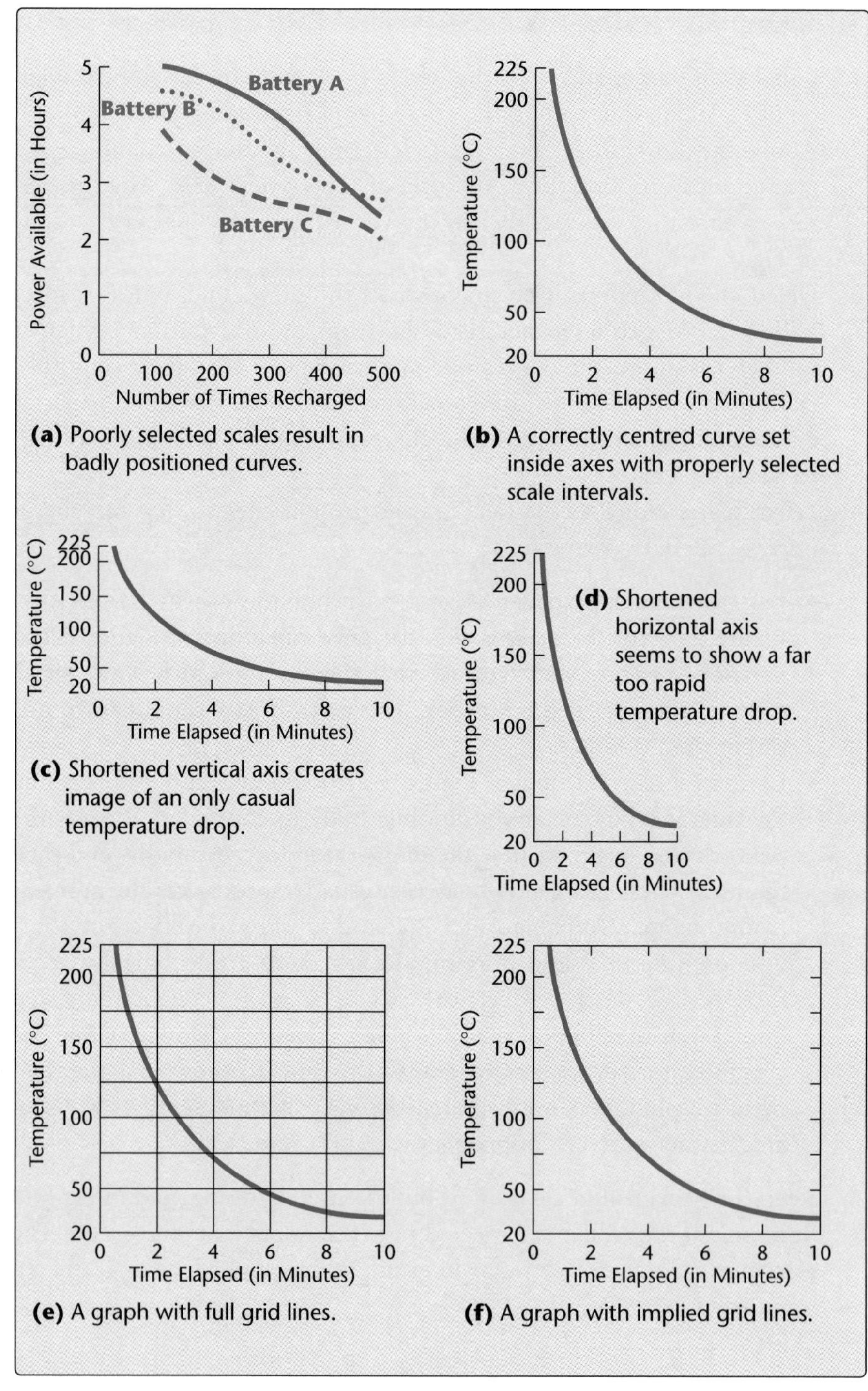

(a) Poorly selected scales result in badly positioned curves.

(b) A correctly centred curve set inside axes with properly selected scale intervals.

(c) Shortened vertical axis creates image of an only casual temperature drop.

(d) Shortened horizontal axis seems to show a far too rapid temperature drop.

(e) A graph with full grid lines.

(f) A graph with implied grid lines.

Figure 9-2 Factors affecting the visual presentation of a graph

To depict the comparison she selects the simplest of all illustrations: the pie chart. She constructs two pie charts, one for 1991 and one for 2000, and places them side by side as shown in Figure 9-3. A primary requirement for constructing a pie chart is that the quantities within the pie *must* add up to a round figure such as "1," "10," "100," or "100%." This means that Sheena

A pie chart is easy to understand but has limited illustrative potential

- cannot use the pure dollar values for each currency listed in Table 9-1, but must convert them to percentages, and
- must include the small quantity of "Other Currencies" if she is to achieve a full 100% within the pie.

Sheena also follows three other guidelines that enhance the presentation of a pie chart:

1. Ensure that one of the primary dividing lines between two segments is a vertical line originating at the centre of the pie and ending at the "12 o'clock" position.
2. Ensure that, if there is more than one pie chart, the segments follow the same sequence clockwise around the pie in all the charts.
3. Shade each pie's segments so they can be compared easily.

Keep the pies parallel

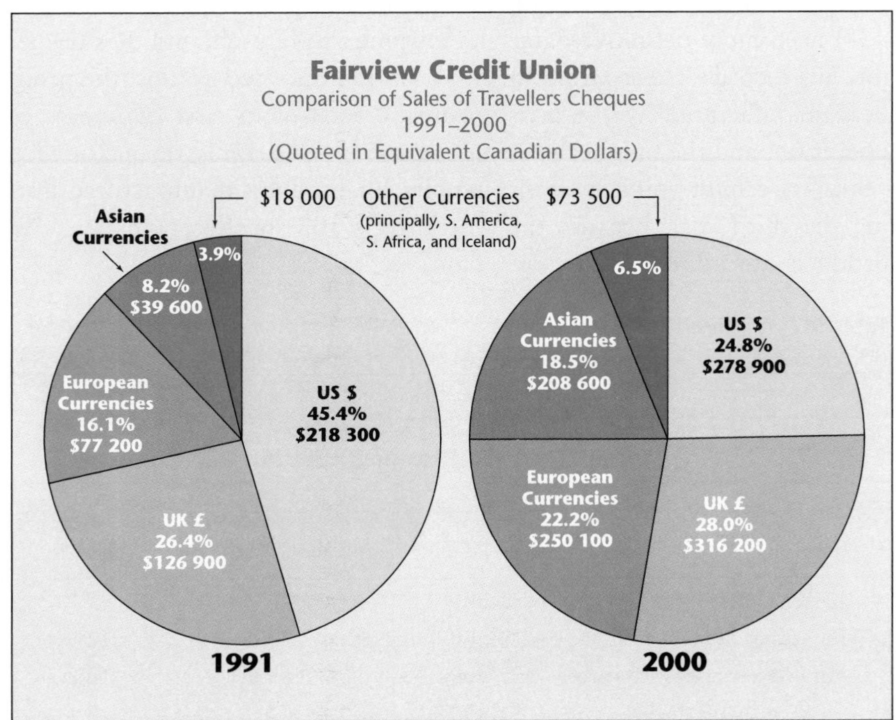

Figure 9-3 Two pie charts (Two are used to demonstrate the changes in sales patterns.)

Credit Union manager Lynn Mahaffey likes both of Sheena's illustrations and is particularly pleased with the pair of pie charts. "You couldn't have found a better way to show the shift in travel patterns," she muses. "Although the table and graph seem to show that purchases of travellers cheques in US dollars have risen slowly but steadily throughout the period, the pie charts show that in effect they have *fallen* in comparison to the volume of purchases in other major currencies."

Bar Charts

Ross Huguenot is preparing a report on product quality for his company's head office in Toronto. (Ross is supervisor of quality control at the three-year-old Electrical Products Division of Com-Nor Manufacturers Limited.) Management has asked him to identify how many items of the five major product lines manufactured by the Electrical Products Division during its first two years of operation were returned for warranty repairs.

A simple table and bar chart convey simple data

Ross first assembles data on warranty returns into a table (see Table 9-2), and then constructs a bar chart (see Figure 9-4). But when he starts to describe his data he finds he has little information to convey, other than that quality control for the electric skillet was excellent, for the electronic wok terrible, and for the other three products about average.

"I need more definitive data," he murmurs to himself, and digs deeper into his records. He separates his information into two groups: the products manufactured by the division during each of its first two years of operation, and the number of items returned for warranty repair for each year. (He cannot count warranty repairs for products manufactured during the third year, because the warranty is still in effect and defective products are still coming in for repair.)

Table 9-2 A "closed" table

Warranty Repairs for Products Manufactured in 1999 and 2000
Small Electrical Products Division

Product Name	*Number Manufactured*	*Number Returned for Warranty Repairs*	*Percent Returns*
Toaster D101	74 000	7215	9.7
Humidifier 300S	26 400	3407	12.9
Hand Mixer Series M	87 500	8953	10.2
Electronic Wok W40	41 200	7438	18.1
Electric Skillet 700	58 000	3588	6.2

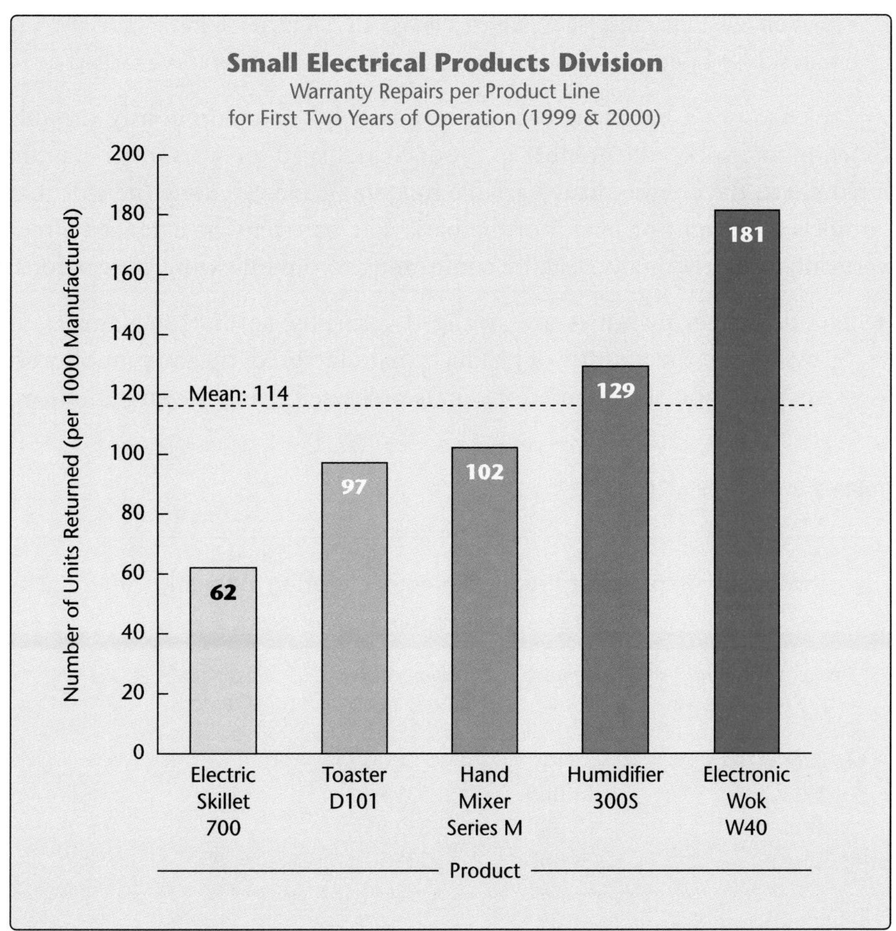

Figure 9-4 A simple bar chart

Ross constructs a second table (see Table 9-3), and sees that there are changes in the frequency of repairs for each item. So he prepares a second bar chart to illustrate the trends that developed over the two years (see Figure 9-5). These trends were not apparent in his first table and chart. Now Ross is able to write in his report:

A more detailed table and bar chart convey more definitive data

> For four product lines the number of units returned for warranty repair decreased from year one to year two (see bar chart), demonstrating that the revised quality control measures introduced at the start of the second production year were taking effect. This was particularly true of the electronic wok (model W40), with which we experienced a disastrous first year with a 21.2% return rate, created chiefly by poor soldering of a printed circuit board purchased from an independent supplier. After the fault was pinpointed, however, we experienced a greatly improved second year with a 9.6% return rate. The

A paragraph like this needs definitive data to support it

exception was Humidifier 300S, which showed a 2.3% increase in the rate of return from year one to year two. I am currently investigating this anomaly.

A bar chart has only one continuous variable

Ross chooses a bar chart because he has only one continuously variable function to display: the number of products returned for warranty repair. In a bar chart, the continuously variable function is placed along the axis that parallels the height or length of the bars. The bars may be arranged either vertically or horizontally, usually conforming to the following conventions:

- Bars depicting quantities are arranged vertically, so that they appear to "grow" (as in the number of products manufactured, the amount of profit recorded, and the number of claims processed over a given period).

Table 9-3 An "open" table

Warranty Repairs for Products Manufactured in 1999 and 2000
Small Electrical Products Division

Product Name and Year of Manufacture	*Number Made*	*Number of Warranty Returns*	*Returns per 1000 Made*	*Percent Returns*
Toaster D101				
1999	33 000	3894	118	11.8
2000	41 000	3321	81	8.1
Totals	74 000	7215	97	9.7
Humidifier 300S				
1999	11 400	1322	116	11.6
2000	15 000	2085	139	13.9
Totals	26 400	3407	129	12.9
Hand Mixer Series M				
1999	42 000	5586	133	13.3
2000	45 500	3367	74	7.4
Totals	87 500	8953	102	10.2
Electronic Wok W40				
1999	30 000	6360	212	21.2
2000	11 200	1078	96	9.6
Totals	41 200	7438	181	18.1
Electric Skillet 700				
1999	16 000	1152	72	7.2
2000	42 000	2436	58	5.8
Totals	58 000	3588	62	6.2

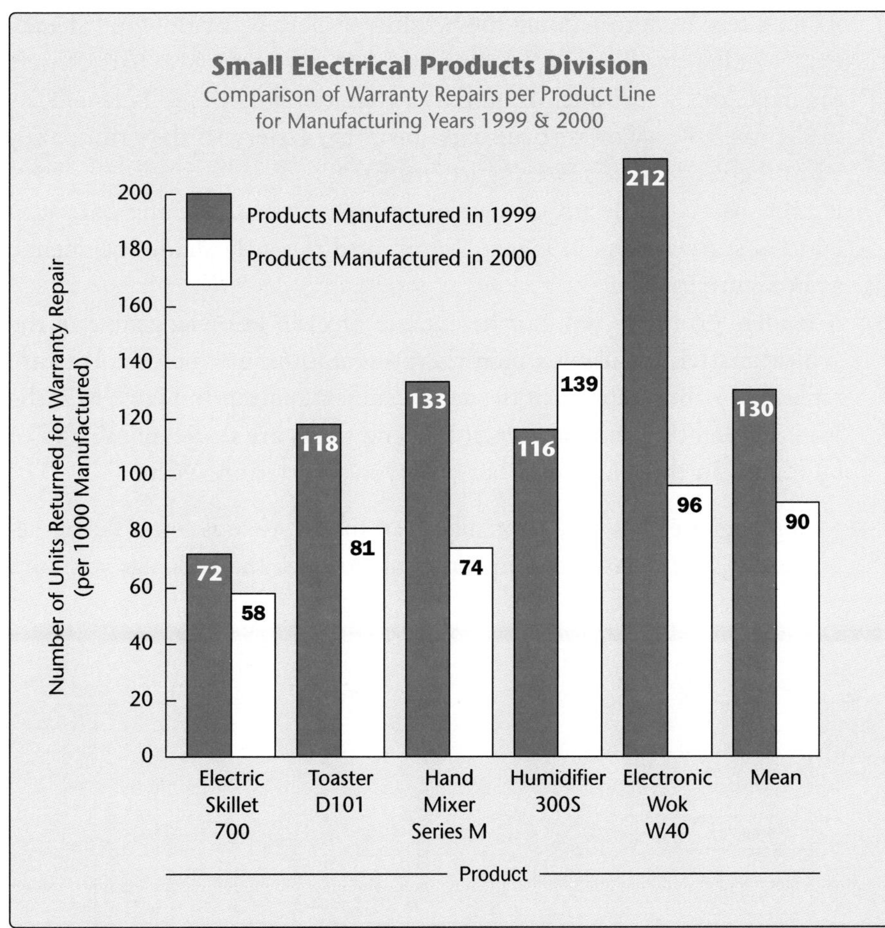

Figure 9-5 A multiple-column bar chart

Shaded bars help readers differentiate between two sets of information

- Bars depicting elapsed time normally are arranged horizontally, so that they appear to be placed along a continuum (as in life expectancy of different categories of people, and the time it takes to introduce a new product line from initial development to production). Figure 9-6(a) is an example.

Choose vertical or horizontal bars to help convey your message

Here are six additional guidelines Ross considers when designing his bar chart, which you can use when designing yours:

1. Position the bars so that the spaces between them are the same width as an individual bar. (In software-created bar charts, the space between the bars may be considerably less.)
2. Shade the bars so that they stand out.
3. If readers are likely to need more than a general idea of the totals depicted by the bars, insert the total at the top or the end of each bar, as Ross has done in Figures 9-4 and 9-5.

4. As an alternative to naming the product or activity at the foot of each bar, as in Figures 9-4 and 9-5 (or to the left, for horizontal bars), insert the name of the product or activity *inside* the bar, along its length, as in Figure 9-6(a). For vertical bars, print the letters so they run parallel to the vertical axis (see Figure 9-6[b]).

Manipulate the bars to make them more informative

5. If each bar is made up of several components, divide the bars into labelled segments, as in Figure 9-6(c), or differently shaded segments, as in Figure 9-6(d).
6. If readers probably will not be experts or even knowledgeable in the subject matter, try using a pictorial presentation in which the bars are replaced by illustrations of the actual subject matter. In Figure 9-7, the bars representing the number of housing starts are depicted as rows of buildings. In this particular bar chart, two variations occur:

   - The bars are shown horizontally, even though time is not a factor, because it would have been inappropriate to stack the buildings vertically.

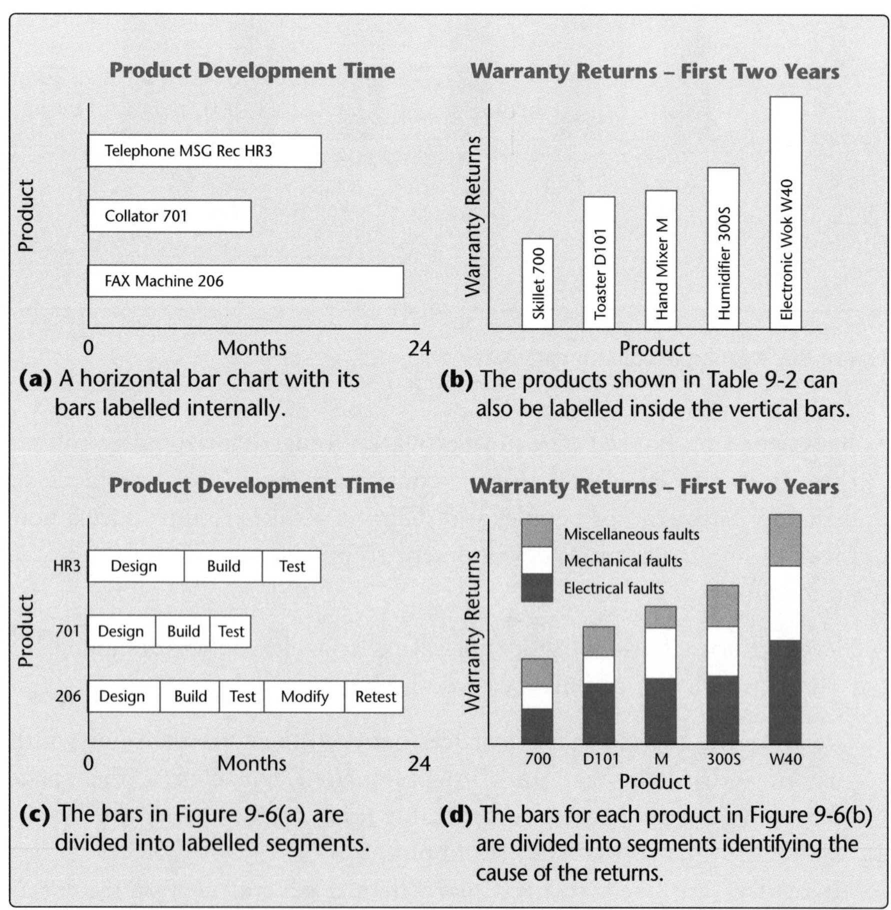

Figure 9-6 Different configurations for bar charts

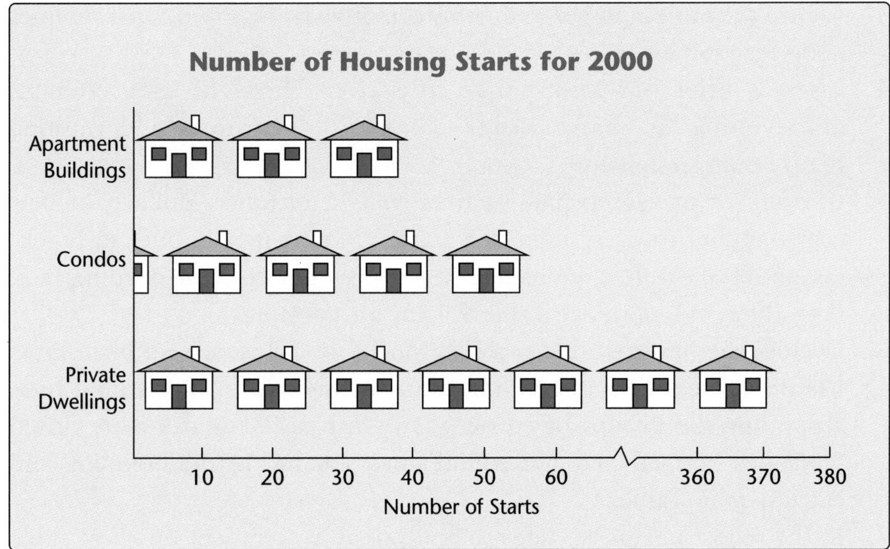

Figure 9-7 Alternative method for depicting the bars in a bar chart

Pictorial charts are used in magazines and newspapers more than in business reports

- The horizontal axis is broken between 60 and 360, to avoid creating a disproportionately long bar.

Another alternative is to depict three-dimensional bars, which can be done easily with computer graphics.

Tables

Both Sheena Dhalmi and Ross Huguenot insert tables as well as graphs and charts into their reports (see Tables 9-1, 9-2, and 9-3). The tables provide detailed data that helps establish the validity of the writers' information and offer evidence for readers to examine in depth.

A table does more than collect bits of data amassed during a study. Rather, it has to be carefully constructed so that it presents essential information in an economical and easily accessible form. The following guidelines apply:

Tables should be lean and mean: facts; no frills!

1. If readers need to refer to the data in a table while they read a report, insert the table inside the report narrative, ideally on the same or the facing page. However, if readers will not need to study the table as they read, place the table in an attachment or appendix at the back of the report, and refer to it and quote one or two key factors from it in the report narrative. (Readers should not have to flip back to the appendix while they read.)
2. Keep the table "lean"; create as few columns as possible and insert only essential data.

3. Centre the table number and an informative title as two separate lines *above* the table.
4. Insert a brief but informative title at the head of each column, abbreviating as many words as possible without undermining reader comprehension.
5. If a unit of measurement—such as weight, distance, dollars, or percent—applies to every item in a column, insert it only once in brackets above the table, immediately beneath the column heading: e.g. (kg), (km), ($), (%). See Table 9-1 for an example.

Open tables are tidy; closed tables help you compartmentalize data

6. Decide whether the table is to be "open" or "closed." An open table has no vertical lines separating the columns and no horizontal lines separating the groups of entries, as in Tables 9-1 and 9-3. A closed table has vertical and horizontal lines separating the columns and entries, as in Table 9-2.
7. In the report narrative, refer to and possibly comment on every table accompanying the report.
8. Refrain from copying tables of data in a report directly onto slides to accompany an oral presentation. Even the relatively simple Table 9-2 would be too detailed for projecting onto a screen in front of an audience.

Histograms and Surface Charts

Two lesser-used charts

Two additional charts have properties of both a bar chart and a graph. A histogram looks like a bar chart, but has no spaces between the bars. A surface chart appears to have curves, but really is a series of bars. Both have a specific application and neither is widely used.

Histogram

A histogram is used when a writer has insufficient data along one axis to construct a graph. Ross Huguenot constructs the histogram in Figure 9-8 to depict the incomplete figures on product warranty returns for his division's third year of operation. In the accompanying narrative he explains that the preliminary returns for the third year seem to show a similar pattern to those for the second year (shown in Figure 9-5).

Surface Chart

A surface chart appears to have curves but really is made up of bars that, like those in a histogram, are set without spaces between them. The bottom curve is plotted in first (in Figure 9-9 it represents the number of drivers who were 100% responsible for causing the accidents in which they

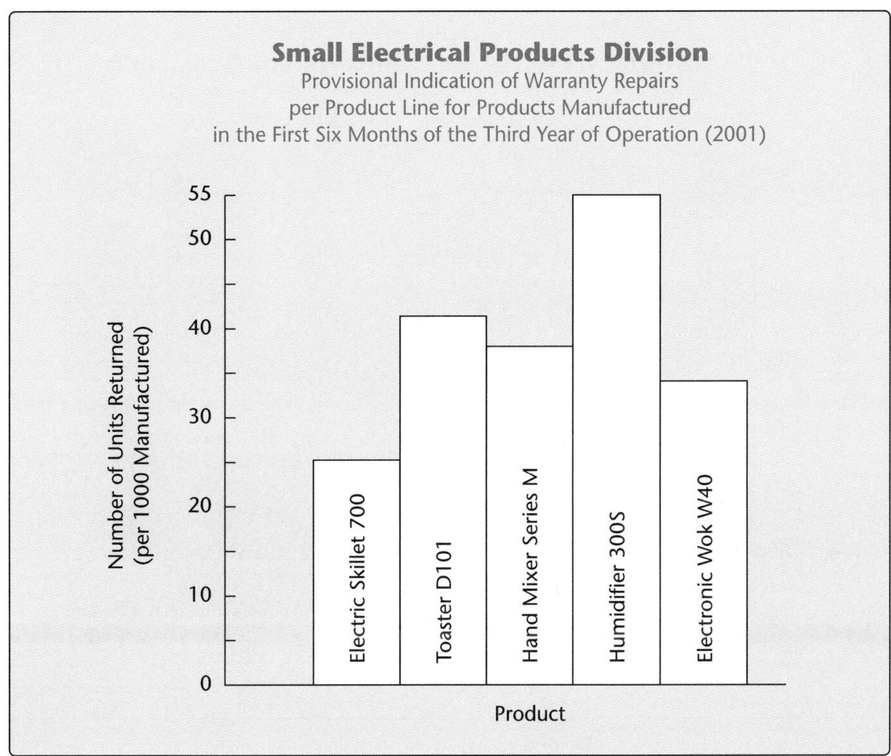

Figure 9-8 A histogram is based on sparse or incomplete data. Because he is presenting incomplete figures, the designer of this histogram has neither inserted quantities at the top of each column nor shown an average or mean.

A histogram depicts only a general trend

were involved). The second curve is then plotted in (in Figure 9-9 it represents claims where another party is 100% responsible for causing the accident), but it *uses the first curve as its base*. In its turn, the third curve (both parties 50% responsible), which uses the second curve as its base, represents the total of the three curves.

A surface chart shows how various components "add up" to a whole

For example, in Figure 9-9 the accident claim records for 2000 show that 697 claims were processed in January. In these claims

- the claimant was 100% responsible in 312 cases,
- another party was 100% responsible in 231 cases, and
- the claimant was 50% responsible in 154 cases.

To construct the January column of the chart, the number of claimants who were 100% responsible (312) was plotted in first at the 312 level of the vertical axis. The number of other parties who were 100% responsible (231) was plotted in next; it was added to the first number (312 + 231 = 543) and the total was plotted against the 543 mark of the vertical axis.

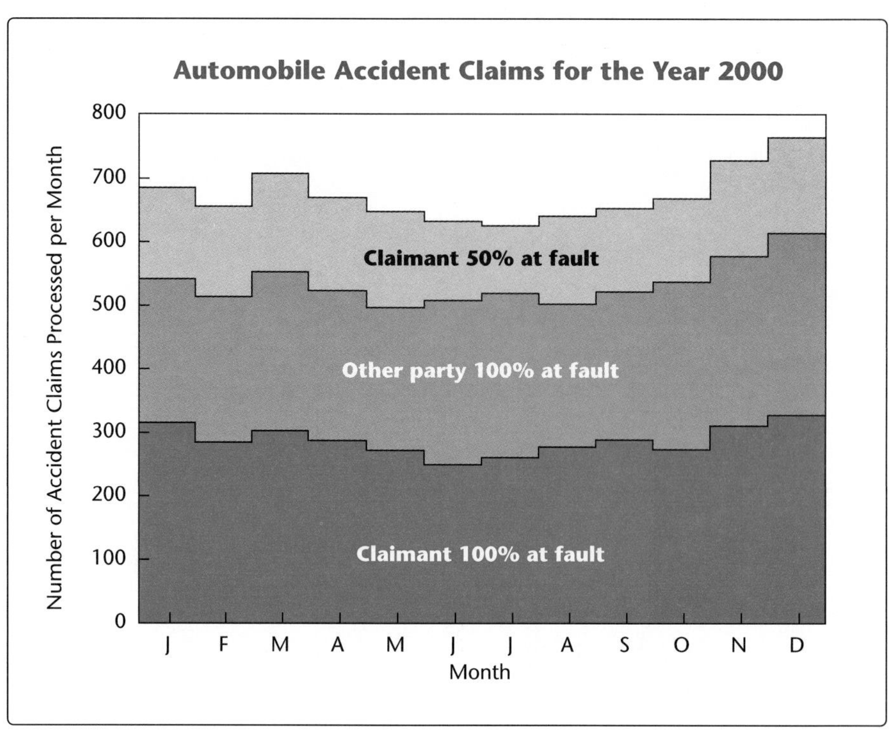

Figure 9-9 A surface chart is like a segmented bar chart (see Figure 9-6[d]), but has no spaces between the bars.

Similarly, the number of claimants who were 50% responsible (154) was added to the total for the previous curve (543 + 154) and plotted in at the 697 level. This process was repeated 12 times, once for each month.

There are three additional guidelines affecting the construction of surface charts:

1. Normally place the largest or most stable segment at the base of the chart.
2. Shade the areas within the curves, normally with the darkest shading at the bottom and the lightest shading at the top.
3. Optionally, smooth out the "steps" to form a true curve for each level. (This was not done for the surface chart in Figure 9-9 because its designer wanted to depict the variances as a series of monthly steps.)

"Massage" the curves to create a smoother effect

Other Illustrations

A flow chart can simplify a complex written procedure

Various other diagrams and charts, such as maps, site plans, sketches, flow charts, and photographs, can be designed to illustrate a particular point. The flow chart in Figure 9-10 is a typical example.

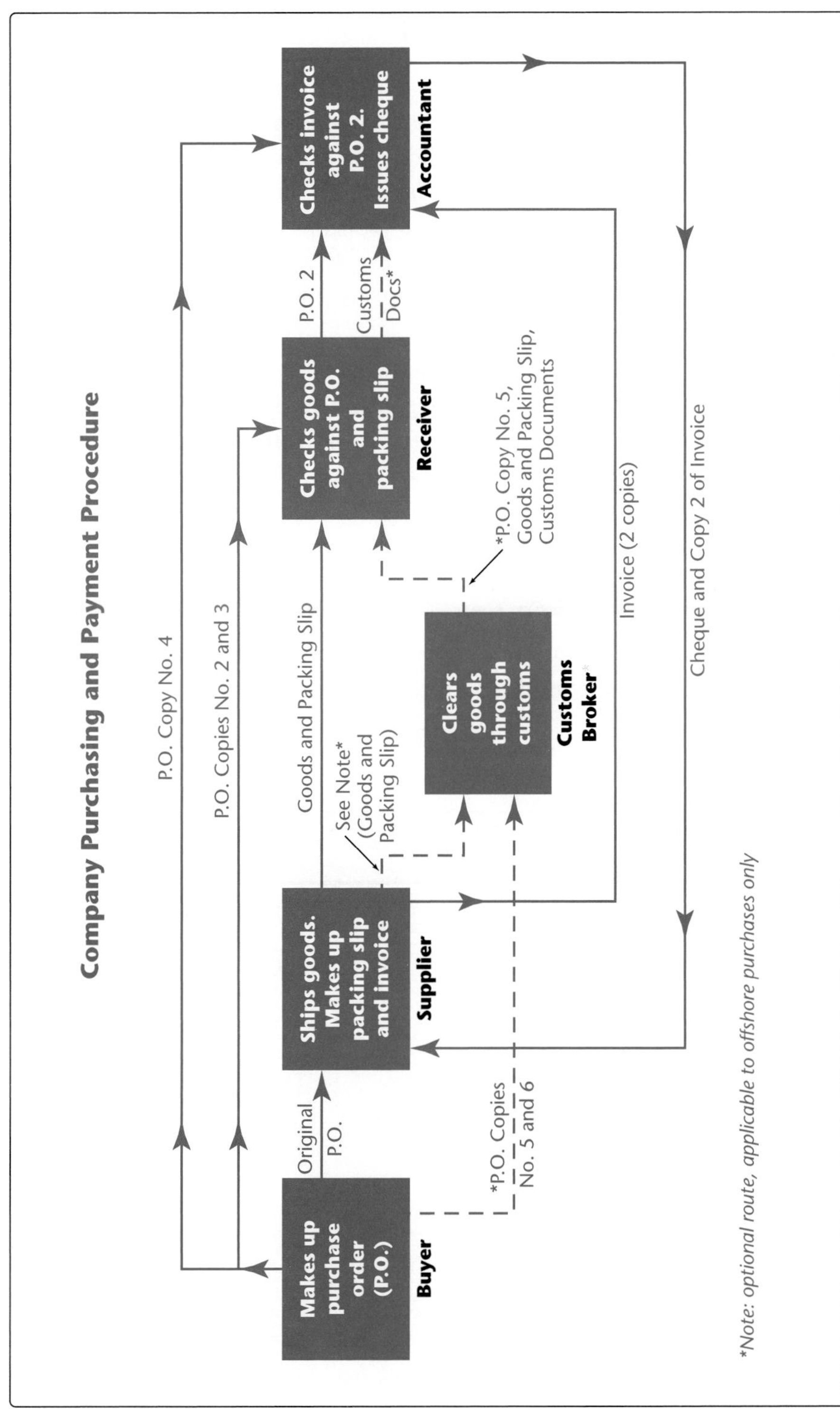

Figure 9-10 A flow chart (Courtesy Floral West Imports Ltd, Vancouver, BC; reproduced with permission.)

Positioning Illustrations

The ideal place for an illustration is on the same page as the text that refers to it, or on a facing page, so that readers can see the illustration as they read. Full-page illustrations, however, can create a problem if a report is printed on only one side of the paper, since they cannot be placed on a facing page. The same holds for illustrations that are referred to more than once, on different pages of the report. In both cases some way must be found to prevent readers from having to flip pages back and forth as they read.

A possible solution is to place the illustration on the right-hand half of an 11 inch by 17 inch sheet of paper and fold it inside the report, as shown in Figure 9-11. Readers can then fold out the sheet and keep it open beside the report as they read.

A similar problem arises over full-page illustrations that are wider horizontally than they are vertically and so have to be placed sideways on the page. The rule is to turn the illustration so that it can be read naturally from the right (see Figures 9-10 and 9-12), even though the words along the vertical axis of a graph may appear upside-down when the report is viewed normally (i.e. from the bottom of the page).

Position illustrations for maximum effect

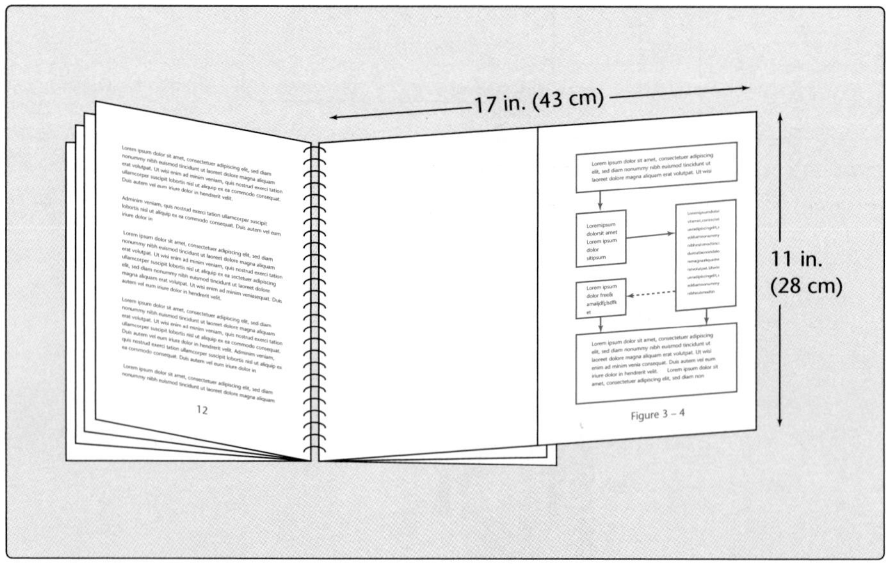

Figure 9-11 Illustrations that are referred to several times can be placed on an oversize page that folds out beside the report

Illustrations for an Oral Presentation

The guidelines for preparing illustrations to be shown during an oral presentation—as 35 mm slides, overhead transparencies, or digital images to be shown by an LCD projector—are similar to those for preparing illustrations for a report: keep them simple and ensure they support the speaker's words (a speaker should rarely have to explain an illustration). The following are specific guidelines:

1. Before designing illustrations for a talk, find out how large the hall will be and the distance the farthest viewer will be from the chart or screen. Use this information to select the size of lettering you will use.
2. Use bold lines for drawings, and simple, bold letters for the call-outs.
3. Use color to create variety and to differentiate between items (but remember that some colors look the same from a distance).
4. Make only one point or describe only one aspect in each illustration.
5. Avoid cluttering the drawing with unessential details.
6. Place a tiny, unobtrusive identifying number in one corner of each illustration (ideally, always the same corner), so that if the slides or transparencies get out of sequence they can be easily sorted.
7. Take the prepared illustrations to the room where they will be presented (or a similar-sized room), project them onto a screen, and walk to the back of the room to check that they can be read easily. Do the same for large charts, placing them on an easel, and for computer-generated slides.

Use strong lines and simple details

For further suggestions, see "Illustrate Your Talk" on page 267 of Chapter 10.

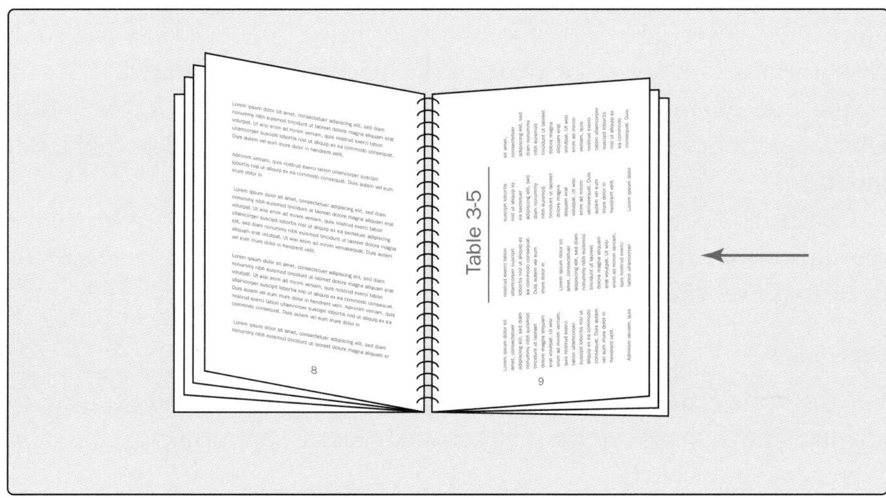

Figure 9-12 A full-page horizontally oriented illustration is turned 90° and positioned so that it can be read from the right

TO SUM UP

Authors insert charts and graphs in their reports, or project them onto a screen if they are making an oral presentation, to help their audience better understand the ideas they are presenting.

Illustrations must be kept simple, positioned close to the accompanying text, tailored to a specific audience, and never need to be explained. Before choosing an illustration, an author or speaker must first clearly identify the audience and then determine which type of illustration will best meet that audience's needs.

EXERCISES

Exercise 9.1

You are part-owner of a consulting firm known as AKA Business Consultants Ltd, and you have been working on a contract for Normandy Beverages, a manufacturer of soft drinks. Over a year ago, on April 1, Normandy Beverages introduced a new soft drink onto the market. Called "Rite On!" the soft drink quickly became popular. Now Normandy Beverages has asked you to study sales of Rite On! for the first year it was on the market and to compare sales with those of two other similar soft drinks that have been popular for several years: Pacific Plus and Bon Kool. Normandy Beverages already knows how many soft drinks it has sold; now it wants to know what share of the market it has captured.

Compare sales of soft drinks for a general view . . .

You first obtain sales figures for all three beverages (see Table 9-4, in which quantities represent the number of 355 mL bottles sold each month).

Construct a graph or chart to accompany your written report. Make the illustration show how the sales of each product have increased or decreased over the 12-month period.

Exercise 9.2

For the same report (see Exercise 9.1) construct a second illustration to compare how much of the market share each soft drink captured in September and March.

Table 9-4 Sales of comparable soft drinks

Month	Pacific Plus	Bon Kool	Rite On!
April	6 870 200	5 293 600	307 100
May	7 005 900	5 188 900	699 600
June	6 990 800	4 926 400	1 105 400
July	7 514 000	5 009 800	2 049 300
August	7 798 700	5 124 300	3 018 800
September	7 602 400	4 916 800	3 941 500
October	7 193 100	4 526 300	4 328 000
November	7 004 700	4 078 000	4 794 100
December	6 825 900	3 456 800	5 316 900
January	6 493 500	3 007 100	5 725 400
February	6 311 100	2 796 200	6 450 300
March	6 157 200	2 424 800	7 223 600

Exercise 9.3

You are writing the report on sales of Rite On! (see Exercise 9.1) when the marketing manager of Normandy Beverages calls you and says, "I'd also like you to show how sales of Rite On! have differed in different regions of Canada over the first year it was marketed. Can you include that?"

You agree to do so and separate the sales records into four regions: Ontario, Quebec, Atlantic Provinces, and Western Provinces. You also divide the sales year into three periods: April to July, August to November, and December to March. The sales for these regions and periods are shown in Table 9-5. Design a graph or chart to illustrate this data.

. . . and a more specific view

Table 9-5 Sales of "Rite On!"

	Sales Period		
Region	*April–July*	*Aug.–Nov.*	*Dec.–March*
Ontario	2 980 100	6 271 300	7 806 700
Quebec*	—	4 077 200	5 281 000
Atlantic Provinces	1 181 300	3 435 400	4 922 300
Western Provinces*	—	2 298 500	6 706 100
Total	**4 161 400**	**16 082 400**	**24 716 100**

**Rite On! was not marketed in Quebec and the Western Provinces until August.*

Exercise 9.4

Six months ago you were hired as administrative assistant to Arlene Blair, executive editor of *Dolphin*, a Canadian magazine for wildlife lovers. Last week Arlene called you in to her office and said: "Our circulation gets audited annually by the Circulation Board, and their reports establish how much we can charge for advertising. But we've never done a study to show how we're doing compared to the competition. I'd like you to go to the Circulation Board and get figures for the past five years, and then do a comparative analysis."

You identify the competition as four other magazines that appeal to wildlife-loving readers. They are:

Wildlife magazine circulation under the microscope

1. *Wetlands and Marshes*, published monthly in Yorkton, Saskatchewan, since 1974. Its history includes

   - Circulation: Five years ago: 7620 per month; four years ago: 8010; three years ago: 7830; two years ago: 8250; last year: 8900.
   - Price: \$2.25 five years ago; \$2.50 for years four through two; \$2.75 last year.
   - Average number of pages per issue: 56–64.

2. *Wildlife Canada*, published twice-monthly since 1964. Originally it was an American magazine called *Wildlife America*. A Canadian version came into effect just two years ago. The Canadianization involves a Canadian name and an eight-page insert of purely Canadian content as the central pages (the remaining 72 pages are exactly the same as in the US edition). The US head office is in Detroit, Michigan; the Canadian office is across the river in Windsor, Ontario. Specific details are

   - Circulation: Five years ago: 14 320; four years ago: 13 160; three years ago: 11 980; two years ago: 12 640: last year: 12 910.
   - Price: \$2.00 five years ago; \$2.40 four years ago; \$2.30 three years ago; \$2.50 two years ago; \$2.50 last year.
   - Average number of pages per issue: 80.

3. *Fish, Fur & Fowl*, published every two weeks in Vancouver, British Columbia, since 1978. Originally it was published as a newspaper, but three years ago the publisher changed it to a glossy magazine. Publication details are

   - Circulation: Five years ago: 15 300; four years ago: 15 860; three years ago: 16 670; two years ago: 16 320; last year: 14 960.
   - Price: Five and four years ago: \$1.25; three and two years ago: \$2.75; last year: \$3.00. Note: magazine format started three years ago.

- Average number of pages per issue: In newspaper format: 32; as a magazine: 80.

4. *Indigenous Species*, published every two months since 1988 in Peterborough, Ontario. Its publication history comprises
    - Circulation: Five years ago: 9320; four years ago: 9600; three years ago: 7650; two years ago: 9320; last year: 9830.
    - Price: Five and four years ago: $2.95; three years ago through last year: $3.25.
    - Pages per issue: 56–64.

How *Dolphin*—your magazine—performs

Dolphin, your company's magazine, publishes every month and has the following publication record:

- Circulation: Five years ago: 8210; four years ago: 9600; three years ago: 11 020; two years ago: 12 700; last year: 13 320.
- Price: Five years ago: $2.50; since four years ago: $3.00.
- Average number of pages per issue: 64–80.

Part 1

Create a table showing circulation figures for all five magazines. Describe the circulation trends you can identify from this table.

Part 2

Create a chart or graph to illustrate circulation trends. Describe why you chose the particular style of graph or chart.

Part 3

From your inspection of the graph or chart, describe how well *Dolphin* is performing in relation to *Wildlife Canada*.

Exercise 9.5

Calculate exchange rates

Go to your local college, university, or public library and ask for 12 back issues of the *National Post*, the *Globe and Mail*, or the business section of your local newspaper (one from each month of the year). From these newspapers find the weekly closing rates for buying and selling of the US dollar, the British pound, and the Euro, in Canadian dollars.

Part 1

Construct a table showing these figures, all expressed in Canadian dollars.

Part 2

Construct a chart or a graph that depicts the changes in exchange rates over the 12-month period. Ensure that the difference between the buying and selling rates is apparent.

Exercise 9.6

Construct a graph or chart that Tom Kirfauver could use to accompany his report in Figure 5-6 (see page 108). Explain why you chose that particular type of illustration.

WEBLINKS

Format

www.cs.unc.edu/~jbs/sm/Part2_format.html

This site discusses how to format your writing to ensure your message is communicated effectively. It includes topics such as levels of headings and use of bold and italic type.

Graphics Guidelines

darkstar.engr.wisc.edu/zwickel/397/graphguide.html

Visit this site to read about the characteristics and importance of pie and bar charts, graphs, flowcharts, tables, and other visuals.

Visuals and Writing

www.io.com/~hcexres/tcm1603/acchtml/graphics.html

Here you will find helpful tips on determining which types of visuals (graphics, photos, tables, charts) to use in a report and how to present them properly with labels, captions, titles, and cross references.

Speaking Before a Business Audience

chapter 10

Brenda Wilkins is standing in a corner of Tots Unlimited Day Care Centre, a clipboard resting on her left arm and a pencil in her right hand. She is watching child care worker Mary Chiroski as she reads a story to three-year-olds, and every now and then Brenda writes a note on her pad, commenting on the way Mary is holding the children's interest.

Vivian Shewchuk—Brenda's supervisor—tiptoes up behind Brenda and taps her on the shoulder. "Can you break off for a moment?" she whispers. "I need to ask you a favor." She inclines her head to one side, and the two women retreat quietly into an alcove.

"The president of the Grosvenor Club has asked me to give a luncheon talk to the members," Vivian starts, a little hesitant. "He wants me to describe the Challenge Program you're working on."

"Oh, good!" Brenda exclaims, glad to hear that the program will get some publicity.

"Yes, but . . . well, I'd rather not," Vivian continues. "I wonder . . . would you do it for me?"

"Me? But it's your project! I'm only helping you."

"Yes, I know," Vivian explains. "It's not that I don't want to, but I'm a member of the Grosvenor Club, and, frankly, it would sound like I'm blowing my own horn. You know what I mean?"

Brenda nods, but then immediately shakes her head. "Oh, I don't think anybody would even—"

"I wish you would!" Vivian interrupts. "I really need someone to talk to them who has been working closely with the program. And you have."

Brenda shakes her head again. "I don't have any experience speaking to a large group like that."

"You've got six weeks," Vivian adds. "It's not until March 9."

Brenda sighs, still very doubtful. "Well . . . "

"Please?"

"All right then," Brenda agrees reluctantly. (Secretly, she is terrified by the thought.)

Vivian squeezes her elbow and heads toward the door. "Thanks, Bren!"
"But you'll have to help me," Brenda calls after her, "to make sure I'm saying what you want me to say!"

IN THIS CHAPTER

You will learn how to make a speech in front of a large audience and a briefing or presentation to a small audience. Specifically, you will learn how to

- prepare thoroughly for either a major or minor presentation, including the development of speaking notes and preparation of visual aids for an LCD projector and transparencies for an overhead projector,
- rehearse your presentation,
- use platform techniques to help you deliver your material effectively, and
- answer an audience's questions.

So, you have to give a talk!

Making a Formal Presentation

Don't be afraid to ask for help

Vivian turns back and faces Brenda.
"I know I'll be nervous," Brenda explains, embarrassed that she has let her feelings show. "I always am when I have to stand up in front of people and say something."
"Everyone is," Vivian consoles her. "Even the most experienced speakers."
"But that doesn't help *me*!"
"Yes, it does, if you take the same steps they do," Vivian suggests. "If you want to make a really confident presentation, start early. Give yourself ample time to prepare."

Establish the Setting

"Go to the person who is arranging your talk," Vivian tells Brenda, "and ask four questions: Who will be in your audience? What do they expect to hear? How long should you talk? Where will you be speaking? The answers will establish the circumstances for any presentation."

Ask questions

Brenda makes a note on her pad (see Figure 10-1).
"But there is more to the four questions than is immediately apparent," Vivian continues, and for each question she explains why.

Establish the Setting

Ask:

1. To whom will I be speaking?
2. What do they want to hear?
3. How long am I to speak?
4. Where am I to speak?

Figure 10-1 Four questions to ask before preparing a talk

Question 1: To whom will I be speaking?

"You will seldom know your listeners' names," Vivian says, "but you should have some idea of their occupations, backgrounds, and sometimes even their education. Details like these will help you tailor your talk to suit their interests."

"Well, who *will* I be speaking to?" Brenda asks.

"About 60 members of the Grosvenor Club."

"Who are . . . ?"

"Accountants, lawyers, social workers, doctors, and managers from a variety of local businesses."

"And what do they do, as members of the Club?"

"Oh, they get involved in various community projects," Vivian explains, "such as setting up the Age and Opportunity Bureau that has been in the news lately. And the Child Care Challenge Program you will be talking about."

Know clearly to whom you will be speaking

Question 2: What do they want to hear?

Vivian tells Brenda that she needs to answer three questions about her audience:

1. ***What do they know about the topic?*** ("This will give you a starting point," Vivian explains. "You don't want to bore your audience by covering aspects they already know. Nor do you want to confuse them by omitting facts they know nothing about.")
2. ***What do they want to know?*** ("That is, what are they most interested in hearing?")
3. ***What do they need to be told?*** (" . . . which may differ from what they are expecting or hoping to hear," Vivian adds.)

Identify your audience's expectations

"Well, how much will they know about the Child Care Challenge Program?" Brenda asks.

"You will have a mixed audience," Vivian says. "Some will be familiar with what we're doing, but others will know very little about it."

"So I had better start with some history?" Brenda suggests.

"Yes, but keep it brief. Give them just the essentials."

Brenda makes a note on her pad, and then asks, "But when I've done that, what will they *want* to hear?"

"A progress report, mostly. Tell them the program they have sponsored is a success."

"They should like that!" Brenda nods, making another note. "But is there anything I *need* to tell them? News they may not be expecting to hear?"

Vivian considers for a moment. "See if you can work in that we need to broaden the program to involve more child care workers."

"Which will cost more money?" Brenda asks.

"Yes."

Question 3: How long will I be expected to speak?

Establish the time frame

Vivian says: "You need to know how long your talk should be so you can plan how much information to present. There is nothing worse than planning a 40-minute presentation only to discover at the last moment you are expected to speak for 20 minutes. Or vice versa!"

"What is normal for a Grosvenor Club luncheon speaker?" Brenda asks.

"About 25 minutes," Vivian recommends. "Twenty minutes for your talk and five minutes for the audience to ask questions."

Question 4: Where will I speak?

Vivian explains that Brenda needs to know whether she will be in a large hall or a small conference room. "Then you can estimate how far you will be from your audience and how large you need to make the lettering on your slides. And you need to determine what kind of projection equipment they have."

Determine room size and facilities

"And where will I be speaking?" Brenda asks.

"In the Connaught Room of the Shaftesbury Inn, up on the second floor. The Grosvenor Club meets there on the second Wednesday of every month. Normally it's set up with 10 round tables, with six members sitting at each. You'll speak from a raised platform at one end of the room."

"Will there be a slide projector?"

"If you need one," Vivian says. "But let me know in plenty of time, so I can arrange for it."

Now Brenda has a good idea of what to expect, all of it background information that will help her as she prepares her talk.

Plan the Talk

"When you give your talk," Vivian says, "you have to capture your audience's attention right away, and then hold it all the way through your presentation. And that's not easy, because many factors will be working against you."

Counteract "mental drift"

She explains that the time of day, temperature of the room, and whether it's immediately before or after a meal, can affect an audience's ability to concentrate. So do personal factors, such as the individual listener's interest in the topic, concern over a sick family member, argument with a partner or spouse early in the day, or annoyance over a scraped fender in a minor traffic accident on the way to the session.

"Because listeners' attention may drift, you have to present your information three times," Vivian adds.

"Three times?!"

"Yes," Vivian nods. She draws a sheet of paper toward her and sketches the diagram in Figure 10-2. She explains that Brenda can adopt the pyramid technique, just as she would for a written report:

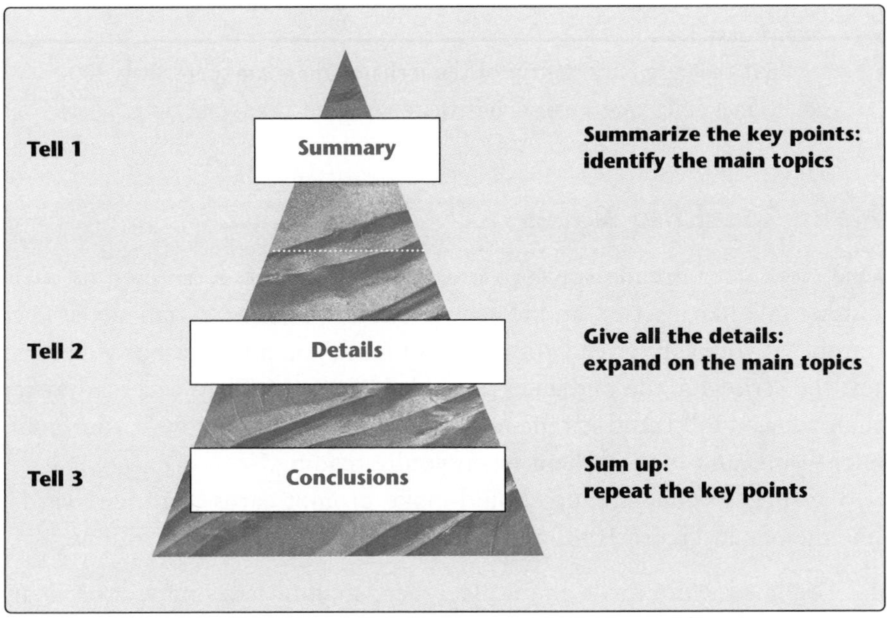

Tell 1	**Summary**	**Summarize the key points: identify the main topics**
Tell 2	**Details**	**Give all the details: expand on the main topics**
Tell 3	**Conclusions**	**Sum up: repeat the key points**

Figure 10-2 The main parts of an oral presentation

1. Start with a Summary that tells listeners what they most need to hear, comments briefly on the purpose of the talk, and outlines the main points you will cover. For example:

Tell your story once . . .

> "Ladies and gentlemen: I want to report to you this afternoon that your moral and financial endorsement of the Child Care Challenge Program has been a worthy investment that is already achieving excellent results. By the time the program ends in 18 months, we expect to graduate 56 participants.
>
> "First, I'll outline how the program started, for those of you who were not here at its inception. Then I'll describe how it has been put into practice and the results we have achieved. And I'll close with some thoughts on the feasibility of making the program available to a wider range of students."

Tell it twice . . .

2. Continue with all the Details. Cover the points you want to make in sufficient depth so your listeners will fully understand them, and present them in the same sequence in which they were mentioned in the Summary.
3. Finish with the Conclusions. Repeat two or three of the key points from the Details and, if appropriate, offer a recommendation:

Tell it thrice!

> "There are 56 child care workers in the Challenge Program, all working toward accreditation and all still working at their jobs. Fifty-six experienced para-professionals who, without your help, the community would have lost.
>
> "But they are only the tip of the iceberg. There are more than 200 additional child care workers out there who still need your help."

Make Speaking Notes

Resist the temptation to write your talk, like a speech

One week later Brenda starts to prepare. At first she is tempted to write out her talk like a script, and to rehearse from that, but Vivian advises her not to. "If you plan to read your talk out loud, you might just as well hand out the script for the audience to read themselves. They can read faster than you can talk! And it's the fastest way to lose contact with your audience—you can't look at them when you're reading."

She suggests that Brenda should make prompt cards (on index cards) like the one in Figure 10-3, and gives her eight guidelines to follow:

1. Use lined white cards and a black pen, so your lettering will be clear.
2. Write in bold letters that can be read easily at arm's length (when the card is lying flat on a table, for example, and you are standing behind or beside the table).

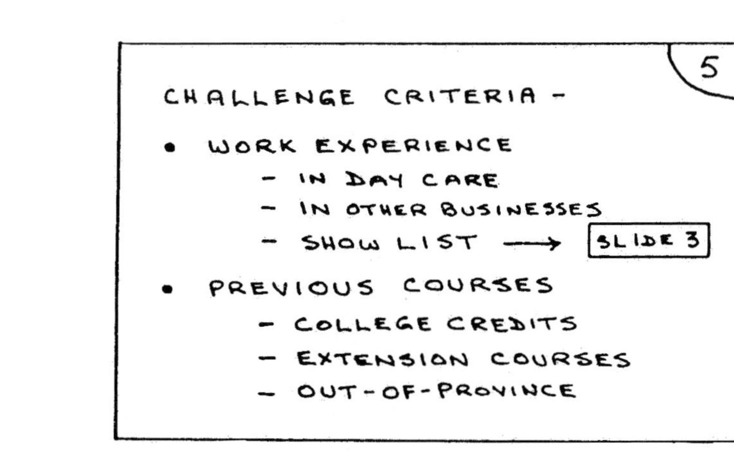

Figure 10-3 A speaker's prompt card

3. Use key words and short phrases to identify what you want to talk about at a particular moment (see Figure 10-3).
4. Indent the key words into three levels of importance:

Primary Topic Heading
  1. Secondary Topic Heading
    • **Supporting Details**

5. Avoid crowding the cards. Start a new card for each new topic.
6. Identify clearly on the card when you are going to show a slide or do a demonstration. Draw a box around the entry (see Figure 10-3) or use a different color of ink.
7. On a separate card list all the items you need to take with you, such as handout notes, computer (for use with an LCD projector), transparencies or slides, a spare projector bulb, and items to demonstrate. Use this card as your "readiness checklist" and place it at the front of the set, as the first card of your speaking notes.
8. Number your cards clearly, so that if they accidentally become jumbled you can easily put them back in order.

Use brief notes as memory prompts

Prepare a pre-talk checklist

Illustrate Your Talk

"Are you planning to use an LCD projector, 35 mm slides, or transparencies?" Vivian asks.

"I have some photographs of children working at the art table and playing in the housekeeping area," Brenda says.

"Slides or prints?"

"Slides."

"Good. Prints have to be scanned and would be more difficult to use."

Vivian explains that prints and drawings are too small to display to an audience, but slides and overhead transparencies can add life to a presentation. However, 35 mm slides need a darkened room whereas LCD projection slides and transparencies usually can be used in a normally lit room.

Liven up your presentation with creative graphics

"But ensure that every illustration contributes to your talk," Vivian cautions her. "Never use an illustration just because you particularly like it or think it's pretty."

She says that the rules for preparing an illustration to accompany a talk are similar to those for an illustration that accompanies a report (see Chapter 9, page 255), but the following additional factors must be kept in mind:

- Keep illustrations simple: too much detail may conceal the point you are trying to make.
- Let each illustration tell only one story.
- Ensure that the illustration will be easily understood (a speaker should rarely have to explain an illustration).
- Use large, bold letters and only a few words on each illustration.
- Use color to accentuate key words or features, but remember that greens and blues, and reds and oranges, are difficult to differentiate from a distance.
- Place a short explanatory title above or below each illustration.
- Prepare blank opaque slides or transparencies to insert when you do not want to project an illustration (to save you from having to switch the projector on and off during your talk).
- If you plan to demonstrate a process or equipment, check that it will be large enough for everyone in the audience to see. Keep the demonstration item out of sight until the appropriate moment in your talk to prevent the audience from studying it and wondering how you are going to use it (when they should really be listening to what you have to say).

By all means use new technology, but take precautions

Show Computer-Generated Images

LCD projectors have taken over as the primary projection medium for talks and presentations

"If you plan to create slides on a computer and then project them through an LCD projector," Vivian continues, "an additional set of guidelines comes into play."

Vivian explains that using an LCD projector offers significant advantages but also presents some constraints. The advantages concern the quality and uniqueness of your presentation: the transitions between slides are slick and smooth, you have much more control over the images, you can make them move, and you can inject sound. The disadvantage is that, unless you take a projector with you, you may experience compatibility problems between your computer and the LCD projector, or find that the light source in the projector may have deteriorated and so cause your slides to look washed out.

Creating Slides. You can create your slides using a software program such as *PowerPoint* or *Astound*. The software program you use will offer an immense range of colors, fonts, graphics, sounds, and backgrounds for creating your slides, and transition methods for changing from one slide to the next. Follow these guidelines:

- Select a background and a color scheme that is appealing and also provides a good contrast between the colors of the background and the lettering you will place in front of it.
- Be conservative in your choice of transitions. Dazzling your audience with special effects may generate "Oohs!" and "Ahs!" but it may also distract your audience from the message the slide is conveying. If you are tempted by the wide range of transitions available to you, such as a wipe from top left to bottom right, a fade out of one image and fade in to the next, or a dazzle as one slide is broken into fragments and the next is inserted in its place, apply the brakes! You would do far better to choose a small range of simpler transitions and use them consistently throughout a particular presentation.
- Develop a progression from slide to slide. If you have several points to make, let each point appear in turn, then leave it visible but in a less noticeable color as you introduce the next point.
- When your slides are complete, print them as a series of images on sheets of 8.5 × 11 inch paper, probably four to a page, so you can refer to them as you speak.
- If you plan to give printouts of your slides to your audience, use an outliner package available with most presentation software before you print them. Doing so will permit your listeners to annotate the slides with additional comments, so that when they refer to the handout later, it does not appear as a series of disjointed images.

Making Your Presentation. Your presentation techniques remain the same as those for a presentation with overhead transparencies and 35 mm slides, with the following additions:

Even with a powerful light source, some LCD projectors need some dimming of the lights

- You need to practise using your computer with the projector before the presentation. You also have more freedom of movement, particularly if the LCD projector has a remote control.

- If you will be projecting video, pay particular attention to the position of light switches and dimmers and determine which you will need to switch off when you are showing video excerpts (projected video needs some darkening of the room, even with a high-intensity overhead projector).
- Practise using your slides in advance and get to know their sequence well. In this sense they are like 35 mm slides: you cannot stop and look at what's coming next, as you can with overhead transparencies.
- In case a questioner asks to see a particular slide you showed earlier, know how to leap back to it without having to work backward through all the slides.
- Consider taking an emergency back up, such as a set of prepared transparencies, just in case you have an equipment failure or the computer and LCD projector prove to be incompatible.

"Finally," Vivian says, "decide whether your presentation and the subject matter really require that you use an LCD projector." She explains that some visual presentations are better if prepared as a transparency (for example, when a lot of words need to be projected) or as a flip chart (if you want to develop an idea or a process step by step, using input from the audience).

Practice . . . and More Practice

"Simply reading over your speaking notes and imagining you are hearing the words is not the same as standing up and saying the words out loud," Vivian tells Brenda. "If you only read them to yourself you will not be able to correct the hesitations or close the gaps in your delivery that inevitably will occur on the day you give your talk." If Brenda rehearses her talk several times, Vivian adds, she will be able to achieve a much smoother delivery and simultaneously overcome some of her nervousness. She suggests a six-step rehearsal plan:

1. Find a location where you will not be interrupted and set up a table with a projector beside it. (If you also will be demonstrating equipment, you should also have the equipment there.)
2. Note the time, or start a stopwatch, and begin speaking aloud from your notes, as if you are addressing a real audience.
3. Each time you have difficulty finding the correct words, pause just long enough to make an "X" on the card, beside the word or phrase that has caused you to pause or stumble. (Do not stop to write additional key words onto your notes at this moment.)

Rehearse until you feel reasonably confident

4. Go on to the next point and talk about it.
5. Each time you have to display a slide or transparency, pause, switch on the projector, and talk about the illustration. Then return to the proper point in your notes and continue speaking from them. (Do the same for equipment demonstrations.)
6. At the end of your talk, note the time or stop your stopwatch. Now you will know roughly how long your talk will take and where you need to insert additional key words.

"When you have improved your speaking notes," Vivian continues, "repeat the six practice steps. Over the next few days continue practising and improving the notes until the words begin to form naturally as you glance at them, and key phrases leap into mind. At this point you will know that your rehearsing has begun to pay dividends."

"How many practice runs should I make?" Brenda asks.

"Much will depend on the speaking event. If you are preparing to make an in-house presentation to other employees, two or three practices probably will be sufficient. But if you will be speaking at a conference, then you should rehearse more."

Make Two Pre-Platform Checks

Go back to your checklist

The day before Brenda is to speak, she holds a final practice run and then places all the materials she will need into her briefcase. As she slides each item into place, she checks it off against the list she has made as the first card of her speaker's notes. When every item has a check mark against it, she wraps an elastic band around the cards and slips them into her briefcase. This completes her first pre-platform check.

Arrive early and check out the facilities

Brenda performs her second pre-platform check in the Connaught Room at the Shaftesbury Inn, where she is to speak. She arrives early and, remembering Vivian's advice, checks all the equipment she will be using. First she places the carousel holding her slides onto the 35 mm projector and checks the size, height, and focus of the image on the screen. Then she checks that there is a spare bulb beside the projector, and that the remote control beside the speaker's stand works properly. She spends a few moments familiarizing herself with the buttons on the remote control so she will not fumble when she selects slides during her talk. And finally she checks that the lamp on the speaker's stand is working, adjusts the height of the microphone, and tests that it is operating (she asks a waiter to tell her when she is the best distance from it as she speaks). "Now," Brenda says to herself, "I am ready."

Stand Up and Deliver

A week earlier, after she had completed her third rehearsal, Brenda stepped into Vivian's office. "How do you control nervousness?" she asked. "Stop your hands from trembling?"

Vivian shook her head. "You don't."

"But *you* do!"

"Not really . . . "

"I've seen you!" Brenda argued. "At the MARM conference. You were as cool as—"

"Uh-uh!" Vivian shook her head again. "Only on the outside."

"You were totally in control!"

"Not on the inside."

"It didn't show," Brenda said.

"You'll be the same," Vivian reassured her.

Brenda looked doubtful.

Thorough preparation helps ease nervousness

"Look, nervousness stems from uncertainty—uncertainty about your audience and your ability to meet their expectations." Vivian explained that even the most seasoned speakers experience some nervousness, but if they have prepared thoroughly their nervousness begins to slip away soon after they start speaking. "You'll find all the preparatory work, and the rehearsing you have done, will pay dividends when you stand up to speak."

Then Vivian listed 11 guidelines she felt would help Brenda become a more confident speaker, and at the same time ease her nervousness.

1. *Be enthusiastic.* Show that you are interested in the subject. Enthusiasm is contagious; listeners react positively to it.

Remember: you're speaking to individuals, not a crowd

2. *Look at your audience.* Consider each person as an individual and let your eyes engage his or hers for a few seconds before you look at another person (not in a slow sweep from left to right, but randomly all over the audience).
3. *Speak from notes.* Never read your talk, or you will become a dull speaker (you cannot be enthusiastic or develop personal eye contact when you are reading).
4. *Use your voice effectively.* Speak at a moderate speed of about 120 to 140 words per minute, varying the pitch and speed to avoid speaking in a monotone (test yourself with a tape recorder). Use a microphone only if the hall is large or has poor acoustics, because a microphone restricts your mobility and tends to reduce your enthusiasm. If a microphone is essential, ask for a lavalier or a radio mic, both of which clip onto your clothing and don't restrict your movement.
5. *Watch your audience.* Use the audience's body language as an indicator. If your listeners are still and attentive, and even nod occasionally when you make an important point, you are doing fine; however, if

too many of them are leaning well back in their chairs, shifting around a lot, or fiddling with something on the table in front of them, take their inattentiveness as a signal that you need to put more "zip" into your presentation.

6. *Lean into your audience.* When you have a particularly important point to make, lean toward your audience and slow your speech a little, as though you are confiding something to them. Your listeners will automatically recognize that you are stressing a point, far more than if you were to raise your voice to drive the words home.

Use body language to reach out to your listeners

7. *Show illustrations confidently.* Regardless of whether you are showing charts, equipment, slides, or transparencies, build them in as an integral part of your presentation. Here are some suggestions:

   - Keep illustrations and demonstration items out of sight until the right moment in your presentation.
   - Give the audience a moment or two to become accustomed to a display item or illustration before you discuss it.
   - Avoid reading aloud the words on a slide or transparency: it wastes time and insults your audience's intelligence. Rather, offer additional comments about the illustration.
   - Keep a demonstration item or slide visible for as long as you are talking about it or the audience needs to understand it, then remove it from view.
   - Never turn to the side, or turn around toward the screen, to speak about a slide or transparency; you will lose contact with your audience.
   - Never apologize for an illustration's deficiencies, because to do so simply draws attention to them. Ideally, correct the deficiencies before you speak.

Visuals are great, but make them *work* for you

8. *Glance at your notes.* Your audience does not expect you to stand up and speak for 20 to 25 minutes without looking down at your notes from time to time to check that you are on track. This also gives you an opportunity to check that you are on time. (Place your wristwatch or a stopwatch beside your notes, so that your time check will not be obvious to your audience.)
9. *Stand comfortably.* Neither stand stiffly at attention nor sprawl over the speaker's stand. Appear relaxed—even if you are not—and in control of the situation.
10. *Avoid distracting movements.* Avoid drawing your audience's attention away from your words by nervously fiddling with objects on the speaker's stand, sliding a pen or pointer through your fingers, drumming your fingertips on the edge of the stand, or (worst of all) cracking your knuckles.

What may be funny to you may be offensive to some listeners

11. *Use humor with care.* Humor is a two-edged weapon: it may work marvellously to enhance your presentation, or it may cause grievous harm by falling flat. If you plan to relate an amusing incident, be absolutely sure that it contributes to your subject; never insert a joke just to warm up your audience. You want your audience to laugh *with* you, not *at* you.

Wrap It All Up

End on a strong note

"This has been a progress report," Brenda says, turning over the last card of her speaking notes. "I wanted to show you that the Child Care Challenge Program you have funded has been—and still is—a success." She pauses slightly, scans the Connaught Room and the 60 members of the Grosvenor Club, who are still sitting attentively. She leans toward them. "But it's only the tip of the iceberg. There are 200 more child care workers out there who still need your help." She pauses for a moment, and then adds, "And that's another challenge!"

She pauses again, glances at her watch (surprised to find she has finished almost a minute earlier than expected), and then says, "If there are any questions, I will be glad to answer them."

There are, and Brenda answers them clearly and confidently, following four additional guidelines Vivian has given her:

1. Not everyone may have heard a question posed by someone in the audience, so repeat the question or at least summarize it at the start of your reply.
2. Answer briefly and in terms everyone will understand. If the questioner is clearly knowledgeable and wants to discuss aspects beyond the scope of your presentation, avoid being drawn into a private "look how well we know the subject" exchange that excludes other listeners. Acknowledge that it is a complex topic and suggest that the questioner see you after your presentation.

Answer questions honestly and politely

3. If you do not know the answer to a question, say so. For example, you could say, "I'm sorry, but I do not have that information with me," then suggest that the questioner see you afterward. Never bluff!
4. Avoid antagonizing your audience:
   - Never use sarcasm when responding to a questioner, no matter how annoying his or her question may seem. (For example, do not say to a questioner who seems to have missed something covered earlier, "Where were you when I was discussing that? Having a snooze?")
   - Never laugh at or make fun of a flustered questioner who unintentionally poses a question in a humorous way.

In either case the audience will take the questioner's side and you will rapidly lose the audience's respect.

Show interest in a questioner's enquiry

Audiences appreciate a speaker who takes the trouble to prepare the topic thoroughly and present good information effectively. You may never become a professional speaker, but you *will* earn a resounding round of applause from an audience that senses your enthusiasm and recognizes the work you have put into your presentation.

Making an Informal Presentation

Production supervisor Darren Korolik feels that he wastes time attending office meetings, so in his workshop he builds a meeting timer.

"It's like a gasoline pump," he announces at the next meeting, and places his gadget on the table with its dials facing the group. "You set the number of people present on this dial, and their average salary on this one. Then when the meeting starts you press this button and the counter starts recording—for everyone to see, minute by minute—just how much the meeting has cost." He grins. "It's bound to inhibit long-windedness!"

Darren tries to shorten meetings

The seven people attending the meeting laugh at Darren's gadget, and agree with him that too much time is wasted at office meetings. As he explains, "It's no wonder we come away from meetings feeling frustrated. If I go to a meeting, I want to feel we have achieved something."

Many people think the chairperson has the major responsibility for conducting effective meetings, but that is only partly true. The participants themselves can do much to streamline the meetings they attend, particularly if they know how to present information efficiently and how to conduct themselves when others are presenting information.

An average office meeting is attended by a chairperson, several meeting participants, and a secretary (who often is one of the participants) who records the topics that are discussed and the outcome of each discussion. The role of each person is discussed here.

The Chairperson as Meeting Manager

A chairperson has two primary functions: to set the scene for the meeting, and to run the meeting. Setting the scene means preparing and distributing an agenda at least 48 hours before the meeting. The agenda lists who should attend, what will be discussed, and where and when the meeting will be held. Ideally, the chairperson will separate the list of topics into two groups, with a heading in front of each:

Divide the agenda into "decision" and "discussion" topics

1. Action (or decision) items.
2. Discussion items.

This strategy ensures that the more urgent items will be dealt with early in the meeting. A typical agenda is shown in Figure 10-4.

To run an efficient meeting, the chairperson can adopt several strategies to demonstrate that he or she means business. (Being businesslike does not mean being officious; it simply means getting on with the job.) For example, an effective chairperson will follow these guidelines:

Tips for chairing a meeting

- Start the meeting on time, even if everyone has not arrived. Participants tend to be punctual when they know a meeting manager starts the proceedings promptly.
- Follow the agenda in the sequence in which it was issued, unless someone who has to arrive late or leave early has specifically asked for a topic to be delayed or moved ahead.
- Run the meeting, but avoid "railroading" it; remember that the outcome of each point should be a consensus of the participants' opinions, not a reflection of the chairperson's opinion.
- Establish among meeting participants that they are *expected* to catch the chairperson's eye and obtain approval before interjecting information.
- Discourage participants from talking to one another while another person is speaking or presenting. (A useful way to do this is to interrupt them and say: "Can we have just one meeting at a time, please!")
- Promote discussion by encouraging input from those who tend to be less outspoken, and dampen the ardor of those who have too much to say.
- Watch out for individuals who introduce side issues that divert the focus of the discussion, and for others who hold private discussions at one end of the table.
- Sense when a topic has been discussed sufficiently, and then sum up the main points and ask for a decision or vote.

The chairperson may use *Robert's Rules of Order* to run the meeting (the *Rules* are commonly used for major government meetings and for conducting society business), but is more likely to conduct the business of a routine office meeting less formally. He or she will invite the participants to discuss each point of the agenda, and then sense the mood of the meeting or even ask individuals whether they agree or disagree with the consensus that seems to be evolving.

The Participant as Presenter of Information

As a meeting member, your role also has two components: preparation and participation. As soon as the agenda arrives on your desk, start

Mid-Town Society of Business Administrators

To: Members, Executive Committee

Date: January 4, 2001

Here is the agenda for the January meeting of the MSBA executive, which will be held at 6 p.m. on Wednesday, January 10, 2001, in the Liberty Room of the Highlander Inn.

Action Items

1. Awarding of scholarship: Moorhaven College. (*Margaret Nurens*)
2. Proposal to hold Year 2005 International Conference of Society of Business Administrators. (*Reg Hill; Pat Voisin*)
3. Participation in curling bonspiel, Saskatoon. (*Dave Kelly*)

Discussion Items

4. Feasibility of holding joint meetings with Business Communication Society. (*Karen Beasley*)
5. Plans for Spring wind-up barbecue. (*Dave Kelly*)
6. Ideas for boosting membership.

Secretary for this meeting: Pat Voisin.

David Kelly

David Kelly, President

Figure 10-4 An agenda for a meeting. The names in italics identify the meeting member who will introduce or lead the discussion on a particular topic.

preparing for the meeting (never leave it until 20 minutes before the meeting starts). This preparation is particularly important if you have to make a presentation.

The key to an effective presentation is to divide your information into two parts:

1. What your listeners need to know.
2. What your listeners would find only nice to know.

Discriminate between "need to know" and "nice to know" information

That is, separate your information into facts your listeners *must* hear if they are to make an intelligent decision following your presentation, and details they only *might* want to hear. Then plan to offer only the "need to know" information, and to let the meeting participants ask about the "nice to know" details (they may, or they may not).

From the need to know information, identify one or two particularly important items and plan to say them first, in no more than two or three sentences. This three-step approach is illustrated in Figure 10-5.

For example, when Darren Korolik investigates how flexible working hours have been implemented at other organizations, and is asked to present his findings at a meeting, he starts like this:

Open with the key point(s) you want to make

> "My investigation of flexible working hours at local companies shows that on average their experiments have been only 60% successful. Organizations having the greatest success were engaged mostly in engineering and marketing. Those experiencing less success were involved primarily in manufacturing and customer service."

By placing the most interesting points in a Main Message at the front of his presentation, Darren knows he will capture his audience's attention much more readily than if he starts with the history of the project and how

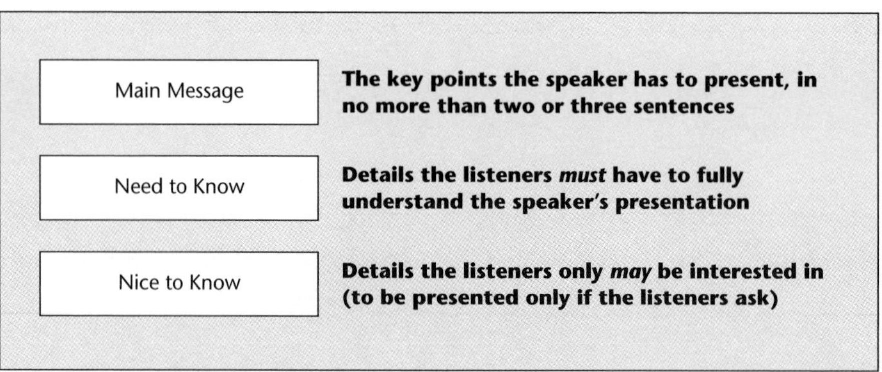

Main Message
The key points the speaker has to present, in no more than two or three sentences
Need to Know
Details the listeners *must* have to fully understand the speaker's presentation
Nice to Know
Details the listeners only *may* be interested in (to be presented only if the listeners ask)

Figure 10-5 A speaking plan for a presentation at an office meeting

he conducted his research.

He continues with the need to know details, such as where he gleaned his information, where the most significant differences were apparent, and the implications that his findings have for his company. Then he stops and invites questions. For his answers he draws on the nice to know information he assembled earlier.

Support your opening with "need to know" details

Adopting this three-stage method for presenting information can be one of the most effective ways for participants to speed up meetings. If, as a meeting presenter, you also remember the following guidelines, you will contribute even more to meeting efficiency.

Tips for presenting information

- Use charts, slides, or transparencies to draw attention to key points.
- Address your remarks primarily to the chairperson, but also remember to look at and speak to the group as a whole.
- Know your topic well enough, and rehearse it often enough, so that your delivery is clear and definite.
- Lean toward the meeting members when you want to stress a particularly important point.
- Avoid handing out sheaves of pages for the meeting members to look over—it wastes meeting time. If you have extensive written material to show them, give the pages to the chairperson well in advance of the meeting so they can be distributed with the agenda.
- If someone interrupts during the Main Message or need to know segments of your presentation, tell the interrupter you will address that point toward the end of the presentation (rather than allow the distraction to destroy the continuity).
- When you are answering questions, avoid becoming defensive if another meeting member challenges your statements provocatively. You win far more points by listening and answering seriously, pleasantly, and cooperatively.

The Participant as Meeting Member

Much of the time you will be a meeting member, often listening to others as they present their information. Occasionally you will make a comment, contribute an additional piece of information, or ask questions. Here are five guidelines for you to follow as a meeting participant:

Tips for being an observer

- Arrive on time, and do not expect the chairperson to "fill you in" on what has transpired if you arrive late. If you know you will be delayed, inform the chairperson *in advance*.
- Be recognized as a valued contributor to every meeting you attend, speaking only when you have something useful to offer, and listening

the rest of the time.

- Catch the chairperson's eye, and gain his or her approval to speak, before offering an opinion.
- Address your remarks to the chairperson, particularly as you start to make an observation, and then share the idea with the other meeting members by looking toward them as well.
- Avoid letting your neighbor draw you into a private conversation while the meeting is in progress, which can be very distracting to other meeting members.

The Participant as Secretary

If the chairperson asks you to record the minutes of the meeting, you have to divide your time between being a meeting participant and taking notes. As a result, you have to be astute at recording the essential details. Here are some suggestions:

Tips for recording meeting minutes

- Divide two or three sheets of paper with a vertical line down the middle. To the left of this line write brief notes (often in code form, with initials for the names of people) as the meeting progresses. Use the right side of the page after the meeting, to fill in the details.
- Remember that minutes should record only the essential *outcomes*, and therefore will be short. Rather than try to record each person's opinion, limit your minutes to
  — conclusions reached,
  — decisions made, and
  — actions taken (or to be taken), and who took or is to take the action.
  Occasionally you may also need to record the exact wording of a policy agreed to by the committee.
- List the participants under three headings:
  — *In attendance* (those who were there)
  — *Regrets* (those who informed the chairperson they could not be present)
  — *Absent* (those who did not forewarn the chairperson they would not be present)

Listen to the chairperson

- Note particularly how the chairperson sums up the outcome of the discussion of each topic. From his or her remarks you often can identify the key words to write in the minutes.
- As soon as the meeting ends, verify any doubtful points with the chairperson (identify these query points as the meeting progresses by inserting a question mark beside them).
- Write the minutes the same day, or no more than 24 hours later, while your memory of the meeting is fresh and you can still remember what your code letters mean.

Mid-Town Society of Business Administrators

Minutes of Executive Committee Meeting
6 p.m., Wednesday, January 10, 2001

Present:	David Kelly (chair)	Margaret Nurens
	Pat Voisin (Secretary)	Reg Hill
	Karen Beasley	Jan Turton
	Tom Woodhaus	
Regrets:	Pat Duraille	

Minutes	*Action*
1. Jan Turton proposed, and Reg Hill seconded, that the minutes of the previous meeting and the agenda for the current meeting be accepted. Carried.	
Action Items	
2. Margaret Nurens proposed that the Society award a scholarship of $300 to a student enrolled in Business Administration at Moorhaven College, for the college year ending June 8, 2001. Carried.	M Nurens
3. The Committee decided to bid on hosting the year 2005 International Conference of the Society of Business Administrators. Reg Hill will prepare a proposal and present a draft copy for approval at the February 7 meeting.	R Hill
4. The Mid-Town Chapter decided not to send a team to the 2005 SBA curling bonspiel in Saskatoon.	
Discussion Items	
5. Pat Voisin suggested that the Mid-Town Chapter should hold some joint meetings with the Business Communication Society, since the two Societies have similar objectives. The Committee expressed interest. Pat will contact the other Society to determine whether they also are interested.	P Voisin
6. A date and location for the annual Spring wind-up barbecue was discussed, but no decision was reached. The topic will be re-introduced at the next meeting.	D Kelly
7. The Society's declining membership was discussed, and each member agreed to present ideas for increasing the membership at the next meeting.	All
8. Next meeting: 6 p.m., February 7, 2001, Highlander Inn.	

Pat Voisin

Pat Voisin, Secretary

Figure 10-6 Minutes of a meeting

The minutes you issue can take several forms, one of which is shown in Figure 10-6 on page 281. This format provides a column on the right-hand side of the page in which to insert the names of people who will be acting on a decision or gathering more information to present at the next meeting. Its purpose is twofold: to act as a reminder for the named meeting participants, and to help the chairperson identify items to be listed for action or discussion in the agenda for the next meeting.

Using Voice Mail

Voice mail is the spoken equivalent of electronic mail, in that you can leave a message for the recipient to access at his or her convenience. Although the transmission medium for voice mail is the telephone, you rarely have a listener waiting at the other end to give you immediate feedback.

In voice mail there are two speakers: the person who records the greeting in which you are asked to leave a message; and the caller who listens to the greeting and then responds by leaving a message. Because there is no immediate feedback, both speakers must articulate their messages clearly and coherently.

Recording the Announcement. Whatever announcement you make, keep it short. A short message will be particularly appreciated by people who call you long distance. In the message, announce your name and the company you work for, say that you are unavailable to take the call, and suggest the caller leave you a number so you can call back. Here is an example:

> "This is Dan Clements, at the Multiple Industries' office in New Westminster. I am in the office today but I may have stepped out for a moment or may be on another line. Please leave your name, your telephone number, and the time you called, and I will return your call shortly."

That announcement has 52 words and lasts approximately 15 seconds.

Because we know our name and telephone number well, we tend to rush them and slur them

When recording your announcement, speak at a normal conversational speed and articulate your name and the company name very clearly. If you will be away from the office for more than a day, say so and if possible offer an alternative number that callers can access if their message is urgent. If you work from your home, or alone in an office, do *not* say you will be absent for an extended time (it's an invitation for someone to break in). Rather, say something like this:

> "I'm working on assignment today, but will be checking my messages regularly."

Some people tend never to answer their telephone personally. They make everyone leave a message and answer only those they feel like returning, or answer them in the order they choose. Using this technique may seem efficient, but in reality it is bad manners. After a while callers realize what the person they can never reach is doing, and so quickly downgrade their opinion of him or her as a person with whom they want to do business.

Leaving a Message. You call Dan Clements and listen to his recorded message. Now it's your turn. Here are some guidelines:

- Anticipate that you may hear a recorded voice, and be ready to give your message.
- Before you dial the number, know clearly what you plan to say or ask.
- Announce who you are and the time that you called. Say your name slowly and clearly, and do the same with your telephone number. (Braydon Houlihan says that people used to think his name was *Craven Who-ann.* He says: "It was a wonder anyone bothered to answer my calls!")
- Present your message pyramid style:
  1. Announce yourself and then immediately state why you are calling:

     "Hello, Dan. This is Braydon Houlihan at 306-488-7077. Can you give me a specific date and time when we can meet?"

  2. Continue with details that expand on your initial statement:

     "There are two opportunities: from Monday, February 8th to Thursday, February 11th, when I'll be staying at the Coast Plaza on Denman Street.

     "Alternatively, we could meet when I come back through Vancouver on Monday, February 15th. We'd have to meet at the airport: I'll be there from 11:20 a.m. to 1:35 p.m."

  3. End with a closing statement, which also will be an action statement if you want your listener to reply. Be specific:

     "Leave me a message saying which date suits you best and where I should meet you. My number again: 306-488-7077. Thanks."

     If you need a reply by a definite time or date, say so in your closing statement.

Get right to the point: voice mail is *not* a medium for chitchat

Like electronic mail, voice mail is not a medium in which you should chat on endlessly. Keep your message brief and businesslike (the example above lasts 42 seconds). Your listeners will appreciate it and will more readily respond quickly to you.

Communicating with One Person

When Kai Tazumi walks into division manager Frank Hawkes's office, he is not prepared for what Frank has to say.

"I'm taking you out of the customer relations department," Frank announces, "and moving you into the production department. At the same time I'm promoting you to supervisor of expediting and material control. Congratulations!"

Frank shakes Kai's hand and motions for him to sit in one of three chairs set around a small table at one side of the office.

Kai expresses his appreciation for being selected, and his surprise.

A promotion brings additional communication responsibilities

"I've been waiting for a vacancy to come up," Frank continues. He crosses to the door, shuts it, then sits in one of the other chairs. "You've been ready for promotion for some time, but I needed a different department for you to work in. It's not a sound strategy to promote someone within their own department, so that they suddenly become boss over the employees they previously worked with."

Kai says he is concerned because he does not have any supervisory experience.

"I'm aware of that," Frank reassures him. "That's why I asked you to come in for a few minutes, so I could talk to you before you take over your new responsibilities."

Frank tells Kai he wants him to enroll in a supervisory management program offered at night by the local community college, and says that the company will pay the tuition fees. And then he adds, "For the moment you'll just have to listen to advice—mostly mine."

Frank explains that good supervision mostly means applying good judgment. And to do that, a supervisor needs good communication skills.

He points to his desk. "Why do you think we are sitting in these chairs, rather than on either side of my desk?"

Kai shakes his head.

Avoid creating a physical communication barrier

Frank explains that the desk would have placed a barrier between them that would have subtly impeded interpersonal communication. "When you talk to an employee—or anyone in a private, one-to-one conversation—you don't want anything to interfere with the comfortable, natural level of communication you want to develop. If I sit behind my desk and you sit on the other side, I immediately create an 'I am the manager and you are the employee' environment. Then we would not talk nearly as easily to one another."

Frank says he has closed the door for exactly the same reason and that Kai should do the same when an employee comes in to see him. "You want to show that you are giving that person your undivided attention. In fact, before you came in I asked my secretary to take messages so that we will not be disturbed by the telephone ringing."

One-to-One Speaking Techniques

Frank explains that communicating information to one person is very much like communicating information to a group. The same guidelines apply.

1. *Know your listener.* Ask yourself exactly the same questions you would ask before making an oral presentation to several people:

   - What does the listener know now?
   - What does the listener want to know?
   - What does the listener need to be told?

   Identify your listener

   The answers will tell you how much background information to include, and how detailed you need to make your explanation or description.
2. *Know clearly what you want to say.* Identify specifically why you want to speak to the person and assemble the facts you have to present in advance. Discriminate between need to know and nice to know details and, just as you would when presenting information at a meeting, plan to

   - offer the need to know information, and
   - store the nice to know information (hold it in readiness in case the listener asks about it).

3. *Know what reaction you expect.* Determine clearly in your mind what action you want the listener to take as a result of your conversation.
4. *Identify your main message.* From the need to know information, pick out the item(s) you feel will be of most interest or most importance to your listener.
5. *Open with a summary statement.* State your purpose (your reason for communicating) and the Main Message right at the start, so the listener will know immediately why you are speaking to him or her.
6. *Continue with the main details.* Support what you have already said by providing *relevant* details (see Figure 10-7). Take care to stick to the facts and not be led into a discussion of irrelevant details that tend to shift the emphasis away from the point you are trying to make or the response you are trying to evoke.

Listening Techniques

"Don't overlook that every person-to-person communication has two participants," Frank continues. "In an exchange of information, at any given moment one person is speaking and the other is listening. And the roles switch back and forth."

Encourage a speaker to "open up"

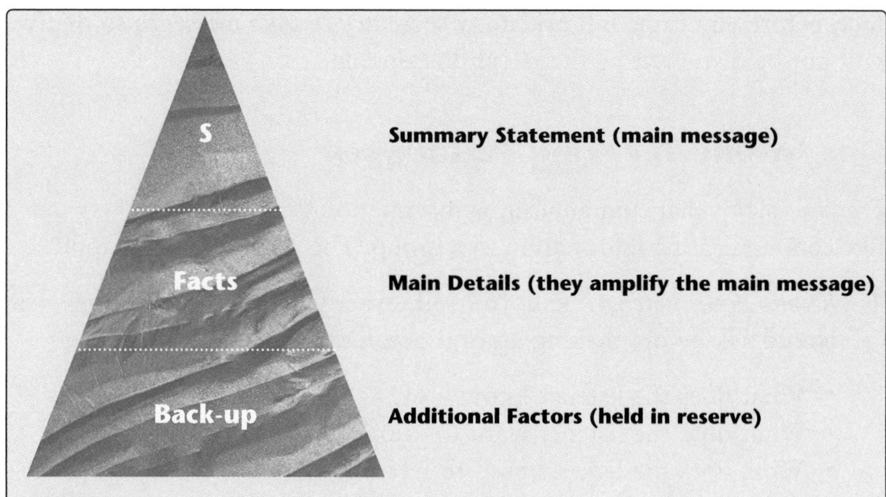

Figure 10-7 The speaker's basic pyramid

Don't just "hear": *listen*!

He tells Kai that interpersonal communication is not only the responsibility of the speaker. If at a particular moment the listener does not use good listening techniques, he or she contributes to information loss and the resulting misunderstanding that can occur. "The trouble," he adds, "is that we take listening for granted. Nobody taught us to listen—that happened naturally—but our parents, and later our teachers, told us if we did not speak well."

Frank explains that a supervisor, in particular, must develop the ability to listen well, and he outlines five guidelines that Kai can follow to improve his listening skills:

Give the speaker your full attention

1. *Be a "switched on" listener.* Go to, or make sure you are in, a location where you will not be disturbed (closing the office door and cutting off telephone calls is the first step). Look the person in the eye and avoid fiddling with objects on the desk or table in front of you. Show that you are interested in the speaker's topic, or concerned about his or her problem. Avoid comparing his or her situation with situations you have experienced (which suggests you are more concerned with what happens to you than with what happens to the speaker).
2. *Encourage the speaker to articulate his or her concerns.* If the speaker is reticent or having difficulty explaining some of the facts, become adept at using the "echo" technique: when the speaker pauses, repeat a key phrase from his or her last sentence. For example, if the speaker says

"Well, I really don't know what to do. I mean, up to now Gabriel has been a good friend, but . . . ."

If the speaker hesitates or stops, you can murmur a single phrase drawn from his or her last words, such as

"Good friend . . . ?" or "Gabriel . . . ?"

The "echo" encourages the speaker to say more, to expand on what was incompletely said.

3. *Avoid taking sides.* If an employee comes to you with a complaint, listen sympathetically but without making comments that indicate you support either the speaker or the person who is the object of the complaint. Become adept at using a sub-branch of the echo technique: murmur non-partisan remarks such as, "Is that right?" "Uh-huh," "That's when you came in . . . ?" "Have you told anyone else?" and "Is that the first time it has happened?"

Be completely impartial

4. *Be known for your integrity.* Integrity is not an obvious attribute. Integrity is built over time, as those who work for you or with you gradually learn that, when they confide something to you, it stays with you; you respect their confidence.
5. *Avoid making hasty judgments.* When a person comes to you who is clearly agitated or angry, or seems to respond with a defensive attitude, allow time to pass before you mentally pass judgment. As a listener you won't know—at least initially—the cause of the individual's exasperation or anger, or the circumstances that have led the person into a particular mood. If the person is angry, give him or her time to simmer down. If the person is agitated, remind yourself that personal circumstances, or events that occurred before you encountered the person, may be coloring his or her attitude. And if a normally friendly person is silent, try not to assume that he or she is sulking. The silence may be concern for a sick relative or worry following a disagreement with a close friend. At such times the individual needs your silent presence and support. Explanations can come later.

Listen without bias

"Relationships are built on good communication," Frank says as he escorts Kai to the door, "regardless of whether you are involved in a supervisor–employee relationship or an employee–employee relationship. As human beings we have been given the unique capacity to speak and listen to one another. It's up to us to make the best possible use of that capability and not to waste it."

He shakes Kai's hand. "Good luck in your new job," he adds.

This short list "says it all"

TO SUM UP

To be an effective presenter of information, either before a large audience or a small group, such as those attending an office meeting, means
- preparing early, and thoroughly,
- identifying your potential audience, and their interest in and knowledge of the topic,
- dividing your information into "need to know" and "nice to know" topics,
- presenting the key information right up front,
- using visual aids to enhance your presentation, but ensuring that they actively support your data (that they are not there "just to look pretty"),
- rehearsing carefully, and out loud,
- using body language to drive points home, and
- being enthusiastic.

To be an effective communicator in a person-to-person situation means
- as a speaker, identifying the listener and the message you want to convey, and
- as a listener, focusing your attention on the speaker and the message he or she is conveying.

EXERCISES

Suggest shorter meetings

Exercise 10.1

Your supervisor is frustrated by the amount of time wasted in attending unfocused meetings. Darren Korolik has shown you his "Meeting Timer" (see page 275) and you are impressed with his idea. You make a sketch of it (you will have to use your imagination!) and show it to your supervisor. He likes the idea and asks you to describe the Meeting Timer, how it operates, and its advantages, at the next supervisors' meeting.

Part 1

Prepare speaking notes and the visual aids you will use for your presentation.

Part 2

Present your idea at the meeting.

Exercise 10.2

The exercises below all evolve from assignments in earlier chapters. In each case, read the assignment details for the previous exercise (ideally, you will have already written the assignment), and then make the suggested oral presentation.

1. *Exercise 3.2.* You meet Tania and tell her how to open up and close down the computer.
2. *Exercise 3.3.* You knock on Joe and Wendy Raphael's office door and tell the substance of the conversation you have just had.
3. *Exercise 3.5.* Bev Maydan, who has had a vehicle on rent for two weeks, telephones to ask where she should leave the car. Tell her.
4. *Exercise 3.8.* Rather than write the announcement, announce the meeting personally to the MSBA members attending the previous month's meeting. (Refer to Exercise 3.7 for more details regarding this situation.)
5. *Exercise 4.4.* You have your written request ready to hand to Georges and Maria Popondopolos, but when you go in to see them they ask you to explain exactly what it is you want.
6. *Exercise 4.5.* Although you have written a request to Sunshine Services Ltd, you decide to go round to their small office on Ebby Street and personally explain the situation and your request.
7. *Exercise 4.6.* You are ready to hand your written request to attend the conference to Rita Shirling, but decide to brief her yourself to explain what you are asking for, just before you give her the request.

   Request conference attendance in person
8. *Exercise 4.7.* Instead of writing to Joe and Wendy Raphael, go to them and explain your request.
9. *Exercise 4.8, Part 1.* When you take your proposal to Maria Cantafio, you say, "I've written a proposal for a faster, more efficient way to take orders from local businesses."
   - Maria says: "Tell me about it. I'll read your proposal afterward."
   - Describe your plan to her.
10. *Exercise 4.8, Part 2.* Maria Cantafio invites 12 local business managers to lunch and tells you that you are to brief them about the new Web-based lunch-ordering service. Describe the service to them.

    Describe an email ordering service
11. *Exercise 4.10.* You receive a telephone call from Mr Edgar Farlinger, at No. 493 Princess Street. He says he has read your flyer describing the home and yard maintenance services you provide, and wants you to make a personal presentation to him, in his home, so that you can identify specifically what you can do for him.
    - Write down five questions you would ask him, while he is on the telephone, so that later you will give him a focused presentation.

- Consider what you believe his answers would be, then make your presentation to Mr Farlinger.

12. *Exercise 5.1.* It's the day following the accident at High Gear Truck and Car Rentals. You receive a telephone call from Fern Whitmore, High Gear's area superintendent, asking you to drive to the downtown office and describe the incident in person. Do so.
13. *Exercise 5.2.* You write the recommendation report to Fern Whitmore, but decide you will go down personally and brief Fern about your findings before you hand in your report.

Describe a neat car rental idea

14. *Exercise 5.3.* Area Superintendent Fern Whitmore happens to call in to the High Gear Truck and Car Rental outlet where you work. She asks about the airport parking space. Describe the situation to her.
15. *Exercise 5.4.* Area Superintendent Fern Whitmore again calls in at the rental outlet. Tell her about the problem you are having and describe how you are going to remedy it.
16. *Exercise 5.5.* When you take your report in to Winona Taverner, she asks you to describe the results of the audit at the Mini-Copyshop to her. *(Note: to do this oral communication exercise, you first need to do the calculations in Exercise 5.5 and, ideally, write that report.)*
17. *Exercise 5.6.* Bill Korton asks you to brief him personally as well as submit a written report about the situation at the Kimberley branch. Tell him your findings.
18. *Exercise 6.1.* When you have written the proposal, you attend a meeting with the College Administration, during which you are asked to describe your plan orally before handing out the proposal.
19. *Exercise 6.2.* Your proposal is ready to send to the head office of Kleyton and Johnston Insurance Services Limited. You give it to Corinne Mahoney, who wants to write the cover letter. She asks you to brief her on the report's contents.
20. *Exercise 6.3.* Your proposal is ready. Now present it orally to a meeting of the Student Council.
21. *Exercise 6.4.* When you take your finished proposal to Karla Vipond, she says: "That sounds fine. I would like you to attend the executive meeting with me and present your findings in person." Do so.
22. *Exercise 7.1.* You have completed your investigation report on new rental accommodation for Northwinds Loan and Investment Corporation, and telephone Pierre Charlebois to let him know that your report is ready. He asks you to attend a meeting of division managers, at which you are to describe your findings and recommend which you think is the best site. You will hand in your report *after* making your presentation.

Present your research into new office space

23. *Exercise 7.2.* Report the findings of your investigation into LCD projection panels to the department heads attending this month's meeting at Wilson, McGee, and Associates.

Exercise 10.3

You are sent to the college library or learning resource centre with the following instructions: "Find an article on oral communication that particularly interests you in a recent journal or magazine. Check that no other student in your class is using the same article for the same purpose, then carry out the following three assignments."

Research a new product or process

Part 1
Write a summary of the key points presented in the article.

Part 2
Make speaker's notes for a five-minute oral presentation of the article's key points to the other members of your class.

Part 3
Make the presentation.

Exercise 10.4

Attend a meeting, or part of one, of your college or university's student association.

Attend and report on a meeting

Part 1
Write a brief comment on how well the meeting's participants present their information.

Part 2
Write minutes covering the chief outcomes of the meeting, or the segment you attend.

WEBLINKS

Ten Tips for Successful Public Speaking
www.toastmasters.org/tips.htm
Part of the Toastmasters site, an international organization designed to help people improve their public speaking skills.

Crossing a Bridge of Shyness: Public Speaking for Communicators
www.eeicommunications.com/eye/shyness.html
Diane Ullius, the author of this article published in *The Editorial Eye*, teaches oral and written communication skills at Editorial Experts Inc. and at Georgetown University. She offers practical advice about getting over the fear of public speaking.

Preparing Outstanding Presentations

www.ieee.org/organizations/society/pcs/creimold.html

This is a series of articles by Cheryl Reimold that includes sections on understanding your audience; basic presentation structure; the introduction, body, and summary of a presentation; effective visuals; and making visuals memorable.

Presenting Yourself to a Prospective Employer

chapter 11

Twins Kelley and Richard Emburgh live far apart, but both have the same goal: to find a better job. Kelley is a receptionist for an environmental protection agency in Saint John, New Brunswick, but really wants to work as a computer programmer. Richard has travelled widely but now has settled in New Westminster, British Columbia, where he is an exceptionally successful telemarketer; however, he really wants to be a contracts administrator.

Both are admirably qualified to hold their desired positions: Kelley has been interested in computers since she entered high school, has completed a computer analyst/programmer course at the local community college, and continually develops software for her own and her friends' personal computers. Richard has excellent oral communication skills (which account for his success as a telemarketer) and was top student in a "Contracts and Marketing Studies" evening course at Douglas College. Yet, although both have applied for several positions advertised in the careers sections of their local newspapers, neither has been invited to attend an interview.

"I don't understand it," Richard complains to his friend Shiro, "I have just the right qualifications for that Quonset Corporation job I showed you, yet all I get is a letter telling me the position has been filled by someone more qualified!"

Richard and Kelley have yet to learn that applicants are selected for interviews based *solely on the evidence they submit in their resumes and letters of application*. Documentation that is interesting, informative, and well presented will appeal to a prospective employer, whereas documentation that is dull, incomplete, too opinionated, or poorly presented will discourage an employer from placing the applicant on the short list of people to be interviewed.

They also have to learn that the Internet has opened up a world of opportunities and possibilities for people seeking employment. They could have used the Internet to research information about companies, search for job postings, enter information about themselves into an electronic database, post a resume, or place an international classified advertisement. Alternatively there are commercially run Internet services that specialize in matching people to positions, and nonprofit Bulletin Board networks that allow anyone to list or look at job openings.

IN THIS CHAPTER

You will learn how to

- prepare four types of resumes, each suited to a particular situation,
- shape your resume so that it focuses attention on the key points in your background that will appeal to a particular employer,
- prepare a resume specifically for posting on the Internet,
- write an application letter that will encourage a potential employer to interview you, and
- present yourself well at an interview.

Show what *you* can bring to a potential employer

An employer who receives 25 or 30 responses to an advertisement screens them initially by asking of each, "What can this applicant do for me?" (or, more specifically, "What will this applicant bring with him or her that will enhance the quality of my product or service?") If the resume and letter of application demonstrate right away that the applicant has something significant to offer, the employer places that person's documentation in an "I'd like to interview" pile. If they do not, the employer places the resume and letter in either an "Only possibly" pile or a "Thank you, but I'm not interested" pile.

The Traditional Resume

Kelley's and Richard's applications are consistently placed in the "Thank you, but no" pile. They both follow a traditional format for their resumes that, when jobs were easy to obtain, was perfectly acceptable:

Personal Data
Education
Experience
Additional Information
References

This format documents an applicant's history in a logical sequence, but does not focus employers' attention on the critical information that will make them want to interview the applicant. To capture an employer's attention, the "Personal Data" section should be replaced with a short paragraph called "Objective," which very briefly covers two primary pieces of information.

Beware the unfocused traditional resume

1. What the applicant can do for the employer.
2. What the applicant has done that makes him or her the ideal person for the position.

This information should be conveyed in no more than two sentences. Here is an example:

Create a snappy opening

> OBJECTIVE:
>
> To become an information writer for a major Canadian corporation, power utility, or government department, applying my experience as a book editor and my Diploma in Journalism.

This writer is really saying, "I want a job, and this is the kind of job I would like." But, by quoting her experience in terms that will appeal to a corporate employer, she seems to be saying, "This is what I can do for you, and these are my credentials."

Figure 11-1 shows the same Objective at the head of a resume written in the traditional format. Corinne LePage does not have extensive work experience, so the arrangement suits her background. Further comments are keyed to the resume by the circled numbers beside Figure 11-1.

Eliminate the Personal Data section

Rather than using a separate Personal Data section, Corinne assembles essential information about herself into a block centred at the head of the page. She omits personal data such as her age, sex, marital status, religion, and ethnic background, because they do not belong on *any* application documents (under Canadian human rights legislation an employer cannot even ask for such information until an applicant has been hired).

As well as focusing attention on an applicant's key attributes, the Objective should be tailored to suit each potential employer (word processing technology makes this easy to do). For example, if Corinne were also to apply for a junior management position with the City of Calgary's Department of Parks and Recreation, she should change her Objective so that it draws attention to her experience as coordinator of a water ski team.

Corinne G LePage
4719–38th Street
Camrose AB T4V 3W9
Tel: (403) 489-8143 ❶

Objective

To become an information writer for a major Canadian corporation, power utility, or government department, applying my experience as a book editor and my Diploma in Journalism. ❷

Education

- Diploma in Journalism, Southern Alberta Institute of Technology, Calgary, Alberta, 2001. ❸
- Graduate of Frobisher High School, Winnipeg, Manitoba, 1998.

Experience

May 1999 to present	**Western Prairie Publishers,** Calgary, Alberta. I work under contract as a part-time editor of trade book manuscripts. I review manuscripts for readability, continuity, language, and punctuation, and check correctness of references and legal implications.	❹
July 1998 to August 1999	**The Bay,** Winnipeg, Manitoba. Sales clerk in household linens (6 months) and home electronics department (8 months).	❺

Other Activities

- Feature writer for high school yearbook for two years (1996–98): yearbook editor for senior year (1998). ❻
- Winner of Kale McCreary award for Creative Communication, S.A.I.T., June 2000.
- Active skier since 2000: cross-country skiing in winter and water skiing in summer. Member of Wave-Topps Water Ski Display Team since 1995, giving displays at resort locations from Ontario to British Columbia. I have been Team Secretary for the past year and a half, developing and maintaining schedules and corresponding with event managers.

References

The following persons have agreed to supply references: ❼

Ms Shirley Chung-Hien Acquisitions Editor Western Prairie Publishers 1480–7th Avenue NW Calgary AB T2N 0Z2 Tel: (403) 475-6661	Mr David Wheeler President Wave-Topps Water Ski Club 917–15th Street SW Calgary AB T3C 1E5 Tel: (403) 452-6437

Let your resume's *appearance* depict you as an efficient person

Figure 11-1 A resume in the traditional format, prepared by an applicant with limited work experience

3

Although traditionally the Education section of a resume precedes the Work Experience section, in today's job market it is just as common for the Work Experience to appear first. This arrangement is particularly effective if the reader is likely to be more interested in what work the applicant has done rather than in what education he or she has completed (for an example, see Figure 11-2 on page 300). In Corinne's case she can present the two sections in either order, because both her education details and her work experience strongly support her Objective. She chooses to adopt the more traditional sequence.

Focus readers' attention on what you have done

In describing her work, Corinne does more than say that she has held a particular job for a specified length of time. She satisfies her reader's interest by describing what the work involves and what responsibilities she has had. (She does this again further down the page, when she describes her role as secretary of the water ski display team.) Note, however, that when a past job has little bearing on the work she is seeking, or is several years further back in her work experience, she provides only a few details about the job.

Work Experience is listed *in reverse order*, with the most recent work described first and the earliest work listed last.

Details of an applicant's activities and achievements outside the workplace help paint an image of an active person who will bring a strong personality to the job. This section should include sport and hobby interests, any scholastic or sport awards the applicant has received, and both past and current activities.

Opinions differ as to whether an applicant should include references in a resume. Some people claim that it is better to write "References will be supplied on request." Others insist that references should appear on the resume. I agree with the latter group, simply because employers tell me that, when deciding which applicants to interview, they tend to select

Include references; don't make the employer ask for them

those who provide *complete* information. ("Why," a personnel manager has confided to me, "should I take an additional step to find information when other applicants give it to me in their resumes?")

Follow these two guidelines when selecting suitable referees:

- Ensure that there is a visible connection between the person you are listing and the job or position you held. An employer wants to see why you have listed a particular person, and will tend to discount anyone who might be construed to be just a neighbor, relative, or friend.
- Before including referees' names in your list, check that they are willing to provide a reference for you. This step is not only a courtesy but also an assurance that your referees will think about what they plan to say before they are called.

There are several other factors to consider when preparing a resume, and they apply to all resumes, regardless of their format.

- Limit the length of a resume to two pages. An applicant with only limited work experience should strive to write a one-page resume, as Corinne has done in Figure 11-1. Only in exceptional circumstances (when an applicant has extensive experience or has published many papers) should a resume fill three or more pages.
- Use "white space" around and between the information to make the resume more appealing. For example, Corinne has not allowed her work experience to run back to the left margin, under the dates, even though it would have saved space. Similarly, try to centre the resume vertically and horizontally on the page so that the overall effect is a balanced, well-presented document. This subtlety appeals to a reader, since it conveys the impression that the applicant is a well-organized person.

Appeal to the reader's "eye"

- Prepare the resume as a word-processed document and print it using a laser jet or ink-jet printer.
- If you make copies of your resume, use a high-quality copier.

The Focused Resume

Debra Craven feels that a potential employer will be more interested in her practical experience than her education, so she alters the sequence of information in her resume and divides her experience into two sections (see Figure 11-2). The sequence becomes

Objective
Related Experience
Other Experience
Education and Training

Achievements/Other Activities
References

Comments on Debra's focused resume, and comparisons with Corinne's more traditional resume in Figure 11-1, are keyed to the circled numbers beside Figure 11-2.

Debra's address and telephone number are centred at the top of the page, and are followed by her Objective.

Her practical experience follows immediately, and is divided into two sections: experience that relates specifically to the Objective, and experience that does not. These sections help to focus the resume even more. If she had placed her work experience in only one reverse-sequence section, the description of her figure skating work would have interrupted the continuity between the two sets of child care experience.

Target your information to a *particular* employer

For each entry in the Experience section, Debra has chosen to describe her role first, and set it in boldface type, rather than place the name of her employer first (as Corinne has done in her more traditional resume). This arrangement is particularly suitable here because it draws attention even more quickly to Debra's practical experience.

Rather than offer a list of duties, a description of one's work should use descriptive verbs that create an image of personal involvement and responsibility, words such as

Paint strong images

administering	analysing	arranging	conceiving
coordinating	creating	designing	developing
directing	evaluating	implementing	initiating
investigating	managing	monitoring	observing
organizing	planning	presenting	researching
resolving	supervising	training	writing

Debra used *planning, developing, guiding, preparing,* and *coordinating* in her resume.

DEBRA L CRAVEN
414–806 Taylor Avenue
Winnipeg Manitoba R3P 2R2
Tel: (204) 488-7094 ❶

Objective

To obtain a full-time position in a registered day care centre in Manitoba. I hold a Child Care Services Diploma and have accumulated over four years' experience working with young children.

Child Care Experience ❷

Focused experience up front immediately proves assertions in the Objective

1999–2001 **Practical Day Care Placement.** Five months' cumulative experience in child care work at four day care centres in Winnipeg, as the practical part of my training in the Child Care Services program at Red River College. At each centre I was responsible for planning and developing curriculum activities such as art, music, and science, for guiding children in their free play and daily routines, and for providing nurturing care. ❸

1995–1998 **Assistant Child Care Worker** in the School-Age Day Care Program at River Forks Elementary School, Winnipeg. I was responsible for planning and implementing school-age activities, guiding children's play, preparing nutritious snacks, and caring for children until their parents arrived.

Other Experience

1996–1999 **Teacher of Figure Skating** to children aged 4 to 12 for City of Winnipeg Parks and Recreation Department. Taught Saturday programs at Century Arena for two years, then worked full-time as figure-skating coordinator at Grant Park Arena for one year. As such I was responsible for preparing schedules, coordinating figure skating with other activities, maintaining student progress records, and teaching 15 hours a week.

/2 . . .

Figure 11-2 A focused resume

5

Debra L Craven – Page 2

6

Education and Training

June 2001	Graduated with a Diploma in Child Care Services from Red River College, Winnipeg, Manitoba. Classified by the Manitoba Child Day Care office as a Child Care Worker Level III.
April 1999	Completed up to Level 6 of the Canadian Figure Skating Association program. (Became a Registered Teacher of Figure Skating in 1996.)
June 1998	Graduated from Riverview Collegiate, Winnipeg, having completed Senior Level 4 with university entrance options.

Achievements

7

Winner of two awards:

- Marjorie Majurski Scholarship for excellence in first year Child Care Studies (Red River College, 2000).
- Campbellton Trophy, as top figure skater in under 17 category (1998).

Selected as one of four high school students to represent Manitoba in interprovincial high school debating contest (Western Provinces), held in Saskatoon, Saskatchewan, November 1997. Team placed second.

Extra-curricular activities contribute to the overall picture

References

The following people have agreed to provide references on request:

8

Mavis Gallard
Supervisor, Skating and Skiing Programs
City of Winnipeg Parks and Recreation Department
70 Main Street
Winnipeg MB R3B 1B7
Phone: (204) 946-3700, Ext 206

Karen Marquadt
Director, River Forks Day Care Centre
East Wing
River Forks Elementary School
328 Meander Avenue
Winnipeg MB R3A 4R6
Phone: (204) 453-8806

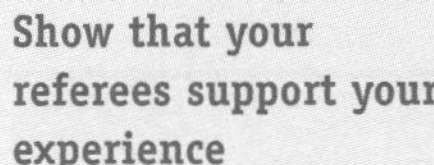
Show that your referees support your experience

5

Debra incorporates enough information to warrant using a second page for her resume, which permits her to insert an additional blank line between each entry and use more white space. She takes care to indicate at the foot of page 1 that there is a second page, and to identify herself at the head of page 2. This precaution is necessary in case the two pages become separated.

Debra has expanded the Education heading to include Training because she wants to include her certification as a teacher of figure skating.

Because her figure skating activities have been covered under Other Experience, Debra uses the single word "Achievements" rather than "Other Activities" as the heading for this section. Awards and achievements can cover past as well as current events.

Ensure relevance of referees

An employer can easily trace the connection between Debra and her two referees: one has been her skating instruction supervisor, and the other the manager of the after-school day care centre where she worked part-time for three years.

The Functional Resume

A functional resume takes a nontraditional approach by listing specific qualities that show the applicant is especially suited for a particular job. These attributes describe what the applicant can do for the potential employer, and identify what he or she has done for previous employers (to demonstrate his or her capability). This information is placed immediately after the Objective and before the employment history and education details. The resume's parts become

Objective
Qualifications
Major Achievements
Employment Experience
Education
Awards/Other Activities
References

The intent is to target the resume not only to a particular employer, but also to a particular job. It is a useful method for an applicant who has proven practical experience but a lean educational background. It also focuses employers' attention on the answer to their primary question: "What can you contribute to the quality of my product or service?"

A special approach for a nontraditional applicant

The resume in Figure 11-3 shows how Paul DeGagne uses the functional method to capture the attention of an automobile leasing agency's divisional manager. The numbered comments are keyed to the circled numbers beside the resume.

The Objective clearly identifies what Paul can do for the organization that hires him. Now Paul must follow it *immediately* with facts that show he can do what he claims he will do. He demonstrates this claim by listing his qualities, and then he proves they are more than just opinions by describing some of his achievements.

Start selling in the first line

Paul adds strength to his qualifications by starting each with an action verb (*target*, *write*, *manage*, *follow through*, and *maintain*). Keeping each statement short increases the overall impact.

He again uses action verbs, this time to introduce each achievement, but now they are in the past tense. He particularly quotes specific quantities rather than generalizations, because specifics such as "42%" and "a 12-month period" convey a much stronger impression than generalizations such as "a significant increase" and "a whole year." For the same reason he identifies the name of his employer, and the year, in brackets at the end of each achievement.

❹

Since Paul has already described his major achievements, he needs to write only short descriptions of each position he has held (this helps keep his resume to two pages). In each case he identifies the company, its location, and his main jobs and responsibilities.

Paul E DeGagne
1727 Phillbrook Crescent
London ON N5X 2Z7
Tel: (519) 472-0383

Objective

To be instrumental in increasing market share for a Canadian automobile rental and leasing company. 1

Qualifications

Use short, sharp, definite statements . . .

I have the particular ability to
- target special-interest groups and develop innovative marketing strategies for them, 2
- write results-oriented proposals and present them persuasively to all levels of management,
- manage a task or project independently, identify and resolve problems quickly, and report progress regularly,
- follow through with clients, both before and after a contract has been signed, and
- maintain effective interpersonal relations with clients, peers, and staff.

Major Achievements

. . . supported by specific details

For previous employers I have
- devised a rapid-response automobile replacement plan for customers of insurance companies, resulting in a 42% increase in fleet size and a 78% increase in insurance-generated rentals over a 12-month period (Carillon Car Rentals, 1999), 3
- increased new printing contracts by 26% and repeat sales by 21% over a nine-month period (Talisman Printing, 2001),
- received the automobile salesperson of the month award for three consecutive months (Atlantic Auto Sales, 1996), and
- advised a Junior Achievement Group that won the Southern Ontario "Junior Achievers Award" for project ingenuity and marketing prowess two years in succession (Carillon Car Rentals, 1998).

/2 . . .

Figure 11-3 A functional resume

Paul E DeGagne – Page 2

Employment Experience

4 2000 to present	**Talisman Printing Limited,** London, Ontario. Marketing manager, responsible for developing commercial printing contracts with new clients and generating repeat business with existing clients.
January 1996 to September 1999	**Carillon Car Rentals,** London, Ontario. For first two years: rentals agent at various daily rental outlets; for latter 20 months: contract and fleet leasing agent at head office, responsible for creating new markets in the commercial leasing field.
July 1993 to December 1996	**Atlantic Auto Sales, Inc,** Fredericton, New Brunswick. Used car salesman for 18 months, then new car salesman for remaining two years.
September 1990 to June 1993	**PROVO Department Stores,** Woodstock, Ontario. Part-time while attending high school (12–15 hours per week), as stock clerk for one year and sales clerk for two years.

For other resume forms, these experience descriptions would be too brief (but they are fine here)

Education

June 1999	Graduated with Certificate in Commercial and Industrial Sales from Broughton Community College, London, Ontario (placed 2nd in course with GPA of 3.76).
5 June 1993	Graduated from Darrell Patterson Collegiate, Woodstock, Ontario.

Awards and Other Activities

1997 to 1999	Member, Toastmasters International. Received "Southern Ontario Master Toastmaster" Award, 1998.
1996 to 1999	Adviser to three "Carillon Junior Achiever" groups, two of whom won major awards.

References

Two immediate references, with others available on request:

6

Gordon Hutchinson	Dianne G Neufeldt
Vice President, Marketing	Dean, Business Administration
Carillon Car Rentals	Broughton Community College
80 Bridge Street	24 Knightsbridge Road
London ON N4J 2R3	London ON N6K 3S9
Tel: (519) 661-2407	Tel: (519) 661-3800

Include your references

Figure 11-3 A functional resume (*continued*)

Pay attention to the appearance

The way in which Paul arranges his information on the page is worth noting. On the first page he uses bullets to introduce each item, which aligns the information neatly and provides continuity throughout the page. On the second page he provides two columns, the left showing dates and the right containing information. This arrangement is easy to read and provides continuity, and is also a familiar arrangement for employers.

Paul does not want to list his current employer as a reference, so he lists a previous employer and a college official, both of whom are familiar with his work. He indicates he has other references, whom he will quote when he is reasonably sure he will be offered a position.

The functional resume is an effective way to present oneself to a prospective employer, but it must be done well if it is to create the right impact. In addition, an applicant should use it only when he or she is confident that the employer will not be "turned off" by a nontraditional resume. In the sales and marketing field the functional approach works well. For more conservative organizations, such as a university or a government office, an applicant should first consider whether the employer may feel the functional format is too nontraditional.

Dare to be different, but don't overdo it!

The two-page resumes prepared by Debra Craven and Paul DeGagne would normally be printed on two sheets of paper held together by a single staple at the top left corner. An alternative arrangement—suitable only for a two-page resume—is to print them as two side-by-side pages on an 11 inch by 17 inch sheet of paper, and then to fold the paper so that the resume is on the inside (see Figure 11-4). With this arrangement, a title for the document and the name of the person can be printed in bold letters on the front of the resume. Then, if the applicant has additional information he or she wishes to present (such as a bibliography of publications or a list of projects worked on), it can be tabulated on the outside back cover.

Such an arrangement not only holds the two pages of the resume permanently together, but also offers more space for applicants with a lot of data to present. It is a simple yet imaginative way for an applicant to demonstrate his or her capabilities. It also shows that you are not limited to the formats illustrated here; indeed, you may manipulate them to match your particular skills, experience, and potential, or tailor them to meet the needs of a specific employer.

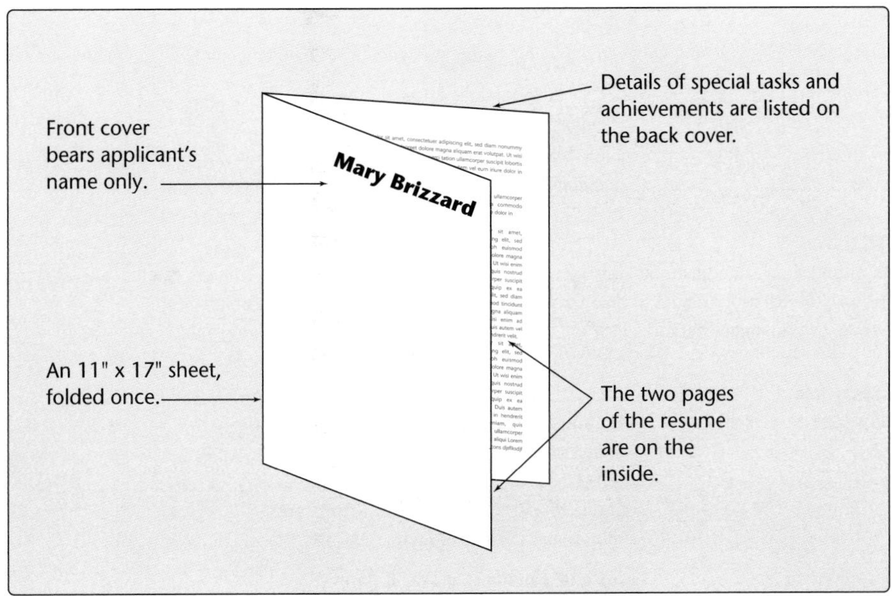
Front cover
bears applicant's
name only.
Mary Brizzard
Details of special tasks and
achievements are listed on
the back cover.
An 11" x 17" sheet,
folded once.
The two pages
of the resume
are on the
inside.

Figure 11-4 An alternative way to present a two-page resume

The Electronic Resume

In today's competitive workplace there are more people looking for fewer jobs, which means that Human Resources departments are often overwhelmed by the number of resumes they receive in response to a job advertisement. So, instead of advertising a position, Human Resources' staff may prefer to maximize their hiring time by using automated computer systems that narrow the search for them. In effect, instead of posting a job and seeing who applies, they first go into the databases to see who is out there.

So, from a job-seeker's viewpoint it can be a smart move to register or submit your resume to one or more independent databases. An electronic resume can be scanned, coded (e.g. in HTML), or both, so the computer can read and categorize it. Sarah Holland, for example, developed two "electronic" resumes:

The Internet has changed how employers seek fresh talent

- A resume she sent to an independent database service (Figure 11-5).
- An HTML version she used on her personal World Wide Web Home Page (Figure 11-6 on page 310).

For the latter, she used a basic menu structure with links to additional information. She also made arrangements with her Internet Service Provider to collect data on who accesses her page, so she can follow up by sending an email message to each organization.

Sarah Ann Holland
245 - 608 Trafalgar Road
London Ontario N5Q 2G7
Tel/Fax: 519 426 0881
s.holland@interact.on.ca

Objective
To obtain a position as an administrator for a Southern Ontario business, where I can use my 10 years experience in organizing and coordinating business and community events to maximum effect.

Experience

Nov 1999 to present	**Child and Family Services**, Cambridge, Ontario Administrator Contract position, coordinating and scheduling counsellors and respite workers with clients (children and their families).
May 1997 to Nov 1999	**Eaton's of Canada**, London, Ontario Human Resources Administrator Coordinating HR services, organizing interviews and meetings, and arranging work and vacation schedules, for a staff of 1870.
June 1993 to April 1997	**City of London, Sports and Social Services Department,** London, Ontario Administrative Assistant One year full-time, after high school graduation; two years part-time, while attending community college. Responsibilities included • coordinating sports and social events, and education courses • arranging travel and accommodation for community club sports and social events • training temporary staff
Education	Diploma in Business Administration, Seneca College, Ontario, 1997, GPA 3.85 Senior Project: Designed software for sports equipment control system. East Elms High School, Stratford, Ontario, 1993, 83.7%

Figure 11-5 Electronic resume prepared by Sarah Holland, which she submitted to an independent database service

Extracurricular Activities	Westferry Gliding Club, London, Ontario, 1992 to present Initially glider pilot in training; received Transport Canada Glider Pilot licence in 1994; served as club secretary 1996–1999; achieved instructor rating in 1998. Instructor, 1999 to present. Teach "Theory of Flight" and "Navigation Principles" during winter ground school for entry-level candidates; give flying instruction during summer months.
Special Awards	Recipient of Cavanaugh Scholarship in Administrative Studies, Seneca College, Ontario, 1996 Awarded Provincial Trophy for best overall performance, East Elms High School, 1992

References

The following people will provide more information about my work and involvement in company activities. Additional references can be provided on request:

Margeurite LeFievre
Waverley Consultants Inc
(previously HR Director, Eaton's of Canada, London)
313 Overland Avenue
London ON N2S D6K
Tel: 519 434 1168
Fax: 519 434 1287
email: lefievre@waverleycon.on.ca

Gary Millies
Chief Flying Instructor
Westferry Gliding Club
PO Box 3190
London ON N5A 6N6
Tel: 519 448 6177
email: g.millies@westferry.net

Figure 11-5 Electronic resume *(continued)*

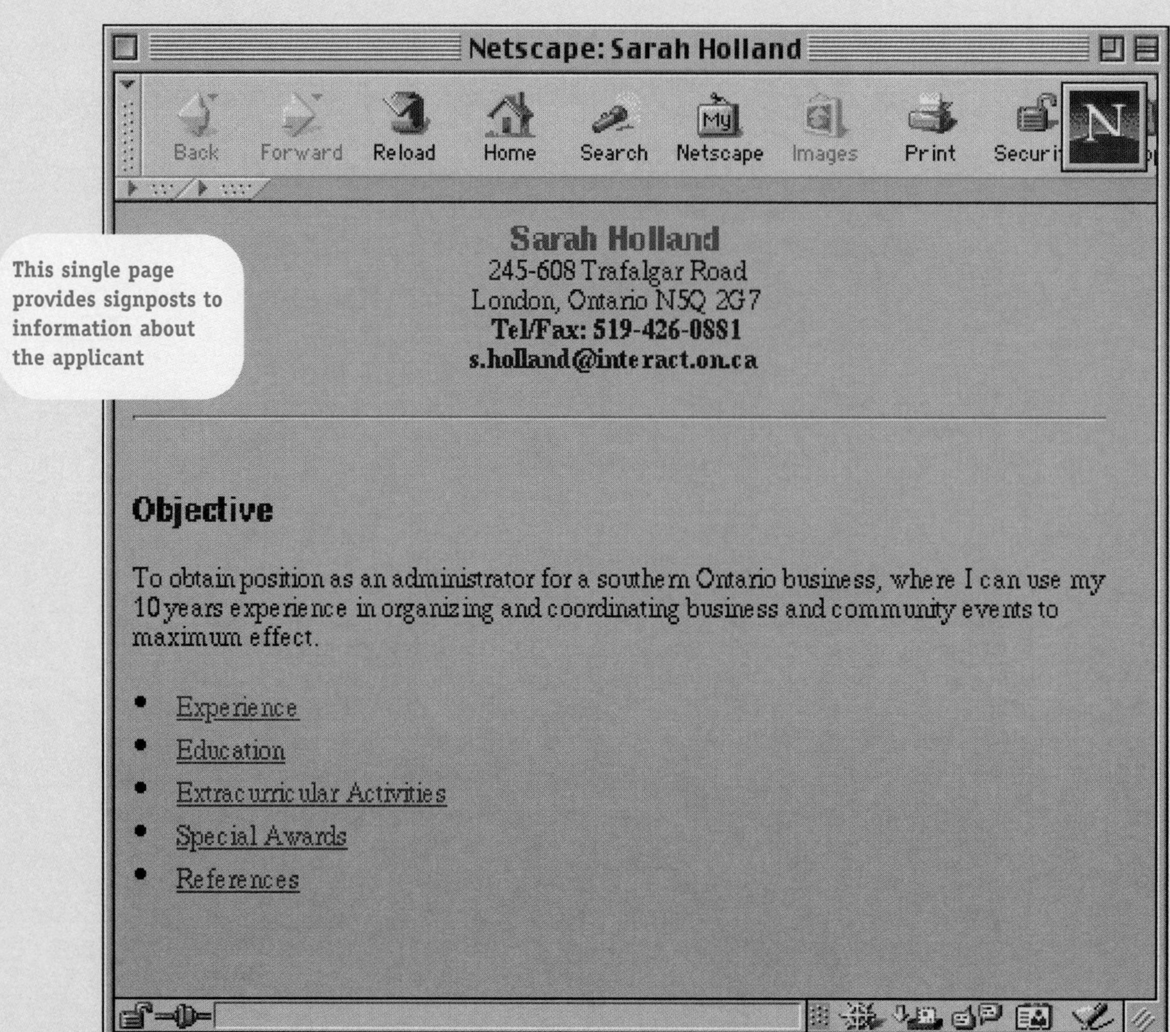

Figure 11-6 An HTML-coded resume prepared by Sarah Holland, which she used on her World Wide Web personal Home Page

When you submit your resume to an independent database service, usually it is scanned in and categorized, labelled, and keyworded in several variations. For example, it might be categorized by **education**, and then by **experience**, and yet again by **location** or a certain **skill.** An employer who is entering a request into the system provides specific keywords to describe the requisites for the position to be filled, such as "administrator," "B.Comm," "marketing," "sales," "telemarketing." The system searches through resumes in its database to locate any that match these keywords, and presents the resumes to the employer. Consequently, it's important to choose your keywords carefully, so they not only describe your qualifications well but also help searchers find you.

Choose keywords that *employers* will list

All this does not mean that the traditional paper resume is obsolete: it just offers a greater range of options for marketing yourself to potential employers. All three types of "paper" resumes described earlier can be scanned by a resume provider service and entered into the system. However, I suggest you prepare a special version of your regular resume if it is to be posted as an electronic resume. Here are some factors to consider.

Keywords

The resumes that get listed first by a potential employer are those in which the keywords most match those the employer has listed. So, when developing an electronic resume, you need to think like a Human Resources Manager and include as many keywords as possible.

A keyword is usually a noun, not an action verb. A Human Resources Manager will search for words that describe the qualities or skills needed for a particular position, words like *account manager, Excel skills, member ARMA* (Association of Records Managers). The searcher may also enter other company names, particular tools or technologies, or even hobbies.

Readability

When a resume is scanned, the quality is often compromised. I suggest using simple fonts and formatting and recommend a sans-serif font such as Arial. When a serif font is scanned, the letters tend to run together, making the words difficult to read. The same is true for small-sized fonts. Consequently, I recommend using a 12 pt font. Similarly, bold fonts should be used for emphasis, rather than italics and underlining, since the latter do not scan well.

Avoid tricky formatting

When formatting your resume avoid using graphics, shading, or horizontal or vertical lines, since a scanner may not be able to handle them or may not interpret them correctly. This includes commas, parentheses, and extra periods. Keep the formatting as simple as possible, as in Sarah Holland's resume in Figure 11-5.

Make sure that your name is the first thing listed on your resume since that is how the computer will index you. That is, avoid placing "Resume" at the top of the page (you don't want to be known as "Resume"!).

Submitting an Original

Before sending your resume to an independent database service, ask them for specific guidelines on preparing and submitting it. Then *mail* your resume (do not send it by email or fax, to eliminate another electronic conversion it has to go through). When mailing it, insert a sheet of cardboard to ensure your resume will not be folded or crumpled, which can create markings when it is scanned. Similarly, never staple the pages of your resume together, because the staples will be removed to scan it and the holes left behind will show up as black blobs on the electronic version. Print it on white paper with a laser printer to obtain the clearest, cleanest original.

The Letter of Application (Cover Letter)

Unfocused applications prompt form-letter replies

Although you may personally give your resume to an employer, more often you will mail it. Rather than send your resume alone in the envelope, you would be wise to include a cover letter. The cover letter then acts like an executive summary that precedes a report, in that it can highlight the key features about yourself that will appeal to an employer. An alternative name for this kind of cover letter is Letter of Application.

There are two kinds of application letters. A *solicited* letter applies for a job that has been advertised or is known to be open. An *unsolicited* letter applies for a position when none has been advertised or is known to be available. The letters take the same shape, although the approach differs slightly (particularly in the opening paragraph).

Because a Letter of Application also is a business letter, it should conform to the business letter style discussed in Chapters 3 and 4. Its writing plan (see Figure 11-7) has three parts:

1. In the Initial Contact—equivalent to a Summary Statement—the applicant states that he or she is applying for a job and has the credentials to hold it.
2. In the Evidence, which should be no longer than three paragraphs, the applicant provides facts to support what has been written in the opening paragraph.

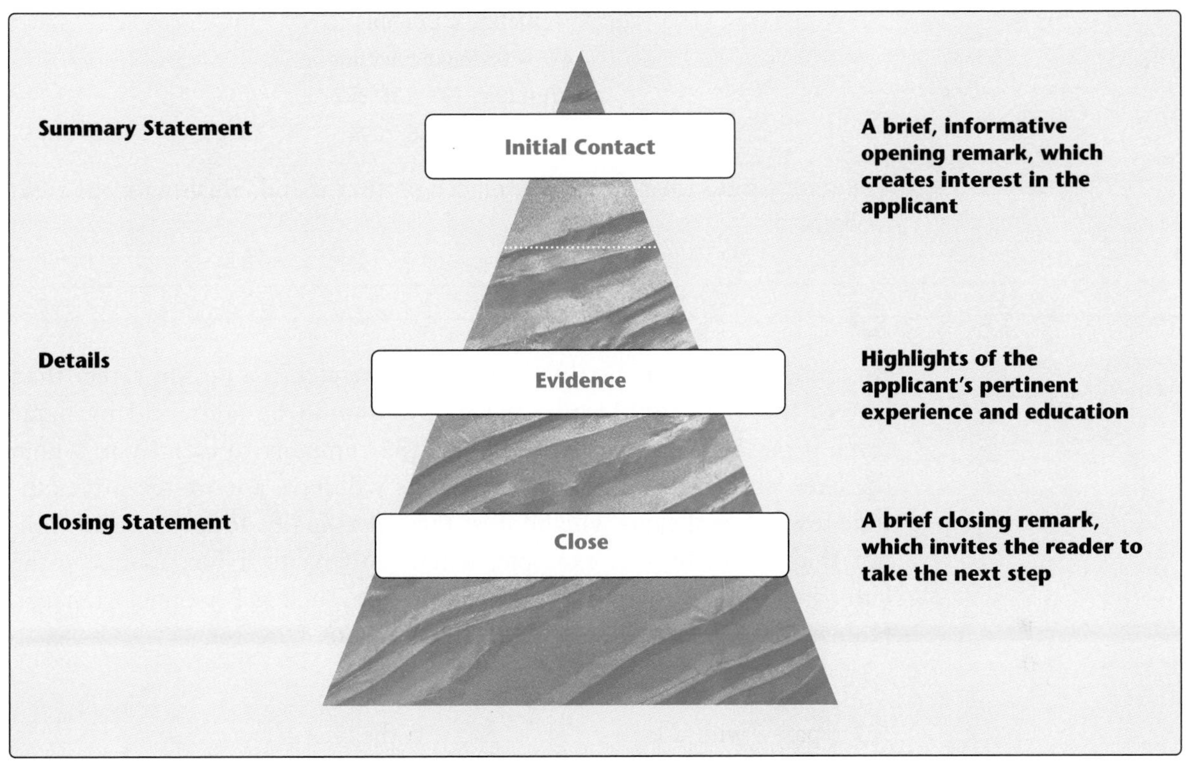

Figure 11-7 Writing plan for an application letter

3. In the Closing Statement, the applicant encourages the employer to place the letter and its accompanying resume in the "Let's interview" pile.

When Debra Craven saw an advertisement for a child care worker at Lawn Park Day Care, she prepared the resume shown in Figure 11-2 and attached it to the cover letter in Figure 11-8 on page 315. As she was applying for an advertised position, her letter was a *solicited* application. The paragraphs that follow comment on Debra's letter and offer guidelines for writing both solicited and unsolicited application letters. Each comment is numbered and keyed to the circled numbers in Figure 11-8.

Let the appearance reflect anticipated reader reaction

Debra chose the modified block letter format because it is less formal and so appears more personable. She also chose to start each line of her address slightly right of the centreline of the page (and later to balance the page by also starting the complimentary close and signature block right of the centreline). Alternatively, she could have centred each line at the head of the page, like this:

Debra L Craven
414–806 Taylor Avenue
Winnipeg MB R3P 2R2
Tel: (204) 488-7094

The date would then have been placed so that it ends flush with the right margin.

Target a specific reader

An application letter should always be addressed to a person rather than just to the company. Ideally, the person should be addressed by name (even if the applicant has to telephone the company to identify to whom the letter should be sent), since recipients will have a more receptive attitude toward applicants who address them personally. If the applicant cannot find the name (for example, when replying to a box number), the letter should be addressed to the position title, such as Personnel Manager, Human Resources Manager, or, in Debra's case, Director.

Greeting the employer by her first name in the salutation is unusual. Debra did so because she worked in that day care centre on a job placement while attending college and so got to know the director on a first-name basis (which is customary in the day care business). In a letter to a day care centre where she is not known, Debra would greet the director by her last name.

Be assertive, but not aggressive

This is the Initial Contact (or Summary Statement) in which Debra states that she is responding to the advertisement and identifies some key points about herself that will create interest and so cause the employer to read further. An applicant must be positive when saying that he or she is applying for a job, writing *I am applying . . .* , *I enclose my application . . .* , or *Please accept my application . . .* , rather than the weak-sounding *I would like to apply. . . .*

This paragraph and the next are the Evidence section of the letter. They provide facts to support what Debra has said in her opening paragraph, and excerpt key points from her resume that will most interest the employer.

Debra L Craven
1 414–806 Taylor Avenue
Winnipeg MB R3P 2R2
Tel: (204) 488-7094

September 10, 2001

2 Carla Donato
Director
Lawn Park Day Care Ltd
2159 Notre Dame Avenue
Winnipeg MB R3H 2J9

3 Dear Carla

Please accept this letter and the enclosed resume as my application for the
"Child Care Professional" position you advertised in the Winnipeg Free Press
4 on September 6. I hold a Diploma in Child Care Services from Red River
College and have been classified at the Child Care Worker III level through
the Manitoba Child Day Care office. I have also accumulated three years'
experience working in day care centres, and another four years as a teacher
of figure skating for young children.

My child care experience was acquired primarily in the School-Age Day Care
5 Program at River Forks Elementary School, and during four placements at
local day care centres as part of the R.R.C. program. Yours was one of the
four centres I was placed in, which has led me to write to you since I particularly enjoyed working with your staff and children.

My teaching experience was achieved with the City of Winnipeg Parks and
Recreation Department, both as a teacher of figure skating for 4- to
6 12-year-olds and as a program coordinator at Grant Park Arena. More
concrete details are contained in the enclosed resume.

7 I would welcome the opportunity to visit your centre again and discuss
the position with you. Would an afternoon next week (September 17 to
21) be suitable?

Regards

8 *[signature]*

Debra L Craven

enc

Show you're good . . .

. . . prove it, and . . .

. . . *ask* for an interview

Figure 11-8 A solicited letter of application

Somewhere in the Evidence section—preferably near the end—an applicant must refer to the enclosed resume. This reference not only draws the employer's attention to it, but also ensures that, should it become detached from the letter, the employer will know to look for it. (It is not enough to assume the employer will notice the "enc" at the foot of the letter.)

Encourage the employer to interview you

The Closing Statement must "open the door" for the employer to make the next move (that is, invite the applicant to come in for an interview). Polite but bland closing remarks such as "I look forward to hearing from you at your earliest convenience" or "Should my qualifications meet your requirements, I would appreciate attending an interview," close rather than open the door. Debra's closing paragraph may seem too direct—even pushy—but if competition is strong she *must* create a firm, positive impression. By quoting possible dates, she creates an opportunity for herself to phone and ask for an appointment if she has not heard from the director by, say, September 18.

In the signature block, an applicant should always quote his or her first name rather than use just an initial. This invites the employer to reply with a first name, either when writing or telephoning, which helps set an informal mood.

How would Debra's letter have differed if she had not been responding to an advertisement, and had to prepare an *unsolicited* application? The main difference would have been in the Initial Contact, in which she would have identified her qualifications first (in what is known as a "hook" or eye-grabber), and then indicated she is seeking a position. For example:

> Dear Ms Donato
>
> As a graduate (Level III) Child Care Worker who has several years of experience in day care, I am seeking a position where I can also utilize my experience in teaching sports activities to young children.

Try to meet the employer's needs

If Debra senses that a day care director may be interested in her administrative experience, she can insert four more words at the end of the paragraph:

"... in teaching sports activities to young children *and administering sports programs.*"

This "tailoring" of the Initial Contact helps the resume meet a specific employer's needs.

The Job Interview

Contrary to what many applicants think, a job interview is much more than simply an occasion for an employer to take a look at a short list of applicants and decide which one to hire. Properly conducted employment interviews permit both parties to survey each other: for the employer to evaluate the applicants, and for the applicants to assess whether they want to work for that particular organization. Consequently, you must come to an interview ready to ask as well as answer questions.

Preparing for the Interview

Thorough preparation is essential. You need to

- learn as much as possible about the potential employer,
- consider what questions the employer might ask and how they should be answered, and
- list any questions you want to ask.

You cannot do all of this overnight.

Do your homework

Learn Something About the Employer. Researching the employer means determining the size of the company or organization, its principal products or services, whether it is a head or branch office, where other branches or offices exist, what major contracts it has won recently or large projects it has handled, how many people it employs, and its involvement as a participating member of the community. With such information you will be ready to ask knowledgeable, intelligent questions during the interview and so demonstrate that you are a well-prepared, worthy candidate who is not treating the interview casually.

Do *more* homework!

Anticipate Difficult Questions. Preparing to answer questions is difficult, because you have no way of knowing what a particular interviewer will ask. There are, however, certain questions that surface at many interviews, and you can prepare for them. For example, the interviewer might ask:

- Why do you want to work for us?
- What will you be bringing to our organization to make it worth our while to hire you?

- Why do you want to leave your present employer? (*Or:* What prompted you to leave your previous employer?)
- What do you enjoy most (or dislike most) about your present job? (*Or:* What did you like or dislike most about your previous job?)
- What do you expect to be doing in five years? In 10 years? (*Or:* Tell me about your career plans.)
- If we were to hire you, what salary would you expect?

If you are asked any of these questions without having considered them beforehand, you will probably pause, gasp, stumble over your words, apologize for not really knowing, and in one way or another demonstrate that you are either not willing or not ready to answer. You will show that you are ill-prepared, and thus reduce your chance of selection. But if you have already thought about these and similar questions, you will answer much more confidently and so increase your image in the interviewer's eyes.

You may ask, "Why should an interviewer want to know what salary I want, when the company already has a pay scale for the position and knows what it expects to pay?" In most cases the interviewer is testing both how well prepared you are and how you value yourself. If you hesitate, or say something like "Well, I . . . er . . . I'm willing to accept the established pay level," or "Umm . . . oh . . . somewhere between $18 000 and $22 000, I guess," the interviewer will sense a lack of certainty on your part. But if you reply, "With my experience and education, I expect about $21 000," you again will create a confident impression. If you feel your price may be a bit high, and thus may jeopardize your chance of selection, you can add, "The exact figure will depend on your company's fringe benefits." What you really will be implying is, "I know what I want, but I'm also reasonable and willing to negotiate."

Avoid undue hesitation

Know What You Want to Ask. Near the end of the interview, the interviewer will inquire, "Now, are there any questions you would like to ask?" In case your mind suddenly goes blank and you find yourself frantically trying to remember what you had in mind, prepare a small card beforehand and on it jot down some questions (just short key words that will trigger the questions in your mind, not a long list). This does not look like a "crib sheet" to the interviewer; rather, it shows that you have prepared thoroughly. Keep the card easily accessible, and limit it to questions that really show you have thought about the job, such as, "Does the company help pay for education courses I would take in my own time?" "Will I be expected to provide my own car, or does the company provide one?" and "Will I always work in the local branch, or is there a chance I will be transferred to another branch or even head office?"

Don't rely on your memory

Getting Off to a Good Start

Many job applicants think an interview does not begin until they are comfortably seated and the interviewer and applicant have exchanged greetings and opening remarks. In reality, however, interviewers are subtly influenced by the applicant's manner right from the start, and the initial impression they gain may color their reaction throughout the interview. So walk purposefully into the interview room, look directly into the interviewer's eyes, smile as you shake hands, and offer a firm grip. If you do, you will create the image of a confident person—one who deserves the interviewer's full attention.

Exude confidence

You may be interviewed by only one person, or by a board of two to four people. Facing only one interviewer is easier, but a board probably will draw more information from you: while you are being questioned by one member of the board, the others will be listening and preparing for the next question. Although this creates a more intense situation for you, it also ensures you are given more opportunity to demonstrate your strengths. In general, a board interview can be an excellent experience for a well-prepared applicant, but may be a disaster for an inadequately prepared applicant.

If you face a board, try to repeat each person's name as you shake hands when the chairperson introduces the board members to you. You will create the impression you are a friendly person, and perhaps help yourself remember the name to use later in the interview. Addressing a board member by name, if you turn to him or her to ask a question, creates a positive response from that person.

Responding to Questions

Experienced interviewers ask questions that elicit well-developed replies, whereas less experienced interviewers may ask questions that require only one-word answers. For example, an open-ended question like this one will encourage you to provide a thoroughly developed answer:

Experienced Interviewer:

"Earlier you mentioned that in your last position you had to train employees to use new software. Can you give me some idea what that involved?"

Applicant:

"Yes, well, two years ago the company instituted a computerized procedure for monitoring customer accounts. I tested it for the company when they were thinking of buying the program, so when they did buy it they asked me to train the operators."

***Develop* your answers**

A less experienced interviewer might ask the same question this way:

Inexperienced Interviewer:

"You mentioned earlier that in your last position you trained employees to use new accounting software." (Slight pause.)

Applicant:

"Right."

Interviewer:

"Er . . . how many did you train?"

Avoid staccato responses

Applicant:

"About 30."

Interviewer:

"Over what period?"

Applicant:

"Two years."

This interviewer is learning facts piece by piece, and struggling to think of the next question while the prior question is being answered. If you face an interviewer who asks "closed-end" questions like these, help him or her along by *developing* your answers. Let's see the difference:

Inexperienced Interviewer:

"You mentioned earlier that in your last position you trained employees to use new accounting software." (Slight pause.)

Applicant:

"Right. That was two years ago, shortly after I had evaluated the software when the company was thinking of purchasing it. When they did, I was asked to train all the existing operators and any new ones who were hired, about 30 altogether."

Expanding your answers like this does not mean you should take over the interview or monopolize the conversation! Your role should be to offer quality answers that reveal details about you as a person. You should judge how much information to give by assessing what the interviewer is trying to elicit from you. At the same time you should look for opportunities, within an answer, to present facts about yourself that you feel are important but which you sense the interviewer may not elicit.

Here are additional suggestions on how to answer questions:

Establish and maintain eye contact

- Speak up, using a natural, moderate speed of delivery.
- Look at the interviewer(s), not at your hands, shoes, or objects on a desk or table.

- Let your enthusiasm *show*, both in your voice and your body language. When you have a particularly important point to make, lean toward your interviewer(s) to stress the importance of your words.
- If you do not know the answer to a question, say so. Neither hesitate nor bluff.
- If you do not understand a question, again do not bluff. Either say you do not understand or, if you think you do but would prefer to check, rephrase the question and ask if you have interpreted it properly (*never* imply that the interviewer has worded a question badly).
- Deal with stress questions honestly but briefly. (In a stress question, the interviewer describes a situation for which two or more possible actions can be taken. You are asked to say what action you would take.) Think momentarily about it, then give the answer you honestly believe to be best. The interviewer(s) will undoubtedly challenge you, no matter which answer you give, to see how well you respond under stress. Remember that often they are more interested in seeing *how* you respond than in the actual answer you give, and that if you try to anticipate what the "correct" answer is (the one you *think* they are looking for), you are more likely to be disturbed by the stress questions and respond weakly to them.

Anticipate "stress" questions

- If you are interviewed by a board, address your answers mainly to the board chairperson. When giving a long answer, also look at each of the other board members in turn, so that you draw them into the topic. If a question is posed by one of the other board members, address your answer to him or her at the start, then look at the other members.
- Be careful about injecting humor into your answers. Remember that what may seem extremely funny to you may not appeal to the interviewer's sense of humor.

Be wary about using humor . . .

- *Never* say bad things about a previous employer (i.e. never backstab the company, a manager, or a supervisor), or even a teacher or person you have worked with. Interviewers will look negatively at such information and suspect that, if they did hire you, you would bad-mouth their company and staff to a subsequent interviewer. Even if you left a previous company hating your boss's guts, just say you left "following a difference of opinion."

. . . or bad-mouthing others

- Be natural. If you try to be the kind of applicant you *think* the employer is looking for, you will probably create a false impression that rings hollow to the interviewers and makes them doubt your suitability for the job.

Asking Questions

When you have an opportunity to ask a question, use these pointers as a guide:

Now it's your turn!

- Ensure that the question is relevant to the topic currently under discussion.
- Know exactly why you are asking the question (interviewers recognize a good question and the clarity of thought that created it).
- If you are facing a board, direct most of your questions to the board chairperson.
- If one board member has been introduced as a specialist in a particular subject, and your question clearly concerns that subject, address the question specifically to that person.
- If the interviewer has not mentioned the salary range or pay scale earlier in the discussion, ask about it just before the interview ends. An interview should not close without addressing this topic.
- Try to avoid questioning how long your vacation would be, or you will sound as though you are more interested in the holidays you will earn than the work you will do! You can, however, ask the interviewer to outline the company's benefits, and hope that he or she will mention vacations along with the pension, health, and dental plans.

Post-Interview Letters

You may have occasion to write to the potential employer after the interview. Sometimes you may feel it would be appropriate to write a follow-up letter, to remind the employer you are still available. Or, if you are fortunate, you may need to write a letter accepting a job offer, or even perhaps rejecting it (for example, if you have already accepted another offer).

Writing a Follow-up Letter

And after the interview?

Although it is not obligatory, a week or 10 days after the interview you may feel it would be appropriate to write a short letter to thank the interviewer for providing you with the opportunity to present yourself. (Such a letter reminds an employer that you are still "out there.") The letter should be short and contain two pieces of information:

1. Your thanks for being given the interview.
2. An offer to provide any additional information the interviewer may need.

Writing an Acceptance Letter

The telephone rings and the caller (who was your interviewer) announces that you are the successful applicant. She asks if you will accept a certain salary, and when you can start. You agree on a specific date and then she asks you to write a letter accepting the position. Your letter should

- accept the offer,
- repeat the important details (rather like a contract), and
- thank the interviewer.

Here is an example:

> Dear Ms Weiss
>
> I am confirming my telephone acceptance of your September 11 offer of employment as a market analyst in your financial services division. I understand that my starting salary will be $26 000 per year, and that I am to start on October 16, 2000.
>
> Thank you for considering me for this position. I look forward with pleasure to working for Multiple Industries Inc.
>
> Regards

The letter no one minds writing!

Suppose, however, that you have just accepted another position and then Multiple Industries' employment manager writes you a letter rather than telephoning the acceptance to you. Now you must phone and decline the offer, and then follow it with a letter saying "Thanks, but no thanks." For example:

> Dear Ms Weiss
>
> I regret that I will be unable to accept your kind offer of employment, because I have already accepted a position with another firm.
>
> Thank you for considering me for this position.
>
> Sincerely

How lucky can you get?

Always decline a job offer politely, and preferably in writing, because one day you may want to work for that firm. Similarly, if you decided earlier—perhaps shortly after the interview—that you would not accept the position even if it were offered to you, you should write immediately to the employer to ask for your name to be withdrawn from the list of candidates.

Every step is important

TO SUM UP

Every step of the job application process is important, because if you present yourself poorly at *any* stage you severely limit your chance of selection.

A successful job search campaign requires that you

- treat each employer as a separate entity rather than one of a group of potential hirers of your talents,
- research each employer and the company's requirements before preparing your documentation (i.e. resume and application letter) or attending an interview,
- prepare your information in electronic as well as the traditional format,
- shape your documentation so that it meets a particular employer's needs,
- focus your documentation so the potential employer can see immediately that you have something useful to offer, and
- anticipate what you may be asked, and what you want to ask, before attending each employment interview, and then present yourself honestly, clearly, and confidently.

EXERCISES

Exercise 11.1: Applying for a Locally Advertised Position

At a Canada Employment Centre or from your local newspaper, identify a local firm currently advertising a position you could apply for when you have completed the course you are enrolled in.

Part 1

Prepare a resume you could use to apply for the position (assume you are within six weeks of course completion).

Part 2

Write a letter applying for the position, to which you will attach your resume. (*Note:* If you are responding to a newspaper advertisement, attach a copy of the advertisement to your letter.)

Part 3

Assume that the personnel manager of the company you applied to in Parts 1 and 2 telephones you and asks you to attend an interview next

Monday. Write five questions you would ask during the interview. After each question, describe why it is important and what answer you hope it will elicit.

Exercise 11.2: Applying for a Widely Advertised Position

Respond to one of the following advertisements, all of which appeared in the careers section of last Saturday's edition of your local newspaper. Assume that the advertiser is located in the same city as your college or university.

A

The Connaught Inn
invites applications for the position of
SENIOR DESK CLERK

In addition to regular front desk duties, you will be responsible for coordinating meetings, receptions, and conferences held at the hotel, and for consulting with representatives of sponsoring organizations. This junior management position will be of interest to recent or upcoming graduates of business administration or hotel/motel management courses. Apply to

Melvyn G Demetrius
Manager, The Connaught Inn
2720 Morton Highway

B

LCD Projection Systems Ltd
requires an
ASSISTANT MANAGER

We are distributors for ZETA state-of-the-art computer-driven LCD projectors and related equipment. Our small office is staffed by the owner/manager and two sales representatives, all of whom are frequently out on sales or service calls. We need an assistant manager responsible for administrative and clerical work, scheduling appointments, ordering and shipping supplies, and demonstrating the ZETA equipment in the absence of the manager and sales staff. Apply in writing to

John Meridian
Manager, LCD Projection Systems Ltd
28A Horton Street

C

H L Winman and Associates
Consulting Engineers
have an opening for an
ADMINISTRATIVE ASSISTANT
who will report to the Manager of Administration

Responsibilities:

- Supervise the business office and accounting staff.
- Coordinate the preparation of proposals and bids.
- Maintain liaison with clients and contractors.
- Assist in administrative and personnel functions.

Experience and/or Education Required:

- Three years as a business administrator, or
- Graduation from a business administration course, or
- A combination of both.

Submit resume and salary requirements to

Tanys Young
Head, Administration and Personnel
H L Winman and Associates
P.O. Box 220

D

A PRODUCTION ASSISTANT
is required by
Metro Videos Inc

Metro Videos Inc specializes in producing short documentaries and promotional programs for a variety of clients. We need a production assistant who also will be our office administrator. Duties will range from coordinating a "shoot," keeping a shot list, and making video dubs, to arranging meetings with clients, answering the telephone, and ordering stationery and video supplies. Experience in either television production or business administration will be an asset. Write, enclosing a resume, to

Harley Kirzan
Metro Videos Inc
316 St Mary's Boulevard

E

An ASSISTANT TO THE ADMINISTRATOR
is required at
Triple-H Medical Centre

Responsibilities will include administering and coordinating the business functions associated with a 150-bed hospital (i.e. accounting, laundry, catering, personnel selection, and training). Applicants must be able to communicate effectively at all levels, both orally and in writing. Persons applying should be graduates of or currently enrolled in a university or two-year college business administration program.

Submit a resume detailing education and experience to

Valerie Treherne
Administrator
Hawthorne Heights Hospital
Triple-H Medical Centre
PO Box 2250

F

LOG-ON INC
A premiere Internet company requires
TELEPHONE ADVISERS

You will provide telephone and online assistance to users of the Log-On email and database service. We will provide extensive training at our head office in Toronto, provide you with software, instruction manuals, and a dedicated telephone line into your home. You will then work either the day, evening, or night shift, responding to local customer calls. Obviously, excellent oral and interpersonal communication skills are essential. We are particularly, but not solely, seeking bilingual applicants (English and French). Previous experience in telemarketing will be an asset.

Email your resume and an application letter to **d.remple@log-on.ho.com**.

G

Vancourt Business Systems Inc
requires a
MANAGER OF INFORMATION SERVICES

who will control inventory and anticipate manufacturing requirements using a Vancourt 660 computer. Duties will include developing schedules and lead-times for project components and materials, monitoring inventory, expediting delivery of materials, and corresponding with suppliers. Applicants should have graduated—or be expecting to graduate shortly—from a recognized business administration or computer analyst course. Proficiency in interpersonal communication and report writing will be a definite asset.

Mail applications to
Karen Schmidt
Manager, Human Resources
Vancourt Business Systems Inc
2 Sherburn Avenue

Exercise 11.3: Applying for a Sales Position

Apply for one of the sales representative positions described below. These advertisements appeared in last Saturday's edition of your local newspaper. Assume that all advertisers are located in your city.

A

Europe's No. 1 discount supply company is ready to open retail outlets in major Canadian cities. We are looking for sales staff for the electronics department. If you are knowledgeable about personal and notebook computers, printers, modems, fax machines, operating systems, and related software, email or fax your resume to us (no letters or telephone calls, please). In a separate paragraph describe why you feel we should hire you.

Majur Computer and Electronics
email: **mazur@supply.ca**
fax: 1-800-632-1000

B

A garment manufacturer invites applications from university and community college undergraduates with a major in marketing. The successful applicant will represent us to wholesale and retail buyers of outerwear and sports apparel, and will be responsible for customer service. Training will be provided in all aspects of garment manufacturing. Excellent starting salary and commissions. Apply in writing only, stating expected annual earnings, to

Supervisor, Human Resources
Outerwear Manufacturers Limited
1950 Norris Avenue

C

A sales representative is required by a national manufacturer of office business systems. Some in-province travel will be required. Previous knowledge of, or experience with, word-processing software, copiers, and facsimile machines will be an advantage. Applicants should be graduates of a recognized business course. Write, describing education, experience, and expected salary, and enclose a resume.

Holly Charadee
Total Business Systems Ltd
220–440 River Avenue

D

Increased sales of our LCD projection systems means that we have to hire an additional salesperson. You will be responsible for establishing leads and demonstrating computer-driven LCD projection equipment, both fixed and portable. For more information see our advertisement for an assistant manager (item B on page 325). Apply in writing to

John Meridian
Manager, LCD Projection Systems Ltd
28A Horton Street

E

> The most progressive truck dealership in the province is hiring salespeople. Previous experience in truck sales is not important, because our training scheme will quickly transform you into a top producer. We prefer well-groomed, well-spoken applicants who have a strong "presence." Submit your resume to
>
> Tony Garylock
> Midtown Truck Centre
> 444 Carling Avenue

F

> A locally based insurance company has openings for two sales representatives, one for selling personal insurance and RRSPs to the public, and one for selling business insurance to local industries. We provide a comprehensive training scheme and a fixed salary during the first six months. Previous experience in direct sales and/or graduation (or imminent graduation) from a community college or university marketing course is essential. Send details of previous work experience and education or training, and indicate which position you are applying for, to
>
> Matthew Wolski
> Mansask Insurance Company Ltd
> 330 Centre Street

Exercise 11.4: Applying for an Unadvertised Position

Part 1

Identify a local firm that you believe could use a person with your talents, experience, and education/training. Assume that in two months you will graduate from the course in which you are enrolled. Prepare an application letter and resume for this particular firm, and address it by name and title to the person you believe would be most interested in you as a potential employee.

Part 2

On a separate sheet describe

1. why you chose the particular firm,
2. why you selected the particular person to whom you are addressing your letter, and

3. which of your talents, education, or experience you feel would be most useful to the firm.

Exercise 11.5: Applying for a Summer Job

Apply for one of these positions

A

> The Provincial Department of Highways will be hiring students for assignment to highway maintenance crews from June 1 to August 31. The work will involve controlling and diverting traffic, and assisting crews in repairing and resurfacing highways. Preference will be given to applicants residing near the areas where work will be done. Write, stating previous experience (if any) and the area of the province where you would be able to work (no accommodation can be provided). Address your application to
>
> Martin E Doumalin
> Senior Administrative Officer
> Department of Highways
> PO Box 808
> (Your city or town)

B

> Holidays Canada offers university and college students summer employment at various resorts in Quebec, Ontario, Manitoba, and British Columbia. Positions are available for kitchen staff, front desk clerks, dining room help, housekeeping staff, marina operators, and general maintenance personnel. We offer top wages plus free accommodation, meals, and air transportation. Write to
>
> Holidays Canada
> Suite 1706–1200 Sheppard Avenue East
> Willowdale ON M4N 7Y7

C

> The Agency for Casual Farm Labor (ACFL) is seeking students who want healthy outdoor work next summer! For a pleasant job in a farm environment, with accommodation and meals provided, write to ACFL stating your availability and preferred province. We have farms located in Quebec, southern Ontario, and the three prairie provinces. The ACFL offices are in Winnipeg, but interviews will be held in most cities across Canada. Apply to William Lockey, Director, ACFL, Box 181, RPO Corydon, Winnipeg, Manitoba, R3M 3S7.

D

> Monteith Construction Company requires students to work on airport maintenance for commercial and military airfields in June, July, and August. This will be mostly outside work and will be conducted in most provinces. Write to PO Box 2200, Ottawa, Ontario, K1G 5A1. Outline why you want the work, the length of time you will be available, and the province in which you would prefer to work. Enclose a resume describing your previous work experience and education.

E Write to the administration office of the university or college you are attending and apply for a summer job.

WEBLINKS

Career Mosaic: Resume Writing Center
www.careermosaic.com/cm/rwc/rwc1.html
The Career Mosaic resume resource page includes sample resumes, electronic resume information, how to contact employers online, cover letters, thank-you letters, resume tips, and links.

Writing in the Job Search
owl.english.purdue.edu/writers/by-topic.html#bw
The Online Writing Lab at Purdue University has a section devoted to writing job search materials, including applications, resumes, cover letters, acceptance letters, and references.

Canadian Jobs Catalogue
www.kenevacorp.mb.ca/
Canadian Jobs Catalogue contains links to more than a thousand Canadian employment-related sites, including job and resume banks, employer sites, and related Internet sites.

Writing Businesslike Language

chapter 12

When Tina Mactiere hires Beth Doland as her executive secretary, she says, "As you will be writing much of my correspondence, it's important you know my views on letter writing."

Beth nods.

Tina repeats her views on the appearance of letters and reports (see Chapter 8, pages 223 and 230), and then adds, "I expect every letter you write to be faultless. No misspelled, fuzzy, or abrasive words, no convoluted sentences, and no directionless, rambling paragraphs."

Beth says she knows what Tina means, except for the word "convoluted."

"Any sentence that is structured confusingly, that says something in a roundabout way, so the meaning is hard to understand," Tina explains.

She says that when she receives a well-written letter, it influences her impression of the letter writer and the company he or she works for. "If the words are vague, or the sentences and paragraphs are clumsily put together, I imagine a sloppy writer. But if the right words are in the right place at the right moment, and the sentences and paragraphs are crisply and clearly written, I imagine an efficient writer—a person I want to correspond with."

IN THIS CHAPTER

You will learn how the words you choose and the way you use them, and how you construct your sentences and paragraphs, combine to create either a positive or a negative image—an image that either enhances or downgrades the message you are conveying. Specifically, you will learn how to

- paint clear pictures with words, spell words correctly, avoid words that offend or are wordy, and form compound words,
- construct strong sentences that are emphatic and properly constructed and punctuated, and
- develop coherent paragraphs that are constructed pyramid-style, have good internal continuity, and in longer documents are separated by effective headings.

You will also learn how to abbreviate words and expressions, insert numerals correctly in narrative, and write metric symbols and quantities correctly.

Words, Words, and More Words

"Look after the words and the sentences will look after themselves." That's not entirely correct, I'm afraid!

Words can be examined in two ways: as words that stand alone, and as words assembled into groups to form expressions, phrases, and clauses. There are four aspects to consider: choosing words that will be readily understood, making sure they paint strong images, spelling them correctly, and checking that the reader will not find them abrasive. You also need to know how to compound multiword expressions correctly and avoid wordy expressions.

Choose Words to Suit Your Audience

The more knowledgeable a business writer is about a subject, the more likely he or she is to use words that less knowledgeable readers may not understand. Jeannine is an experienced medical technician in a children's hospital, and she recently wrote in a patient's report that " . . . the patient was injected with 0.5 cc of radioactive material, then sent to Nuclear Medicine for diagnostics." The doctors who read her report knew exactly what she meant.

But when Jeannine was called away to cope with an emergency, she left the clipboard, with her report on it, lying on the windowsill of the patient's room where the patient's father picked it up and read it. He immediately hurried down to the nursing station, where he indignantly stated that the hospital had no right to expose his daughter to nuclear radiation. It took two doctors and a senior hospital administrator to convince him that the tests were not dangerous.

Choosing the correct words depends on the audience you are reaching. Jeannine knew that every medical person connected with the patient would understand the words she was using. If she had been writing for the family, she would have written a simpler description and explained some of the terms.

Be wary of jargon

Perhaps Jeannine's case is extreme, but it does point out that in each of our areas of specialty we tend to use words that may be incomprehensible to many of our readers. Accountants tend to write about remuneration and superannuation, when they could just as easily say wages, pay, salary, and pension, and be understood by everyone. A manager may write, "John has furthered his cognizance of the Wexlar program," when he would do much better to write that "John has increased his knowledge of the Wexlar program."

What's clear to you and me may be misunderstood by uninitiated readers

The message is clear: if you have a choice between two words that have the same meaning, always try to use the simpler word, which will be understood by everyone.

Paint Strong Images

When Phil Terrhaus slips into his chair at the company's quarterly budget meeting, he apologizes to the chairperson and the other members for being 35 minutes late. "I'm sorry," he says, "but there was an accident in my department. I had to send one of my staff to the hospital."

But his terse statement does not say enough for the other members, who shoot questions at him.

"Who was it?"

"What happened?"

"Which hospital?"

"Will he be all right?"

The advantage of face-to-face communication is that listeners can ask questions if a speaker does not make himself clear. Yet Phil's general statement wastes the committee's time while he answers their questions. He should have anticipated their concern and phrased his apology like this: "Sorry I'm late. I had to send Paul Mariner to the hospital—a bookshelf fell and crushed his hand. He's pretty uncomfortable, but he'll be all right." His listeners would have raised their eyebrows and murmured "Mmmm," but they probably would not have asked any questions.

Suppose, however, the incident had been more serious, so that just before the meeting Phil had to scribble a note to the chairperson: *I'll have*

Be wary when using generalizations

to miss the meeting. There has been an accident in my department and I'm sending one of my staff to the hospital. Now the chairperson knows Phil will not be there, but the vagueness of Phil's note adds to his concern and creates questions in his mind that he cannot ask until later. If Phil had taken just a moment or two longer to explain who was involved and how badly he had been hurt, he would have communicated more effectively.

Speaking vaguely wastes people's time. Writing vaguely wastes their time even more, because they have to visit, telephone, write, fax, or email the writer to ask questions and obtain answers.

Use Descriptive Words. Every word in a sentence, particularly verbs, contributes to the clarity or vagueness of a message. Vague verbs can range from simple words such as *sent, went, got,* and *put* to more complex words such as *contacted* and *communicated (with)*. Each vague verb should be replaced by a more descriptive verb. For example:

. . . particularly the verbs

when you are going to write:	**pause first and search for a word such as:**
sent	mailed, shipped, air-expressed
went	drove, walked, flew
got	purchased, rented, bought, borrowed
put	dropped, inserted, threw (but not placed)
contacted	spoke to, telephoned, emailed, wrote to
communicated with	emailed, spoke to, talked to, telephoned, faxed

The two sentences below demonstrate how vague verbs and nondescriptive words can contribute to a message's lack of clarity.

Vague Shortly after Ms Keeler contacted me, I sent her a copy of the Westland report.

Clear Twenty-four hours after Ms Keeler telephoned, I faxed her a copy of the Westland Mall traffic report.

Vague When the crew went to the management conference at Lake Freeling, they were held up by fog and got there late.

Clear When the crew drove to the management conference at Lake Freeling, they were delayed by fog and arrived two hours late.

Now reread the four sentences and consider the *impression* that each creates of the person who wrote them. The two vague sentences convey an image of a nice but rather fuzzy person who has only partly grasped what is going on. The two clear sentences convey an image of a writer who knows exactly what is happening and is fully in control. How would you prefer your readers to view you?

Use Specifics. Dale and Mark are supervising the installation of computerized documentation equipment at different branch libraries, and then training the library staff to use the equipment. At the end of the second week each writes a brief memorandum to the city's chief librarian.

Dale's Report The computerized documentation conversion program at Braintree Library is experiencing a little difficulty, but not enough to prevent completion in time for the planned system changeover date.

Specifics instill confidence

Mark's Report A defective sensor has delayed the computerized documentation conversion program at the North End Library by two days. The installation contractor has agreed to work the Saturdays of March 1 and 8 so the project will be completed in time for the March 15 system changeover date.

Dale's report makes him sound hazily competent. Mark's report makes him sound knowledgeable and confident. The chief librarian will sense that Mark has much better control of the project because he has quoted specific details (the number of days behind schedule, exactly what will be done to make up the lost time, and specific dates). Dale probably has made similar arrangements, but his vaguely worded report keeps them hidden.

You can subtly convince your readers that you have good control of the task you are working on by quoting exact details rather than providing only generalizations. It takes a little longer, but the aura of confidence it injects into your memos, letters, and reports adds immensely to your prestige in management's eyes. (If you hesitate to predict an exact completion date because there are many variables affecting the job, you can precede the date with the words *I estimate that . . . .*)

The one word your reader inevitably *knows* how to spell is the one you have misspelled!

Check Spelling

The first, and most natural, step to take is to check for spelling errors using your word-processor's spell-check program. But use spell-check programs with caution: they do not identify misspelled words that form another word (for example, if you write "affect" or "arises" when you should have written "effect" or "arisen," the spell-checker will not recognize the words as errors). Alternatively, refer to the glossary at this end of this book (it starts on page 397).

The second step is to consider the unique situation that exists in Canada. Canadians fall into two camps when it comes to spelling: some feel more comfortable with the British spelling of words such as "centre," "labour," and "programme," while others feel more at home using the American spelling (center, labor, program). Who is correct? Both, of course.

The important thing for writers in Canada is to decide which style they feel most comfortable with, and then to stick to that style. If almost all of their letters and reports go to readers in Canada or the UK, and even much of Europe, they can safely use the more traditional British spellings. But if some of their correspondence goes to readers in the US, they should consider adopting the US style of spelling. (Although in Canada we are accustomed to seeing words such as "theatre" and "analyse," we have to remember that to an American they may look quaint.) One style is not better: they both have their place.

To help you decide which style to follow, particularly in spelling words not listed in this book's glossary, I suggest you keep a good dictionary on your bookshelf, and offer two choices:

- For British-based spellings: *The Canadian Oxford Dictionary*.[1]
- For US-based spellings: *Funk and Wagnalls Canadian College Dictionary*.[2]

Both identify the alternative spellings, but in different ways. For example, the *Oxford* dictionary lists

centre, *center (the asterisk means "chiefly US").

The *Funk & Wagnalls* dictionary lists

center Brit., centre

Because these alternatives exist, the glossary at the end of *Communicating at Work* does not tell you exactly how you should spell such words. Rather, it shows both spellings and indicates which I recommend: you will find that generally I recommend the "-re" ending for words such as "centre" and "litre," but the "-or" ending for words such as "harbor" and "labor." These also are the spellings recommended by the Canadian Press in the most widely used style guide in the Canadian newspaper publishing industry: the *CP Stylebook*[3] and *Caps and Spelling*.[4] I have chosen them to provide the spelling standards for this book, because they are the most widely recognized in Canada.

[1]*The Canadian Oxford Dictionary* (Don Mills, Ontario: Oxford University Press, 1998)

[2]*Funk & Wagnalls Canadian College Dictionary* (Toronto, Ontario: Fitzhenry & Whiteside, 1989).

[3]*The Canadian Press Stylebook* (Toronto, Ontario: The Canadian Press, 1999).

[4]*Caps and Spelling* (Toronto, Ontario: The Canadian Press, 1998).

Avoid Abrasive Words

Beware of treading on your readers' toes

Certain words or groups of words can cause a reader to react negatively to your remarks. For example, suppose you wrote the following note to a customer:

> When you filled in the form, you failed to enter your expenses for the third quarter.

The customer's reply may be cool, or even resentful, because by using the word "failed" you subconsciously implied that the customer is "a bit of a failure."

I recommend that you avoid using any expression that might be interpreted as abrasive, and which may subtly downgrade your relationship with the reader. These expressions fall into three groups, and are italicized in the left-hand column of Table 12-1. The right-hand column shows reworked, much more positive versions of the abrasive sentences.

Compound Words Consistently

Coral Sharma is writing a report describing how her department will take over a warehouse and its contents in Moncton, New Brunswick. In it she writes:

> The takeover will be achieved in three stages, which is one stage less than recommended in the take-over plan dated October 12, 2000. In stage 1 we will take over the inventory . . .

Should Coral use two words, insert a hyphen, or join the words?

At this point Coral stops, realizing she has written "take over" three different ways: as *takeover*, *take-over*, and *take over*. She feels somehow she should be consistent but cannot decide which form is correct.

Coral's difficulty is faced daily by many business writers, who question when and under what circumstances they should retain a multiword expression as two words, join the words with a hyphen, or combine them into a single, solid expression. Coral's choice of two words for the verb (". . . we will *take over*. . .") was correct. However, because the trend today is to compound fully rather than hyphenate many multiword expressions, she should have used a solid combination for the noun ("The *takeover* will. . .") and the adjective (". . .the *takeover* plan. . .").

Most multiword terms are written as compound adjectives, which are always joined by a hyphen or combined into a single term:

> the *takeover* plan
> a *low-budget* production
> the *readout* window
> an *eight-column* table

Table 12-2 Expressions that May Prove Abrasive

Sentences containing abrasive words	Much more positive sentences
1. Words that make a reader feel inadequate or guilty:	
When completing your application *you neglected* to include your tax number.	Your tax number needs to be included on your application.
Clearly, *you have not understood* the implications.	Let me explain the implications in more detail.
We could not accept your bid because *you failed* to submit a complete price proposal.	We could not accept your bid because it did not include a complete price proposal.
You ought to know that staff working after 11 p.m. have to be sent home by taxi.	It's company policy that staff working after 11 p.m. have to be sent home by taxi.
When rejecting the request *you overlooked* human rights legislation.	Before rejecting the request you needed to consider human rights legislation.
2. Words that provoke and so create resistance in a reader:	
I am sure you will agree that our decision is correct.	Kindly note that our decision is correct.
We must insist that you return the form by November 30.	Please return the form by November 30.
To ensure prompt payment *we demand* that you file your invoice within three days of job completion.	To ensure prompt payment please file your invoice within three days of job completion.
You must bring the application to room 117.	Please bring the application to room 117.
In your letter *you claim* that the food processor was incorrectly priced.	In your letter you state that the food processor was incorrectly priced.
3. Words that imply the writer is "talking down" to the reader:	
We have to assume that you understand the problem.	We assume that you understand the problem.
Undoubtedly you will be present at the hearings.	We request your presence at the hearings.
We simply do not understand how you misinterpreted our instructions.	Apparently you misinterpreted our instructions.
You must understand that we cannot reopen the file.	I regret we cannot reopen the file.
If you are applying for reassessment, then *I must request* that you attend a preliminary hearing on October 5.	If you are applying for reassessment, then I request that you attend a preliminary hearing on October 5.

Don't use patronizing language

Here are two guidelines:

Compounding Guideline 1

1. As a general rule, multiword terms are normally joined by a hyphen if they are formed from an adjective and a noun:

Words to be Combined		*Compound* +	*Primary*
adjective	*noun*	*adjective*	*noun*
low	budget	low-budget	production
heavy	duty	heavy-duty	battery
quick	release	quick-release	harness
eight	column	eight-column	table

Compounding Guideline 2

2. However, if one of the combining words is a verb, they are more often combined into a single expression in the noun and adjective forms:

Words to be Combined (verb form)	*If used as a noun*	*If used as a compound adjective*
to take over	the takeover	takeover (plan)
to read out	a readout	readout (window)
to mark up	the markup	markup (percentage)
to write off	a writeoff	writeoff (action)

These guidelines can help you form your own compound adjectives with reasonable accuracy, if they are not listed in the glossary or shown in the compound form in your dictionary.

Avoid Wordy Expressions

"Some of my staff don't know how to convey a message in only a few words," Tina Mactiere has been heard to say more than once. "I'm certainly not looking for letters so brief that they read like telegrams, but I am looking for properly constructed letters and reports written in clear, taut language, not sentences full of needless words that don't contribute anything."

The "needless words" she is referring to are low-information-content (LIC) expressions such as these:

LIC expressions obfuscate understanding

LIC expression:	**Replace with:**
due to the fact that	because
it will be necessary to	we must
pursuant to your request	as you requested
for the purpose of	to *or* for

Wordy expressions are "untidy lodgers": they not only take up space but also muddy the true meaning of a message. Here are three examples:

Original sentence:	**Delete:**
At this point in time there is no evidence of negligence.	At this point in time
A night shift was started in an effort to increase productivity.	in an effort
The local accounting procedure was revised in such a manner as to integrate it with the head office procedure.	in such a manner as

Wordy expressions are difficult to avoid because you see many other writers using them, and so they drop easily into your own writing. Yet if you do not remove them, many of your readers will view you as a ponderous, wordy writer. If you do remove them, your readers will think of you as a straightforward, informative writer.

Table 12-2 lists some commonly used LIC expressions and suggests how to correct them. Table 12-3 contains overworked expressions known as clichés, which in most cases you can simply delete.

Write Strong Sentences

A sentence is a single unit of information with a major responsibility

Sentences have to be constructed carefully if they are to achieve their dual roles. Each sentence must be able to stand alone and convey a complete thought, yet it must also be part of a larger unit—the paragraph—in which it interlocks with other sentences to convey a complete, coherent idea. In sentence building, there are three factors to consider: achieving the proper emphasis, arranging the words to create the best effect, and punctuating the sentences carefully to ensure they read smoothly and are properly constructed.

Be Emphatic

The following four sentences contain exactly the same information, yet one conveys its information more effectively than the others:

A Our representative at this year's business management conference was Angie Ruttner.

B We were represented at this year's business management conference by Angie Ruttner.

C At this year's business conference we were represented by Angie Ruttner.

D Angie Ruttner represented us at this year's business management conference.

Table 12-2 Typical low-information-content words and expressions

These words and phrases should be eliminated (indicated by X) or written in a shorter form (shown in brackets).

actually (X)
a majority of (most)
a number of (many, several)
as a means of (for, to)
as a result (so)
as necessary (X)
at present (X)
at the rate of (at)
at the same time as (while)
at this time (X)
bring to a conclusion (conclude)
by the use of (by)
communicate with (talk to, telephone, email, write to)
connected together (connected)
contact (talk to, telephone, email, write to)
due to the fact that (because)
during the course of (during)
during the time that (while)
end result (result)
exhibit a tendency to (tend to)
for a period of (for)
for the purpose of (for, to)
for the reason that, for this reason (because)
in all probability (probably)
in an area where (where)
in an effort to (to)
in close proximity to (close to, near)
in color, in length, in number, in size (X)
in connection with (about)
in fact, in point of fact (X)
in order to (to)
in such a manner as to (X)
in terms of (in, for)
in the course of (during)
in the direction of (toward)
in the event that (if)
in the form of (as)
by means of (by)
in the light of (X)
in the neighborhood of, in the vicinity of (about, approximately, near)
involve the use of (employ, use)
involve the necessity of (demand, require)
is a person who (X)
is designed to be (is)
it can be seen that (thus, so)
it is considered desirable (I or we want to)
it will be necessary to (I, you, or we must)
of considerable magnitude (large)
on account of (because)
on the part of (X)
previous to, prior to (before)
subsequent to (after)
utilize (use)
with the aid of (with)
with the result that (so, therefore)

This is just a short list of LIC expressions

Many people select sentence A, B, or C because they feel sentence D is too direct. Yet most business managers say they prefer sentence D because it tells them right away *who did what*.

Here is some more wordy bureaucratese!

Table 12-3 Typical overworked expressions

a matter of concern	in the long run
and/or	in the matter of
all things being equal	it stands to reason
as a last resort	last but not least
as a matter of fact	many and diverse
as per	needless to say
attached hereto	on the right track
at this point in time	par for the course
beef up	pick up the tab
by no means	please feel free to
conspicuous by its absence	pursuant to your request
easier said than done	regarding the matter of
enclosed herewith	slowly but surely
for your information (as an introductory phrase)	the stage is set
if and when	this will acknowledge
in reference to	we are pleased to advise
in short supply	we wish to state
in the foreseeable future	with reference to
	you are hereby advised

Straight-line communication is better . . .

Write in the Active Voice. The words *who did what* can help you write more emphatically. Whenever possible, arrange the parts of a sentence so that they form a subject-verb-object sequence known as the active voice:

WHO (or WHAT)	DID	WHAT
(Subject)	*(Verb)*	*(Object)*
Frank Ng	issued	the receipt.
I	request	a refund.
A broken cable.	stopped	the printer.
Angie Ruttner	attended	the conference.

In the earlier examples (at the foot of page 342), sentences A, B, and C employ the passive voice, which uses a less emphatic *what was done by whom* construction (the reverse of the subject-verb-object sequence). If the four who-did-what sentences immediately above this paragraph had been written in the passive voice, they would have been much less emphatic:

The receipt was issued by Frank Ng.
A refund is requested. ("by me" is implied)
The printer was stopped by a broken cable.
The conference was attended by Angie Ruttner.

. . . than roundabout communication

Note particularly that the word "by" appears in three of these sentences, and is implied in the fourth sentence. Often, you can look for the word "by" to help you identify if you are writing in the passive voice.

To write in the active voice,

- place the "doer" (a person or thing) at the beginning of the sentence so that it starts the action, as in *Frank Ng issued . . .* and *A broken cable stopped . . .* , and
- if you are the "doer," write in the first person ("I" or "We," as in *I request . . .* or *We request . . .*).

If you do not know who the doer is, or if you prefer not to name the doer, you have to write in the passive voice:

The budget was cut by 15%. *(We do not know who made the cut.)*

Use the First Person. You may feel uncomfortable starting a sentence or paragraph with "I," particularly if at school or college you were told that doing so promotes yourself too much. Yet it is logical to write in the first person if you are describing actions you took or were responsible for.

Don't be afraid to use "I"

Here are five guidelines to help you use the active voice and the first person:

1. Use "I" when writing a memo or letter from yourself to another person.
2. Use "we" when writing a memo or letter that represents the joint opinion or decision of several people. ("We" is still the first person, but plural.)
3. Use either "I" or "we" when writing from your department to another department within the same organization, depending on the informality of the message and how well you know the person or people in the other department.
4. Use "we" when writing a memo or letter from your company to another company.
5. Use "I" or "we" rather than refer to yourself as "this writer" or "the author," because the latter expressions will make you sound pompous.

Position Words with Care

How you position or arrange the words in a sentence has a marked effect on how your readers will react to your messages.

Seek Out Impact-Bearing Positions. Readers particularly notice the first and last words in a sentence, so make sure both ends contain an important word or phrase. The following sentence loses impact because its opening and closing words carry only marginally useful information:

> Enclosed with this letter is a report describing the advantages to a small business owner of leasing rather than buying a computer, as you requested.

Put quality information in the engine and the caboose

The important information here concerns the report and its topic, yet the opening and closing words refer to an enclosure and a request. Rearranging the sentence improves its impact:

> The enclosed report describes the advantages to a small business owner of leasing rather than buying a computer.

Now the opening and closing words contain words of greater interest to the reader:

> The enclosed report describes . . .
> . . . leasing rather than buying a computer.

In the first paragraph of this section, notice how the opening and closing words of its two sentences contain important information:

> *Readers particularly notice . . .*
> *. . . important word or phrase.*

> *The following sentence loses impact . . .*
> . . . marginally useful *information.*

Here are more examples:

Impact lost:	At least twice a day check the fax machine to see if any important messages have arrived.
Impact restored:	Check the fax machine at least twice a day for important messages.
Impact lost:	It is of interest that each time there has been an accounting error it has occurred overnight, although the dollar figure has been small.

Impact restored	Each time there has been an accounting error, even though it has been only small, it has occurred overnight.

Try to place important words (important from the reader's point of view) in these impact-bearing positions whenever you can, but recognize that to maintain continuity there may be occasions when you cannot do it for every sentence.

Keep verbs on parallel tracks

Keep the Parts Parallel. Readers rarely notice the rhythm in a sentence, unless you disturb their reading by using verbs, and sometimes nouns, that are not parallel. This can be particularly true of long sentences in which the sentence parts are separated by a comma, or by connecting words such as *and, but, or, either . . . or, neither . . . nor,* and *not only . . . but also.* The following sentence lacks rhythm because the verbs *noticed* and *fax* are not in the same form:

> When the accountant noticed the billing error, his immediate reaction was to fax a credit note to the client.

Keeping the verbs parallel (in the same form) restores the rhythm:

> When the accountant *noticed* the billing error, he immediately *faxed* a credit note to the client.

Here are more examples:

Instead of	My inspection of the crates revealed that seven were damaged and four had no labelling.
Write	My inspection of the crates revealed that seven *were damaged* and four *were unlabelled.*
Instead of	All supervisors were given training in administering first aid and how to recognize and treat heart-attack victims.
Write	All supervisors were trained *to administer* first aid and *recognize and treat* heart-attack victims.
Instead of	The sales representative neither presented the product well nor was successful in closing the sale.
Write	The sales representative neither *presented* the product well nor *closed* the deal successfully.

Offer your readers a smooth ride

Poor parallelism has a negative effect, partly because it upsets reading continuity and partly because it distracts the reader's attention. The following sentence does both, and violates parallelism twice:

> Improper punctuation not only *disturbs* sentence rhythm but also *is implying* that the author is either *careless* or *a person who writes poorly.*

Read the next sentence (at the start of the next paragraph) to see how the above sentence has been corrected.

Punctuate Properly

Improper punctuation not only disturbs sentence rhythm but also implies that the author is either careless or a poor writer. Here is a review of six general punctuation guidelines:

Place a buffer at the end of the line . . .

1. Place a period at the end of every sentence, unless the sentence is introducing an example, a list of items, or two or more subparagraphs. For example, if a list follows, end the sentence with a colon (*not* a semicolon):

   Three items still have to arrive before the order is complete:
   1. Liquid paper, 12 bottles.
   2. Lined paper, $8^1/_2 \times 11$ in., 10 pads.
   3. White envelopes, 9×4 in., 500.

   Do not insert a dash after the colon.

2. If a sentence ends with a quotation mark, place the period *inside* the quotation mark:

   . . . except when there is a quotation mark . . .

   On reading the report, Ms Chewallader said, "Now, these are the results we have been waiting for."

   (Note, however, that in the UK it is common practice to place the period *outside* the quotation mark.)

3. If the sentence ends with a closing bracket, place the period *outside* the bracket:

   Sound levels were highest in the printing room (see table 3).

   . . . or a closing bracket

   However, if the bracketed words form a complete sentence, and follow a sentence that ends with a period, place the period *inside* the bracket. (See the bracketed item at the end of suggestion 2, above, and at the end of this sentence.)

4. Decide whether you will insert or omit the comma after the penultimate (second last) item in a series:

   The project comprised a preliminary study, a thorough investigation, and a detailed report.

   (This comma is optional.)

This is known as a serial comma. In most writing it is omitted, however if a sentence is particularly complex, I suggest you insert the last comma to assist reader understanding:

> During the first quarter we hired three clerks to work in the administrative services division, two additional buyers for the materiel control department, and four field services representatives for customer services.

5. Check that every sentence has a subject, verb, and object. This simple precaution will prevent you from inadvertently writing a sentence fragment, such as

Make each sentence a *complete* unit

> The 1999 audit was completed on March 11. Two weeks earlier than usual.

The first sentence is complete: it has a subject-verb-object construction. The second sentence is incomplete—it has no verb—and so is a sentence fragment. It can be corrected in two ways:

- By replacing the period separating the two sentences with a comma, thus combining the two sentences into one:

  > The 1999 audit was completed on March 11, two weeks earlier than usual.

- By inserting a subject and verb ("This was . . . ") into the start of the second sentence:

  > The 1999 audit was completed on March 11. This was two weeks earlier than usual.

Here is another example:

> With reference to your letter of September 12 and subsequent telephone call of September 19. We have reduced your September 15 payment to $500.

This time the second sentence is complete but the first sentence is not (it has a long subject but no verb and object). To correct it, change the period to a comma:

> With reference to your letter of September 12 and subsequent telephone call of September 19, we have reduced your September 15 payment to $500.

In particular, check any sentence that opens with a word ending in "-ing" (e.g. "Referring" or "Replying") or starts with an expression that ends with the preposition "to" (e.g. "With reference to . . . " or "In response to . . . "). In both cases you may inadvertently insert a period before the sentence is complete—as the writer did in the previous example.

Watch that opening phrase!

Check for careless commas!

6. Check that each sentence develops only one thought, and separate each part of the sentence with a comma or a connecting word such as *and, but,* or *because*. If you insert only a comma, check that you have not inadvertently written a run-on sentence like the one following:

   If you buy one or two desks the price will be $525 each, buy three or more desks and the price will drop to $475 each.

   Here there are two separate thoughts:

   1. One or two desks will be price A.
   2. Three or more desks will be price B.

   You can either separate them into two sentences or combine them into one sentence.

   - For two sentences, insert a period between the sentences and insert a word or two to start the second sentence:

     If you buy one or two desks the price will be $525 each. *If you* buy three or more desks, the price will drop to $475 each.

   - For a single sentence, retain the comma and insert linking words:

     If you buy one or two desks, the price will be $525 each, *but if you* buy three or more desks the price will drop to $475 each.

   The same can be done with this run-on sentence:

   Avery Schilling has been selected for promotion to cost control clerk III she will accept the position even though she is unhappy that she will have to move to the Main Street building.

Link separate thoughts with proper punctuation

   If you prefer to create two sentences, insert a period:

   . . . to cost control clerk III. She will accept . . .

   Or, if you prefer to create one properly punctuated sentence, insert a comma and a linking word (and possibly delete "she"):

. . . or connecting words

   . . . to cost control clerk III, and will accept . . .

Dealing with the Semicolon. A semicolon separates two complete thoughts, each of which *must* be a complete sentence:

The investigation resulted in unexpected results that disproved our theory; three of the seven samples showed traces of drug use.

Inserting the Colon Correctly. You can use a colon to introduce a thought that evolves directly from the sentence immediately before the colon (and this time the thought that follows the colon does not have to be a complete sentence):

Take care when lifting the lid: the steam can scald!

Alternatively, you can use a colon to introduce a list:

I need you to ship the following items by air express:

1. Computer model A700.
2. Printer model 2020.
3. Scanner, Nabuchi type 300.

Here are some more guidelines for using the colon:

1. When using a colon at the end of a sentence, to introduce a list,
   - the words before the colon must form a complete sentence (as in the example above), and
   - each item in the list must start with a capital letter and end with a period.
2. However, when the line introducing a list does *not* form a complete sentence,
   - do not place a colon after the introductory line,
   - start each item in the list with a lower-case letter,
   - follow each line, except the last line, with a comma, and
   - follow the last line with a period.

   For example:

   I need you to ship
   - a computer model A700,
   - a printer model 2020, and
   - a scanner type 300.

This is exactly the same as if the words had formed a single sentence:

I need you to ship a computer model A700, a printer model 2020, and a scanner type 300.

Note, however, that in the two examples immediately above, it's much easier to identify the individual items when they are presented as a list.

These guidelines can help you correct the more common punctuation errors made in business writing. For more rules and guidelines concerning punctuation, refer to a comprehensive handbook such as *The Canadian Writer's Handbook*.[5]

[5]William E Messenger and Jan DeBruyn, *The Canadian Writer's Handbook*, 3rd ed (Scarborough, Ontario: Prentice Hall Canada, 1994).

Construct Coherent Paragraphs

Construct each paragraph as a complete, coherent statement

In an ideal paragraph the sentences are arranged very much like the basic writing plan for a short letter or report (see Figure 12-1, which demonstrates how this paragraph has been developed). The opening sentence should summarize what the paragraph is about, several central sentences should develop the information in detail, and the closing sentence should sum up the key point(s) in a mini-conclusion. Each sentence should develop a single thought that contributes to the overall idea presented by the paragraph, and no sentence should stray from that central theme. Ideally, the final sentence should also provide a bridge or link to the first sentence of the next paragraph.

Build Paragraphs Pyramid-Style

Paragraphs can be constructed like miniature writing pyramids (see Figure 12-2), which also ensures that every paragraph has a topic sentence. Do you remember the rule drilled into you by your English composition teacher?

> "Always identify one sentence as your topic sentence, and place key information in it that sums up what the paragraph is all about. Then follow or precede your topic sentence with additional sentences that either amplify or support it, and are always related to it."

Summary Statement	In an ideal paragraph the sentences are arranged very much like the basic writing plan for a short letter or report (see Figure 12-1, which demonstrates how this paragraph has been developed). The opening sentence should summarize what the paragraph is about,	**The Main Idea**
Details	several central sentences should develop the information in detail, and the closing sentence should sum up the key point(s) in a mini-conclusion. Each sentence should develop a single thought that contributes to the overall idea presented by the paragraph, and no sentence should stray from that central theme.	**Supporting Sentences (Evidence)**
Outcome	Ideally, the final sentence should also provide a bridge or link to the first sentence of the next paragraph.	**Mini-Conclusion**

Figure 12-1 The parts of an ideal paragraph parallel those of a short letter or report

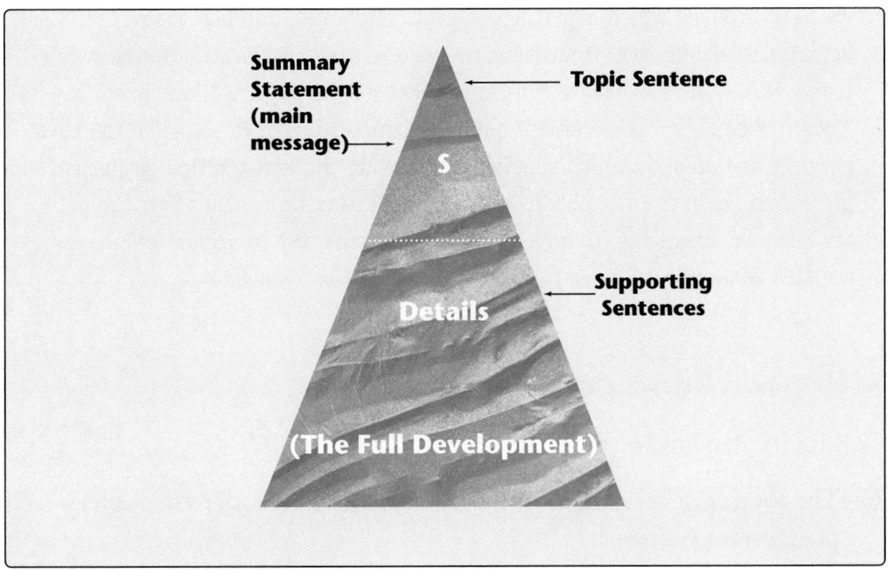

Figure 12-2 The pyramid writing plan applied to the paragraph

Topic Sentence = Summary Statement

Your English teacher probably also told you that you could place the topic sentence at the start of a paragraph, at the end, at the start and the end, or let it be only implied. For most short business letters and reports, however, I recommend that you place your topic sentence up front, where it will tell your readers immediately what the paragraph is about, in the same way that a Summary Statement presents readers with the main message at the start of a pyramid-style letter or report. The topic sentence is at the front of the following paragraph excerpted from a business letter (its topic sentence is in italics):

> *I suggest you insert "Renovations" as an early discussion item on the agenda for the next meeting.* I will need extra time to describe the building renovations that will occur over the summer. In particular, I will have to identify those offices in which asbestos cladding will be removed from the steel beams, and stress the need to completely vacate these offices. Because this will create a major disturbance, I want the department heads to have time to discuss how they can temporarily accommodate the disrupted staff, furniture, and equipment.

When you are an experienced writer and write longer letters and reports, then you can try positioning the topic sentence at the end of a paragraph. The following paragraph is excerpted from the Conclusions section of a report (again, the topic sentence is in italics):

This paragraph is constructed like an inverted pyramid

We need to know which departments want cellphones, and how many per department. From each department we need written justification for each cellphone requested, so that we can assess whether the need is "must have" or "nice to have," and so determine priorities. We also need to establish the cost per unit and identify which supplier can provide the best multiple-acquisition price. And we have to establish whether purchasing or leasing offers the better financial advantage. *Clearly, before deciding whether to acquire cellphones we must conduct both a needs analysis and a cost assessment.*

Strive for Good Continuity

Continuity depends on two factors:

1. The logical development of information as the reader encounters each progressive sentence.
2. Natural links between the sentences that carry the reader smoothly through the paragraph.

No matter how well each individual sentence is written, a reader will be disoriented if the sentences do not work together to develop the topic logically and coherently. The following paragraph lacks continuity:

Badly written sentences provide an uncomfortable ride

The movers jolted the hard disk on personal computer 8281706A yesterday, causing damage to its surface. Another operator switched on the system after the regular operator had parked the drive head. This second operator booted up the system and used the computer, but did not repark the head by simultaneously depressing the "Control," "Alt," and "Break" keys. All of this happened between 2 p.m., when the regular operator parked the disk drive and left, and 3:30 p.m., when the movers picked up the computer. The computer was being moved as part of the department's relocation from the sixth to the eighth floor. The jolting caused the drive head to slide across the disk and scratch the surface, damaging it sufficiently to prevent retrieval of about 40% of the stored data.

Revising the paragraph to achieve better continuity between its sentences enhances reader comprehension considerably:

To achieve a smooth ride . . .

The hard disk in personal computer 8281706A was damaged yesterday, during the department's relocation from the sixth to the eighth floor. Before leaving for the new office at 2 p.m., the computer operator parked the disk by simultaneously depressing the "Control," "Alt," and "Break" keys. However, before the movers picked up the computer at 3:30 p.m., another operator switched it on, booted up the system, did some work, and then switched it off without reparking the drive. The jolting during the move caused the head to move across the disk's surface, and damaged it sufficiently to prevent retrieval of about 40% of the stored data.

To achieve continuity within a paragraph, you need to present your information in a prescribed sequence, which may be

. . . find a comfortable route

- the order in which the events occurred (known as chronological development),
- from what happened to what effect the occurrence has had (known as cause and effect), or
- a carefully developed presentation of the facts, from which a conclusion can be drawn (known as evidence to conclusion).

In each sequence the information is presented systematically so that the reader can readily understand what has happened. The earlier paragraph about the meeting agenda (page 353) follows a basic cause-and-effect sequence, while the paragraph discussing cellular telephones (page 354) uses an evidence-to-conclusion sequence. Sometimes there can be a combination of two methods, as there is in the coherent paragraph describing hard disk damage (it combines cause and effect with chronological development). For more information about narrative patterns and paragraph development, consult a comprehensive handbook of English usage such as *The Canadian Writer's Handbook* referenced earlier.

Control Paragraph Length

The *appearance* of your paragraphs has a subtle influence on the readers' initial reaction to your information, even before they have read a word:

A paragraph's visual appearance . . .

- Very long paragraphs (more than about eight lines) create the impression that reading your information will be "heavy going."
- Too many paragraphs of the same length make a reader feel your information will be dull.
- Too many very short paragraphs—particularly one-sentence paragraphs—will give the impression you have made up a list rather than written a properly developed narrative.

To prevent readers from gaining a wrong impression, and also to draw their attention to particular information, follow these guidelines:

1. Vary the length of your paragraphs to create an interesting, informative image.
2. Place simple, easy-to-understand details in slightly longer paragraphs.
3. Place complex, more difficult-to-understand details in shorter paragraphs.

. . . affects readers' initial reaction

4. Place a key piece of information in a short paragraph surrounded by longer paragraphs (or do the reverse).

Use Headings as Visual Signposts

Headings have a dual purpose: they act as signposts, telling readers what to expect in the next piece of narrative; and they visually break up long stretches of narrative. When combined with a series of main paragraphs and indented subparagraphs, they also show your readers how you have arranged the main ideas and subordinated the secondary ideas.

Use headings to help shape the narrative

Figure 12-3 shows an effective way to arrange headings and paragraphs. Word-processing technology permits you to use different sizes of type to differentiate between different levels of headings, and to use subparagraphing to illustrate how you have subordinated your ideas. Figure 12-4 (page 358) also shows indented side headings and how to insert paragraph headings into the text.

Still another arrangement of headings, rapidly gaining popularity because it embraces information design in its makeup, is to create two columns of information, with the headings set in a narrower column on the left and the text on the right, which is illustrated in Figure 12-5 (page 359).

Additional Factors to Consider

Four other aspects of business writing also have to be taken into account:

- Using capital letters
- Abbreviating words and expressions
- Writing numbers in narrative
- Writing metric terms

These features are discussed in general below and shown in detail as individual entries in the Glossary of Business Usage.

Using Capital Letters Appropriately

Compare these two paragraphs:

A The Branch Manager insisted that Department Heads provide a weekly Statement of Absenteeism for their Departments. The totals were to be summarized on an Attachment that could be removed by the Branch Manager and forwarded directly to Head Office for the Attention of Ms Wynn Topolinski, Manager of Human Resources, who would compile a Monthly Record of Absenteeism Chart for the whole Company.

Title of Document

Main Section Heading

This example shows several levels of headings. The two centred headings above are set in Times New Roman 16 pt and 14 point respectively. All headings should be set in boldface type, and major headings can be set in larger type than subsidiary headings. Leave one, one-and-a-half, or two blank lines between centred headings, and between the section heading and the first line of text.

Set main paragraphs flush with the left margin and leave at least one blank line between each paragraph. Leave one-and-a-half or two blank lines before a heading.

Main Side Heading

The text throughout is set in Times New Roman 12 point type. The main side heading preceding this paragraph has been set in 14 point type (the same as for the lower centred headings). Subsidiary side headings are set in smaller type. Leave one blank line between the side heading and the paragraph that follows it.

Set all main paragraphs against the left margin and leave one-and-a-half blank lines after a paragraph that immediately precedes a subsidiary side heading, as has been done here.

Subsidiary Side Heading

Leave one blank line before starting a paragraph that follows a subsidiary side heading, and continue to set main paragraphs against the left margin.

When you want to use subparagraphs, provide your readers with a visual clue that you are subordinating your ideas. Use the techniques suggested below.

- This is the first of three subparagraphs. Indent the whole subparagraph 0.5 to 1.0 cm to the right.
- Precede the first line of each indented subparagraph with a bullet (used here) or a number set against the left margin. Use bullets for general subparagraphs, and numbers when you want to show clearly there is a definite sequence or prioritization of ideas, or when you will refer to the subparagraph later in your letter or report.
- If you continue into a second level of subparagraphs, use the same procedure but keep the sub-subparagraphs short and use a different symbol:
    * Set the whole sub-subparagraph a further 0.5 to 1.0 cm to the right.
    * Use a different subparagraph identification, such as an asterisk or a number.

Figure 12-3 How to use headings, paragraphs, and subparagraphs to create a visually pleasing effect

Normal Side Heading

This is a normal paragraph of text following a side heading (there may be more than one paragraph), used to introduce some subordinate thoughts which are preceded by a subordinate side heading:

Indented Side Heading

The subordinate side heading and the paragraphs are both indented 0.5 to 1.0 cm to the right. There may be only a single paragraph or there may be several. If there is more than one, leave a single blank line between the paragraphs.

Paragraph Heading. An alternative is to build a subordinate heading into the paragraph, as has been done here. Normally, the paragraph heading precedes only a single paragraph.

If you are using bullets or paragraph numbers to introduce subpoints within an indented subparagraph, the bullets should be set flush with the left-hand edge of the subparagraph, and the points should be indented a further 0.5 to 1.0 cm to the right:

- First subparagraph. . .
- Second subparagraph. . .

Try this alternative arrangement for sub-headings

Figure 12-4 Subheadings used within subparagraphs

Use as few captial letters as possible

B The branch manager insisted that department heads provide a weekly statement of absenteeism for their departments. The totals were to be summarized on an attachment that could be removed by the branch manager and forwarded directly to head office for the attention of Ms Wynn Topolinski, Manager of Human Resources, who would compile a monthly record of absenteeism chart for the whole company.

The preponderance of capital letters in paragraph A makes it look much more cluttered than paragraph B. Paragraph B not only looks tidier but also, because there are fewer capital letters, helps draw attention to Wynn Topolinski.

The guidelines for using capital letters in the narrative parts of a letter or report are listed here.

Guidelines for using (or not using) capital letters

1. Capitalize the first letter of

   - people's names and their specific titles or job positions (if they are being referred to directly):

     Frank J Llewellyn, Vice-President, Operations

Know Why You Are Writing

Know Your Purpose

Before you pick up your pen or place your hands on your computer keyboard, decide what kind of message you want to convey. There are only two to choose from:

- Messages that *tell* about facts and events.
- Messages that *sell* an idea or concept.

• *Tell* Messages

Communications that *tell* are primarily *informative:* they simply pass along information and do not expect the reader to respond. Consequently they need to be clear, concise, and definite. Because they deal with tangibles (facts, events, occurrences, happenings), you can get straight to the point and need describe only the essential details.

First, however, you must decide your purpose:

- Do you want to *inform* somebody about something that has happened or is happening?
- Or do you want to *instruct* somebody to do something, or tell them how to go about doing it?

• *Sell* Messages

Communications that *sell* have to be *persuasive:* they present an idea or concept and require the reader to act or react, by agreeing with, approving, or implementing the idea, suggestion, or proposal. Consequently, if your reader is to react in the way you want, your communication must be *convincing.*

Because sell messages deal with intangibles (ideas, concepts, suggestions, proposals), you must develop the background and details in sufficient depth so that the reader has all the information he or she needs to make a decision or take the appropriate action. Yet you have to be prudent and avoid presenting too much information, so that your message does not become obscure.

Again, first you must decide your purpose:

- Do you want to *request* something?
- Do you want to *propose* that something be done?
- Or do you want to *get approval* to do something?

Make your page arrangement "easy on the eye"

Figure 12-5 A well-designed page (Courtesy RGI International; reproduced with permission.)

- the name of a specific manufacturer's equipment:

  The Arbutus Corporation's Model 3001 Photocopier

- the names of specific business and government offices:

  Canadian Broadcasting Corporation
  Department of Mines and Resources

2. Do not capitalize the first letter of

   - business and government offices, and job titles and positions, that you refer to only generally:

     The records have been taken to the department for verification . . .
     No government has levied such a tax . . .
     There will be a meeting of vice-presidents . . .
     In most cases a manager of human resources conducts the interview . . .

   - abbreviations of general words and symbols:

     a.m. (morning)
     approx (approximately)
     cw (clockwise)
     kg (kilogram)

     For some exceptions to this rule, see the section "Writing Metric Terms Correctly" on page 363.

Abbreviating Words and Expressions

When you use a particularly long word or a multiword expression frequently in a letter or report, you may want to shorten it to a handier size. Spell the word or expression in full the first time you use it, and show the abbreviated form in parentheses immediately after it:

> Before selecting particular word-processing (wp) software to use within our local area network (LAN), we evaluated the four most popular wp programs currently on the market.

You may form an abbreviation of any word or expression you wish, providing you follow these guidelines:

Rules for forming effective abbreviations

1. Never form a new abbreviation for a word or expression that already has a commonly recognized abbreviation. (It would be wrong, for example, to form the abbreviation 2RC for Red River College in Winnipeg, which is commonly abbreviated to RRC.)

2. Whenever possible use lower-case letters for abbreviations (these letters are in lower case), because capital letters may give an abbreviation unwanted emphasis (for example, you should write "approx," not "APPROX"). The abbreviations for names of organizations, however, normally carry capital letters, as do certain common terms where the capital letter is needed to avoid ambiguity or the public has become accustomed to seeing it in the capitalized form. For example:

   ABC — Association for Business Communication
   No. — number
   LAN — local area network
   L — litre

   For further guidance, particularly when abbreviating symbols for quantities, see item 2 of the section "Writing Metric Terms Corrrectly."
3. Omit periods from an abbreviation unless the abbreviation forms another word. For example, there should be no period following "approx" or between the letters ABC, but there should be a period after "No." because it foms the short word "no". (An abbreviation at the end of a sentence also would be followed by a period.)
4. Do not add an "s" to plural abbreviations of quantities; treat them exactly the same way you would a singular abbreviation (e.g. 1 kg, 27 kg). For a more specific rule, see item 4 of the section "Writing Metric Terms Correctly."

There are a few exceptions to these rules because some abbreviations have evolved over many years and people are accustomed to using them in their original form. For example, the abbreviation "No." carries a capital N, and periods are inserted between the letters a.m., p.m., e.g., and i.e. Where such differences exist, they are identified in the Glossary of Business Usage.

But there are exceptions

Writing Numbers in Narrative

If you write numbers in a column or as part of a table, you know automatically to use numerals rather than spell out the numbers. But when you write a number as part of a sentence or paragraph, you have to decide whether to spell the number or show it as numerals. Follow these guidelines:

Rules for writing numbers within paragraphs

1. As a basic rule, spell out numbers one to nine, and use numerals for 10 and up. For example:
   - There are 17 power outlets on the seventh floor.
   - We have hired three temporary staff.

But know that there are exceptions to this rule, as discussed in items 2 and 3, below.

2. Use numerals when writing the following:

But there are exceptions

- Dimensions, tolerances, speeds, temperatures—any number that is followed by a unit of measurement: 5 mm, 3 kg, 8 L.
- Any number that contains a decimal or a fraction greater than "1": 6.45, 23.6, 4 $^1/_2$.
- Percentages (7%) and sums of money (5 cents or $0.05 [preferred], $8, $5000).
- Years, dates, and times: January 2002, August 11, 2001; 8 p.m.; 20:00 h. *Never* use three numerals for a date, as in 7/9/01, because readers may read them incorrectly (in the example, the date could be read as either July 9 or 7 September).
- Book or publication references, such as section 4, chapter 6, page 81, figure 3, and table 5.
- Ages of persons, such as 6 years old or age 34.

3. Spell out

- any number that starts a sentence (or recast the sentence so that the number is not the first word),
- any fraction less than "1": *One quarter of the members form a quorum.*

4. In addition, remember to

- insert a zero before a decimal if the whole number is less than "1": 0.25, 0.008, and
- insert spaces (instead of commas) in numbers that are five digits or greater: 3820; 33 500; 235 617.

Writing Metric Terms Correctly

The rules for writing, typing, keystroking, and printing SI (metric) units are rigid but straightforward:

1. Print all metric units in upright type (this type is upright), never in sloping *(italic)* type. This rule applies even if the rest of the sentence in which the metric unit appears is printed in italic letters.
2. Use lower-case letters for all symbols (g, mg, kg, etc), except when a symbol is derived from a person's name (120 V, 200 kV, because the symbol for volt is derived from Alessandro Volta). An exception is "L" for litre, because a lower-case "l" can be mistaken for the number "1."

3. Insert a space between the last numeral of a quantity and the first letter of the symbol, as in 165 g and 120 V (*not* 165g and 120V), but leave *no* spaces between the letters of the symbol, as in kV, cm, and km/h. (Percentages and temperatures are exceptions: write 75%, 20.2°C, 78°F.)
4. Do not add an "s" after a plural symbol (2 kL, 25 m, 180 kg) or place a period after the symbol.
5. Use an oblique stroke (/) to represent the word "per" (as in km/h), and insert a dot at midletter height to denote that the two symbols on either side of the dot are multiplied (as in 2·4).
6. Insert a space instead of a comma between the thousands of large numbers such as 23 612 and 3 000 000.
7. Never allow a metric symbol to stand alone in a sentence of narrative, without a number immediately in front of it. That is, you should not write *the weight in* kg *exceeds the prescribed limit* (write: *the weight in kilograms exceeds . . .*).

TO SUM UP

For an email message, memo, letter, or report to convey information clearly, its words, sentences, and paragraphs must work together to contribute a cohesive, coherent, and often persuasive impression to the reader. In particular,

- the words must be specific rather than general, and positioned to achieve maximum impact,
- the sentences must be complete, parallel, properly punctuated, and, whenever possible, presented in the active voice and first person, and
- the paragraphs must have a topic sentence, be written in pyramid style, and have internal continuity.

Good language instills confidence and increases reader receptiveness

EXERCISES

Exercise 12.1

Delete the low-information-content words, clichés, and hackneyed expressions from the following sentences. In some cases you may have to revise part of the sentence.

Tighten up these wordy sentences

1. The end result was in the form of a compromise.
2. If you find any further errors, it would be appreciated if you would feel free to contact me at any time.
3. Overhead costs have been reduced as necessary to achieve a profit margin in the neighborhood of 22.7%.
4. The *4Tell* software will be introduced as a means of preventing slippage of the schedule in the future.
5. Writing this report brings the Woodward project to a conclusion.
6. In an attempt to consolidate purchases of like items by different departments, it is our intention to route all purchase requisitions through a central clearing office.
7. Attached hereto are the records of delinquent loans that have accumulated in the course of the past two years.
8. For your information, this is an opportune moment to transfer responsibility for hiring part-time staff to individual department heads.
9. Concerning the matter of your Vancourt model 270 copier, serial number 2126321, if you wish to convert your current rental agreement to outright purchase, it may be done by completing the enclosed form 115E.
10. We will introduce the Newton-Appleton method of cost control in an effort to avoid a projected cost overrun of $35 000 to $40 000.
11. We wish to state that preparation of a proposal for supplying the maintenance services you requested has been advanced by five days in order to email it to you on or about, but no later than, April 20.
12. It is suggested that you should not use the Roving 2.7 software program at this point in time, since it has some bugs and it is entirely within the realm of possibility that it may be discontinued in the not too far distant future.

Exercise 12.2

Make the following sentences sound more definite and more confident, principally by changing statements written in the passive voice to the active voice.

Change roundabout routes into straight-line statements

1. Your attendance is requested at a December 2 committee meeting to be held at noon in conference room A.
2. The meeting was adjourned by the chairperson at 4:30 p.m.
3. It is recommended that the Westport travel insurance program be adopted for Vancourt Business Systems' international staff.
4. A Cost Control Monitoring course was attended by Lianne Briggs and Phillipe Larriviere at the Inn on the Park on June 13. It was presented by Carla Rohnstein of The Capital Group.

5. It is our recommendation that next year's major capital equipment acquisitions should be leased rather than purchased.
6. All international travel requests are to be approved by the manager of administration and, following approval, all travel arrangements are to be made *only* by Boccacio Travel at 2130 Gordon Valley Road.
7. The product analysis report was written by Mavis Barnes, edited by Vic Darwin, and illustrated by Richard Gagné.
8. When the proposal was examined in detail by the selection team, a disparity was noticed between the project management structure specified by the client and the management plan provided by the vendor.
9. To apply for transfer to another branch, form 2720 must be completed and handed to the personnel department. If a transfer has not occurred within six months, this procedure must be repeated (because six months is the maximum length of time that transfer applications are held on file).
10. When the service request was phoned in to Ms Tallenquist on February 5, she was instructed by the service manager that it should be forwarded to the Montrose area representative.
11. Our application for a licence to use the Mosaic project management software program on a company-wide basis has been approved by Mosaic Information Systems, Mississauga, Ontario. The software will be installed on May 7 and 8 by Mosaic's senior program developer.
12. An email was circulated by Jimen Ashwal to all division managers on June 18, proposing that one I.T. professional be selected by each manager for attendance at next October's International Software Exposition in Toronto.

Exercise 12.3

Correct any faulty parallelism evident in the following sentences.

1. Print your name, full address, and postal code in spaces A, B, and C on the application form, and in space D insert a telephone number where you can be reached during the day.
2. We selected the model AS800 portable computer because of its small size, high speed, and because its battery has a 4.5-hour life between charges.
3. We requested an independent audit for two reasons: to satisfy management's demands and because there was a need to alleviate shareholders' concerns.
4. Jeff Freiburg is to coordinate the project, administration responsibilities have been assigned to Jane Swystun, and a study of the documentation process is to be initiated by Hal Kominisky.

Keep the tracks parallel

5. When we counted cellphones we found that the accounting department has 4, the purchasing and materiel control departments have 2, customer services has 5, and, distributed among various offices throughout the building are 14 owned by the office services department.
6. If we buy three copies of program WS-22 the cost will be $187 each, but it will drop to $145 apiece if we buy eight or more copies.
7. Version 7.1 of the 4Tell software not only provides direct Internet access but also the problem of printer interface exhibited by version 7.0 is corrected.
8. The two new contracts forced us to recruit additional staff: three I.T. professionals from Montreal, 2 technical writers from Winnipeg, and from the west coast of British Columbia, four marketing agents.
9. All supervisors are to attend a 10-hour First Aid course during which they will be given training in administering first aid and how to recognize and help heart-attack victims.
10. The main conclusions drawn from Provo Department Stores' job-sharing experiment show that job sharing
    - demands managers' cooperation,
    - requires compatible participants,
    - employee attendance is improved, and
    - individual productivity is increased.
11. A survey of staff shows that 32% favor a 30-minute lunch break, 13% would like a 60-minute lunch break, and retention of the existing 45-minute lunch hour is preferred by 48%. The remaining 7% indicated they had no preference.
12. Three errors caused us to quote an incorrect price: the clerk who took the telephone order wrote 150 rather than 105 units; the estimator who calculated the assembly time based his calculations on a wage of $7.45 instead of $6.75 an hour; and then an additional $280 was added when I mistakenly assumed the units were to be shipped by air express rather than by surface transport.

Exercise 12.4

Identify and correct any punctuation errors, sentence fragments, and run-on sentences in the following sentences.

1. I have examined your Nabuchi model 400 Bubble Jet printer, repairs will cost you $85 plus tax.
2. Please book me flights to Beijing on October 16, return on October 22. Aisle seat.
3. Minutes of the meeting were recorded by Dirk Haans. In the absence of Keith Toews.

Smooth out that rough road

4. Although Marie Helweg did not want to be transferred to head office she accepted the company's offer, (she liked the increased pay package that came with the transfer.)
5. The request for quotation was not received until July 8. Too late, then, to prepare a bid.
6. We have installed a twelve-line telephone system, right now we need only eight lines. Four held for planned expansion next year.
7. We have examined your Maestro 707 dishwasher and estimate repairs will cost $254.62 tax included, probably more than you might want to spend on a nine-year-old dishwasher we suspect.
8. In yesterday's email you described a problem with the software we shipped to you last week. Purchase order 3215A. Received wet, CD-ROM disk bent, unusable. I have arranged for Zipper Courier to pick it up, replace with repeat order shipped with same courier.
9. The order from Nesbitt Industries came in by courier at noon on July 5, they had been trying to fax us for three days, the connector had been pulled out of the telephone jack.
10. Please transfer our account to your Loudon Avenue branch which is much closer to our office, this confirms my telephone call of yesterday afternoon.
11. With reference to your July 6 email regarding problems with your Model 1700 copier. The problem has been sent to Craig Newton, he will look into it. This is to acknowledge and confirm.
12. As requested in the client's purchase order of May 16 you are to prepare a separate invoice for each shipment rather than consolidate all shipments onto one invoice and submit the invoices in triplicate so that they reach the client by June 30.

Exercise 12.5

Select the correct word in each of the following sentences:

1. The members of the project group (is/are) requested to attend a planning meeting on July 13.
2. Please inform me if the software to be shipped with the Nabuchi 2020A computer and Artec 300 monitor (is/are) ready.
3. The team responsible for developing the dual maintenance programs (has/have) completed 80% of (its/their) work.
4. A full description of the three problems (follow/follows).
5. Responsibility for developing the programs (was/were) shared by Marnie Gaynes and Brian Wolchuk.
6. The sequence of service calls (is/are) described on page 8.
7. The details of the proposed follow-up training (is/are) not described in this document.

Make sure the verb *agrees* with the subject it refers to

8. Documentation, such as passports and visas, for Phil, Chris, and Steve's flights to Sweden and Norway next week (has/have) been checked and (is/are) current.
9. There are three levels of administration on the fourth floor of the Waltham Centre at 3880 E 41st Avenue in Vancouver, which (provide/provides) centralized administrative services to the company's operating division.
10. The full complement of customer service representatives in our Vancouver office (amount to/amounts to) 24 full-time and 10 part-time staff.
11. The call centre, which is staffed 24 hours a day by operators fluent in five different languages, (respond to/responds to) enquiries from all over the world.
12. The Calgary office has eight technicians each of whom (is/are) responsible for servicing computers in a particular area of the city.

Exercise 12.6

Select the correct word from those shown in brackets in each of the following sentences.

Choose the right words

1. The June order for (stationary/stationery) was placed with Midtown Paper Products Ltd.
2. The report showed that the (amount/number) of service orders handled in 2000 was 30% higher than in 1999.
3. Two weeks following the (enquiry/inquiry) the committee submitted (its/it's/their/there/they're) report.
4. The questionnaire was designed to (elicit/illicit) responses from the staff regarding their preference for a no-smoking ban throughout the office.
5. Regulation 720-2 (supercedes/superceeds/superseeds/supersedes) regulation 715-1, and takes (affect/effect) from January 1.
6. The March 21, 2001, break-in was the second such (occurance/occurrance/occurence/occurrence) in three months.
7. Email has become an (indispensable/indispensible) means of communication.
8. Documentation provided by applicants is confidential and consequently must be handled (discretely/discreetly).
9. The tight budget for the project left little room for the team members to (maneuvre/manoeuver/manoeuvre).
10. When you have completed the form in duplicate, please (forward/foreward/foreword) the pink copy to the personnel department.
11. If we receive your request before November 30, we will (wave/waive) the videotape rental fee but will ask you to confirm in writing that *all* the viewing data (has/have) been collected.

12. We can either retain the current price list for a (farther/further) 12 months or, (alternately/alternatively), we can institute a 5% across-the-board price increase on January 1.
13. Our investigation shows that 78% of the surveys were completed in June. The (balance/remainder) will be ready by July 10.
14. A (preventative/preventive) (maintenence/maintenance) program instituted on February 1 has reduced printing equipment breakdowns by 30%.
15. In her opening remarks to the safety committee, Ms Shawcross (inferred/implied) that the Mondaco division had a better accident record than the Westview Division.
16. My (principal/principle) reason for inserting the 16 sentences of Exercise 12.6 is to ensure you refer to the Glossary of Business Usage on page 397.

Exercise 12.7

Improve these sentences to make them more human and more personal.

1. You are hereby advised that all failure reports are to be emailed to this office monthly.
2. It is respectfully requested that you attend a meeting on Tuesday March 1.
3. The person corresponding with you is alarmed that your files have been subjected to a virus infection.
4. The recommendations should not be implemented because an installation plan is not yet in place; it has yet to be developed.
5. When travelling in remote areas it is considered wise by this office that extra protective clothing and supplies be carried.
6. It would be advisable if all inquiries could be sent to *customer_support@provo.com*
7. It is evident from this office's examination that an error of considerable magnitude has been perpetrated by the programmer.
8. It is our considered opinion that the implications of failing to file a complete report apparently has not been understood by the user.

Can *an office* take action or offer an opinion?

Exercise 12.8

Improve the following sentences to make them better conveyors of information.

1. For your information, attached hereto are the employment records in respect of D Evers and T Parkinson.
2. The newly occupied Halderstone Street office is much closer in proximity to the transit system than the recently vacated Main Street office.

Try your hand at editing . . .

3. If you have any further questions in regard to the aforementioned delivery delays, please do not hesitate to give this office a call at 292-3617.
4. The auditors will arrive at your office on or about, but no earlier than, Monday March tenth, and will depart on or before, but no later than, Friday 16th of May. They will be with you for a period of five consecutive working days.
5. Sincere apologies are extended for the prolonged delay in settling your account, enclosed herewith is our cheque in the amount of $387.50.
6. This letter acknowledges your fax request of March 10 and encloses a number of examples of forms we use for the purpose of monitoring stock levels.
7. A decision to purchase an LCD projector was reached by the executive committee on August 25, the day following a demonstration by Vicki Feldman showing how the projector would assist in improving company presentations.
8. The meeting on May Tenth was drawn to a conclusion by chairperson Milly Sampson by showing the videotape "Six Around the Table."
9. It has come to our attention that payments on your loan have been listed as being 10 or more days late on three separate occasions: the May 10 payment was received on May 24; the June 10 payment was received on June 27; and it was August 6 before we received your July 10 payment.
10. Although we actually have the capability to market the Wendell software, we did not submit a bid due to the fact that the staff who would be effected are already fully committed for the full duration of the planned marketing period.
11. If it is your considered intention to implement the introduction of multimedia instruction into your training programs, it would be advisable first to investigate the cost of installing 15 multimedia work stations.
12. The form should be completed in quadruplicate and distributed as follows:
    1. attach the white original to the goods, ship both to the customer by surface transport.
    2. Mail the yellow "Confirmation" copy to the purchaser (use first-class mail,)
    3. the green copy should be sent to accounts receivable, and
    4. the pink copy should be filed.
13. An examination of your account at this point in time shows that the balance has remained consistently below the minimum we negotiated on May 17.
14. Regarding the Mainstay Proposal, it has come to our attention that an error of considerable magnitude has been perpetrated on page 7.

In the calculation of operating expenses for the second and third years no allowance has been made for the anticipated decrease in staff that will result from the company's amalgamation with Excell Enterprises.

15. The ManTor product line incurred a net loss of $87 361 due to the fact that the program was underfunded, the staff were under-trained, and the marketing department underestimated consumer acceptance.
16. Our booth at the Business and Trade Fair will be staffed from 10 a.m. to 5 p.m. by G Horlund and F Martinez, and, to ensure double coverage during the peak hours between 2 p.m. and 5 p.m., it will be staffed by A Mahoney and R Turko from 2 p.m. to 9 p.m.

Exercise 12.9

Improve the following letters to make them more personal and more businesslike. At the same time correct poorly worded sentences and misspelled words, and remove low-information-content expressions.

. . . and here too!

1. Email

To: r.grealey@KBBEngco.ns.ca
From: j.enfers@mancom.sk.ca
Date: 22:01:01
Re: Proposal Info

Rob

What's yr reaction to draft proposal sent you 12:01:01? Not heard anything fm you yet, speed is essence: deadline end month. Client expects input fm yr office as well as ours, won't except bid after 31st. Problem! We need 5 days to put it all together, you know? Gotta here fm you 25th latest, w. all changes entered. Could you email it? faster, ok?

Too choppy . . .

Jason

2. Fax

To: Customer Service Manager, Remick Airlines
Fax No.: 1-888-166-0541
From: Greg Howarth, Multiple Industries
Date: December 1, 2000

Subject: Overcharged air fare

I am writing with reference to a reservation I made by telephone last week. This isn't the first time I've had problems with one of your booking agents, the last time was February 1999. And this is the second time its costing me money.

. . . and too many words

On November 20, Monday, I phoned your agent (1-800-265-8897) and booked a flight from Saskatoon through Wpg to Montreal for the 12th of January 2001 (that's a Wensday.) She said her name was Sharon. Anyway, she quoted me $389 for the round trip, returning nine days later, on the 21st. That was a special discount fare and it had to be confirmed by the end of the week.

I phoned again on Friday (24th), this time I talked to Tom. But he said he couldn't find my reservation, not all of it, just the bit from Saskatoon to Wpg, Flight 186 (return flight 187.) So he made me a new reservation for the Wpg to Montreal bit, on Flight 232 going and 235 coming back. Then he said the fair would be $616!! I said no, that wasn't right, the fare Sharon quoted was $389. He said it might've been that then, if there were Q class space available. Now he said there wasn't any—only V class—and the difference between Q and V was $227 more for the Winnipeg to Mont leg.

Mr service manager, your careless reservation people are costing me $227! So what are you going to do about it?

3. Email

To: All field staff
From: sharleen.dobie@multindco.com
Date: November 13, 2000
Re: Christmas Pay Cheques

Too vague . . .

With Christmas fast approaching it is time again to think about Christmas pay cheques. Last year there were real problems because some people planned to travel but failed to warn me they would need their cheques early and omitted to remember that anyway mail deliveries are slower at this time of year.

This year you can save yourself a heap of problems if you can get your request for an early pay cheque in to me by December 1. For my part, I'll see your cheque goes out at least one full week before you need it.

Your speedy reply would be appreciated.

Sharleen

P.S. Don't forget to tell me *the date* on which you will need your cheque!

4. Letter

September 1st

Dear Mr and Ms French

. . . and too wordy

It is with pleasure that we recognize that you have been a long-term and valued customer of Provo Department Stores. Yet, regrettably, and this comes as somewhat of a surprise, it has been brought to our attention that we have not received payment for our invoice No. 17616, with reference to a washer and dryer purchased from our Maplewood store on May 20 and delivered to your residence at 1310 Curzon Drive on 27 May which, as no doubt you are aware, under the terms of the "no interest for 45 days" purchase agreement, should have been paid in full by 5 July, which is what you agreed at the time of purchase as you did not wish to incur interest charges.

However as no payment has been received we have instituted interest, not, as you might be expecting, from July 5, but from the original purchase date of May 20, as stipulated in para 4(a) of the purchase agreement which at this point in time calculates out at $31.30 based on an interest rate of 0.85% per month for 3.33 months on the original purchase price of $1115.87 including tax.

So, as you must by now have realized, it is in your best interests to finalize this account immediately, especially as from now on we will be calculating interest at a *compound* rate of 0.85% per month (so far, the interest has not been compounded). We look forward to receiving your cheque for $1147.17 and, thanking you in advance for your cooperation, we remain,

Yours very truly

Penelope D Ambrose

Assistant Manager, Customer Accounts

5. Letter

Dear Ms Furneaux

We are writing in response to your letter of July 16 and concurrently expressing our extraordinary dismay that you should have experienced so many problems with your refridgerator since it's purchase on the fifteenth of January last year. It is indeed unusual for a customer to experience four breakdowns in a period of such short length (18 months), and we wish now that we had pressed you harder to avail yourself of the opportunity to invest in our three-year appliance agreement six months ago, just prior to the end of your refridgerator's warranty period.

Too much explaining . . .

I have telephoned to the manufacturer and have explained the problem described heretofore, but must regretfully admit his or her lack of sympathy and unwillingness at this point in time to allow any farther warranty repair work to be carried out.

However, we would like to assure you that we feel that, as you are a regular customer with us, that we are to some extent responsible for your complete satisfaction with the products we sell. For this reason, we are therefore willing to offer you, for this time only, free labor for the current repairs, providing you are willing to buy the parts at cost, and, as no doubt you are aware, labor often is the major part of any repair work.

If this offer is exceptable to your good self, please feel free to call me at any time so that I may arrange for our service technician to come in and carry out the necessary repairs.

Yours very truly

Barry Hurlburt

Exercise 12.10

Read the following letter, then respond to the questions that follow.

. . . and too roundabout

Dear Mr Caulfield

Thank you for your letter of March 2 and for bringing your snow thrower problem to our attention. With reference to your letter, I must say I was more than surprised to read that you have been having problems with your snow thrower. As you know, the Weston 700 is our top-of-the-line model and it is indeed rare to receive complaints about it.

It is extremely possible that the problem you describe is being caused by snow melting on the engine housing and running down the throttle cable to the point where it enters the gear assembly, where there probably is a cracked seal, and then freezing when you park the snow thrower (have you been remembering to run the snow thrower for five minutes after you finish clearing snow?) This undoubtedly would prevent you from advancing the throttle to "High" when you want to start the engine, as you describe.

Unfortunately, you purchased your snow thrower all of seventeen months ago, which you will realize puts it well outside the warranty period. What this means is that we are prevented from servicing the snow thrower free of charge as you request in your letter. However, if you care to write to the manufacturer yourself, and explain your problem, it is entirely within the realms of possibility that they will authorize us to repair it at no cost to you (they usually are amenable to authorizing reasonable repair costs for the model 700, up to 2 years from the date of purchase). But they do need you — not me — to contact them. There address is: Weston Machine and Tool Works, 210 Wales Avenue, Weston, Manitoba, R3H 2J7.

I wish you the very best luck!

Sincerely
Walter Solanger, Manager
Customer Services

1. How would you react if you received this letter?
2. What is your opinion of Walter Solanger's sincerity?
3. Rewrite the letter, also correcting the spelling and punctuation errors.

WEBLINKS

Ask Miss Grammar

www.protrainco.com/info/grammar.htm

This site allows you to search articles on grammar and ask specific questions about various grammatical problems.

Proofreading Strikes the Mark

www.csun.edu/~vcecn006/proof.htm

This site talks about the importance of proofreading, gives tips, and provides exercises to improve your proof.

Dave's Truly Canadian Dictionary Of Canadian Spelling

www.luther.bc.ca/~dave7cnv/cdnspelling/cdnspelling.html

An opinionated list of words, terms, and proper names in their Canadian forms. Includes American and British equivalents for comparison.

chapter 13

The Personal Aspects of Business Writing

Tomorrow Charles Bolingbroke retires as president of Independent Research Labs Limited, Atlantic Division. Today he visits each department and says farewell to the staff who have worked with and for him, some for more than two decades.

In the marketing department he finds manager Louise Fournier sitting in front of a computer with marketing analyst Marie Dassault beside her. Together they are writing a proposal for a major software development plan.

"Writing seems so much faster now," Charles comments, "so much easier."

He says that when he joined Independent Research Labs 28 years ago, an employee traditionally handwrote the first draft, had it typed, edited the typed draft, had the drafting department prepare illustrations, and then had the final copy typed with spaces left for the illustrations.

"But there is more to contend with now," Louise suggests. "Then, all you had to do was write. Now, you have to know how to make the document look good when it's printed, or when it's read online. There is no typist in between, to format the document for you, or to catch your spelling and punctuation errors."

"Or your grammar!" Marie interjects.

"True," Charles agrees. "But, you know, with today's broader international markets there's even more to think about." He explains how writing for international audiences means being aware of cultural differences that affect how a person responds or reacts to information. "I know that in Canada and the US we prefer to open a letter with the main message—what we most want the reader to know or to do—right up front, but in some cultures being so direct would be considered impolite. We have to be aware what effect our words may create."

Marie looks up from the computer screen: "And you have to avoid being sexist. You know, not labelling people with old-fashioned roles."

Charles looks at her quizzically over the top of his glasses. "You mean, like assuming a secretary is always female and an engineer is always male?"

"Exactly!"

IN THIS CHAPTER

You will learn how to
- design your letters, reports, and proposals to make them visually appealing,
- write efficient, effective email, and
- eliminate sexual bias from your writing.

You will also be introduced to some of the factors that affect how one writes for an international audience.

How we write has changed significantly

Now there is so much more to consider

Designing Information for Maximum Effect

You can help your readers understand and access your information more easily by incorporating *Information Design* techniques into the letters, reports, and proposals you write. These techniques include selecting an appropriate font, adjusting column and margin widths, using subparagraphs to help readers *see* how you have subordinated your ideas, and inserting tables to make details more readily available.

Choose an Appropriate Font

Match your choice of type to the document's purpose

The font you choose will project an image of you, your company, and your document. A font such as Times New Roman or Arial is a set of printing type consisting of the same features. Some fonts are called *serif* (they have a slight finishing stroke—**T**) and some are called *sans-serif* (they do not have a finishing stroke—**T**). Statistics show that a *serif* font, like Times New Roman, is easier to read and should be used for longer documents. For example, this book is printed in **Sabon**, which is a *serif* font. The serifs help lead the reader's eyes from letter to letter. A *sans-serif* font, such as Arial or Century Gothic, is clean and clear and portrays a neat and modern image, yet is not as easy to read. Consequently, *sans-serif* fonts are more suitable for short documents. There is an example of a *sans-serif* font in the indented text following the heading "Break Up Long Paragraphs" on page 379.

Once you have decided on a particular font, you should stay with it. Avoid changing to a different font inside the document (some people do this in a mistaken attempt to create emphasis). Rather, use **Bold,** *italic,* or a larger character size to emphasize text. The only exception is letterhead and logos, in which the font often is not the same as in the rest of the document.

Make sure that the font and character size you choose is appropriate for your document and for your audience. For *serif* fonts I recommend 11 pt or 12 pt type ("pt" = "point," or type size). For *sans-serif* fonts I recommend 10 pt or 11 pt type, because the plainer font looks larger than the *serif* fonts.

Justify Text Only on the Left

To justify or not to justify?

Word processors make it easy to justify both the left and right margins, which means all lines are exactly the same length. However, I recommend you justify the text only on the left and leave the right side "ragged." If you justify both margins the computer will generate spaces between words and characters to force the right margin to be straight. These spaces make it stressful for readers' eyes, since they constantly have to adjust to the uneven spaces. It is a subtle difference, but it's something you as a letter or report writer can control.

Adjust the Margins to Draw Attention

Many technical people hesitate to change the standard settings (the defaults) that come with word-processing packages, which usually give you a 6 inch (153 mm) wide typing line within two 1.25 inch (31 mm) margins. For longer documents such as formal reports and proposals, I encourage you to use a larger left margin and place the headings all the way to the left. This helps draw the readers' eyes and therefore their attention to the headings. It also helps readers retrieve information faster. I suggest a 1.75 inch (45 mm) wide margin for inserting the headings, and a 4.25 inch (108 mm) wide column for the text.

The model pages in Figure 13-1 show the same proposal presented with normal paragraphs and headings (a), and with a wider left margin and left-justified headings (b). The latter may take up more space, but it makes the information more accessible.

For an example of a proposal written using a wider margin and left-justified headings, see Figure 6-5 on page 147 of Chapter 6.

Break Up Long Paragraphs

I encourage you to use bulleted lists to break up big chunks of text and so make the information more visually accessible. Here's an excerpt of a report written without Information Design.

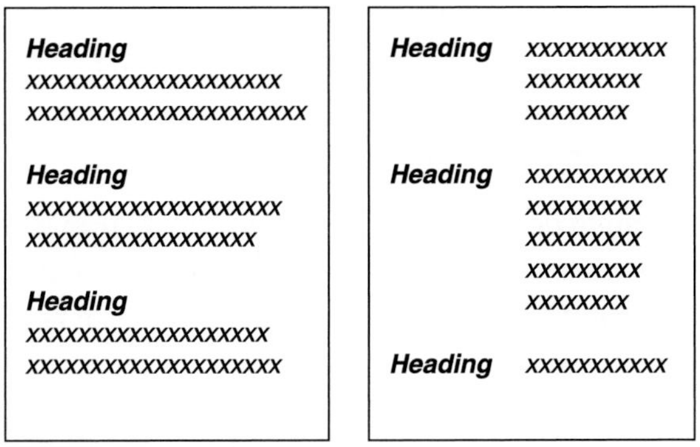

Heading
xxxxxxxxxxxxxxxxxxxx
xxxxxxxxxxxxxxxxxxxxxx
Heading
xxxxxxxxxxxxxxxxxxxx
xxxxxxxxxxxxxxxxxx
Heading
xxxxxxxxxxxxxxxxxxx
xxxxxxxxxxxxxxxxxxxx

(a) Regular Margins and Headings

Heading	xxxxxxxxxxx
	xxxxxxxxx
	xxxxxxxx
Heading	xxxxxxxxxxx
	xxxxxxxxx
	xxxxxxxxx
	xxxxxxxxx
	xxxxxxxx
Heading	xxxxxxxxxxx

(b) Wider Margins and Left-Justified Headings

Figure 13-1 Comparing regular text and headings with text and headings arranged for easier access to the information

Let the reader *see* how well you have organized your information

> I have analyzed our present capabilities and estimate we can increase our commercial business from 20% to 30% per month. To meet this objective we will have to shift the emphasis from purely local customers to clients in major centres. To increase business from local customers alone will require an extensive sales effort for only a small increase in revenue, whereas a similar sales effort in a major centre will attract a 30% to 40% increase in revenue. We will also have to increase our staff and manufacturing facilities. The cost of additional personnel and new equipment will in turn have to be offset by an even larger increase in business. Properly administered, such a program should result in an ever-increasing workload. And, third, we will have to create a separate department for handling commercial business. If we remove the department from the existing production organization it will carry a lower overhead, which will result in products that are more competitively priced.

If you break up the second long sentence by converting it into a lead-in sentence with a colon at the end, and then make a numbered list of the actions, the information is much easier to read and understand:

Present bite-size morsels of information

> I have analyzed our present capabilities and estimate we can increase our commercial business from 20% to 30% per month. To meet this objective we will have to take three parallel steps:
>
> 1. Shift the emphasis from purely local customers to clients in major centres. To increase business from local customers alone will require extensive sales effort for only a small increase in revenue, whereas a similar sales effort in a major centre will attract a 30% to 40% increase in revenue.

2. Increase our staff and manufacturing facilities. The cost of additional personnel and new equipment will in turn have to be offset by an even larger increase in business. Properly administered, such a program should result in an ever-increasing workload.

3. Create a separate department for handling commercial business. If we remove the department from the existing production organization it will carry a lower overhead, which will result in products that are more competitively priced.

Use Tables to Display Information

Many people reserve tables for numerical data, but we suggest you also use them to present text. Figure 13-2 shows three ways to present information:

- Panel 1 is a standard-style paragraph without headings.
- Panel 2 contains the same information, but this time it is separated by headings inserted in appropriate places.
- Panel 3 also contains the same information, but this time it is separated into compartments.

Match the design to the reader

Opinion among readers is almost equally divided: some prefer the presentation design in panel 2, while others prefer the compartments in panel 3. Be aware of this before *automatically* choosing to assign your information to a table: some information is more suitable for the approach in panel 2.

Use Columns to Increase Readability

Although columns are not suitable for correspondence, they certainly can be used for reports or as an attachment to a letter. The value of using columns is described in Figure 13-3 on page 382.

"Netiquette": Tips for Writing Electronic Mail

The word "Netiquette" has only recently become a part of our language. It means, roughly, "the etiquette of writing email on the Internet." There are no established Netiquette guidelines, but here are some suggestions that will help you be an efficient email communicator.

Three Examples of Information Design

(From a Notice Board Announcement)

1

Travel Expense Guidelines

Certain guidelines apply to travel expenses. All air travel must be booked with Haynes Travel Services and the cost charged to account A78641. Attach Haynes's invoice and the ticket stub to your expense claim. Request hotel/motel accommodation at our corporate rate (quote file 2120), pay with a company Visa card, and attach hotel receipt. The per diem rate for meals is $30. No receipts are necessary except for meals over $25 (excluding tip).

2

Travel Expense Guidelines

For Air Travel
All air travel must be booked with Haynes Travel Services and the cost charged to account A78641. Attach Haynes's invoice and the ticket stub to your expense claim.

For Hotel/Motel Accommodation
Book at corporate rate (quote file 2120), pay with company Visa card, and attach hotel receipt.

For Meals
The per diem rate is $30. No receipts are required except for meals over $25 (excluding tip).

3

Travel Expense Guidelines

Expense	Guidelines	Receipts Required
Air Travel	• Book with Haynes Travel Services • Charge to Account A78641	• Haynes's invoice • Ticket stub
Accommodation	• Request corporate rate (quote file 2120) • Pay with company Visa card	• Hotel/motel receipt
Meals	• Per diem rate is $30	• Receipt not required unless meal cost is over $25 (excluding tip)

Which layout do you prefer?

Figure 13-2 Using a table to compartmentalize information

Narrow columns mean *short* paragraphs

Setting Text in Two Columns Increases Readability

Using a newspaper-style, two-column printed text area helps guide the reader. The line length is forced to be shorter so a reader's eye can follow the line easily and therefore is less stressed. Imagine how difficult it would be to read a newspaper that was printed in one long six-inch (153 mm) wide column!

I don't recommend this format for letters or short reports, but it can have a good impact for longer reports, case studies, and, particularly, technical proposals.

This column format is especially useful when you insert graphics into a document. Text and graphics can be clearly integrated by wrapping text around the image. The two are then visually linked.

Graphics used in two-column format also help to balance the page. Often a graphic is inserted and seems to be isolated because there is too much white space around it. With two columns, each column offsets the other.

Another benefit of the two-column format is that it forces the author to write shorter paragraphs. Otherwise the column would be just one big block of text without any breaks.

Figure 13-3 Using dual columns rather than a single, wide column of text

Write Properly Formed Sentences

Email does not give you a licence to write fragmented, poorly punctuated, badly spelled, or abrupt messages. Neither, however, is it a forum for telling long stories and anecdotes. (You can use regular mail—"snail mail"—for that!)

Write "Pyramid Style"

Use the pyramid structure for email messages

You can use the pyramid method for writing email messages, just as you do for ordinary mail:

1. Start with the most important information and, if appropriate, what action you want the reader to take.
2. Follow with any background information the reader may need to understand the reason for your message, and provide details about any point that may need further explanation.

Check that each message contains only the information your reader will need to respond or act—and no more. That is, take care to separate the essential "need to know" information from the less important "nice to know" details.

Be Careful and Prudent

Proofread email *very* carefully: the informality of the medium and the speed with which you can create and answer messages can invite carelessness. It may sound contradictory to suggest that you *print* your email message and edit it on hard copy before you send it, but I recommend you do so if the message is long or its contents are particularly important.

Email is no place to share confidences

Remember that email is not a good medium for conveying confidential information, and particularly is *not* a medium for making uncomplimentary remarks about other people! Email messages can too easily be forwarded or copied to other readers, and then you have no control over who else may see what you have written. Be just as professional as you are when writing regular letters and memorandums. Similarly, be just as sensitive when deciding to copy a message to another person. Be sure that the original sender would want his or her message distributed to a wider audience.

Follow These Guidelines

Here are some additional suggestions:

- Remember that busy readers who receive many messages want them to be concise yet complete. Feed their needs.
- If you are writing to multiple readers, consider sending *two* messages rather than a single all-embracing message:
  - — Send a short summary for readers interested only in the main event and the result.
  - — Write a detailed message for readers who need all the details.
- Similarly, be selective when replying to a multiple-audience message. Simply clicking the "Reply All" button rather than taking the time to address your reply to a specific reader means that your reply will go to everyone, not just the person who needs it. If other people reply in the same way, the system will quickly become overloaded.

  Don't "broadcast" your replies
- When accessing email, download it immediately so that you remain online only briefly. Read and answer your mail offline (i.e. when you are not connected to the service). As well, avoid letting messages accumulate for too long after reading them. If you want to keep a message or may need to refer to it later, archive it.

- Avoid printing copies of every message you receive: creating extra paper defeats the aim of email!
- When replying to a message, particularly if your reply will go to multiple addressees, quote a line or two from the original message to help put your reply in context. Your email program most likely will insert “>” before the excerpt, and “<” immediately after it. If it does not, identify the excerpt by placing the signs there yourself.

A message that says only "Yes, I agree" will be meaningless to most readers

```
Dan Reitsma wrote on May 12:
> The Society's constitution was last updated in 1984
> and needs amending.
<
I agree, but first we need to check how much editing
was done by Karen Ellsberg before she retired in 1995.
```

- Write your name at the foot of every message you create, even though your name appears as the sender. If a recipient decides to forward the message to other people, frequently only the text will be forwarded and recipients will not be able to identify the originator.
- If you are annoyed or irritated by a message you receive, cool down before replying. Email is ideal for transmitting facts but it's the wrong medium for sending emotionally charged messages.
- Use only simple formatting. Write short paragraphs with line lengths of no more than 60 characters, and separate each paragraph with a blank line. Avoid creating columns and subparagraphs, because what you see on screen may not be what your readers see. For example, your screen may look like this:

Avoid formatting email messages

Facilities are located as follows:

Facility	Location	Distance
Master Control	Calgary, AB	28.6 km south of transmitter
Remote Site 1	Regina, SK	Downtown
Remote Site 2	Thunder Bay, ON	2.5 km north of university

But your reader will probably see something like this:

```
Facilities are located as follows:
Facility Location Distance
Master Control Calgary, AB 28.6 km south of
transmitter
Remote Site 1 Regina, SK Downtown
Remote Site 2 Thunder Bay, ON 2.5 km north
of university
```

- If you need to format columns, consider creating a separate document and sending it as an attachment to an email message.
- Avoid inserting "cute" graphics or humorous remarks—they make you appear unprofessional.
- AVOID BELLOWING! PARAGRAPHS COMPOSED OF ALL CAPITAL LETTERS ARE HARD TO READ. Use upper- and lower-case letters, just as this sentence has been written.

Shouting is completely out of place

Writing Non-Gender-Specific Language

History has provided us with a scenario in which men were the warriors and hunters, and subsequently the breadwinners, and women were the caregivers who cooked the meals, reared children, and catered to their men's needs.

Today, however, it is universally recognized in developed countries that women and men are equal and can perform equally well in most occupations and roles. Consequently, we now see, for example, men as secretaries, nurses, and child care workers, and women as airline captains, engineers, truck drivers, and backhoe operators. Unfortunately, our language hasn't kept pace with these changes and we still see some people use sexually biased language like this:

A change in the way we write is long overdue!

> A secretary will be brought in to record the minutes of the executive committee meeting. *She* will also be responsible for making travel arrangements for the meeting participants.
>
> The committee has decided to hire an engineer. *He* will evaluate the erosion caused when the river overflowed its banks.

In neither case do these writers know whether the secretary and the engineer are going to be male or female. They simply *assumed* the secretary would be female and the engineer would be male, because they have been influenced by generations who practised that stereotype. Now it's our job to consciously eradicate gender-specific references like these from our writing, until we automatically write non-gender-specific references. For example:

> A secretary will be brought in to write the minutes of the meeting and to make travel arrangements for the meeting participants.
>
> The committee decided to hire an engineer to evaluate the erosion caused when the river overflowed its banks last summer.

These examples are straightforward and fairly obvious. However, some subtle gender-specific references are more difficult to detect and correct.

For example, the script for a recent educational video depicted a 12-year-old boy arriving home from school:

Even a greeting can create a false image

> Exterior: Gavin walks up the path and leaps up the steps. He inserts a key into the front door.
>
> Cut to interior: We hear a radio playing. The door opens and Gavin enters. He drops his books on a side table, peers into the living room and the kitchen, but sees no one. He leans against the stair rail and calls up the stairs.
>
> GAVIN: Mom? I'm home!

The scriptwriter assumed that it would always be a mother who is at home. Before shooting the scene, the script was changed so that Gavin said:

> GAVIN: Dad? Mom? I'm home!

Eliminate Masculine Pronouns

It can be particularly difficult to remove masculine pronouns

When describing managers, supervisors, architects, technical people, and even accountants and lawyers, historically our language has abounded with masculine pronouns. The engineer described earlier is a typical example. Here is another, this time an excerpt from a company's operating procedures.

> **4.3 Training Coordinator.** *His* primary role is to plan, organize, and coordinate all training courses held at DEF company. *He* also is responsible for promoting (advertising) the courses to staff and counselling employees *he* feels should attend.

There are several ways you can remove the male pronouns:

Here are six suggestions for writing gender-neutral sentences

1. Repeat the job title, and abbreviate it:

   > **4.3 Training Coordinator.** The primary role of the training coordinator (TC) is to plan, organize, and coordinate all training courses held at DEF company. The TC also is responsible for promoting (advertising) courses to staff and counselling employees who should attend.

2. Use a bulleted list:

   > **4.3 Training Coordinator.** The training coordinator is responsible for
   > - planning, organizing, and coordinating all training courses held at DEF company,
   > - promoting (advertising) courses to staff, and
   > - counselling employees who should attend.

3. Create a table:

4.3 Training Coordinator

Primary Responsibility	**Secondary Responsibilities**
To plan, organize, and coordinate all training courses held at DEF company	1. To promote (advertise) courses to staff 2. To counsel employees who should attend

4. Replace the male pronoun with "you" and "your":

4.3 Training Coordinator. Your primary role is to plan, organize, and coordinate all training courses held at DEF company. You also are responsible for promoting (advertising) courses to staff and counselling employees whom you feel should attend.

(*Note*: If you use "you" in one part of a document, be consistent and use it throughout the document. Avoid bouncing back and forth between "you" and "he" or "she.")

5. Replace the male pronoun with "he or she":

Try to avoid writing "(s)he" or "his/her"

4.3 Training Coordinator. The training coordinator's primary role is to plan, organize, and coordinate all training courses held at DEF company. *His or her* responsibilities also include promoting (advertising) the courses to staff and counselling employees *he or she* feels should attend.

(*Note*: This is the least recommended method.)

6. Change singular pronouns to plural pronouns:

4.3 Training Coordinators. *Their* primary role is to plan, organize, and coordinate all training courses held at DEF company. *They* also are responsible for promoting (advertising) the courses to staff and counselling employees *they* feel should attend.

(*Note*: This method can be used only when the description lends itself to using plural nouns and pronouns.)

Replace Gender-Specific Nouns

Each province has its Workers Compensation Board, an organization that provides financial help to employees who are injured at work. Yet, not many years ago, all Workers Compensation Boards in Canada were

Eliminate sexually biased titles

known as *Workmans* Compensation Boards. The previous title seemed to imply that the Board provided help *only* to male workers, which was not true. Similarly, until about 15 years ago, flight attendants on airlines were known as stewardesses, implying that the job was held only by females. Again, particularly today, this assumption is plainly inaccurate.

Many other job titles are equally gender-specific and predominantly male-oriented. These have been changed in recent years so that the title refers to both male and female employees. Table 13-1 lists gender-specific titles and suggests better alternatives.

Be Consistent When Referring to Men and Women

Men throughout recent history have used the courtesy title *Mr* to precede their names. Until 20 years ago, women had two courtesy titles, which denoted whether they were married or single: *Mrs* and *Miss*. Today, a woman's marital status is *never* implied in the title: all women should be referred to as *Ms*. (English is not the only language to have created this anomaly. For example, in France men are referred to as *Monsieur* and women as *Madame* or *Mademoiselle*. In Russia, a sex-identifying title is not placed before a person's name, but a woman's

Masculine labels are slowly being eradicated

Table 13-1 Alternative (and preferred) names for gender-specific titles

If you are tempted to write:	Consider replacing the word with:
actor; actress	actor (for both sexes)
chairman	chairperson (*or* chair)
cowboy	cattle rancher
fireman	firefighter
foreman	supervisor
newsman	reporter
policeman; policewoman	police officer
postman	letter (*or* mail) carrier
repairman	service technician
salesman	sales representative
spokesman	spokesperson
workman	worker; employee
waiter; waitress	server (*or* "waiter") for both sexes

Still another is the term "man-hours," which was previously used to define the time that would be expended on a particular job. Today we write *work-hours* or *staff hours*.

family name often has an "a" added to the end to denote the person is female: for example, Boris Serov; Svetlana Serova.) And a final thought: *never* address a letter to "Dear Sir or Madam."

Communicating with an International Audience

Three years ago, when Independent Research Labs Limited started doing business with companies in Eastern Europe, Marie Dassault had to learn a different set of rules for communicating with the company's new customers and business associates. She found it strange that she had to change the way in which she wrote her letters and memos. "I took it for granted that everyone used the pyramid method to construct their letters," she explained. "But then I found that in many Eastern European and Asian countries, starting immediately with the Main Message—getting right down to business—is considered downright rude."

Writing Business Correspondence

Eons of tradition surround eastern communication practices

At first Marie thought it would be just a matter of explaining to her Russian, Lithuanian, and Ukrainian clients that she wrote this way because western writers considered it more efficient. She thought it would be helpful if they adopted our methods. But she had forgotten the hundreds of years of history that have fashioned the Eastern European and Asian cultures, and found that *she* had to adapt her methods to suit them. "You have to understand the culture prevalent in each society and adjust to it," she says now.

Marie didn't entirely discard the pyramid method. She decided she could still use the pyramid for the central part of her letters, but that she would have to precede it with a personal greeting and polite remarks concerning the health and happiness of her reader (and, often, also of her reader's family). And she would have to follow the pyramid with a polite closing remark, such as wishing the reader continuing good health and prosperity in the months and years ahead. So at first she constructed her letters to Eastern Europe as shown in Figure 13-4. Here is an email letter Marie wrote to a business associate in Moscow:

> 10 May 2000
>
> Dear Dr Kirislov
>
> I am very pleased to be writing to you again and hope this letter finds both ❶ you and Svetlana, and your son Boris, in good health. I still carry with me happy memories of the very pleasant evening Dan Collings and I spent with you last November. You and Svetlana were excellent hosts.

Nest the writing pyramid *within* the traditional letter format

Now I would like to tell you about an idea I have in mind. In September 2001, the Canadian Association for International Business Communication will be holding its annual meeting in Montreal, Canada. During the meeting we plan to hold a three-way video conference between Montreal, Cambridge University in England, and the Institute for International Studies in Moscow. I would be honored if you would agree to be the moderator of the Moscow panel. 2

Dan Collings has agreed to be the moderator in Montreal, and Philip Reidiger will be the moderator in Cambridge. (You may remember the paper on electronic mail Philip presented last November, at the International Centre for Scientific and Technical Information in Moscow.) I would particularly like you to be the moderator in Moscow, because your knowledge of international communication practices will be a valuable asset during the discussion, and you already know the two other moderators. 3

There will be no cost to your association, because a major international electronics corporation has agreed to sponsor the video conference. Their contribution will include providing the television facilities in all three countries, and also the satellite links. All I will be asking you to do is to find two 4

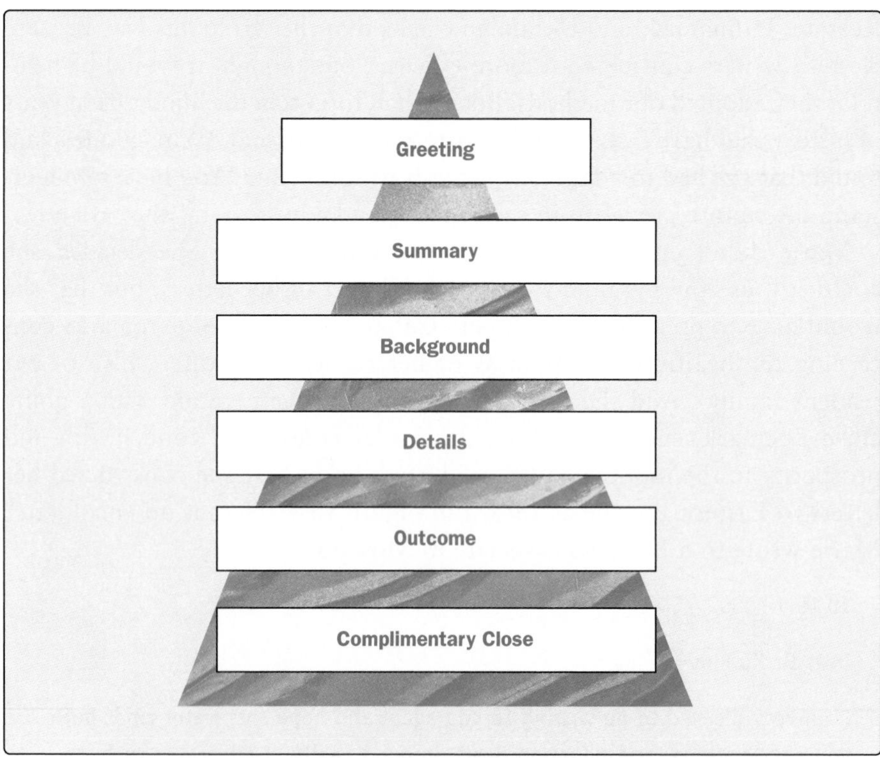

Figure 13-4 "Adapted" pyramid for a letter to an Eastern European or Asian reader

more people who can speak knowledgeably about communication practices in Russia, and to bring them to a particular Moscow studio on 10 September. Ideally these two people will be fluent in speaking English.

Could you let me know by 8 June whether you will be my third moderator? I hope you will, because you have so much experience to share with us. 5

In the meantime, please pass my good wishes to Svetlana and Boris. I very much look forward to hearing from you.

A complimentary close *politely* concludes the letter

Best wishes, from your very good friend,

Marie Dassault

In the above example,

- paragraph 1 is Marie's Greeting,
- paragraph 2 is her Summary and the Background,
- paragraphs 3 and 4 are the Details,
- paragraph 5 is the Outcome (in this case, it's an Action Statement), and
- the final paragraph is Marie's Complimentary Close.

"Yet even then I had to be cautious," Marie continued. "I learned fairly quickly that this arrangement was fine for readers I had corresponded with before, but to new readers—particularly older, more traditional readers—it would still seem too abrupt. For them, I would have to move the Summary Statement further down in the letter." Marie's revised writing plan looked like this:

1. Greeting
2. Background
3. Details
4. Outcome and Summary Statement (combined)
5. Complimentary Close

This inverted pyramid is the reverse of the sequence promoted in previous chapters. And it applies not only to formal business letters but also to memos and electronic means of communication: faxes and particularly email.

However, changing the focus is not the only part of a message to an Eastern or Asian country that requires attention. When you write in English to readers who normally speak another language—German, French, Italian, Spanish, Malayan, or Chinese, for example—you have to choose words that will be clearly understood. (This also holds true for different cultures who speak the same language. In Great Britain, for instance, the word "fortnight" is commonly used to mean "two weeks," yet in the United States and even in parts of Canada it would not be understood. Similarly, the word "presently" has different meanings in the US and Great Britain.) Here are some guidelines:

Use simple words, simple sentences, and simple paragraphs

- Avoid long, complex sentences.
- Avoid long, complex words. If you have to choose between two or more words or expressions that have roughly the same meaning, choose the simpler one. For example, write "pay" rather than "salary" or "remuneration."
- Use the same word to describe the same action or product consistently throughout your letter. Decide, for example, whether you will refer to money in the bank as *funds, currency, deposits, capital,* or *money*.
- Use a word always in the same sense. You would confuse a foreign-language reader if you wrote "It would not be *appropriate* to transfer funds from Account A to Account B" (meaning it would not be suitable to do it), and then in another sentence you wrote "We had insufficient capital to *appropriate* Company A" (meaning to take over Company A, or buy it out).

Meeting and Speaking

It's essential to adapt to local meeting protocol

Ted Cavanaugh was one of Multiple Industries' first supervisors to visit clients in Russia and Estonia, and while he was there he discovered some major but subtle differences between western and eastern perceptions of good manners and effective communication techniques. When he went to a meeting, he learned that it was inappropriate to start the meeting by immediately describing why he was there and what he wanted to accomplish. First, members of both companies would sit around a table, drink coffee or soft drinks, eat small cakes or biscuits, introduce themselves, and engage in polite conversation about travel, where they lived, the weather, the health of each other's families, but *never* about business. (He learned, too, that it was bad manners to get up from his chair and pour himself a second cup of coffee: it was *always* the host's prerogative. Nothing was said, but the sudden pause in the conversation told Ted he had committed a faux pas.)

The business discussion did not start until the topic was introduced by a member of the host country. Only then could Ted start describing his plans and ideas, and even then he discovered it had to be done in a roundabout way. Where Ted was accustomed to putting the main message right up front, using the method described in Chapter 10, he found that in the host country it was more customary to start with some history about the subject and then lead gently toward the point he wanted to make. He also discovered that the words he used had to be chosen carefully, because he and his hosts interpreted some words differently.

In one country he visited, his host told him, "It really would not be convenient to pay your hotel expenses by credit card." Ted assumed that it could be done but it was the less-preferred method. But he subsequently discovered that, when his host had said, "It would not be convenient," really he was saying, as politely as he could, that it simply could not be done (because they had no facilities for accepting credit cards). Similarly, Marie discovered that in some Asian countries it is severely impolite to directly contradict a speaker or to say "no" to a suggestion; in their culture she should nod her head and say something like, "That is a possibility," or "We will consider that." (In Japan this technique is known as Bokashi, and it has a long historical background.)

Pay close attention to "dress" customs

Ted noticed that in many Eastern European countries businesspeople always wear a dark suit and black shoes to a meeting, and soon realized that for him to wear the new grey sports jacket, contrasting dark slacks, and light grey shoes he had bought especially for his visit would be considered a slight in his hosts' eyes. And when Marie visited manufacturers in Europe, she was at first surprised by how much, the farther east she travelled, people would shake hands with her: always when they first met each day, and sometimes several times afterward if they parted for a time and then rejoined each other.

Now Ted and Marie are seasoned world travellers and communicators, yet they both would admit that, as world markets expand and boundaries between countries become less apparent, they have to become even more sensitive to the cultural differences that affect how people in other countries act and react to the way we conduct ourselves, and particularly to the way we present information.

Every culture has a different "set of rules"

Here, I have room to offer only a few illustrations and suggestions. If you are going to be doing business with other nations, I recommend you visit your local library and research information on communicating with businesspeople in other cultures. A good starting point would be these journals: the Association for Business Communication's (ABC) *Journal of Business Communication*, the IEEE Professional Communication Society's (PCS) *IEEE Transactions on Professional Communication*, and the Society for Technical Communication's (STC) *Technical Communication* and *InterCom*.

TO SUM UP

Designing information so that it is visually appealing is an ideal way to capture readers' attention, even before they start reading your words.

The guidelines for writing email are similar to those for writing regular correspondence, but there are limitations on how you can format your messages.

We need to be vigilant and check that we never use gender-specific expressions in our writing. Similarly, now that the doors are wide open for global communication, we need to take care that we respect the customs and writing modes of other cultures.

EXERCISES

Exercise 13.1

Rewrite this notice, which is posted at bus stops, to make the information more accessible.

Route 18 Bus Intervals

Buses on route 18 start operating at 6 a.m. Monday through Saturday, and are spaced at 6-minute intervals until 10 a.m. and from 4 p.m. until 6 p.m. Between these times they run at 10-minute intervals, and also from 6 p.m. to midnight. On Sundays buses start operating at 6:30 a.m. with 10-minute intervals, then from 9 a.m. until 6 p.m. operate at 8-minute intervals, reverting to 10-minute intervals during the evening hours until the last bus at midnight.

***Design* your information to help your readers grasp the facts**

Exercise 13.2

Rewrite this announcement, which was emailed to all company employees:

To: allstaff@multind.org
From: d.hollabrin@hr.multind.org
Date: October 19
Subject: Revised Vacation Schedule

In previous years the company has provided a three-week annual vacation for all employees who have been with the company for 15 months or more, with the option of taking their vacation at any time of the year, providing their choice meshed with the vacation choices of co-workers in their department. Next year we are embarking on something new: we are offering you the opportunity to avail yourself of a four-week annual vacation (after the statutory 15 months of service). If you still choose to take only a three-week vacation, you may do so at any time of the year, including the high-season priority period (June 1 to September 30). But next year, if you would like a four-week vacation, and providing you are willing to forgo the high-season priority months, then you may do so; and you may take your vacation in one four-week block, or break it into smaller blocks. There is, however, one limitation: you cannot include the Christmas-New Year season (i.e. Dec 20 to Jan 5). To avail yourself of an extended vacation, you will need to inform the Human Resources Department of your intention by December 15, either by responding to this email message or by phoning extension 234.

Exercise 13.3

Explain why you should avoid using gender-specific terms.

Exercise 13.4

Correct the following passages so they show no signs of sexual bias:

Writing without using gender-specific language

1. Under no circumstances should a duty nurse attempt to hook up or disconnect electronic imaging equipment. If equipment is needed or has to be removed, she must immediately contact a technician from the medical electronics department at extension 2261. (If he does not respond within five minutes, she may page him at extension 2050.)
2. Employees' wives attending the company's annual picnic are requested to bring either an item of baked goods or a salad. It would be best if they were to contact Janice Adams first, to ensure there is no duplication of dishes.
3. The chief auditor is responsible for arranging the annual financial audit of each branch. Normally, he will inform *only* the selected auditors of the date and time, so that the branch will be unaware that the audit is about to occur.
4. Our company-wide medical insurance coverage has been extended to include both each individual employee and his wife and dependent children.
5. A child care centre for employees' children aged 18 months to six years is about to be set up in room 2420. If you know of a certified child care worker who is seeking employment, either pass her name and address to the Personnel Department or, alternatively, suggest to her that she apply for one of the six positions that will be staffed in the centre.

Exercise 13.5

Different cultures employ different writing styles

In three weeks' time, the company you work for will be sending you to work with a team of local people setting up a training centre in ______________. *(Your instructor will tell you which country.)* From your local library, research information on customs that will influence how you write, speak, and deport yourself in the host country. Write three short paragraphs describing the factors you will have to consider when you

1. write letters to the host country,
2. speak to your hosts at a conference, and
3. attend meetings or business lunches.

WEBLINKS

Effectively Communicate across Cultures
www.bena.com/ewinters/xculture.html
Become an effective multicultural communicator by reading the practical tips for writing for an international audience on this site.

University Press Bias-Free Guidelines – At Last
www.eeicommunications.com/eye/biasfree.html
This review from *The Editorial Eye* of the *University Press Bias-Free Guidelines* by Priscilla S. Taylor discusses the problems of gender-biased, racist, and ethnocentric language and how to avoid them.

Netiquette Home Page
www.albion.com/netiquette/
This site teaches you proper "netiquette"—or network etiquette—the "do's and don'ts of online communication."

Glossary of Business Usage

When Tom flops grumpily into the chair on the other side of Pam's desk, she can't tell whether he is angry at someone or just concentrating on a knotty problem. So she asks him.

"A bit of both," he admits, sliding a dozen typed pages toward her. "Take a look at these!"

Pam leafs through the pages.

"Oh!" she says, "this is your report on the Blackthorn account."

"Right!"

"And you have been revising it," she adds, pointing to the red-ink changes on the first page.

"Not me!" Tom complains. "I haven't revised anything. Mr Sawatsky has. And it's like that on every page!"

Mr Sawatsky is the branch manager.

Pam examines some of the changes. "He likes 'programme' with an 'me' at the end," she says, "and you don't."

"And he's put a second 'u' in 'rumour' and switched to 're' at the end of 'centre' and 'theatre' and 'litre!'"

"Do you prefer the 'er' spelling?" Pam asks. "The American way?"

"That's what I was taught at school," Tom grumbles. He grabs a page and points to the word *coordinate*, which has been changed to *co-ordinate*. "But there's much more than that. I don't insert a hyphen in compound words, but he does." Tom turns to the third page and points to *checklist*, which has been changed to *check-list*. "See?"

"Well, what do you want me to do about it?" Pam asks.

"Tell me who's right! If I am, then I'll go back to him and ask if I can do it my way. If he is, then I'll have to live with his changes."

Pam laughs, but sympathetically. "You're both correct, really. There's more than one school of thought."

"Thanks! You're a lot of help!" Tom interjects. "I need guidelines! Clear guidelines."

"They're hard to find," Pam explains, "and when you do find them, you'll discover each 'authority' has a different opinion."

"Oh, no!" Tom groans, sinking back in his chair.

IN THE GLOSSARY

You will be able to find how to

- choose the appropriate spelling for words that have alternative spellings in Canada,
- identify the correct spelling for words that are frequently misspelled,
- form abbreviations of frequently used words and expressions, and
- write numbers and metric symbols correctly in narrative.

A dictionary especially for business writers

A glossary at the end of a textbook is rather like a small dictionary, in that it lists in alphabetical order words and expressions that the book's readers are most likely to have trouble with. To keep the glossary down to a manageable size, the choice of words is limited to those most applicable to the readers' field of work (in your case, words and expressions used in a business setting). Consequently, a business glossary contains considerably fewer standard words than a dictionary but, in proportion, significantly more business terms and expressions.

The Glossary's Main Features

In the glossary you will find

- words that are often misspelled (such as *across*, *forty*, and *irrelevant*),
- words that are often confused for one another (such as *elicit* and *illicit*, and *principal* and *principle*),
- words for which there are alternative spellings (such as *maneuver* and *manoeuvre*, and *program* and *programme*),
- words and expressions often used incorrectly (such as *disinterested* and *very unique*),
- rules for words that might or might not be capitalized, and
- abbreviations for frequently used words.

Where appropriate, definitions are provided to help you identify a word's proper usage, together with an example of the word used in a typical sentence. Where a word stands alone in the glossary, it is there because it has often proved to be a spelling problem for business writers.

Definitions Used in the Glossary

To conserve space, the following words and expressions are abbreviated in the glossary:

abbreviated; abbreviation	abbr
Britain, British	Br
Canada; Canadian	Can.
Canadian Press	CP
definition	def
lower case	lc
plural	pl
prefer; preferred; preference	pref
recommend; recommended	rec
International System of Units (Metric Units)	SI
United States	US

Glossary of Business Usage

A

a; an use *an* before words that begin with a silent *h* or a vowel; use *a* when the *h* is sounded or if the vowel is sounded as *w* or *y*; *an hour* but *a hotel, an onion* but *a European*

aberration

ab initio def: from the beginning

above- as a prefix, *above-* combines erratically; *aboveboard, above-cited, aboveground, above-mentioned*

absence

accelerate; accelerating; accelerator

accept; except *accept* means to receive (normally willingly), as in *she accepted the company's offer of employment; except* generally means exclude, as in *the report has been typed except for the table of contents*

access; accessed; accessible

accidental(ly); accident-prone

accommodate; accommodation

account abbr: **acct**

accrue; accrual

accumulate; accumulator

achieve means to conclude successfully, usually after considerable effort; avoid using *achieve* when the intended meaning is simply to reach or to get

acknowledg(e)ment *acknowledgment* pref in US, rec in Can.; *acknowledgement* pref in Br

acquaint; acquainted; acquaintance

acquiesce def: agree to

acquire; acquisition

across not *accross*

actually omit this word; it is rarely necessary in business writing

A.D. def: Anno Domini

adapt; adept; adopt *adapt* means to adjust to; *adept* means skilled, proficient; *adopt* means to acquire and use

adaptation pref spelling; *adaption* is also common in US

adapter; adaptor adapter pref

addendum pl: *addenda*

adhere to never use *adhere by*

ad hoc def: set up for one occasion

adjective (compound) two or more words that combine to form an adjective are either joined by a hyphen or compounded into a single word; see page 339; abbr: **adj**

advance plan(ning) *advance* is redundant; delete it

advantageous

advertise; advertisement; advertiser

advice; advise use *advice* as a noun and *advise* as a verb: *the consultant's advice was valuable; the receptionist advised the customer to return the goods;* spell: **adviser, advisable**

ae; e *ae* pref in Br and common in Can., as in *aesthetic* and *anaemic*; *e* pref in US and rec for Can. by CP, as in *esthetic* and *anemic*

affect; effect *affect* is used only as a verb, never as a noun; it means to produce an effect upon or to influence (e.g. *the color affects consumer response*); *effect* can be used either as a verb or as a noun; as a verb it means to cause or to accomplish (as in *to effect a change*); as a noun it means the consequences or result of an occurrence (as in *the detrimental effect upon the environment*), or it refers to property, such as *personal effects*

affidavit

affiliate; affiliation

aforementioned, aforesaid avoid using these awkward, ambiguous expressions

after- as a prefix usually combines to form one word: *aftercare, aftereffect, aftermath, afterthought, afterword*; but: *after-hours*

agenda although plural, *agenda* is generally treated as singular: *the agenda is complete*

aggravate the correct definition of *aggravate* is to increase or intensify (worsen) a situation; try not to use it when the meaning is *annoy*

aggregate

aging; ageing *aging* pref in US, rec in Can.; *ageing* pref in Br

agree to; agree with to be correct, you should *agree to* a suggestion or proposal, but *agree with* another person

air- as a prefix normally combines to form one word: *airborne, airfield, airflow*; exceptions are: *air-condition(ed)(er)(ing), air-cool(ed)(ing)*

airline; air line an *airline* provides aviation services; an *air line* is a line or pipe that carries air

allege; alleged; alleging

alleviate def: to ease, to relieve the stress

allot; allotted; allotment

all ready; already *all ready* means that all (everyone or everything) is ready; *already* means by this time: *the samples are all ready; the samples have already been tested*

all right def: everything is satisfactory; never use *alright*

all together; altogether *all together* means all collectively, as a group; *altogether* means completely, entirely: *the samples have been gathered all together, ready for testing; the samples are altogether useless*

allude; elude *allude* means refer to; *elude* means avoid

almost never contract *almost* to *most*; it is correct to write *most of the letters have been typed*, but wrong to write *the letters are most ready*

alphanumeric def: in alphabetical, then numerical sequence

alternate; alternative *alternate(ly)* means by turn; *the inspector alternated among the four construction sites*; *alternative(ly)* should offer a choice, most often between only two things: *the alternative was to return the samples*; however, it is becoming common for *alternative* to refer to more than two, as in *there are three alternatives*

a.m. def: before noon (ante meridiem)

amateur

ambiguous; ambiguity

among; between use *among* when referring to three or more items: *she circulated among the guests*; use *between* when referring to only two: *he had to choose between flying and driving to Cold Lake*; avoid using *amongst*

amount; number use *amount* to refer to general quantity: *the amount of time taken as sick leave has decreased*; use *number* to refer to items that can be counted: *the number of people attending the conference exceeded our expectations*

an see **a**

anaemic; anemic see **ae**

analog(ue) *analog* pref in US, rec in Can.; *analogue* pref in Br

analogy; analogous

analyse; analyze *analyse* pref in Br, rec in Can.; *analyze* pref in US; also: **analyser**

and/or avoid using this term; in most cases it can be replaced by either *and* or *or*

annul; annulled; annulling; annulment

antarctic see **arctic**

ante- a prefix that means before; combines to form one word: *antecedent, anteroom*

ante meridiem def: before noon; abbr: **a.m.**

anti- a prefix meaning opposite or contradictory to; generally combines to form one word: *anticlimax, anticlockwise, antidepressant, antiseptic, antitrust*; if combining word starts with *i* or is a proper noun, insert a hyphen: *anti-icing, anti-English*

anxious although *anxious* really implies anxiety, current usage permits it to be used when the meaning is simply keen or eager

anybody; any body *anybody* means any person; *any body* means any object: *anybody can attend; discard the batch if you find any body containing foreign matter*

anyone; any one *anyone* means any person; *any one* means any single item: *you may take anyone with you to the meeting; you may take any one of the samples*

anyway; any way *anyway* means in any case or in any event; *any way* means in any manner: *the results may not be good, but we want to see them anyway; the work may be done in any way you wish*

apology; apologize; apologetic

apparent; apparently

appear(s); seem(s) use *appears* to describe a condition that can be seen: *the computer appears to be new*; use *seems* to describe a condition that cannot be seen: *it seems to operate faster*

appendix def: the part of a report that contains supporting data; pl: *appendices* (pref) or *appendixes*

appreciate although *appreciate* is often (wrongly) used to mean understand (as in *we appreciate the difficulties your team faced*), its proper meaning is to value or cherish, as in *I appreciate your help*

approximate(ly) abbr: **approx**; but *about* is a better word to use

arbitrary

arctic capitalize when referring to a specific area: *beyond the Arctic Circle*; otherwise use lc letters: *in the arctic*; do not omit the first *c*

around def: on all sides, surrounding; avoid confusing with *round* (circular); in UK, *round* is commonly used to mean *around*

artwork one word

as avoid using when the intended meaning is *since* or *because*; to write *he could not open his desk as he left his keys at home* is incorrect (replace *as* with *because*)

ASCII American standard code for information interchange

as per avoid using this hackneyed expression, except in specifications

assess; assessment; assessor

assure means to state with confidence that something has been or will be made certain; it is sometimes confused with *ensure* and *insure*, which it does not replace; see **ensure**

as well as avoid using when the meaning is *and*

audible; audibility

audiovisual one word

audit; auditor

aural def: that which is heard; it should not be confused with *oral*, which means that which is spoken

author; writer avoid referring to yourself as *the author* or *the writer*; use *I*, *me*, or *my*

authoritative

authorize; authorise *authorize* pref

auto- a prefix meaning self; combines to form one word: *autobiography, autoload(ing), autosuggestion*

auxiliary

average see **mean**

avocation def: an interest or hobby; avoid confusing with *vocation*, which means one's trade or work, such as teaching or carpentry

ax; axe *axe* pref in Br, rec in Can.; *ax* pref in US; pl for both forms: *axes*

axis def: the pivot or centre; its plural also is axes

B

back- as a prefix normally combines into one word: *backboard, backdate(d), backlog, backorder(ed), backpay*

balance; remainder use *balance* to describe a state of equilibrium (as in *a marginal business venture delicately balanced between profitability and bankruptcy*), or as an accounting term; use *remainder* when the meaning is the rest of: the *remainder of the shipment will be delivered next week*

balk(ed); baulk(ed) *balk(ed)* pref

bare; bear *bare* means barren or exposed; *bear* means to withstand or to carry (or an animal)

barring def: preventing, excepting

bases this is the plural of both *base* and *basis*

basically

baulk(ed) see **balk(ed)**

B.C. def: Before Christ

because; for use *because* when the clause it introduces identifies the cause of a situation: *he could not open his desk because he left his keys at home*; use *for* when the clause introduces something less tangible: *he failed to complete the project on schedule, for reasons he preferred not to divulge*

behavio(u)r; behavio(u)rism *behavior* pref in US, rec in Can.; *behaviour* pref in Br

benefit; benefit(t)ed; benefit(t)ing single *t* pref

beside; besides *beside* means alongside, at the side of; *besides* means as well as

between see **among**

bi- a prefix meaning two or twice; combines to form one word: *biangular, bicultural, bidirectional, bilateral*

biannual(ly); biennial(ly) *biannual(ly)* means twice a year; *biennial(ly)* means every two years; the *bi* of *bimonthly* and *biweekly* means every two

bias; biased; biases; biasing

billion def: one thousand million, 10^9 (Can. and US); one million million, 10^{12} (Br); *billionaire* has only one *n*

Bill of Materials abbr: **BOM**

bimonthly def: every two months

bits per second abbr: **bps**

blur; blurred; blurring; blurry

bona fide def: in good faith, authentic, genuine

bonus, bonuses

book- as a prefix normally combines to form one word: *bookcase, bookkeeper, booklist, bookstore*; exception; *book club*

borderline

brand-new

break- when used as a prefix to form a compound noun or adjective, *break* combines into one word: *breakaway, breakdown, breakup*; in the verb form it retains its single-word identity: *it was time to break up the meeting*

bulletin

burned; burnt *burned* pref in Can. and US; *burnt* pref in Br

buses; bused; busing

business; businesslike; businessperson avoid using *businessman* or *businesswoman*

busywork

by- as a prefix, *by-* normally combines to form one word; *byelection, bylaw, byline, bypass, byproduct*

byte def: a unit of computer memory; the expressions are **kilobyte, megabyte, gigabyte**; the abbreviations are **kbyte** or **kb**, **Mbyte** or **Mb**, **Gbyte** or **Gb**; **byte** is also frequently abbr as **B** (as in **kB, MB, GB**)

C

calendar; calender; colander a *calendar* is the arrangement of the days in a year; *calender* is the finish on paper or cloth; a *colander* is a sieve.

calibre; caliber *calibre* pref in Br and rec in Can.; *caliber* pref in US

cancel(l)ed; cancel(l)ing *ll* pref in Br, rec in Can.; single *l* pref in US; **cancel** always has single *l*; **cancellation** always has *ll*

cando(u)r *candor* pref in US, rec in Can.; *candour* pref in Br

cannot one word pref; avoid using *can't* in business writing

canvas; canvass *canvas* is a coarse cloth used for tents, *canvass* means to solicit

capacity for never use *capacity to* or *capacity of*

capital letters abbr: **caps.**; use capital letters as little as possible (see page 356)

car- as a prefix normally combines to form one word: *carload, carlot, carpool, carwash*

case- as a prefix normally combines to form one word: *casebook, casework(er)*; exceptions: *case history, case study*

cassette

caster; castor pref spelling is *caster* when the meaning is to swivel freely; *castor* is used when the reference is to castor oil, etc

catalog(ue) *catalogue, catalogued* and *cataloguing* pref in Br and Can.; *catalog, cataloged,* and *cataloging* pref in US

category; categories; categorical

caveat def: a caution or limitation, usually legal

CD-ROM

-ceed; -cede; -sede only three words end in *-ceed*: *exceed, proceed, succeed*; only one word ends in *-sede*: *supersede*; all others end in *-cede*: e.g. *precede, concede*

census

central processing unit abbr: **cpu** (pref) or **CPU**

centre; center *centre, centred, centring, central* pref in Br, rec in Can.; *center, centered, centering, central* pref in US

chairperson avoid using *chairman* or *chairwoman*

changeable; changeover

channel; channel(l)ed; channel(l)ing *ll* pref in Br, rec in Can.; single *l* pref in US

chargeable

check- as a prefix combines to form one word: *checklist, checkpoint, checkup* (only as noun or adjective)

checksum def: a term used in computer technology

cheque; check *cheque* pref in Can. and Br; *check* pref in US

Christmas avoid writing Xmas

cipher not *cypher*

cite def: to quote; see **site**

citywide

cliché def: an overworked, often redundant expression

clientele

climactic; climatic *climactic* refers to a climax; *climatic* refers to the climate

climate avoid confusing *climate* with weather; *climate* is the average type of weather, determined over a number of years, experienced at a particular place; *weather* is the state of the atmospheric conditions at a specific place at a specific time

co- as a prefix, *co-* generally means jointly or together; it usually combines to form one word; *coauthor, coaxial, coefficient, coequal, coexist, coinsure, cooperate, coordinate (co-owner* and *co-worker* are exceptions)

coarse; course *coarse* means rough in texture or of poor quality: *a coarse granular material; course* implies movement or passage of time: *the business writing course*

coerce; coercible; coercion; coercive

collaborate; collaborator avoid writing *collaborate together* (delete *together*)

collapsible

collateral

collectible; collector

collision

colon when a colon is inserted in the middle of a sentence to introduce an example or short statement, the first word following the colon is not capitalized; a colon rather than a semicolon should be used at the end of a sentence to introduce subparagraphs that follow; a hyphen should not be inserted after the colon; also see page 351

colo(u)r *color* pref in US, rec in Can.; *colour* pref in Br

column; columnist

combustible

comma a comma need not be used immediately before *and, but*, and *or*, but may be inserted if it will increase understanding or avoid ambiguity

commence in business writing, replace *commence* with the more direct *begin* or *start*

commit; commitment; committed; committing

committee

communicate it is vague to write *I communicated the information to the supplier*; use a clearer verb: *I emailed, wrote, faxed*, or *telephoned*

compare; comparable; comparison; comparative use *compared to* when suggesting a general likeness; use *compared with* when making a definite comparison

compatible; compatibility

complement; compliment *complement* means the balance required to make up a full quantity or a complete set: e.g. *in a right angle, the complement of 60° is 30°; to compliment* means to praise, as in *Rita complimented Dave on his success*

composed of; comprises; consists of all three terms mean "made up of" (specific items); if any one of these terms is followed by a list of items, it implies that the list is complete; if the list is not complete, these terms should be replaced by *includes* or *including*; see also **comprise**

compound terms two or more words that combine to form a compound term are joined by a hyphen or are written as one word, depending on accepted usage, and on whether they form a verb, noun, or adjective; the trend is toward one-word compounds; see page 339

comprise; comprised; comprising to write *comprised of* is incorrect, because the verb *comprise* includes the preposition *of*

comptroller; controller *comptroller* is more common in Br, *controller* in the US; *controller* rec for Can.

computer

conceive; conceivable

concur; concurred; concurring; concurrent

confer; conferred; conferring; conference; conferee

conform use *conform to* when the meaning is to abide by; use *conform with* when the meaning is to agree with

connection; connexion *connection* pref in Can. and US; *connexion* is alternative spelling in Br; also **connector**

conscience; conscientious

conscious

consensus means a general agreement of opinion; hence to write *consensus of opinion* is redundant; e.g. *the consensus was to proceed with the project*

consistent with never use *consistent of* or *consistent to*

consists of see **composed of**

conspicuous

contact *contact* should not be used as a verb when *write, visit, speak, email* or *telephone* better describes the action

content; contention; contentious

continual; continuous *continual(ly)* means happens frequently, but not all the time: *the generator is continually being overloaded* (is frequently overloaded); *continuous(ly)* means goes on and on without stopping: *the noise level is continuously above 80 decibels* (it never drops as low as 80 decibels)

continue(d) abbr: **cont**

contra- as a prefix normally combines into a single word

contrast when used as a verb, *contrast* is followed by *with*, as in *the new lamp shades contrast well with the decor*; when used as a noun, it may be followed by either *to* or *with* (*with* pref), as in *the sumptuous dinner was a marked contrast to* (or *with*) *the frugal lunch*

contributor

control; controller; controlled; controlling

convene; convener (pref) or **convenor**

conversant with never use *conversant of*

converter; convertible

conveyor

cooperate

coordinate; coordinator

copyright not *copywrite*

corollary

correlate

correspond *to correspond to* suggests a resemblance; *to correspond with* means to communicate in writing

corroborate

cosigner

council; counsel a *council* is a group of people; a *counsel* is a lawyer; *to counsel* is to give advice

counsel(l)ed; counsel(l)ing; counsel(l)or *ll* pref in Br and rec in Can.; single *l* pref in US

counter- a prefix meaning opposite or reciprocal; combines to form one word: *counteract, counterbalance, counterflow, counterweight*

countrywide

course see **coarse**

crisis pl: *crises*

criteria; criterion the sing. is *criterion*, the pl is *criteria*

criticism; criticize; critique

cross- as a prefix combines erratically: *cross-check, crosshatch, cross-purpose, cross section, crosstalk*

cross-refer(ence) abbr: **x-ref**

cryptic

curb; kerb the verb is always *curb*; the noun is *kerb* in Br, but *curb* in US and Can.

curriculum pl: *curriculums* (pref) or *curricula*

cursor

D

dais def: a platform

data def: gathered facts; although *data* is pl (derived from the sing. *datum*, which is rarely used), it is acceptable to use it as a sing. noun: *when all the data has been received, the analysis will begin*

dateline

date(s) avoid vague statements such as "last month" and "next year" because they soon become indefinite; write a specific date, using day (in numerals), month (spelled out), and year (in numerals): *January 27, 2001* or *27 January 2001* (the latter form has no punctuation); to abbreviate, reduce month to first three letters and year to last two digits: *Jan 27, 01* or *27 Jan 01*

day- as a prefix, generally combines to form one word: *daybook, daylight, daytime, daywork*

days days of the week are capitalized: *Monday, Tuesday*

de- a prefix that generally combines to form one word: *deaccentuate, deactivate, decentralize, decode, deemphasize, deenergize*

dead- as a prefix combines erratically: *deadbeat, dead centre, dead end, deadline, deadweight, deadwood*

debate; debatable; debater

debrief

deceit; deceitful; deceive

decelerate def: to slow down; never use *deaccelerate*

decimals for values less than unity (one), place a zero before the decimal point: *0.17, 0.0017*

decimate def: to reduce by one tenth; can also mean to destroy much of

deductible

defective; deficient *defective* means unserviceable or damaged (generally lacking in quality); *deficient* means lacking in quantity (it is derived from *deficit*) and, in the military sense, incomplete: *a defective smoke detector battery prevented the automatic fire alarm from sounding; the installation is incomplete because the eight deficient smoke detectors will not be delivered until May 15*

defence; defense *defence* pref in Can. and Br; *defense* pref in US; *defensive* always has an *s*; also **defendant**

defer; deferred; deferring; deferrable; deference

definite; definitive *definite* means exact, precise; *definitive* means conclusive, fully evolved; e.g. *a definite price* is a firm price; *a definitive statement* concerns a topic that has been thoroughly considered and evaluated

demonstrate; demonstrator; demonstrable not *demonstratable*

depend; dependence; dependent; dependable *dependant* is also common as a noun in Br and Can.

deposit; depositor

deprecate; depreciate *deprecate* means to disapprove of; *depreciate* means to reduce the value of: *the use of "as per" in business writing is deprecated; the vehicles depreciated by 30% the first year and 20% the second year*

depth

desirable

desktop

desktop publishing abbr: **dtp** (pref) or **DTP**

desktop video conference abbr: **dtv** (pref) or **DTV**

despite def: in spite of; *despite* should never be followed by the word *of*

deter; deterred; deterrence; deterrent; deterring

deteriorate

develop; development not *develope*

device; devise the noun is *device*; the verb is *devise*: *a unique device; she devised a new program*

dext(e)rous *dexterous* pref

diagram(m)ed; diagram(m)ing *mm* pref in Can. and Br; single *m* pref in US; **diagram** always has single *m*; **diagrammatically** always has *mm*

dial(l)ed; dial(l)ing *ll* pref in Br, rec in Can.; single *l* pref in US

dialog(ue) *dialogue* pref

didn't all right for use in speech, but not in writing

dietitian

differ use *differ from* to demonstrate a difference; use *differ with* to describe a difference of opinion

different *different from* is preferred; *different to* is sometimes used; *different than* should never be used

dilemma means to be faced with a choice between two unhappy alternatives; should not be used as a synonym for *difficulty*

directly def: immediately; do not use when the meaning is as soon as

disassemble; dissemble *disassemble* means to take apart; *dissemble* means to conceal the truth

disassociate; dissociate *dissociate* pref

disc; disk *disc* pref in Br, rec in Can. (except in computer technology, where *disk* is used universally); *disk* pref in US

discernible

discolo(u)r *discolor* pref in US, rec in Can.; *discolour* pref in Br

discreet; discrete *discreet* means prudent or discerning: *his answer was discreet*; *discrete* means individually distinctive and separate, as in *discrete stereo channels*; **discretion** is formed from *discreet*, not from *discrete*

disinterested; uninterested *disinterested* means unbiased, impartial; *uninterested* means not interested

dispatch; despatch *dispatch* pref

disseminate

dissimilar

dissipate

dissociate; disassociate *dissociate* pref

distribute; distributor

districtwide

don't; doesn't such contractions are acceptable in speech but should not appear in business writing

DOS disk operating system

double- as a prefix combines erratically: *double-barrelled, doublecheck, doublecross, double-duty, double entry, doublefaced, doubled-park(ed)*

down- as a prefix combines into one word: *downgrade, downtime, downward, downwind*

draw- as a prefix combines to form one word: *drawback, drawdown*

drier; dryer the adjective is always *drier*; a drying machine is a *dryer* in Can. and US, a *drier* in Br; write: *this material is drier; place the others back in the dryer*

drily, dryly *drily* pref in Br, rec in Can.; *dryly* pref in US

drop; droppable; dropped; dropping; but **drop out** (verb or noun)

dtp; dtv desktop publishing; desktop video conference

due to an overused expression; *because of* is pref

duplicator

dutiable; duty-free

E

each abbr: ea

east capitalize only if *east* is part of a name: *East Africa*; otherwise use lc letters; *the east coast of Canada*; also: **eastbound** and **eastward**; abbr: E

echo; echoes

economic; economical use *economic* when writing about economics; use *economical* to describe economy (of funds, effort, time); *an economic disaster* (refers to economics); *an economical operation* (it did not cost much)

effect see **affect**

efficacy; efficiency *efficacy* means effectiveness, ability to do the job intended; *efficiency* is a measurement of capability, the ratio of work done to energy expended: *we hired a consultant to assess the efficacy of our training methods; we have installed a high-efficiency furnace*

e.g. means for example; avoid confusing with **i.e.**; no comma is necessary after *e.g.*; may also be abbr **eg**

eighth (often misspelled)

electronic(s) use *electronic* as an adjective, *electronics* as a noun; *electronic equipment; a career in electronics*

elevator

elicit; illicit *elicit* means to obtain or identify; *illicit* means illegal

eligible; eligibility

elite

email

embarrass; embarrassed; embarrassing; embarrassment

embed; embedded

emigrate; immigrate *emigrate* means to move away from; *immigrate* means to come into

emolument a much-too-big word for salary or pay; avoid using it

employee; employer

emulate; emulation

encipher

enclose; inclose *enclose* pref; *inclose* is used mainly as a legal term; also **enclosure**

endeavo(u)r *endeavor* pref in US, rec in Can.; *endeavour* pref in Br

endorse; indorse *endorse* pref; also **endorsable**

enforce not *inforce*

enquire; inquire *inquire* pref; also **inquiry**

enrol; enroll both are correct, but *enroll* pref; universal usage prefers *ll* for *enrolled* and *enrolling*, but only a single *l* for enrolment

en route def: on the road, on the way; never use *on route*

ensure; insure; assure use *ensure* (pref in Br, rec in Can.) or *insure* (pref in US) when the meaning is to make certain of: *a calculator ensures (or insures) mathematical accuracy*; use *insure* when the meaning is to protect against financial loss: *we insured all our drivers*; use *assure* when the meaning is to state with confidence that something has been or will be made certain: *he assured the meeting that production would increase by 8%*

entrepreneur; entrepreneurial

entrust; intrust *entrust* pref

envelop; envelope *envelop* is a verb that means to surround or cover completely; *envelope* is a noun that means a wrapper or covering

environment; environmental

equal; equal(l)ed; equal(l)ing *equal, equality, equalize* always have single *l*; *equalled; equalling* pref in Br, rec in Can.; *equaled, equaling* pref in US; **equalize** can also be spelled *equalise* in Br

equip; equipped; equipping; equipment

equivalent abbr: equiv

erase; erasable

errata although *errata* is plural (from the singular *erratum*, which is seldom used), it can be used as a singular or plural noun: both *the errata are ready* and *the errata is complete* are acceptable

erratic

erroneous

escalator

especially; specially use *especially* to introduce a phrase: *they were well trained, especially the computer technicians;* use *specially* when referring to an adjective (*a specially trained operator*)

et al. def: and others; now rarely used

etc def: abbr for *et cetera*, and so forth, and so on; use with care in business writing; *etc* can create an impression of vagueness or unsureness: to write *the purchase orders, etc, have been mailed* is much less definite than either *the purchase orders, bills of lading, packing slips, and invoices have been mailed* or (if to restate all the items is too long or repetitious) *the documentation has been mailed*

everybody; every body *everybody* means every person, or all the persons; *every body* means every single body: *everybody was present; every body was examined for gunpowder scars*

everyone; every one *everyone* means every person, or all the persons; *every one* means every single item: *everyone is insured; every one had to be tested in a saline solution*

exaggerate

exceed

excel; excelled; excellent; excelling

except def: to exclude; see **accept**

excerpt

executor

exhaust

exhibit; exhibitor

exhort

exorbitant

expedite; expediter (pref) or **expeditor**

explicit; implicit *explicit* means clearly stated, exact; *implicit* means implied (i.e. the meaning has to be inferred from the words); *the supervisor gave explicit instructions* (they were clear); *that the manager was angry was implicit in the words he used*

extemporaneous

extracurricular

extraordinary

F

face- as a prefix normally combines to form one word: *facedown, facelift, faceplate*; exceptions: *face-saver, face-saving*

facsimile see **fax**

fait accompli def: something done or accomplished, and now too late to change; pl: **faits accomplis**

fallout one word, in the noun form

familiarize; familiarization

farfetched; far-out; far-reaching; farseeing; farsighted

farther; further *farther* means greater distance: *he travelled farther than the other sales staff*; *further* means a continuation of (as an adjective) or to advance (as a verb): *the promotion was a further step in his career plan*, and *to further her education, she took a course in industrial management*

faux pas def: a social blunder; this is both the sing. and pl form

favo(u)r *favor* pref in US, rec in Can.; *favour* pref in Br

fax generally used abbr for facsimile transmission or facsimile machine

feasible; feasibility

February

fewer; less use *fewer* to refer to items that can be counted: *fewer employees than we predicted have been assigned to the project*; use *less* to refer to general quantities: *there was less water available than predicted*

fibre; fiber; fibrous *fibre, fibreglass* pref in Br, rec in Can.; *fiber, fiberglass* pref in US; *Fiberglas* is a US trade name

field- as a prefix normally does not combine into a single word or hyphenated form: *field glasses, field test, field trip;* but *fieldwork(er)*

figure numbers in text, spell out the word *figure* in full, or abbr it to **Fig.**: *refer to the circuit diagram in figure 26*, or *for details, see Fig. 7*; use the abbreviated form beneath an illustration; always use numerals for the figure number

final; finally; finalize; finale

fire- as a prefix combines erratically: *firearm, fire alarm, firebreak, fire drill, fire escape, fire extinguisher, firefighter, firepower, fireproof, fire sale, fire wall*

first to write *the first two* (or *three*, etc) is better than to write the *two first*: never use *firstly*

flammable def: easily ignited; see **inflammable**

flavo(u)r *flavor* pref in US, rec in Can., *flavour* pref in Br

flexible

flier see **flyer**

flight usually combines to form two words: *flight bag, flight control, flight deck, flight plan*

floor- combines erratically: *floor-length, floor manager, floor model, floor sample, floorspace, floorwalker*

flotation this is the correct spelling for an item that floats

flowchart

flu accepted contraction of *influenza*

fluorescence; fluorescent

flyer; flier *flyer* pref in Br, rec in Can.; *flier* pref in US

focus; focused; focuses; focusing

folio; folios

follow-through; follow-up (as noun or adjective)

foot- as a prefix normally combines into one word: *foothold, footnote, footwork*

for see **because**

forceful; forcible use *forceful* to describe a person's character; use *forcible* to describe physical force

fore- def: that which goes before; as a prefix normally combines into one word: *foreclose, forefront, foregoing, foregone, foreground, foreknowledge, foremost, foresee, forestall, forethought, forewarn*

forecast this spelling applies to both present and past tenses

forego; forgo *forego* and *foregoing* mean to go before; *forgo* means to go without

foreman avoid using in a general sense, except when referring to a person specifically, as in *John Harris, the foreman*; never use *forewoman* (a better word for both is *supervisor*)

foresee

forestall

foreword; forward a *foreword* is a preface or preamble to a book; *forward* means onward: *the scope is defined in the foreword to the book; he requested that we bring the meeting date forward*

for example abbr: **e.g.** (pref) or **eg**

former; first use *former* to refer to the first of only two things; use *first* if there are more than two

formula pl: *formulas* (pref in Can. and US) or *formulae* (pref in Br)

fortnight def: two weeks (this Br term is not recognized in US)

forty def: 40; it is not spelled *fourty*

foul-up

fourth def: 4th; it is not spelled *forth*; also: **fourteen**

fractions when writing fractions that are less than unity (one), spell them out in descriptive narrative: *on the completion date, only nine-tenths of the installation work had been finished*; spelled fractions are hyphenated; for technical details, use decimals rather than fractions

franchise; franchisee; franchisor a *franchisee* is the person who receives a franchise; a *franchisor* is the person who grants the franchise

free- as a prefix normally combines into one word: *freehand, freehold, freelance, freestanding, freeway, freewheel*

free from use *free from* rather than *free of*: *he is free from prejudice*

free on board abbr **fob** (pref), **f.o.b.** (commonly used), or **FOB**

fulfil(l) *fulfil, fulfilment* pref in Br, rec in Can.; *fulfill, fulfillment* pref in US; **fulfilled** and **fulfilling** always have *ll*

further see **farther**

G

gauge pref spelling; **gage** also used in US; **gauging** does not retain the *e*

generalize; generalization

ghostwrite; ghostwriter

giftware; giftwrap

gimbal not *gymbal*

giveaway (noun) def: a bargain or free gift

glamor; glamorous; glamorize these are the pref spellings in Can. and US; in Br, *glamour* pref

goodby(e) *goodbye* pref in Br, rec in Can.; *goodby* pref in US

gotten try not to use this expression in business writing; use *have got* or simply *have*

government capitalize when referring to a specific government either directly or by implication; use lc if the meaning is government generally: *the Canadian Government; the Government specifications; no government would sanction such restrictions*

grammar; grammatical; grammatically

grateful not *greatful*

gray this is the US spelling; see **grey**

Greenwich mean time abbr: **GMT**

grievance

grey; gray *grey* pref in Br, rec in Can.; *gray* pref in US

grill(e) use *grill* to describe a cooking method; use *grille* for a loudspeaker covering or a grating

gross national product abbr: **GNP**

guage wrongly spelled; the correct spelling is **gauge**

guarantee never *guaranty*; also: **guarantor**

guesstimate

guideline(s)

H

half; halved; halves; halving as a prefix *half-* combines erratically; some common compounds are: *half-and-half, half-baked, half-dozen, half-full, half-hour(ly), half-month(ly), half pay*; for others, consult your dictionary

hand- as a prefix normally combines to form one word: *handbill, handbook, handful, handfuls, handheld, handmade, handpicked, handshake*

harass; harassment

harbo(u)r *harbor* pref in US and rec in Can.; *harbour* pref in Br

hard- as a prefix normally combines into one word: *hardbound, hardcover, hardfisted, hardhanded, hardhat, hardheaded, hardnosed, hardware*; exceptions: *hard-earned, hard-hitting*

head- as a prefix normally combines into one word: *headfirst, headquarters, headset, headstart, headway*

hectic

height (not *heighth*) abbr: **ht**; also: **heighten, heightfinder**

here- whenever possible avoid using *here-* words that sound like legal terms: *hereafter, hereby, herein, hereinafter, hereof*; they make a writer sound pompous

heterogeneous; homogeneous *heterogeneous* means of the opposite kind; *homogeneous* means of the same kind

high- as a prefix combines into one word or the two words are joined by a hyphen: *highhanded, highlight, high-power, high-priced, high-rise, high-speed*

hinge; hinged; hinging

home- as a prefix normally combines into one word: *homeowner, homeward, homework*

homogeneous see **heterogeneous**

hono(u)r *honor* pref in US and rec in Can.; *honour* pref in Br

hour abbr: **h** or **hr**; do not add an "s" in the pl form: *27 h*

house- as a prefix normally combines into one word: *housebound, householder, housekeeper*

humo(u)r *humor* pref in US and rec in Can.; *humour* pref in Br; but **humorous** in US, Br and Can.

hyperbola; hyperbole a *hyperbola* is a curved line; pl: *hyperbolas* (pref) or *hyperbolae; hyperbole* is an exaggerated statement

hyphen in compound terms you may omit hyphens unless they need to be inserted to avoid ambiguity or to conform to accepted usage; e.g. *preemptive* is preferred without a hyphen, but *photo-offset* and *re-cover* (when the meaning is to cover again) both require one; refer to individual entries and to page 339

I

ibid. def: Latin abbr for *ibidem*, meaning in the same place; used in footnoting, now obsolescent

ID card

i.e. def: that is; avoid confusing with **e.g.**; no comma is necessary after *i.e.*; may also be abbr **ie**

if and when avoid using this expression; use either *if* or *when*

ill- as a prefix combines into a hyphenated expression: *ill-advised, ill-defined, ill-timed*

illegible

illicit def: illegal, avoid confusing with *elicit*

im- see **in-**

imbalance this term should be restricted for use in accounting and medical terminology; use **unbalance** in other situations

immaterial

immeasurable

immigrate see **emigrate**

immovable

impasse

imperceptible

impetus

impinge; impinging

implicit def: implied; also see **explicit**

imply; infer speakers and writers can *imply* something; listeners and readers *infer* from what they hear or read: *in his closing remarks Mr Smith implied that further studies were in order; the accountant inferred from the report that the project is complete*

impostor

impracticable; impractical *impracticable* means not feasible; *impractical* means not practical; a less preferred alternative for *impractical* is *unpractical*

impromptu

in; into *in* is a passive word denoting position; *into* implies action: *ride in the car; step into the car*

in-; im-; un- all three prefixes mean *not*; all combine to form one word: *ineligible, impossible, unintelligible*; if you are not sure whether to use *in-*, *im-*, or *un-*, use *not*

inaccessible

inaccuracy

inadmissible

inadvisable; unadvisable *inadvisable* pref

inasmuch as a better word is *since*

inaudible

incalculable not *incalculatable*

inclose see **enclose**

includes; including abbr: **incl**; when followed by a list of items, *includes* implies that the list is not complete; if the list is complete, use *comprises* or *consists of*

incomparable

incompatible

inconceivable

incumbent def: the person currently holding the position

incur; incurred; incurring

index pl: *indexes* pref, except in mathematics (where *indices* is common)

indifferent to never use *indifferent of*

indiscreet; indiscrete *indiscreet* means imprudent; *indiscrete* means not divided into separate parts

indispensable

indorse *endorse* pref

industrywide

ineligible

inequitable

inessential; unessential both are correct; *unessential* pref

infallible

infer; inferred; inferring; inference see also **imply**

inflammable def: easily ignited (derived from *inflame*); **flammable** is a better word: it prevents readers from mistakenly thinking the *in* of *inflammable* means *not*

inflection; inflexion *inflection* pref in Can. and US; *inflection* and *inflexion* used in Br

inflexible

ingenious; ingenuous *ingenious* means clever, innovative; *ingenuous* means innocent, naive; *ingenuity* is a noun derived from *ingenious*

in-house

initial; initial(l)ed *ll* pref in Br, rec in Can.; single *l* pref in US

innocuous

innovate; innovative; innovator

innumerable

inoculate

inoperable not *inoperatable*

inquire; enquire *enquire* pref in Br and rec in Can.; *inquire* pref in US; also: *enquiry*

inseparable

in situ def: in the normal position

insofar as a wordy expression; not recommended

insolvent; insolvency

instal(l) *install, installed, installer, installing, installation* pref; but *instalment* pref in Br, rec in Can.; *installment* pref in US

instantaneous

insure the pref def is to protect against financial loss; can also mean make certain of (particularly in US); see **ensure**

intelligible

inter- a prefix meaning among or between; normally combines to form one word: *interact, interchangeable, interface, intermittent, interoffice*

Internet

interrupt

into see **in**

intractable

intranet

intrust *entrust* pref

IOU

IQ

irrational

irregardless *never* use this expression; use *regardless*

irrelevant frequently misspelled as *irrevelant*

irremovable

irreversible

its; it's *its* means belonging to; *it's* is an abbr for *it is*: *the computer and its peripheral equipment; if the fault is not in the disk drive, then it's most likely in the CPU*; in most business writing it is better to write *it is* than *it's*

J

jobholder; job-hopper; jobless; jobseeker; but **job lot**

journey; journeys

judg(e)ment *judgment* pref in US, rec in Can.; *judgement* pref in Br

judicial; judicious *judicial* means related to the law; *judicious* means sensible, discerning

K

kerb see **curb**

key- as a prefix normally combines to form one word: *keyboard, keynote, keypunch, keying, keystone, keystroke*; but *key word*

kickback

king-size

know-how

knowledge; knowledgeable

L

label(l)ed; label(l)ing *ll* pref in Br; rec in Can.; single *l* pref in US

labor; labour *labor* pref in US, rec in Can.; *labour* pref in Br; **laborious** pref in Can, Br and US.; also: **labor-saving**

last; latest; latter *last* means final; *latest* means most recent; *latter* refers to the second of two things (if there are more than two, use *last*); write *the last two* (or *three*, etc) rather than *the two last*

latecomer

law- as a prefix generally combines to form one word: *lawbreaker, lawsuit*; but *law-abiding*

lay- as a prefix generally combines to form one word: *layoff, layout, layover* (all nouns)

learned; learnt *learned* pref; *learnt* common in Br

leaseback; leasehold

leeway

lend; loan use *lend* as a verb, *loan* as a noun; to write or say "loan me your calculator" is wrong, but "*lend* me your calculator" is correct

length the SI unit of length is the *metre*, expressed in multiples and submultiples: *kilometres, metres*, and *millimetres;* abbr: **km, m, mm**

lengthy not *lengthly*; also: **lengthening, lengthwise**

letter- as a prefix combines erratically: *letterhead, letter-perfect, letter writer*

letter of intent; letter of transmittal pl: *letters of intent or transmittal*

liable to means under obligation to: avoid using as a synonym for *apt to* or *likely to*

liaison *liaison* is a noun; it is sometimes used uncomfortably as a verb: **liaise**

libel; libel(l)ed; libel(l)ing; libel(l)ous *ll* pref in Br, rec in Can.; single *l* pref in US

licence; license in Can. and Br the noun is *licence* and the verb is *license: a driving licence; I am licensed to drive a semitrailer*; in US, *license* is pref for both noun and verb; **licensee** always has *s*

lieutenant-governor

life- as a prefix generally combines into a single word: *lifelong, lifestyle, lifetime*, but *life-size* and *life insurance*

light- as a prefix *light-* generally combines to form one word: *lightface* (type), *lightweight*; the past tense is *lighted*, but *lit* is common in the UK

lightening; lightning *lightening* means to make lighter; *lightning* is an atmospheric discharge of electricity

lik(e)able *likable* pref in US and rec by CP for Can.; *likeable* pref in Br

lines of communication not *line of communications*

Listserv

litre; liter the SI spelling is *litre* (pref in Can. and Br), but in US *liter* is more common; abbr: **L**

liv(e)able *livable* pref in US, rec in Can.; *liveable* pref in Br

loan see **lend**

loath; loathe *loath* means reluctant; *loathe* means to dislike intensely

lock- as a prefix combines into a single word: *lockout, locksmith, lockstep, lockup*

logbook

logistic(s) use *logistic* as an adjective, and *logistics* as a noun: *logistic control; the logistics of the move*

long- as a prefix normally combines into a single word or is hyphenated:

long-distance, longhand, longplaying, long-term, long-winded; but *long shot*

looseleaf

lose; loose *lose* is a verb that refers to a loss; *loose* is an adjective or a noun that means free or not secured: *three loose nuts caused us to lose a wheel*

M

macro- a prefix meaning very large; combines to form one word: *macroscopic, macroview;* in word processing, *macro* can also be used as a noun meaning "a stored body of text"

mail- as a prefix normally combines to form one word: *mailbag,* but *mail-order* (as an adjective)

maintain; maintained; maintaining; maintenance

majority use *majority* mainly to refer to a number, as in *a majority of 27*; avoid using it as a synonym for *many* or *most*; e.g. do not write "the majority of" when the intended meaning is *most*

make- as a prefix normally combines to form one word: *makeshift, makeup*; but *make-believe*

man to avoid sexist connotations, replace *man* as follows:

for:	*write:*
man(ned), (ning)	staff(ed), (ing)
man-hour(s)	work-hour(s)
manpower	labor
salesman	salesclerk or sales representative
workman	worker

Also see page 385

manage; managed; managing; manageable; management

manoeuvre; maneuver *manoeuvre, manoeuvred, manoeuvring* pref in Br, rec in Can.; *maneuver, maneuvered, maneuvering* pref in US

manufacturer; manufacturing abbr: **mfr; mfg**

markup; markdown (noun and adj)

marketplace

material; materiel *material* is the substance or goods out of which an item is made; when used in the plural, it describes items of a like kind, such as writing materials; *materiel* are all the equipment and supplies necessary to support a project or undertaking (a term commonly used in military operational support)

matrix pl: *matrices* (pref) or *matrixes*

maximum pl: *maximums* (pref) or *maxima*; abbr: **max**; like *minimize, maximize* can be used as a verb

maybe; may be *maybe* means perhaps: *maybe there is more than one supplier*; the verb form *may be* means *perhaps it will be* or *possibly there is/are*: e.g. *the proposal may be accepted*

mean; median the *mean* is the average of a number of quantities; the *median* is the midpoint of a sequence of numbers; e.g. in the sequence of five numbers 1, 2, 3, 7, 8, the mean is 4.2 and the median is 3

mediocre

medium when *medium* is used to mean substances, liquids, materials, or the means for accomplishing something (such as advertising), the pref pl is *media*; in all other senses the pref pl is *mediums*

meetingplace

memorandum pl: *memorandums* (pref in US, rec in Can.) or *memoranda* (pref in Br); abbr: **memo** and **memos**

menu pl: *menus*

merit; merited; meriting

metre; meter def: metric unit of length; the SI spelling is *metre* (pref in Can. and Br), but *meter* is more common in US; abbr **m**; other typical abbr: **km** (kilometre), **m^2** (square metre), **m^3** (cubic metre)

micro- a prefix meaning very small; normally combines to form one word: *microorganism, microprocessor, microview*

mid- a prefix that means in the middle of; generally combines into one word: *midday, midpoint, midterm, midweek*; if used with a proper noun, insert a hyphen: *mid-Atlantic*

mileage; milage *mileage* pref

milli- combines to form one word: *millimetre, milligram*

million in general narrative it is simpler to write *$12 million* than *$12 000 000*; but the full number should be used in legal documents and contracts

mini- as a prefix combines to form one word: *minicomputer, minireport*

miniature; miniaturization

minimum pl: *minimums* (pref) or *minima*; abbr: **min**; also: **minimize**

minority use mainly to refer to a number: *a minority by 2*; avoid using it as a synonym for *several* or *few*; to write *a minority of the technicians* is incorrect when the intended meaning is *a few technicians*

minuscule not *miniscule*; def: minute (very small)

minute (of time) abbr: **min** or **m**; do not add an "s" in the plural form: *the job was completed in 2 h 27 m*

mis- a prefix meaning wrong(ly) or bad(ly); combines to form one word: *misalign, misfired, mismatched, misplaced, misshapen*

miscellaneous

misspelled; misspelt *misspelled* pref

mnemonic

model; model(l)ed; model(l)er; model(l)ing *ll* pref in Br, rec in Can.; single *l* pref in US

momentary; momentarily means *for a moment*, not *in a moment*

money- as a prefix normally combines to form one word: *moneylender, moneymaking, moneysaving*

months the months of the year are always capitalized: *January, February,* etc; if abbr, use only the first three letters: *Jan, Feb*, etc; the abbr for *month* is **mo**

moral; morale often confused; *moral* refers to personal strength of character, the ability to differentiate between right and wrong; *morale* means the general contentedness or happiness of a person or group of people

mortgage; mortgageholder

most never use as a short form for *almost*; to say *most everyone is here* is incorrect

movable; moveable *movable* pref

Mr; Ms address men as *Mr* and women as *Ms*; use *Miss* or *Mrs* only if you know the person prefers to be so addressed; the period (punctuation) may be omitted from or inserted after *Mr.* and *Ms.*

multi- a prefix meaning many; combines to form one word: *multiaddress, multicolored, multifold, multilayered, multinational, multipurpose*

multiple-choice

municipal, municipality

N

nameplate

nationwide

NB means note well, and is the abbr for *nota bene*; it is more common to use the word *NOTE*

necessary; necessarily; necessitate

negligible

neighbo(u)r *neighbor* pref in US, rec in Can.; *neighbour* pref in Br; also: **neighborhood**

nevertheless

newsletter; newsprint

next write *the next two* (or *the next three*, etc) rather than *the two next* (etc)

night never use *nite*; write *nighttime* as one word

nineteen; ninety; ninth all three are frequently misspelled

nitpick; nitpicker; nitpicking

No. abbr for **number**; also **no.**

non- as a prefix meaning not or negative, normally combines to form one word: *noncommittal, nondeductible, nondirectional, nonnegotiable, nonprofit, nonrenewable, nonstop*, but *non-existent*; if combining word is a proper noun, insert a hyphen: *non-Canadian*; avoid forming a new word with *non-* when a similar word that serves the same purpose already exists (e.g. you should not form *nonaudible* because *inaudible* already exists)

none when the meaning is "not one," treat as singular; when the meaning is "not any," treat as plural

no one two words

norm def: the average or normal (distribution, situation, or condition)

normalize

north; northeast; northwest; northbound; northward abbr: **N, NE, NW**; for rule on capitalization, see **east**

no-show

notable

not applicable abbr: **N/A**

note well abbr: **NB**

notice; noticeable; notification

not to exceed an overworked phrase that should be used only in specifications; in all other cases use *not more than*

number although **no.** would appear to be the logical abbr for number (and is pref), **No.** is much more common (the symbol # should not be used as an abbr for number); the abbr *no.* or *No.* must always be followed by a quantity in numerals; it is incorrect to write *we have received a No. of shipments*; for the difference in usage between *amount* and *number*, see **amount**

numbers (in narrative) as a general rule, spell from one to nine and use numerals for 10 and up; for specific rules see page 362

O

oblivious def: unaware or forgetful; although *oblivious* should be followed by *of*, it is becoming common practice to follow it with *to: she was oblivious of the disturbance* is correct; *she was oblivious to the disturbance* is acceptable but less pref

obsolete; obsolescent

obtain; secure use *obtain* when the meaning is simply to get; use *secure* when the meaning is to make safe or to take possession of (possibly after some difficulty); *we obtained four additional samples; we secured space in the prime display area*

occasional; occasionally

occur; occurred; occurrence; occurring

o'clock avoid using; see **time**

of avoid using in place of *have*; write *we should have measured*, not *we should of measured*

off- as a prefix either combines into one word or a hyphen is inserted: *offbeat, off-centre(d), off-scale, offset, offshoot, off-the-shelf*

offence; offense *offence* pref in Can. and Br; *offense* pref in US; *offensive* always has an *s*

offline

off of an awkward construction; omit the word *of*

OK; okay these are slang expressions that should not be used in business writing

omit; omitted; omission

on; onto *on* means positioned generally; *onto* implies action or movement; *the report is on Mr Cord's desk; the speaker stepped onto the platform*

one- as a prefix mostly combines with a hyphen: *one-piece, one-sided, one-*

to-one, one-way; but *oneself* and *onetime*

online

onward(s) *onward* pref

op. cit def: Latin abbr for *opere citato*, meaning in the work cited; used in footnoting, but now obsolescent

operate; operator; operable not *operatable*

optimum pl: *optima* (pref), and sometimes *optimums*; also: **optimal**

oral; orally def: spoken; avoid confusing with **aural**

organize; organizer; organization

orient; oriented; orienting these are the verb forms; the noun is **orientation**

out- as a prefix normally combines to form one word: *outbreak, outcome, outdistance*; when *out-* is followed by *of*, insert hyphens if used as a compound adjective (*an out-of-date list*), but treat as separate words when used in place of a noun (*the printing schedule is out of phase*)

outward(s) *outward* pref

over- as a prefix meaning above or beyond, normally combines to form one word: *overconfident, overemphasis, overestimate, overpopulation, overproduction, overrated, override, oversimplification*, but *over-the-counter*; avoid using *over* as a synonym for more than, particularly when referring to quantities: *more than 17 were serviceable* is better than *over 17 were serviceable*

overage means either too many or too old

overall an overworked word; as an adjective it often gives unnecessary additional emphasis (as in *overall impression*) and should be deleted; avoid using as a synonym for *altogether, average, general,* or *total*

P

pacemaker; pacesetter

page; pages abbr: **p; pp**

paid not *payed*, when the meaning is to spend

pamphlet

panel; panel(l)ed; panel(l)ing *ll* pref in Br, rec in Can.; single *l* pref in US

paper- as a prefix mostly combines to form one word: *paperback, paperbound, paperwork*; but *paper-covered, paper-thin*

paragraph(s) abbr: **para**

parallel; paralleled; paralleling; parallelism; parallelogram both *parallel to* and *parallel with* are correct

parameter; perimeter *parameter* means a guideline; *perimeter* means a border or edge

paraplegic

paraprofessional

parenthesis the pl is *parentheses;* in Can., the term *bracket(s)* is more common

partly; partially use *partly* when the meaning is "a part" or "in part"; use *partially* when the meaning is "to a certain extent," or when preference or bias is implied

part-time

pass- as a prefix normally combines to form one word: *passbook, passkey, passport, password*

passed; past as a general rule, use *passed* as a verb and *past* as an adjective or a noun: *Mr Patrick passed the examination; past experience has shown. . . ; in the past*

pay- as a prefix normally combines to form one word: *paycheque, payload, payroll*; but *pay day* and *pay-as-you-go*

pencil(l)ed; pencil(l)ing *ll* pref in Br, rec in Can.; single *l* pref in US

penultimate def: the next to last

people; persons *people* pref: *all the people were present*; use *persons* to refer only to small numbers of people: *three persons were interviewed* (and even here, *people* could be used); *person* is correct in the singular form

per in business writing it is acceptable to use *per* to mean either *by* or *a(n)*, as in *per diem* (by the day) and *kilometres per hour*; avoid using "as per" in all writing

per cent; percent *percent* is pref in US and common in Can., where it is replacing *per cent*; abbr: **%**; use % after numerals: 35%; use *percent* after a spelled-out number: *about twenty percent*; avoid using the expression *a percentage of* as a synonym for *a part of* or *a small part;* also

percentile

perceptible

per diem def: per day

permissible

permit; permitted; permitting; permit-holder

personal; personnel *personal* means concerning one person; *personnel* means the members of a group, or the staff; *a personal affair; the personnel in the office; personnel* is often misspelled; for *person(s)* see **people**

pharmacy; pharmacist; pharmaceutical

phase def: a stage of transmission or development; it should not be used as a synonym for *aspect*; it is used correctly in *the second phase called for a detailed cost breakdown*

phase-in; phaseout use a hyphenated or compound word for noun and adj, but two words in the verb form

phenomenon pl: *phenomena*

photo- as a prefix, normally combines to form one word: *photocopy, photoelectric, photostat*; if combining word starts with o, insert a hyphen: *photo-offset*

phraseology

piecemeal; piecework

plagiarism def: to copy without acknowledgement to the original source

plateau pl: *plateaus* (pref in US, rec in Can.) or *plateaux* (pref in Br)

p.m. def: after noon (post meridiem)

policyholder

portfolio; portfolios

post- a prefix meaning after or behind; combines to form one word: *postgraduate, posthaste, postmortem, postpaid, postpone*

postage; postmark; post office

post meridiem def: after noon; abbr: **p.m.**

practicable; practical these words have similar meanings but different applications that sometimes are hard to identify; *practicable* means feasible to do: *it was difficult to find a practicable solution* (one that could reasonably be implemented); *practical* means handy, suitable, able to be carried out in practice: *a practical solution would be to combine the two departments*

practice; practise the noun is always *practice*; the verb is *practise* (pref in Br, rec in Can.), but can also be *practice* (pref in US)

pre- a prefix meaning before or prior; normally combines to form one word: *prearrange, predetermined, preeminent, preempt, preexist, preflight, prejudge, preoccupied, prerequisite, preset*; if combining word is a proper noun, insert a hyphen: *pre-1998*

precede; proceed *precede* means to go before; *proceed* generally means carry on or continue: *the dinner was preceded by a brief business meeting; after dinner, we proceeded with the annual presentation of awards*; see **proceed**

precedence; precedent *precedence* means priority (of position, time, etc): *the environmental aspects have precedence* (they must be dealt with first); a *precedent* is an example that is or will be followed by others: *we may set a precedent if we grant her request* (others will expect similar treatment)

précis

predominate; predominant; predominantly

prefer; preferred; preferring; preference; preferable avoid overstating *preferable*, as in *more preferable* and *highly preferable*

prescribe; proscribe *prescribe means to state as a rule or requirement*; *proscribe* means to deny permission or forbid

presently use *presently* only to mean soon or shortly; never use it to mean *now* (use *at present* instead)

prestigious

pretend; pretence/pretense *pretence* pref in Can. and Br; *pretense* pref in US

preventive; preventative *preventive* pref

previous def: earlier, that which went before; avoid writing *previous to* (use *before*); see **prior**

principal; principle as a noun, *principal* means: (1) the first one in importance, the leader, or (2) a sum of money on which interest is paid: *one of the firm's principals is Johannes Van Nuys; the invested principal of $10 000 earned $950 in interest last year*; as an adjective, *principal* means most important or chief: *the principal reason for choosing the Arrow copier was its low operating cost; principle* is always a noun and means a strong guiding rule, a fundamental or primary source (of information, etc): *his principles prevented him from taking advantage of the error*

printout (noun and adj)

prior; previous use only as adjectives meaning earlier: *he had a prior appointment*, or *a previous commitment prevented Ms Goodwin from attending the meeting*; it's often better to write *before* rather than *prior to* or *previous to*

prioritize def: to arange items or events in order of their priority

privilege

proceed use *proceed to* when the meaning is to start something new; use *proceed with* when the meaning is to continue something that was started previously

producible

program(me) single *m* pref in US, rec in Can.; *mm* pref in Br; *programmed, programmer* and *programming* always have *mm* in Can. and Br, and usually in US; a *software program* always has only one *m*

prohibit use *prohibit from*, never *prohibit to*

promissory (note)

proofread

prophecy; prophesy use *prophecy* only as a noun, *prophesy* only as a verb: *it's my prophecy that we will experience a bonanza in sales; it's too early to prophesy that we will have a surplus*

proportion avoid writing "a proportion of" or "a large proportion of" when *some, many*, or a specific quantity would be simpler and more direct

proposition in its proper sense, *proposition* means a suggestion put forward for argument; it should not be used as a synonym for *plan, project*, or *proposal*

pro rata def: assigned proportionally; sometimes used in the verb form as **prorate**: *you are to prorate the cost over two years*

prospectus; prospectuses

proved; proven use *proven* only as an adjective or in the legal sense; otherwise use *proved: he has been proven guilty; she proved that the data was inaccurate*

provincewide

pursuant to avoid using this wordy expression

Q

quality control abbr: QC

quantity; quantitative the abbr of *quantity* is **qty**

question mark insert a question mark after a direct question: *how many booklets will you require?*; omit the question mark when the question posed is really a demand: *may I have your decision by noon on Monday*

questionnaire

quick- as a prefix normally combines with a hyphen: *quick-acting, quick-freeze, quick-tempered, quick-witted*; exceptions: *quicklime, quicksilver*

quorum

R

radio- as a prefix combines to form one word: *radioactive, radiobiology, radioisotope*; if combining word starts with *o*, omit one *o*: radiology

radius pl: *radii* (pref) or *radiuses*

rain- as a prefix normally combines to form one word: *raincoat, rainproof, rainwear*; exception: *rain check*

random-access memory abbr: **ram** or **RAM** (the latter is more common)

ratify; ratified; ratifying

ratio; ratios

rational; rationale *rational* means reasonable, clear-sighted: *John had a rational explanation for the error; rationale* means an underlying reason: *Jane explained the company's rationale for diversifying the product line*

re avoid using *re* in business writing, particularly as an abbr for *regarding, concerning, with reference to*

re- a prefix meaning to do again, to repeat; normally combines to form one word: *readdress, realign, reassess, reexamine, reorganize, rerun, reset*; if the compound term forms an existing word that has a different meaning, insert a hyphen to identify it as a compound: e.g. *re-cover* (to cover again)

reaction *reaction* is better used to describe a chemical or mechanical process rather than as a synonym for *opinion* or *impression*

readability

read-only memory abbr: **rom** or **ROM** (the latter is more common)

readout (noun and adj only)

realize; realization

rebut; rebuttal; rebutted; rebutting

recede

receive; receiver; receiving; receivable; receipt

rechargeable

recipe, receipt often confused; *recipe* means preparation instructions, most often for cooking; *receipt* means a written record that something has been received

recognize; recognizance

recommend; recommendation

reconcile; reconcilable

recordkeeper; recordkeeping

recover; re-cover *recover* means to get back, to regain; *re-cover* means to cover again

recur; recurred; recurring; recurrence; recurrent these are the correct spellings; see *reoccur*

recycle; recyclable

reducible

reenforce; reinforce *reenforce* means to enforce again; *reinforce* means to strengthen: *David Courtland reenforced his original instructions by circulating a second memorandum; the Artmo Building required 34 750 tonnes of reinforced concrete*

refer; referred; referring; referral; referee; reference

referendum both Br and US dictionaries list *referenda* as the pref pl, but *referendums* is much more commonly used and is rec by CP

rein; reign *rein* means to have control; *reign* means to rule

reiterate def: to say again

relaid; relayed *relaid* means laid again, like a carpet; *relayed* means to send on, as a message would be relayed to another person

reminisce

remit; remitted; remitting; remittance; remitter

remodel; remodel(l)ed; remodel(l)ing *ll* pref in Br, rec in Can.; single *l* pref in US

removable

remuneration *pay, salary,* and *wages* are better words; often misspelled as *renumeration*

rent-a-car

reoccur; reoccurrence *recur* and *recurrence* are better words

repairable; reparable both words mean in need of repair and capable of being repaired; *reparable* also implies that the cost to repair the item has been taken into account and it is economically worthwhile to effect the repairs

replaceable

repossess; repossession

representative abbr: **rep**

reproducible

rescind

respective(ly) this overworked word is not really needed in sentences that differentiate between two or more items; it should be deleted from sentences such as: *rooms 3, 5, and 7 are used as a message centre, control room, and storage area respectively*

resume when the meaning is "biography of experience" (rather than to continue) the correct spelling is *résumé* (with two accents), but the no-accent *resume* has become standard usage

retrieve; retrieval

retro- a prefix meaning to take place before, or to be backward; normally combines to form one word: *retroactive, retrofit, retrogression*; if combining word starts with *o*, insert a hyphen: *retro-operative*

rhythm; rhythmic; rhythmically

rigo(u)r *rigor* pref in US, rec in Can.; *rigour* pref in Br; **rigorous** is standard spelling in Can., US, and Br

ripoff (noun form)

road- as a prefix normally combines to form one word: *roadblock, roadmap, roadside*

role; roll a *role* is a person's function or the part that he or she plays (in an organization, project, or play); a *roll* (noun) is a round object; to *roll* (verb) means to rotate: *the assessor's role was to check that the casters rolled smoothly on a pile rug*

rollover (noun and adj)

ROM def: read-only memory

round def: circular; in Br, *round* is used in place of **around**

rumo(u)r *rumor* pref in US, rec in Can.; *rumour* pref in Br

runaround; run-down; run-through

S

sal(e)able; sal(e)ability *salable, salability* pref in US, rec in Can.; *saleable, saleability* pref in Br

salesclerk; salesperson; salespeople avoid using *salesman, salesgirl, saleslady, saleswoman*

sales slip; sales take

salvageable

same avoid using *same* as a pronoun; to write *we have repaired your modem and tested same* is awkward; a better version is *we have repaired and tested your modem*

save; savable

scarce; scarcity

sceptic(al); skeptic(al) *sceptic(al)* pref in Br, common in Can.; *skeptic(al)* pref in US, rec by CP

schedule

schematic although really an adjective (as in *schematic diagram*), *schematic* can also be used as a noun meaning a drawing of a circuit

scissors as a plural word, write *the scissors are*; in the singular form, write *the pair of scissors is*

seasonal; seasonable *seasonal* means affected by or dependent on the season; *seasonable* means appropriate or suited to the time of year: *a seasonal activity; seasonable weather*

seasons the seasons are not capitalized: *spring, summer, autumn* or *fall, winter*

secede; secession

second- combines erratically: *second-class, second-guess, second-hand, second-rate, second sight*

second (of time) abbr: **sec**

secure see **obtain**

-sede *supersede* is the only word to end with *-sede*; others end with *-cede* or *-ceed*

seem(s) see **appear(s)**

self- insert a hyphen when used as a prefix to form a compound term: *self-appointed, self-defence, self-employed, self-service, self-starter*; but there are exceptions: *selfless, selfsame*

semi- a prefix meaning half; normally combines to form one word: *semiactive, semiannually* (every six months), *semimonthly* (half-monthly), *semiofficial, semiskilled, semiweekly* (half-weekly); if combining word starts with *i*, insert a hyphen: *semi-idle, semi-immersed*

separate; separable; separator; separation these words are often misspelled

sequence; sequential

serial number abbr: **ser no.** or **S/N**

serviceable; serviceperson avoid using *serviceman, servicewoman*

setback (noun and adj)

shall *shall* is rarely used in business writing (*will* is pref), except in specifications when its use implies that an action is mandatory

shop- as a prefix normally combines to form one word: *shopkeeper, shoplifter, shoptalk*; but *shop steward*

short- as a prefix may combine with a hyphen (*short-circuit, short-form* [report], *short-lived, short-term*) or into one word (*shortfall, shorthand* [writing], *shorthanded, shortcoming, shortsighted*)

show- as a prefix normally combines to form one word: *showcase, showdown, showpiece, showroom*

sic a Latin word that means a quotation has been copied exactly, even though there is an error in it: e.g. *the report stated: "Our participation will be an issential (sic) requirement."*

sight see **site**

similar not *similiar*

site; sight; cite these three words are often used wrongly; a *site* is a location: *the construction site*; *sight* implies the ability to see: *mud up to the axles became a familiar sight*; *cite* means to quote: *Ms Smedley cited the May progress report*

siz(e)able *sizable* pref in US, rec in Can.; *sizeable* pref in Br

skeptic(al) see **sceptic(al)**

ski; skis; skied; skiing; skier; skiwear

skill; skil(l)ful *skilful* pref in Br, rec in Can.; *skillful* pref in US; note that this is contradictory to most *l* and *ll* situations listed in this glossary

slip- usually combines into a single word: *slippage, slipshod, slipstream*

smelled; smelt *smelled* pref in Can. and US; *smelt* pref in Br

socioeconomic

solely

someone; some one *someone* is correct when the meaning is any one person; *some one* is seldom used

some time; sometime; sometimes *some time* means an indefinite time: *some time ago*; *sometime* is an adjective that means at a particular time, as in *a sometime friend;* the word *sometimes* means occasionally, as in *he sometimes works until after midnight*

sound- combines irregularly: *sound-absorbent, sound-powered, soundproof, sound track, sound wave*

south; southeast; southwest; southbound; southward abbr: **S, SE, SW**; for rule on capitalization, see **east**

space- as a prefix normally combines to form one word: *spacecraft, spaceflight*

spare(s) as a noun, spares is used to mean spare part(s)

specially see **especially**

spelled; spelt *spelled* pref in Can. and US; *spelt* pref in Br

spilled; spilt *spilled* pref in Can. and US; *spilt* pref in Br

spinoff (noun and adj)

spiral; spiral(l)ed; spiral(l)ing *ll* pref in Br, rec in Can.; single *l* pref in US

split infinitive def: to insert a word between the word *to* and a verb: e.g. *to really insist* is a split infinitive; current grammarians say an infinitive can be split to avoid ambiguity, an awkward construction, or extensive rewriting

split-level

spoiled; spoilt *spoiled* pref in Can. and US; *spoilt* pref in Br

standby; standfast; standoff; standstill all combine into one word when used as a noun or adjective; but: **stand-in** (as a noun or adjective)

state-of-the-art

stationary; stationery *stationary* means not moving: *the vehicle was stationary when the incident occurred*; *stationery* refers to writing materials: *the only item in the October stationery requisition was an order for writing pads*

statutory

stencil; stencil(l)ed; stencil(l)ing *ll* pref in Br, rec in Can.; single *l* pref in US

stimulus pl: *stimuli*

stock- as a prefix normally combines to form one word: *stockholder, stocklist, stockpile, stocktaking*; but: *stock market* and *stock in trade*

stop- as a prefix usually combines to form one word: *stopgap, stopnut, stopover, stopwatch*; but *stop payment*; also: **stoppage**

store- as a prefix usually combines to form one word: *storefront, storekeeper, storeroom, storewide*; but *store-bought*

storey; story when the meaning is a certain level of a building, *storey* pref in Br, rec in Can., *story* pref in US

sub- a prefix generally meaning below, beneath, under; combines to form one word: *subassembly, subcommittee, subdivision, subnormal, subpoint*

subparagraph; sub-subparagraph

subpoena; subpoenaed *subpena* also used in US but less pref

subtle; subtlety; subtly

succinct

sufficient in business writing, *enough* is a better word than *sufficient*

summarize

super- a prefix meaning greater or over; combines to form one word: *superabundant, superannuation; supermarket*

superimpose; superpose *superimpose* means to place or impose one thing generally on top of another; *superpose* means to lay or place exactly on top of, so as to be coincident with

supersede see **-sede**

surfeit def: to have more than enough

susceptible

syllabus pl: *syllabuses* (pref) or *syllabi*

sympathize

symposium pl: *symposiums* (pref) or *symposia*

synonymous use *synonymous with*, not *synonymous to*

synopsis pl: *synopses*

systemwide

T

tailor-made

take- as a prefix normally combines to form one word: *takeoff, takeover, takeup*; but *take-home* (pay)

tangible

tape deck

taxable; tax collector; tax-exempt; taxpayer

teamwork

technician

teenage; teenager

telecom; telecon *telecom* is the abbr for *telecommunication(s)*; *telecon* is the abbr for *telephone conversation*

template; templet def: a pattern or guide; both spellings are correct, but *template* pref in Can. and Br

temporary; temporarily

tenfold

tentative; tentatively

tenuous

terminus pl: *terminuses* (pref) or *termini*

textbook

that is abbr: **i.e.** (pref) or **ie**

theatre; theater *theatre* pref in Br, rec in Can.; *theater* pref in US

their; there; they're the first two words are frequently misspelled, more through carelessness than as an outright error; *their* is a possessive meaning belonging to them: *the staff took their holidays earlier than normal*; *there* means in that place: *there are 18 desks in the room*, or *put it there*; *they're* is a contraction of *they are* and should appear as two words in business writing: *they are*

there- as a prefix combines to form one word: *thereafter, thereby, therein, thereupon* (these words are not rec for business writing)

therefor(e) *therefore* pref

thesis pl: *theses*

thirdhand; third-rate

three- when used as a prefix, a hyphen normally is inserted between the combining words: *three-dimensional, three-phase, three-ply*; exceptions are: *threefold, threesome*

threshold

through never write *thru*

tieing; tying *tying* pref

time always write time in numerals, if possible using the 24-hour clock: *08:17* or *8:17 a.m., 15:30* or *3:30 p.m.*; 24-hour times may be written as *20:45* (pref), *20:45 h*, or *20:45 hours*; never use the term "o'clock" in business writing: write *15:00* or *3:00 p.m.* rather than *3 o'clock*

time- as a prefix combines erratically; typical combinations are: *time base, time-card, time clock, time constant, time-consuming, timekeeper, time lag, timesaving, time-sharing, timetable, time-wasting*

titleholder

to; too; two frequently misspelled, most often through carelessness; *to* is a preposition that means in the direction of, against, before, or until; *too* means as well; *two* is the quantity 2.

today; tonight; tomorrow never use *tonite*; *tomorrow* has only one *m*

ton; tonne the metric (SI) tonne is 1000 kg (2204.6 lb) and is abbr **t**; the US ton is 2000 lb and is known as a short ton; the Br ton is 2400 lb and is known as a long ton; also: **tonmile** and **tonnage**

top- as a prefix combines erratically: *top-flight, top-heavy, top-loaded, topnotch*

total; total(l)ed; total(l)ing *ll* pref in Br, rec in Can.; single *l* pref in US

toward(s) *toward* pref

traceable

trade- as a prefix combines most often into a single word: *trademark, tradeoff*; but *trade-in, trade name,* and *trade show*

traffic; trafficked; trafficker; trafficking

trans- a prefix meaning over, across, or through; it normally combines to form one word: *transcontinental, transpacific, transship*; if combining word is a proper noun, insert a hyphen: *trans-Canada* (an exception is *transatlantic*, which, like *transpacific*, has dropped the capital first letter through common usage); *transonic* has only one *s*

transfer; transferred; transferring; transferable; transference

transmit; transmitted; transmitting; transmittal; transmitter; transmission

travel; travel(l)ed; travel(l)er; travel(l)ing *ll* pref in Br, rec in Can.; single *l* pref in US; but **travelogue** in all three countries

tri- a prefix meaning three or every third; combines to form one word: *triangulation, tricolor, trilateral, triweekly*

triple- all compounds are hyphenated: *triple-acting, triple-spaced*

turn- *turnaround* and *turnover* form one word when used as adjectives or nouns; *turnstile* and *turntable* always form one word

two- when used as a prefix to form a compound term, a hyphen normally is inserted: *two-address, two-phase, two-ply, two-position*; an exception is *twofold*

type- as a prefix normally combines to form one word: *typeface, typescript, typeset(ting), typewriter, typewriting*

U

ult; ultimo avoid using these out-of-date expressions in business writing

ultimatum pl: *ultimatums*

un- a prefix generally meaning not or negative; normally combines to form one word: *unaccompanied, unbiased, uncontrolled, uncooperative, uncoordinated, unethical, unnecessary*; if combining word is a proper noun, or if the combined term forms an existing word that has a different meaning, insert a hyphen: *un-Canadian, un-ionized*; if uncertain whether to use *un-*, *in-*, or *im-*, try using *not*

unadvisable; inadvisable both are correct; *inadvisable* pref

unbalance; imbalance *unbalance* pref; see **imbalance**

under- a prefix meaning below or lower; combines to form one word: *underachieve, underestimate, undergraduate, underrated, undersigned, underwrite(r)*

underage def: (1) a shortage or deficit, or (2) too young

unequal(l)ed *unequaled* pref; see **equal**

unessential; inessential *unessential* pref

unforeseeable; unforeseen

uni- a prefix meaning single or only one; combines to form one word: *unidirectional, unilateral, unisex*

uninterested def: not interested; avoid confusing with *disinterested*

unionized; un-ionized *unionized* refers to a group of people who belong to a union; *un-ionized* means not ionized

unique def: the one and only, without equal, incomparable; use with great care and never in any sense where a comparison is implied; you should not write *this is the most unique design*; rewrite as *this design is unique*, or (if a comparison must be made) *this is the most unusual design*

unmistakable

unparalleled

unpractical *impractical* pref

unsanitary *insanitary* pref

unstable; unstability/instability *instability* pref

untie; untied; untying

untraceable

up- as a prefix combines to form one word: *upcoming, update, upend, upgrade, uprange, upswing*, but *upside down*

up-to-date

uppermost

use; usable; usage; using; useful

utilize; utilise *utilize* pref; avoid using *utilizes* when *uses* or *employs* would be a better word

V

vacillate; vacillation

vary; varied; variance; variant write *at variance with*, never *at variance from*

vehicle; vehicular

vender; vendor *vendor* pref

versus def: against; abbr: **vs** or **V** (in legal documents)

veto; vetoed; vetoes; vetoing

vice- can either be hyphenated when used in a combining function, as in *vice-president*, or written as two words, as in *vice president*; *vice-presidential* is always hyphenated

vice versa def: in reverse order

video- as a prefix normally combines to form one word: *videocast, videocassette, videotape*; the abbr for **videocassette recorder** is **VCR** or **vcr**

viewfinder; viewpoint

vigo(u)r *vigor* pref in US, rec in Can.; *vigour* pref in Br; but *vigorous* and *vigorously* are so spelled in all three countries

vocation; avocation *vocation* is a trade or calling; *avocation* means an interest or hobby

vouchsafe

W

waive; waiver/waver *waive* and *waiver* mean to forgo one's claim or give up one's right; *waver* means to hesitate, to be irresolute

warranty

waste; wastage

water- as a prefix combines erratically: *water bed, water-cooled, water cooler, waterflow, water level, waterline, watermark, waterproof, water-resistant, water-soluble, watertight*

waver see **waiver**

wear and tear note: no hyphens

weather use only as a noun: *the weather*; never write "weather conditions"; avoid confusing with *climate* and *whether*

weatherproof

Wednesday often misspelled

weekend

well- as a prefix normally combines with a hyphen: *well-adjusted, well-defined, well-known, well-spoken, well-timed*

west; westbound; westward abbr for *west:* **W**; for rule on capitalization, see **east**

where- as a prefix combines to form one word: *whereas, wherefore, wherein, wherewithal*; when the combining word starts with *e* omit one *e*: *wherever*

whether, weather *whether* means if; *weather* has to do with rain, snow, sunshine, etc

while; whilst *while* pref

whisky; whiskey *whisky* pref in Br, rec in Can.; *whiskey* pref in US

whoever

wholly not *wholely*

wide- as a prefix combines erratically: *wide-screen, wideband, widespread*; the abbr for *wide* and *width* is **wd**

withheld; withhold(ing)

word processor; word processing (as a noun); **word-processing** (as an adjective); the common abbr is **WP** or **wp**

words per minute abbr: **wpm**

work- as a prefix usually combines to form one word: *workbench, workbook, workflow, workload, workout, workshop*; but *work force*

worldwide

World Wide Web abbr: **www** or the **Web**

wrap; wrapped; wrapping; wraparound; wrap-up

writeoff; writeup both combine into one word when used as noun or adjective

writer see **author**

writing only one *t*

www abbr for World Wide Web

X

x- *x-axis, x-ray, x-ref* (abbr for *cross-reference*)

Xerox

Xmas avoid using; write **Christmas**

Y

y- *y-axis*

yardstick

year abbr: **yr**; typical combinations are: *year-end, yearlong, year-round*

your; you're *your* means belonging to or originating from you: *I have examined your proposal*; *you're* is a contraction of *you are* and should not appear in business writing

Z

z- *z-axis*

zero pl: *zeros* (pref) or *zeroes*; typical combinations are: *zero-access, zero-adjust, zero hour, zero level, zero-set*

zoology: zoological

Index

D

E

F

G

H

I

J

L

M

N

O

P

Q

R

S

T

W

"AS IS" LICENSE AGREEMENT AND LIMITED WARRANTY

READ THIS LICENSE CAREFULLY BEFORE OPENING THIS PACKAGE. BY OPENING THIS PACKAGE, YOU ARE AGREEING TO THE TERMS AND CONDITIONS OF THIS LICENSE. IF YOU DO NOT AGREE, DO NOT OPEN THE PACKAGE. PROMPTLY RETURN THE UNOPENED PACKAGE AND ALL ACCOMPANYING ITEMS TO THE PLACE YOU OBTAINED THEM. ***THESE TERMS APPLY TO ALL LICENSED SOFTWARE ON THE DISK EXCEPT THAT THE TERMS FOR USE OF ANY SHAREWARE OR FREEWARE ON THE DISKETTES ARE AS SET FORTH IN THE ELECTRONIC LICENSE LOCATED ON THE DISK:***

1. **GRANT OF LICENSE and OWNERSHIP:** The enclosed computer programs and any data ("Software") are licensed, not sold, to you by Pearson Education Canada Inc. ("We" or the "Company") in consideration of your adoption of the accompanying Company textbooks and/or other materials, and your agreement to these terms. You own only the disk(s) but we and/or our licensors own the Software itself. This license allows instructors and students enrolled in the course using the Company textbook that accompanies this Software (the "Course") to use and display the enclosed copy of the Software for academic use only, so long as you comply with the terms of this Agreement. You may make one copy for back up only. We reserve any rights not granted to you.

2. **USE RESTRICTIONS:** You may not sell or license copies of the Software or the Documentation to others. You may not transfer, distribute or make available the Software or the Documentation, except to instructors and students in your school who are users of the adopted Company textbook that accompanies this Software in connection with the course for which the textbook was adopted. You may not reverse engineer, disassemble, decompile, modify, adapt, translate or create derivative works based on the Software or the Documentation. You may be held legally responsible for any copying or copyright infringement which is caused by your failure to abide by the terms of these restrictions.

3. **TERMINATION:** This license is effective until terminated. This license will terminate automatically without notice from the Company if you fail to comply with any provisions or limitations of this license. Upon termination, you shall destroy the Documentation and all copies of the Software. All provisions of this Agreement as to limitation and disclaimer of warranties, limitation of liability, remedies or damages, and our ownership rights shall survive termination.

4. **DISCLAIMER OF WARRANTY: THE COMPANY AND ITS LICENSORS MAKE NO WARRANTIES ABOUT THE SOFTWARE, WHICH IS PROVIDED "AS-IS." IF THE DISK IS DEFECTIVE IN MATERIALS OR WORKMANSHIP, YOUR ONLY REMEDY IS TO RETURN IT TO THE COMPANY WITHIN 30 DAYS FOR REPLACEMENT UNLESS THE COMPANY DETERMINES IN GOOD FAITH THAT THE DISK HAS BEEN MISUSED OR IMPROPERLY INSTALLED, REPAIRED, ALTERED OR DAMAGED. THE COMPANY DISCLAIMS ALL WARRANTIES, EXPRESS OR IMPLIED, INCLUDING WITHOUT LIMITATION, THE IMPLIED WARRANTIES OF MERCHANTABILITY AND FITNESS FOR A PARTICULAR PURPOSE. THE COMPANY DOES NOT WARRANT, GUARANTEE OR MAKE ANY REPRESENTATION REGARDING THE ACCURACY, RELIABILITY, CURRENTNESS, USE, OR RESULTS OF USE, OF THE SOFTWARE.**

5. **LIMITATION OF REMEDIES AND DAMAGES: IN NO EVENT, SHALL THE COMPANY OR ITS EMPLOYEES, AGENTS, LICENSORS OR CONTRACTORS BE LIABLE FOR ANY INCIDENTAL, INDIRECT, SPECIAL OR CONSEQUENTIAL DAMAGES ARISING OUT OF OR IN CONNECTION WITH THIS LICENSE OR THE SOFTWARE, INCLUDING, WITHOUT LIMITATION, LOSS OF USE, LOSS OF DATA, LOSS OF INCOME OR PROFIT, OR OTHER LOSSES SUSTAINED AS A RESULT OF INJURY TO ANY PERSON, OR LOSS OF OR DAMAGE TO PROPERTY, OR CLAIMS OF THIRD PARTIES, EVEN IF THE COMPANY OR AN AUTHORIZED REPRESENTATIVE OF THE COMPANY HAS BEEN ADVISED OF THE POSSIBILITY OF SUCH DAMAGES.** SOME JURISDICTIONS DO NOT ALLOW THE LIMITATION OF DAMAGES IN CERTAIN CIRCUMSTANCES, SO THE ABOVE LIMITATIONS MAY NOT ALWAYS APPLY.

6. **GENERAL:** THIS AGREEMENT SHALL BE CONSTRUED AND INTERPRETED ACCORDING TO THE LAWS OF THE PROVINCE OF ONTARIO. This Agreement is the complete and exclusive statement of the agreement between you and the Company and supersedes all proposals, prior agreements, oral or written, and any other communications between you and the company or any of its representatives relating to the subject matter.

Should you have any questions concerning this agreement or if you wish to contact the Company for any reason, please contact in writing: Customer Service, Pearson Education Canada, 26 Prince Andrew Place, Don Mills, Ontario M3C 2T8.